Introduction to Politics

Introduction to Politics

Governments and Nations in the Post Cold War Era

Martin Slann
Clemson University

Boston, Massachusetts   Burr Ridge, Illinois   Dubuque, Iowa
Madison, Wisconsin   New York, New York   San Francisco, California   St. Louis, Missouri

McGraw-Hill

*A Division of The **McGraw·Hill** Companies*

INTRODUCTION TO POLITICS: GOVERNMENTS AND NATIONS IN THE POST COLD WAR ERA

Copyright © 1998 by The McGraw-Hill Companies, Inc. All rights reserved. Printed in the
United States of America. Except as permitted under the United States Copyright Act of 1976, no
part of this publication may be reproduced or distributed in any form or by any means, or stored
in a data base or retrieval system, without the prior written permission of the publisher.

 This book is printed on recycled, acid-free paper containing 10% postconsumer waste.

1 2 3 4 5 7 8 9 0 QPF/QPF 9 0 9 8 7

ISBN 0-697-31637-8

Publisher: *Jane Vaicunas*
Sponsoring editor: *Lyn Uhl*
Developmental editor: *Monica Freedman*
Marketing manager: *Annie Mitchell*
Project manager: *Ann Morgan*
Production supervisor: *Sandy Hahn*
Designer: *Kay Fulton Design*
Cover image: © *Lonny Kalfus/Tony Stone Images*
Photo research coordinator: *Lori Hancock*
Art editor: *Joyce Watters*
Compositor: *ElectraGraphics, Inc.*
Typeface: *10/12 Janson*
Printer: *Quebecor Printing Book Group/Fairfield*

Library of Congress Cataloging-in-Publication Data

Slann, Martin W.
    Introduction to politics, governments, and nations in the post
cold war era / Martin Slann. — 1st ed.
      p.   cm.
    Includes index.
    ISBN 0-697-31637-8
    1. Comparative government. 2. Political science. 3. Post-
communism. I. Title.
JF51.S5444 1998
320.3—dc21

                        97-4405
                        CIP

www.mhhe.com

Contents

Part II
The Institutions of Government and the Political Process

8   Political Parties and Electoral Systems   163

Part III
Ingredients of International Politicals

9   The Global Political Economy   191

Part IV
The International Situation at Century's End

Preface

*T*his book was written to provide an introduction to the most important areas of politics within the atmosphere of uncertainty and opportunity created by the end of the Cold War. Sometimes the uncertainties and opportunities are so entwined as to be almost indistinguishable. Communism's demise was a victory for western democracy, but it also presented new challenges in the form of religious radicalism and ethnic violence. After teaching introductory courses in politics for many years, I have come to believe that politics must be presented as a consistently dynamic and inevitable human activity that changes rapidly and often unpredictably. The Cold War's end was generally unanticipated, and it has radically altered the international environment.

The book is divided into four sections into which chapters seemed to naturally fall. Part I's three chapters develop the theme of politics as a creative human activity. It includes a review of the features considered proper ingredients of a political society as well as of the impact of a particular society's history and culture on the conduct of politics. Part II includes four chapters that explain the kind of political institutions and/or processes commonplace throughout political systems, including basic government structures familiar to most students. Part III explores some current themes of politics such as economy, geography, demography, and violence that we cannot ignore as critical considerations of nearly every country's political life. Finally, Part IV reviews the post Cold War international constellation, focusing on the characteristics that have changed it drastically over the past decade and that promise continued influence well into the new century.

The non-American introductory politics course is growing in popularity, but it differs considerably from campus to campus in content and in the way it is taught. No text, including this one, offers coverage that can satisfy all preferences. I have tried to provide coverage of materials and themes that are relatively commonplace and vital to the understanding of politics. Thus, for example, there are chapters devoted to such basic political institutions as the executive, legislature, and judiciary. Most of the time, the treatment of political institutions is comparative. However, where relevant, comparisons have been made to elements of the American political system. American references have been included for two main reasons: (1) to put the student at ease in handling much of the unfamiliar material, and (2) to point out that what is going on in the increasingly global political economy is important to Americans, just as how our country copes with the Cold War's aftermath is important to the rest of the world.

Clarity of language in this book has been a consistent goal. Many students taking this course will not take another course that studies and analyzes politics. Three decades of teaching experience suggest to me that undergraduate students want to learn new material if it is interesting and not unduly cumbersome. My goal in writing this book has been to encourage the reader to become aware that the political conduct of individuals or entire nations is fascinating (if occasionally disturbing). Perhaps no text can completely captivate all students at all times. However, one of the most rewarding comments I receive on student evaluations is simply "This course was a lot more interesting than I thought it would be." It is my hope that readers will think the same of this book.

Throughout the writing process, I have been grateful for the invaluable encouragement and assistance provided by Irv Rockwood, Scott Spoolman, and Lynn Uhl, past and current political science editors, and Marsena Konkle and Monica Freedman, past and current developmental editors, who were always available for advice and ideas, and who served as a gracious link with sanity. Annie Mitchell, marketing manager, Ann Morgan, project manager, and Carol Smith, photo editor, were wonderful, helpful, and reassuring voices on the phone. Finally, an overdue but sincere thanks to my wife, Ruth, who more than lives up to her name. This text is truly a joint effort, though I must accept full responsibility for any and all mistakes you may encounter. Still, I hope it reflects my personal enthusiasm for and advocacy of the study of politics, as well as ignites an answering spark in the students who will read it.

Martin Slann
Clemson University

For My Grandchildren

Introduction: Government and Politics in the Post Cold War Era

Government is actually a recent innovation whose history goes back about eight thousand years, a very tiny percentage of the time humans have inhabited this planet. Governmental institutions were in large part the result of, and certainly coincided with, the development of agriculture and the establishment of permanent human settlements. The essential purpose of government has not changed since its creation: to achieve and guarantee a degree of social order that enables society's members to enjoy a maximum degree of physical security. This purpose is not easily accomplished. A large proportion of the world's population today remains either under uncertain and frequently incomplete governmental authority, or under government whose policies toward citizenries are so harsh that they threaten rather than provide physical security.

Government, whether acting on behalf of people or otherwise, is the result of politics. Politics is often considered a corrupt and debasing profession that no self-respecting person would consider entering. But politics is also a feature common to all human society. It is an activity that "arises from accepting the fact of the simultaneous existence of different groups, hence different interests and different traditions within a territory ruled."[1] We have and participate in politics because we need it.

Politics is not necessarily a complicated phenomenon. The distinguished political scientist Harold Laswell, for example, has succinctly defined it as a process of determining "who gets what, when, and how." More recently, another respected political scientist, David Easton, defined politics simply as "the

---

[1] Bernard Crick, *In Defense of Politics* (Baltimore, Maryland: Penguin Books, 1964), p. 18.

authoritative allocation of values." There is little doubt (although often much disgust) that politics has become an important vehicle in the United States and elsewhere in the world for determining nonmaterial and frequently very intimate and personal values. Decisions on how separate church and state should be, whether homosexuals should be excluded from military service, or even on what language a national or subnational student community will be taught in are dilemmas that have been turned over to the political process.

Politics is far from being an isolated activity that occurs in national capitals such as London, Moscow, Tokyo, or Washington. Politics is a common feature of daily human existence that occurs wherever and whenever decisions are made about "who shall get what, when, and how." Politics may take a variety of forms, some that may be familiar and desirable to us and others that may be neither.

This chapter will introduce you to some of the more current themes in politics as well as activities that continually cause stress in international relations. The chapters that follow will explore all of them in more detail. For the time being, let us develop an acquaintanceship with the issues that influence our lives and promise to continue to do so for the foreseeable future.

GOVERNMENT IN THE POST COLD WAR ERA

Politics and government are not the same thing. Politics often occurs outside of government. Similarly, politics may (and usually does) involve both governmental and nongovernmental actors. Important political actors may not even hold government posts. In the United States, for instance, the very active role First Lady Hillary Rodham Clinton took in developing a national health plan in the early 1990s and trying (in this case, unsuccessfully) to coordinate its passage in Congress was apparent from the beginning of the Clinton presidency. Mrs. Clinton has generally been regarded as President Clinton's closest political advisor.

President Saddam Hussein of Iraq, on the other hand, emphasizes the importance of his eldest son, Uday, who holds no government office, but whose political qualifications consist mainly of driving fast cars, editing a tabloid newspaper, and playing the currency markets. The betting is on Uday to succeed his father,[2] assuming he continues to survive attempts on his life.

Of course, most of us don't really care how policy is made as long as it is done in a rational and humane fashion. Government, then, may be defined simply as the formal social instrument that partially or wholly resolves conflicts that arise among individuals or groups. The primary purpose of government is to manage and resolve conflict, thereby providing security and continuity for society as a whole and for its individual members. Successful governments do this and more. A successful government is also one that is not itself a source of conflict. We tend, for example, to condemn the authoritarian government of

---

[2] "Inheriting the Crown," *The Economist*, May 28, 1994, p. 42.

Iraq because it is the greatest perpetrator of violence in the country: its most visible accomplishment is the war it conducts against segments of its own population. It will come as no surprise that Saddam Hussein is not a fan of Alexander Hamilton, who argued in *Federalist Paper 51* that

> *in framing a government which is to be administered by men over men, the great difficulty lies in this: you must first enable the government to control the governed; and in the next place to oblige it to control itself.*

This is a tall order for most of the world's regimes, who still insist on either ignoring the people's legitimate needs or who are determined to make life miserable for their people by denying them basic human rights.

The collapse of the Soviet Union in 1991 is, in this context, instructive. Its economic system was a disaster that became more blatant during its last years. The Soviet population was stunned by the revelation that the communist regime had avoided economic reforms in order to avoid risking its own political power. To the Soviet communist elite, economic stagnation was a worthwhile price for continued power and privilege. The Soviets had therefore rejected another critical ingredient of successful government by refusing to take the steps necessary to enhance the quality of life for its citizens. During the last two decades of its existence, the Soviet Union became the only industrialized society in history to experience a *decline* in average life expectancy.[3] To the Soviet citizen standing in line for hours to purchase basic foodstuffs, often in subfreezing conditions, it was of little comfort to be told that the Soviet military was achieving parity with the United States. Of more immediate concern was whether meat, bread, and milk would be available when finally reaching the head of the line (after an average wait of two hours).

Throughout the twentieth century, American government has taken on an ever increasing load of responsibility for at least two reasons: (1) we want government to do more for us (even though we are reluctant to pay for additional services with additional taxes) and (2) government is able to do more because of modern technology and increased (if unevenly distributed) economic prosperity. One estimate has it that 85 percent of all scientists who have ever lived are alive today.[4] We are usually the beneficiaries of scientists whose medical and technological breakthroughs are frequently dependent on government funding.

Government in many countries, particularly the more advanced ones in Europe and North America, has unprecedented technological advantages when it comes to delivering services. At the same time, though, government can no longer consider itself the sole monopolizer of information, making pronouncements that the entire citizenry automatically believes. Some governments have a difficult time accepting the fact that satellites and other

---

[3] By the early 1990s, Russian men had a life expectancy of only 68 and women 72 compared to 75 and 82 for Japanese men and women, respectively; 73 and 78 for Israeli men and women; and 72 and 79 for American men and women. See *The Economist*, June 4, p. 4.

[4] Paul Kennedy, *Preparing for the Twenty-First Century* (New York: Random House, 1993).

Part of the reason of the collapse of the Soviet Union: Muscovites waiting in long lines for their turn to purchase food.

communication technologies now provide almost instantaneous information to hundreds of millions of people.

But while government is experiencing both unprecedented assistance in delivering services and unprecedented public scrutiny, the collapse of the Soviet Union suddenly created yet a new challenge. While parts of the former Soviet empire are democratizing, others are suffering breakdowns in governmental authority as ethnic and religious strife reach levels unseen in the modern world for many decades.

Estimates of distinct ethnic groups around the world range from five thousand to six thousand communities. Some are very small indigenous tribes numbering only a few thousand members; the Han Chinese are the largest ethnic group in the world, with perhaps a billion people. Only a tiny percentage of the world's ethnic groups have their own territorial state and are equipped with the trappings of political sovereignty, such as a national flag, currency, language, and military. The number of independent states has increased since 1945 from fewer than 60 to nearly 200, but 96 percent or more of the ethnic communities in the world do not have their own sovereign system, and most are unlikely to acquire one. The potential challenges stateless communities pose for international political stability are serious, as we shall see in chapters to follow.

Ethnic diversity on an American college campus.

Government and Politics

Democratic governments are a lot more accustomed to dealing with challenges than nondemocratic ones because democratic regimes normally have to either respond to problems or risk being replaced at the next election. Politics is apparent in dictatorial regimes, but it is a politics played out within the confines of a political clique or between competing elements within a political elite. This body only reluctantly, if at all, considers public opinion, even if it knows what public opinion is on a given issue. But this is also why authoritarian government is inherently unstable: the government's lack of interest in and/or knowledge of public concerns is an excellent formula for ensuring that people withdraw both loyalty to and cooperation with the regime. If the public perceives the government as uninterested in or incapable of responding to citizen concerns, there is no point in supporting the regime. With this point in mind, we can make some reasonably safe assumptions about the nature of government and politics:

1. *Politics is a natural phenomenon that rises from human diversity. It should not be replaced by political ideology, a set of comprehensive beliefs about what a government should be doing.* If politics is working right, it will consider but not give way to different and often competing expressions of political ideology. The art of politics involves the selection of the best possible choice from a set of imperfect but workable alternatives. Politicians don't have all the answers. If they are honest, they admit to this. Ideologues brag that they have all the answers without understanding that their answers could easily be wrong or even dangerous.

2.   *People create and employ government to help them live more comfortable, secure, and productive lives.* Because it is a human device, government is often a miserable failure when it comes to fulfilling its mission. Governments fail most often, though, when they are guided either by an ideology or a leadership oblivious to what government is all about. To do its job, government must be cognizant of what the citizenry requires and accurate about what it can deliver. Government can do neither if it is uninterested in or intolerant of dissent. Bear in mind, though, that the observation offered by Abraham Lincoln that "government of the people, for the people, and by the people," is less than a century and a half old. It was a radical suggestion when it was first uttered, and it remains so in much of the world today. Most of the history of government is dominated by authoritarian regimes that operate with differing degrees of brutality.

3.   *Political stability is enhanced when as much of the citizenry as possible have legitimate and guaranteed access to government.* Historically speaking, governments have been notoriously lax when it comes to accessibility. Many citizenries today still live under severe limitations on freedom of speech and action. Their governments don't want to hear from them. In numerous cases, a government doesn't even want them around: dozens of countries contain minority ethnic, racial, linguistic, and religious communities that they regard as surly and ill-disposed toward "fitting in" with the prevailing majority. Moreover, many such communities are reluctant to accept the legitimacy of the government that has control over them. Many Sikhs in India, Shiite Muslims in Iraq, Muslims in western China, and Tamils in Sri Lanka do not accept the central authority either because they regard the central authority as a detriment to cultural autonomy (as in India) or because the central government is committed to a program of **genocide** against the community (as in Iraq).

4.   *Economic prosperity and political democracy are interrelated.* There is no satisfactory way to demonstrate this assumption empirically. We know, however, that the most prosperous economies in history have been democratic, and that when the Soviet Union collapsed, its demise was at least in part the result of a deteriorating economy that had not only failed to "catch up" with the West but had become altogether inoperable. Political scientists debate whether it is feasible for every country to establish a combination of political democracy and an economy dominated by the free market. We shall explore the debate in various discussions below.

The Collapse of the Soviet Union and the End of the Cold War Era

The Soviet Union officially ceased to exist on December 25, 1991, when its last president, Mikhail Gorbachev, resigned and the Soviet flag flying over the **Kremlin** in Moscow came down for the last time. Months before, the Soviet Union had, for all practical purposes, politically disintegrated as most of its republics seceded and established independent governments and as more and more of its political leadership broke with the Communist party. Boris Yeltsin, for example, became the Russian Republic's first popularly elected president in 1990 after he had turned his back on the party and created his own popular power base. And before then, the Soviet government had begun to wind down its adversarial position with the United States in a remarkable period of international cooperation unseen since World War II that resulted in a build-down of their respective nuclear arsenals.

In retrospect, it was probably inevitable that the Soviet Union would not only lose the Cold War, but experience an implosion. Its economy had ceased to develop for at least the previous two decades. During this same time, the mostly free markets of Western European, North American, and East Asian countries were expanding to the point that, by the late 1980s, they accounted for nearly four-fifths of the global economy, though their citizenries comprised only about a fifth of the world's population. The Soviet model **command economy** had clearly failed, not only in the Soviet Union but everywhere else it had been tried—Eastern Europe, Southeast Asia, North Korea, Ethiopia, and Cuba. Its economy was lagging so far behind that of the free market democracies that the Soviet Union became increasingly recognized as a **Third World** country, though one that, disconcertingly, possessed thousands of nuclear warheads.

In fact, that was the problem. The Soviet Union was a nuclear power and not much else. It could not even begin to compete economically with the West, and its technology was often woefully inadequate to sustain a modern industrial power. Unless Soviet intentions were to destroy the world (happily, they weren't), there wasn't much use for a nuclear arsenal. It was expensive to build and maintain and, perhaps worst of all, severely detracted from chronically urgent consumer needs. Perhaps even worse, the emphasis on centralized control discouraged innovation. In the last years of its existence, the Soviet Union averaged only 400 patents per year—only a few more than Belgium, whose population was about one-twelfth the size.[5]

The Soviet Union has been referred to as the "last colonial empire." This is because only about half of the Soviet population was Russian. Nearly 150 million other people represented perhaps a hundred different nationalities, most of them conquered and occupied by a Russia that had been expanding its territory since the sixteenth century. Thus, the Soviet state was doomed to disintegration in part because the communist regime had failed to nurture a coherent loyalty of huge sections of its population. Millions of non-Russians retained historical memories of a politically sovereign past free from Moscow's control. The government never eliminated the desire to restore national autonomy. In some cases, the autonomy had never really existed, but that did not detract from the desire to acquire it anyway.

Ironically, the Soviet Union had served an important purpose for Americans. Nearly two generations of Americans had grown up understanding that

---

[5] "The New World Order, Based on Share of Leading Patents," *The New York Times*, May 28, 1991.

Source: *The Christian Science Monitor*, June 2, 1997, p. 10.

Soviet communism was an evil but containable global menace. By the 1980s, most of the American population could not remember or even fantasize about what the world was or would be like without a brutal totalitarian regime that was easy to both condemn and accept as a permanent fixture in our lives. Then, rather suddenly, the Soviet Union under Gorbachev, its youngest leader in decades, seemed to mellow politically. Tensions drained away between the two superpowers, and within the Soviet Union, Gorbachev's government tried to reform both the economic and political systems to make them more efficient and more responsive to the citizenry's needs.

The reform attempts, however, only exposed the Soviet system as hopelessly corrupt and inept. After the failure of a coup in August 1991 to restore a more hard-lined political elite, no defenders of the Soviet system were left to delay what seemed to be an inevitable demise. The leaders of the coup reflected everything that was wrong with the system—they were not only corrupt, but they revealed an astounding incompetence in planning and activating the overthrow. Many of them were also regularly drunk (another chronic problem in Soviet society) or soon became that way after they realized how badly things were going for them.

The United States as the First "Universal Nation"

The Cold War era, roughly 1945 to 1990, was over, and the generation of political leadership that had dominated it and whose perspectives had been forged by the trauma of World War II (1939–1945) was now leaving the scene. George Bush, for example, was the last World War II veteran to become president. His

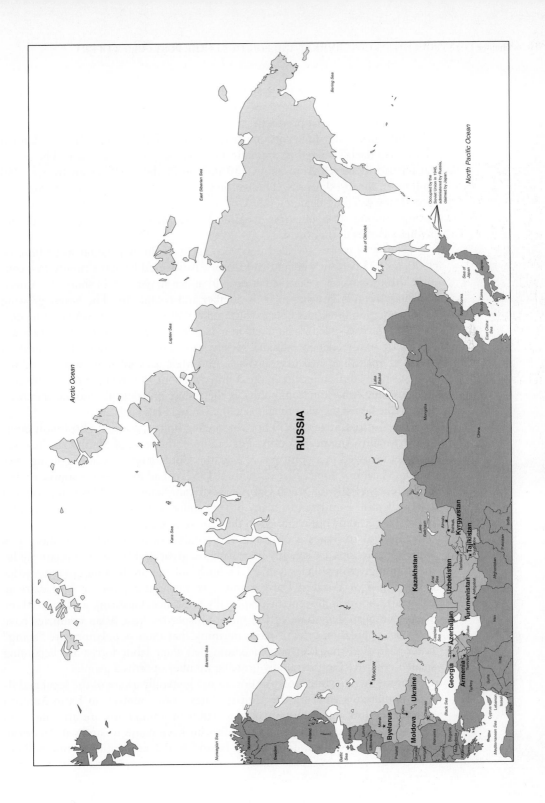

RUSSIA

North Pacific Ocean

Occupied by the
Soviet Union in 1945,
administered by Russia,
claimed by Japan.

Arctic Ocean

Bering Sea

East Siberian Sea

Laptev Sea

Kara Sea

Barents Sea

Norwegian Sea

Sea of Okhotsk

Sea of Japan

Lake Baikal

Mongolia

China

Japan

Sea of Japan

North Korea

South Korea

East China Sea

Lake Balkhash

Almaty

Bishkek

Kyrgyzstan

Tajikistan

Dushanbe

Kazakhstan

Uzbekistan

Tashkent

Aral Sea

Turkmenistan

Ashgabat

Afghanistan

Pakistan

Caspian Sea

Azerbaijan

Baku

Iran

Georgia

Armenia

Yerevan

Turkey

Syria

Iraq

Cyprus

Lebanon

Israel

Egypt

Mediterranean Sea

Moscow

Ukraine

Kiev

Byelarus

Moldova

Black Sea

Finland

Sweden

Norway

Baltic Sea

Poland

Estonia

Latvia

Lithuania

Germany

Romania

Bulgaria

Chisinau

Minsk

successor, Bill Clinton, was elected president in the first post-Cold War American election in 1992. Clinton was born in 1946, just as the Cold War era was beginning, and became president shortly after it ended.

But during the four-and-one-half decades of the Cold War, the United States had itself changed in dramatic and often unpredictable ways. The population had increased from about 150 million in the 1950 census to over 250 million in the 1990 census. The nation's demographic composition underwent even more startling change. The United States now counts 110 distinct ethnic groups among its population, making Americans one of the most heterogeneous societies in the world.

The 1950 census revealed that 90 percent of the population was white; by 1990, only 75 percent were in that category. By the middle of the twenty-first century, this proportion is expected to drop to under 50 percent. In short, the American population is growing in both number and complexity. The fastest growing ethnic group in the United States during the 1980s was the Asian-American community, which doubled its numbers in a decade. At the same time, Americans are becoming an increasingly bilingual society, with about 6 percent of the population speaking Spanish as their first language. And while African-Americans are still the largest single ethnic minority in the country at about 13 percent of the population, the Hispanic-American community is the fastest growing in absolute numbers. One of the fastest growing religions in the United States is Islam.

The United States is still not completely united, and old ghosts still occasionally haunt American society. For example, the state of South Carolina was recently involved in a controversy over the Confederate battle flag flying over the state's capitol dome. Placed there in 1962, it had long been a source of displeasure, especially for South Carolina's African-Americans. This controversy is relatively mild compared to many other gender and ethnic issues that crop up in but are certainly not confined to the United States.

The United States is also one of a handful of industrialized democracies whose populations are steadily increasing, in great part because of relatively lenient immigration policies (table 1.1). Such policies are becoming very restrictive in most of Western Europe and have inspired a resurgence of extreme nationalist political movements, especially in France, Germany, and Italy. Many West European and some of the more prosperous East Asian countries have fairly flat population growth rates, meaning that their populations are "aging" faster than the American populace, and that their labor forces are becoming smaller compared to the rapidly growing number of retired people.

Interestingly, while most Americans are generally aware of the legal and illegal immigrants entering the United States from countries in Latin America and the Caribbean, a substantial proportion of immigrants are arriving from East Asia. Most are university students who have come to study at American universities from China, Taiwan, and Japan.[6] And a substantial portion will de-

---

[6] "Foreign Students in America: Where They Come From—Where They Go," *The New York Times*, November 29, 1989.

TABLE 1.1   Global Migratory Patterns

From	Usual Destination(s)
North Africa (Algeria, Morocco, Tunisia)	France
Turkey, East European countries	Germany
South Asia (Bangladesh, India, Pakistan, Sri Lanka) and West Indies	United Kingdom
Central American countries, Cuba, Haiti, Mexico, East Asia	Canada and United States

Millions of people (at least 17 million during 1995) are on the move, mostly from the less economically developed countries to the more prosperous countries of Western Europe and North America. Most of these immigrants are unwelcome in host countries when unemployment is high.

cide to remain in the United States to live and work (usually in well-paid professions such as medicine and engineering). Like previous immigrants, they have found it easy to adapt to the American economic and social systems.

Unprecedented demographic changes are certainly occurring. As they do, the more established elements of the population sometimes feel threatened by or helpless in a society that they increasingly find full of challenging political agendas. Politically conservative and religious Americans worry, for example, about the huge rise in illegitimate births, at a rate that doubled during the two decades after 1975.[7] In another vein, militant African-Americans have blamed whites for the poor economic status of blacks in the United States.[8]

In reality, of course, it is a waste of time to live in a multiethnic society and be unappreciative of diversity and the material benefits that it can bring. There is growing evidence, for example, that multiethnic societies more fully understand and can more easily operate in a global economy full of cultural nuances.[9] The United States is about as multiethnic as a country can be, with built-in legal structures to ensure mutual toleration. It is thus positioned to continue to be a leading economic and political power.

At the same time, Americans are also becoming a more class-oriented and class-conscious society. We are still a predominantly middle class society, but the middle class is increasingly fragmented. For example, lower-middle class Americans tend to idolize celebrities such as television personality Katie Lee Gifford; middle-middle class Americans prefer Janet Reno, the attorney general; and many upper-middle class Americans are devotees of Rush Limbaugh, a conservative and controversial talk show host and commentator.[10]

The American economy has also experienced terrific change. In 1945, because of the devastation of World War II in Europe and Asia as well as growth in America, the United States accounted for one-half of the world's economy.

---

[7] "Welfare Reform in America," *The Economist*, June 18, 1994, p. 22.

[8] "Free Speech, Foul Speech," *The Economist*, June 4, 1994, p. 30.

[9] "Market Place," *NPR*, July 6, 1994.

[10] Kenneth Labich, "Class in America," *Fortune*, February 7, 1994, p. 115.

Half a century later, that proportion had been cut in half to a fourth of the world's economy. This happened not because Americans were less well off, but because of the recovery and unprecedented economic growth in Western Europe and East Asia. The nearly $8-trillion-dollar American economy was still about as large as the economies of all the countries of western Europe combined and more than twice the size of Japan's, the second biggest economy in the world. In fact, the state of California alone had an economy almost the size of the United Kingdom's. If California were an independent country, it would have had the seventh biggest economy in the world.

For all of these reasons, the United States will frequently appear in this text as a familiar reference point for purposes of comparison. Its economic, political, and cultural impacts throughout the world are not unlimited, but they are so crucial and pervasive that they cannot be ignored in any assessment of comparative and international politics.

THE NEW CONTEXT OF GLOBAL POLITICS

The Cold War era was characterized by a superpower rivalry between the United States and the Soviet Union. This competition consumed trillions of dollars in an arms race and often overshadowed domestic economic concerns and even basic human rights. For nearly half a century, the American-Soviet competition consistently overrode other political considerations. By the time it ended, the Soviet system had disintegrated, but the United States, while clearly the winner, still confronted challenges to international peace, stability, and prosperity from sources that had been submerged until communism's collapse.

As the sole remaining superpower, the United States could naturally be expected to easily get what it wanted: stable, democratic governments with political leaders committed to fostering societies that enhance individual opportunity and welfare. This was a nice prospect, but not very realistic. A former U.S. secretary of state observed that

> . . . the United States is actually in no better a position to dictate the global agenda unilaterally than it was at the beginning of the Cold War. America is more preponderant than it was ten years ago, yet, ironically, power has also become more diffuse. Thus, America's ability to employ it to shape the rest of the world has actually decreased.[11]

By the mid-1990s, it was clear that much of the world was adjusting to the winding down of the Cold War. In fact, many governments as well as antigovernment movements felt free to pursue their own agendas, many of which were far from peaceful and several of which were destructive to the point of genocide. Nationalist movements, radical religious fundamentalism, and the expan-

---

[11] Henry Kissinger, *Diplomacy* (New York: Simon & Schuster, 1994), p. 809.

sionist plans of numerous governments have produced what can only be judged as a less peaceful world.

During any given day of the week, as many as three dozen separate conflicts are going on across the globe. Most of these are in Third World countries, but the First World of Europe and North America are not immune. In Northern Ireland and the former Yugoslavia, for example, ancient animosities have created—or, perhaps more properly, renewed—such violent phenomena as political terrorism and "ethnic cleansing." Clearly, the beginning of a new era in global politics was no guarantee of worldwide peace. What characteristics mark the new context of world politics? Several stand out, including democratization, westernization, religious fundamentalism, and tribalism, and ethnic conflict.

Democratization

We should not confuse democratization with democracy. Democratization is a process that, it is hoped, leads a society to create and sustain democracy. Democratization rarely proceeds at an even pace or exhibits identical characteristics everywhere it occurs. Nor is it always the automatic successor of collapsing authoritarian or totalitarian regimes. As we have seen in the aftermath of the Soviet Union's demise, democracy is far from a sure thing. Democratization itself, or reforms toward democracy, while doing fairly well in some of the former Soviet republics such as the **Baltic states,** is found haphazardly, if at all, in other areas.

It is generally acknowledged that to successfully establish a permanent and stable political democracy, the democratization process must achieve certain minimal economic and social conditions. The following list of conditions is not all-inclusive, but it does set forth several basic conditions that tend to foster democratization and that are fairly commonplace wherever democracy occurs:

A broad, large, and fairly accessible middle class. The middle class is often a vague entity (and a complicated one, since there are various gradations within the class), but by and large its members enjoy a decent standard of living, have the ability to work realistically toward and access to the means for self-improvement, and have at least a modicum of hope that their children will have better lives than they have had.

Literacy. A well-educated citizenry in itself is no guarantee of democratization, but democracy is probably impossible if the bulk of the citizenry cannot read and write its own language. Literacy enables an electorate to become politically well informed. It's not that literate electorates don't make mistakes. After all, the relatively educated nation of Germany produced, mainly through the electoral process, twelve nightmarish years (1933–1945) of **Nazism,** and Russians, whose reading habits tend to be more sophisticated than those of most Americans, endured more than seven decades of totalitarian communism.

Health. A citizenry must enjoy overall adequate sanitation and proper nutrition to be economically productive, let alone be aware of political issues. Chronically sick or undernourished people are unable to build healthy political or economic systems. Some countries still must fear outbreaks of famine or plague that can decimate large segments of the population or wipe out entire settlements. At least a billion of the world's people currently live in grinding poverty and are surviving at a subsistence level at best. The countries they inhabit are hardly suitable places in which to try to establish democratic institutions.

Modern technology. The democratization process requires a modern technological as well as cultural infrastructure. The advent over the last quarter century of personal computers, fax machines, and electronic mail has enabled and encouraged an unprecedented exchange of information between governments and between people. It is no longer possible for government to monopolize information except in the most tightly controlled dictatorships. The democratization requirements of a free press and free speech have been substantially enhanced by the explosion of accessible and affordable technology.

Perhaps most importantly, though, the democratization process cannot occur until a nation has an overall culture conducive to democracy's success. Ethnic conflict, religious violence, gender discrimination, and severe class divisions are all serious hindrances to democratization, and can even destroy it. This is not to say that undemocratic traditions in a society cannot survive a democratization process and exist in a full democracy. The House of Lords in the United Kingdom is an example: it is not a democratically chosen body; rather, its members assume their positions by royal appointment or aristocratic inheritance. It survives in a mostly democratic culture because it is politically insignificant.

On the other hand, a society is ill-suited for democracy if any segment of its population suffers continual persecution or discrimination. In India, a country making a serious and, in many ways, successful effort to pursue democratization, regular elections occur, an uncensored press informs the people, and civilians control the government. But, as table 1.2 strongly suggests, India is also one of several countries in which female infanticide is widely practiced. India is undergoing democratization, but it has yet to achieve a democracy.

Westernization

The appearance of European and, even more emphatically, American products and businesses in the East and South Asia, the Middle East, and Latin America suggests that the globe is undergoing a westernization process that includes the adoption of western value systems as well as western-style economic and political systems. Millions of Asians, for example, happily consume billions of MacDonald's hamburgers and wash them down with either Coca-Cola or Pepsi-Cola. The largest Kentucky Fried Chicken outlet is in Beijing, China's capital city (the largest MacDonald's is in Russia). To an appreciable extent, the westernization process is undeniable. But it is possible to overestimate both its influence and occasional nonwestern resentment of this influence.

It is understandable that some aspects of western culture are neither desired nor appreciated in nonwestern societies. For example, in 1980, the prison population in the United States was 370,000. By the early 1990s, that num-

TABLE 1.2   Missing Women in Populations of Selected Areas

	China	India	Pakistan	Bangladesh	Nepal	West Asia	Egypt
Census data	1990	1991	1981	1981	1981	1985	1986
Actual ratio of males to females	1.066	1.077	1.105	1.064	1.050	1.060	1.047
Expected ratio of males to females	1.010	1.020	1.025	1.025	1.025	1.030	1.020
Number of females (millions)	548.7	406.3	40.0	42.2	7.3	55.0	23.5
Number of missing females (millions)	30.5	22.8	3.1	1.6	0.2	1.7	0.6

Data from *Population and Development Review.*
Source: "Missing Women in Populations of Selected Areas," from "Stark Data on Women: 100 Million Are Missing," *The New York Times.*
November 5, 1991. Copyright © 1991 The New York Times Company. Reprinted by permission.

ber had tripled to over 1.2 million, "a higher figure per 100,000 citizens than anywhere in the world."[12] Even many obviously undemocratic societies have a prison population proportionally lower than our own. Nonwestern cultures would clearly have to be self-destructive to want to emulate such an element of western society. For that matter, even within western society there are communities that question both the superiority and morality of western culture. A number of fundamentalist groups, for instance, have turned their backs on the more materialistic characteristics of what they regard as an immoral culture.

Radical and sometimes violent religious fundamentalism, whether Christian, Jewish, Islamic, or Hindu, and vehement expressions of nationalism are in some sense a reaction to westernization. Such expressions oppose a global culture dominated by western economies, western language (usually English), a "shop 'til you drop" mentality. We will explore this conflict further in a later chapter.

Religious Fundamentalism

The term *fundamentalism* may be variously interpreted. It is often associated with zealots ready to maim and kill at a moment's notice anyone they consider less than adequately enthusiastic about a particular religious viewpoint. Religious radicals do not regard toleration as a virtue, and most treat it as a vice that should be eradicated.

Religion and expressions of nationalism often go together. For example, in sixteenth- and seventeenth-century France, one had to be Catholic to be considered authentically French (both the government and populace regarded Protestants as less than politically loyal), while to be Catholic in England was almost synonymous with treason.[13] Hostility toward religious minorities

---

[12] "Bill Bradley, Commonsense Cop," *The Economist,* July 23, 1994, p. 30.

[13] Even today, members of the British royal family are discouraged from marrying outside of the Anglican Church. This rule makes sense to the British, since the monarch is both head of state and head of the Anglican Church.

Ayatollah Khomeini is the founder of the Islamic Republic of Iran.

can be even more severe. In the 1930s, to be Jewish (or have even one Jewish great-grandparent) in Germany was enough to earn expulsion and confiscation of property; by the 1940s, Jews were the targets of outright genocide. With the depressing exception of Northern Ireland, however, most of western Europe has stopped equating religion with political loyalty.

Residues of religion in politics, however, are still easy to find in the West. Prochoice and prolife advocates in the United States are vocal and active. Both often decide which congressional candidate to support based simply on the view the candidate holds on abortion, without considering other issues that might be important to the electorate. This exceptionally delicate issue (the death penalty is another) only infrequently leads to violence.[14]

Western Europeans (and North Americans) are exceptions to the general rule that religious violence is rather commonplace. And it *is* commonplace, often in religions unfamiliar to many Americans. For example, in Assam, a state in northeastern India, much blood has been shed between the Muslims who migrated there and the indigenous Boro tribe. The Boros would probably attack anyone who was migrating into their ancestral home, but Muslims also represent the largest religious minority in India, and to non-Muslims they are a serious menace. India is a country where a great deal of conflict has already arisen between Muslims and Hindus.[15]

Religious fanatics often view those who oppose their policies as fanatics themselves. For example, Islamic fundamentalists believe American foreign policy advocates the sort of program that is relentlessly hostile to Islam. They view the Jewish state of Israel as an agent of the Christian West in the midst of the Islamic world. Moreover,

> *Christian missionaries . . . loom large for the [Islamic] fundamentalists, who see them as leaders of a systematic assault on Islam. Fundamentalists discern a strong crusading component to U. S. foreign policy. "The U. S. attitude is motivated by several factors, but the most important, in my view," writes Umar al-Talmasani, the Egyptian fundamentalist leader, "[is] religious fanaticism. . . . This attitude is a continuation of the crusader invasion of a thousand years ago."[16]

---

[14] Keep in mind, though, that pro-life advocates regard an abortion as an act violent enough to be termed murder. Two Pensacola, Florida, physicians were murdered by pro-life advocates who subscribe to the notion of "justifiable homicide."

[15] John F. Burns, "60 Die in Separatist Battles in Northeast India," *The New York Times,* July 25, 1994, p. A3.

[16] Daniel Pipes, "Fundamentalist Muslims between America and Russia," *Foreign Affairs,* Vol. 64, No. 5 (Summer 1986), p. 947.

As we shall examine elsewhere, when religious fundamentalists succeed in taking over a government, that government is usually a good deal less than inspired by democratic values. Even dress codes are strictly enforced. In Iran, for instance, government-sponsored religious police are on the lookout for young women who fail to wear sufficient clothing (covering every body part but the eyes), and for young couples who flaunt their affection for one another by holding hands.[17] The state considers the overall moral conduct of Iranians as an activity that government can legitimately regulate according to religious precepts.

In sum, radical religious fundamentalism normally includes the following characteristics:

1. An absolutist doctrine not open to compromise or change
2. An intolerance of dissent and opposition
3. An insistence on a particular life-style and official enforcement of doctrinal values[18]
4. A binding social and familial hierarchy that spells out specific duties by gender, age, and religious status
5. A legal system dependent upon scriptural remedies for crimes and immoral activities and that sees little difference between crime and immorality.

Tribalism and Ethnic Conflict

As the Soviet Union and communism collapsed in eastern and central Europe, ancient ethnic tensions that had been contained for most of the twentieth century bubbled to the surface. Ethnicity is not the only source of conflict in the post Cold War era, but it is easily one of the most important. One scholar, for example, has identified in Russia a total of 204 "ethnoterritorial" conflicts.[19] And these are only in one country. Keep in mind that with anywhere between six thousand and eight thousand distinct ethnic communities crowded into only two hundred states worldwide, the possibilities of conflict are virtually endless.

In fact, the existence of states themselves may be a critical reason for ethnic and tribal violence. Many—perhaps most—states are rather unnatural creations. This point is most vivid in the African continent, where Belgian, British, and French colonizers drew boundary lines between their possessions during the nineteenth century for their convenience rather than for the benefit of the indigenous tribes that lived there. Inevitably, tribes were divided and found

---

[17] *The Economist*, July 23, 1994, p. 39.

[18] An unmarried couple caught holding hands in Iran are liable to prosecution. *The New York Times*, August 3, 1994.

[19] Bogdan Szajkowski, "Will Russia Disintegrate in Bantustans?" *The World Today* (August-September 1993).

themselves in the post-colonial era (after 1945) living in different countries with fellow citizens who spoke different languages, practiced different religions, and were often traditionally hostile to one another.

Again, the West is neither immune nor insulated from the conflict responsible for the numerous wars currently underway all over the globe. Some West European countries have been affected by immigration from the North African countries of Algeria and Morocco. The immigrants may already speak the language of their adopted country, especially if they emigrate to France. But the immigrants are encountering varying degrees of hostility from indigenous populations that see serious economic challenges from workers willing to provide labor for lower wages. Perhaps even more gripping is the fear among indigenous groups in France, Germany, and Britain who see immigrants as destructive of and in competition with native cultures. Nativism is evident when the native inhabitants of a country in effect retreat into a nationalist shell to exclude immigrants they consider undesirable.

The southern European countries of Spain, France, and Italy are feeling the brunt of immigration, much of it illegal from northern Africa. Some of the immigrants raise special concerns because they are suspected Islamic extremists.[20]

At the same time that resentment against immigrants is increasing in the West, western society itself is becoming increasingly multicultural. The United States, for example, currently has the fifth-largest Spanish-speaking population in the world; Germany's capital, Berlin, has more Turkish residents than all but two cities in the world; and one out of every five police officers in London is from Africa or the West Indies.[21] Yet despite their numbers, immigrants are usually the first to lose their jobs in hard economic times: in the Netherlands, for example, the unemployment rate in the middle of 1994 was 7 percent, slightly more than it was that year in the United States. But the Netherlands has large ethnic minorities; unemployment among Turks living there that year was 35 percent, and among Moroccans, 42 percent.[22]

NATIONS AND STATES

There is an inaccurate tendency to use the term *nation* interchangeably with the term *state*. Most nations are, in fact, stateless, and a great many states can actually count several nations within their borders. A genuine nation-state is an unusual entity. For example, the United Kingdom is a state that consists of the English, Scottish, Welsh, and Irish nations. Collectively, these people are frequently referred to as "Britons." But not among themselves: most prefer to be known as English, Scot, Welsh, or Irish.

---

[20] "Something New Out of Africa," *The Economist*, July 16, 1993, pp. 41–42.

[21] David C. Gordon, *Images of the West: Third World Perspectives* (London and New York: Rowman & Littlefield Publishers, 1989), pp. 40–41.

[22] "Europe and the Underclass," *The Economist*, July 30, 1994, p. 19.

When World War II ended in 1945, perhaps five dozen or so sovereign states existed in the world. In the later 1940s, and continuing into the 1950s and 1960s, the British, French, Belgian, and Dutch colonial empires shrank as one colony after another became politically independent. As a result, by the end of the 1980s, there were around 170 sovereign countries. After the collapse of the "last colonial empire," the USSR, more countries emerged as sovereign, while others either dissolved (such as East Germany) or subdivided (as Czechoslovakia and Yugoslavia did). By the middle 1990s, over 200 independent countries were in the world, a record number in modern times.

Some experts believe the process is far from over. Some predict that some countries may, in cell-like fashion, continue to divide and redivide. The possibility of a world with 500 or more countries is a serious possibility, as distinct communities secede and establish their own political structures. This eventuality is not one that most authorities are enthusiastic about, and for good reason:

> There is simply no way in which all the hundreds of peoples who aspire to sovereign independence can be granted a state of their own without loosening fearful anarchy on a planetary scale. . . . An international system made up of several hundred territorial states cannot be a basis for global security and prosperity.[23]

One of the most important challenges for the early years of the next century is how to contain or at least coordinate the unprecedented explosion of states, many of which are not expected to become economically viable.

"Nations Against States"[24]

Very few countries in the world have been ethnically, religiously, and linguistically homogeneous. It helps to live in an out-of-the-way place where no one else lives and where no one else wants to live. The settlers themselves would have to decide to live in an uninhabited land, all originate from the same place, and share an identical cultural and historical background (as in Iceland).[25] These happy circumstances rarely if ever occur; the places where they have occurred could probably be counted on the fingers of one or, at the most, two hands.

Most countries are heterogeneous to some extent. A fortunate few find heterogeneity to be a virtue. The diverse population of the United States, while not without some negative aspects (such as ongoing racism and religious bigotry, as well as local disagreements over whether the United States is a mono- or bilingual country) has found diversity an enriching cultural and economic experience.

---

[23] Gidon Gottleib, *Nation Against State: A New Approach to Ethnic Conflict and the Decline of Sovereignty* (New York: Council of Foreign Relations Press, 1994), pp. 26–27.

[24] This phrase is taken from Gidon Gottleib, *Ibid.*

[25] Iceland's approximately 300,000 inhabitants are nearly all descendants of Scandanavians who established settlements approximately a millenium ago.

Even stable democracies have their problems. A fourth of Canada is French-speaking and Catholic, while most of the remaining three-fourths are English-speaking and Protestant. The French and Catholic part of the country, Quebec, may secede from Canada, perhaps causing substantial economic dislocation and hardship to itself as well as to other parts of the country. But at least secession, if it occurs, will most likely be peaceful in Canada.

Separatism is even more volatile and common in Third World countries. India (with fifteen official languages and several religions), for example, could unravel. Even in western Europe, separatist movements such as the Basques in Spain and the Lombardy League in Italy (which doesn't want to secede so much as throw the southern and poorest third of the country out) have threatened to separate.

In these and dozens of other cases, nations reside in states they are neither loyal to nor consider their own. Moreover, this isn't simply a case of regime loyalty. For instance, while President Saddam Hussein is an especially unpopular ruler of Iraq, the country itself is a good deal less than a natural entity, anyway. The Kurds in the northern third of the country and the Shiite Muslims in the southern third hardly consider themselves Iraqi and were far from loyal to the central government long before Saddam took power. Since then, they have understandably desired to escape the genocidal tendencies not only of Hussein, but of his predecessors (and most likely his successors).

Countries that unravel are not uncommon. The unraveling of a superpower, however, is somewhat frightening. When the Soviet Union disintegrated in 1991, it was replaced by fifteen successor states, four of them with nuclear arsenals. Several of the fifteen were soon embroiled in internal conflicts, usually based on ethnic rivalries, but also on border disputes.

During the dictatorship of Josef Stalin (1924–1953), a favorite pastime of the Soviet government was moving entire national communities hundreds or even thousands of miles from their ancestral homelands. Now some of these peoples are attempting to move back. Some of the Tatars, for example, are trying to return to the Crimea, even though few have ever seen the region. After they were forced out, though, their homes were occupied by Russians and Ukrainians who are still there and who show no desire to be replaced.

Perhaps a situation with even greater potential for havoc is found in countries whose citizenries are (sometimes vastly) outnumbered by noncitizenries. Several of the Persian Gulf states are experiencing this political incongruity (see table 1.3). Very large minorities and often substantial majorities in these countries are simply guest workers who benefit from the jobs generated by the country's oil industry. These people generally are denied access to the political process (as much as one exists) and are not permitted to own businesses of their own. They are often exploited and abused, particularly if they are female house servants. In short, there is no reason for them to demonstrate any loyalty to the regime or to go to the slightest trouble to preserve it.

In the closing years of the twentieth century and in the first years of the twenty-first, the international constellation may be punctuated not by conflicts

TABLE 1.3   Noncitizens in Selected Middle Eastern Countries (percent of total population)

Country	Approximate Percentage of Noncitizens
Bahrain	37
Kuwait	50
Qatar	60
United Arab Emirates	80

Source: Adopted from *CIA World Factbook, 1994,* Central Intelligence Agency, Reston, Virginia.

between states as much as by conflicts within them. Several types of governments or states may be subject to such conflict, including:

1.   Countries that have sizable ethnic and/or religious minorities who wish to establish their own territorial states (for example, French-speaking Canadians)

2.   Countries with noncitizen populations so large that they threaten the political process they are usually denied access to (for example, United Arab Emirates)

3.   Countries that are artificially contrived and that have sizable ethnic and/or religious minorities that want to join their brethren across the borders (for example, Kurds in Iraq who desire to establish a Kurdistan state with the Kurds in Iran and Turkey)

Naturally, most countries consider their territories sacrosanct and will not often see them change in peaceful fashion. Some, though, will probably change one way or another, and this may usher in an era of new and perhaps irresolvable border disputes.

New Political Formulations

Political scientists often enjoy speculating on political scenarios that usually don't come true. However, the scenarios occasionally correspond to reality. Today, speculation even seems appropriate—we are living in a transitional period that began with the end of the Cold War and as yet has no likely end in sight.

What does seem likely is that as states divide and new countries are created, new territorial disputes will arise. Some may actually be resolved peacefully. When Czechoslovakia dissolved in 1993 into two countries, the Czech Republic and Slovakia, the dissolution was without violence. Peaceful examples of secession, though, seem to be the exception rather than the rule.

Regardless of how state boundaries are drawn, some minorities will always get stranded in countries they have little affection for and whose majority populations have little toleration for nonindigenous populations. One of the most serious examples of this situation involves the 25 million Russians living in the non-Russian former Soviet republics. A large proportion are content where they are and have been more or less accepted by the indigenous population. But many aren't either content or accepted. Hundreds of thousands of Russians are residents of the three small Baltic republics, and they complain of all sorts of discriminatory measures that the Baltic governments have taken against them. In some sense, there is a balance: as many as 35 million non-Russians, more than 20 percent of the total population, live in the Russian Federated Republic, and many of them complain and worry about discrimination by the Russian authorities.

Possible Alternatives to the Traditional State

As traditional states experience internal conflicts that cause them to splinter, other alternatives may increasingly come into play.

Mini-States.   A state small in both population and territory has a certain advantage. If such a country lacks valuable natural resources such as oil, it can usually expect to be left alone. Europe has had mini-states for centuries: Andorra, Lietchenstein, Monaco, San Marino, and Vatican City, to name some. The economies of these countries are based on a single product that ranges from smuggling to gambling to banking to religion. A plethora of mini-states has also cropped up in the West Indies and the South Pacific. Most have populations between ten thousand and a hundred thousand and are dependent upon outside economic assistance. These countries are members of the United Nations (where they have a vote equal in weight to that of the United States in the General Assembly), regularly exchange ambassadors with other countries, print their own currency and stamps, and have all the other trappings of a sovereign state.

Regions with Limited Political Autonomy.   Varying degrees of autonomy have become a political fact in several countries that contain diverse linguistic, ethnic, and religious communities. In order to retain political unification, central governments in several countries, from Spain to Russia, have granted substantial degrees of local autonomy to various regions.

The degree is normally dependent upon the deals the central government can work out with the respective regions. Obviously, this is no easy task. The Basque region in Spain has a strong separatist movement that wants complete independence. In Russia, Tatarstan and Chechyna have announced with limited success their departure from the Russian Federated Republic. Tatarstan has had trouble getting by the international community as well as the Russians to take its independence seriously because it is completely surrounded by Russian territory. Hence, it is necessary to travel either across or over Russia to get to or from Tatarstan.

Despite such occasional incongruities, experiments in limited autonomy are going forward, sometimes in unlikely places. Israel and the Palestine Liberation Organization (PLO), for example, have agreed to Israeli withdrawal from parts of the Gaza Strip and the West Bank. The PLO hopes that the withdrawal and the replacement of Israeli authority with its own will eventually lead to a fully sovereign (and enlarged) Palestinian state.

The experimentation with limited political autonomy will no doubt continue as central governments, either voluntarily by coercion, give up at least partial authority over various regions. It is a delicate matter. To give in too completely to local demands may actually cause the collapse of an entire country; on the other hand, for a government to attempt to retain full control over a disaffected region may incite civil war. Several alternatives for providing limited autonomy range from the inhumane to the reasonable:

1. A central government may refuse to grant any local autonomy and may resort without hesitation to genocidal policies to retain control (for example, Iraqi treatment of Kurds and Muslim Shiites)

2. A central government may grant local cultural autonomy, usually including free use of the local language, control over the educational system, and limited political autonomy, but retain control over foreign policy and military forces (for example, Russia's relationship with Tatarstan and other members of the federated republic)

3. A central government may operate in a fairly democratic and commonsense fashion, addressing needs that are more or less national in scope and making itself available to assist in regional and local matters whenever all sides agree it is desirable (for example, most democracies in Western Europe and the United States)

We will refer to all of these alternatives in future chapters.

SUMMARY

1. While government and politics are not identical, they are inseparable. Politics precedes and usually results in government and remains its driving force.

2. The Soviet Union's political regime is an excellent example of how a governmental structure can completely fail to provide for the needs of its citizenry by adhering to an unworkable ideology and institutionalizing corruption and incompetence.

3. Government that actively seeks to provide for the security and overall welfare of its citizenries tends both to survive and to receive the loyalty of those under its jurisdiction.

4. American society and its political system are good reference points because of the economic and political impact the United States has had in the rest of the world and its status as a "universal nation."

5. The Cold War period (1945–1990) was, in retrospect, a simpler time when the world seemingly could be divided into bad and good governments.

6. The post Cold War era is much more complex because of the resurgence of ethnic and/or religious conflicts.

7. Democratization is a not-always-successful process that can lead a society to adopt permanently democratic political institutions.

8. Pillars of durable democracy seem to include a citizenry that enjoys a decent standard of living, widespread literacy, universally available modern technology, overall good physical health, and accessibility to self-improvement.

9. Westernization is widespread and popular in some nonwestern regions, but deeply resented and feared in others, as expressed through religious fundamentalism.

10. The term *nation-state* does not accurately describe most countries on the map. Many societies are breaking down into tribal and clannish affiliations, and the central government is having a difficult time retaining authority in such regions. In many cases, a central government is having difficulty even establishing control over regions and populations it is considered responsible for.

11. Some new political formulations—including mini-states or areas of limited autonomy— may be implemented to cope with the breakdown of countries into smaller, quasi-independent areas.

GLOSSARY

Baltic states   The three small republics (Latvia, Lithuania, and Estonia, with a combined population of about 8 million) that were forcibly annexed by the Soviet Union in 1940 and, in 1989, became the first of the Soviet republics to secede, leading to the eventual collapse of the entire Soviet system.

command economy   The total control and bureaucratization of a national economy from the political capital, which makes often arbitrary economic decisions without consideration of either need or quality.

genocide   The systematic murder, usually planned or at least sponsored by the government, of an entire community or nation of people based on its religion, ethnicity, and/or social status.

Kremlin   The physical and political center of the Russian government in Moscow through the czarist and communist periods for most of Russian history, except when the capital was located in St. Petersburg during the eighteenth and nineteenth centuries.

Nazism   The ideology officially expressed in Germany from 1933 to 1945 that practiced racism and genocide.

Third World   A term traditionally used to denote the 150 or so countries, whose populations include four-fifths of the human race, considered lacking in comprehensive economic modernization.

Government and Politics

*T*he following three chapters offer general discussions on such
perennial subjects as what politics is and what good it does. As
chapter 2 indicates, politics has been a much discussed activity for
as long as recorded history. An entire discipline, political philosophy, devotes
itself to making formulations about what kind of political state is best for most of
us and how we can arrive at it. Chapter 3 reviews the various dimensions and
intricacies of political culture. Each country's overall culture heavily influences
the society's political culture. The latter both shapes and is shaped by the
prevailing political institutions and is guided for better or worse by the country's
overall political history. Chapter 4 concentrates on the two primary current
forms of political system, democracy and authoritarianism. Each can be broken
down into several interpretations and practices. One, democracy, is a
comparatively new political arrangement and is still rather experimental, while
authoritarianism has a long, if not always appealing, tradition.

Government, the State, and Political Philosophy

Why does the human species prefer to live in a political society regardless of its inherent imperfections? Why do we require the state to conduct and guarantee a civilized life-style, and why do we expect the state and those in political authority to be user-friendly? These preferences, which we will discuss in this chapter, led to the birth of political philosophy at least twenty-five hundred years ago. It is important to briefly review some of the most outstanding theories of the state, since theorists have debated political obedience, the rights of the individual versus those of society, and what actually constitutes legitimate government for centuries. These debates are far from resolved and will most likely continue for a long time.

For thousands of years, people have speculated about government: What is the purpose of government? How much government is good for us? How much government is too much? Through what kind of institutions can we balance the need for government with the desire for individual freedoms? And, perhaps most importantly, if we don't like our government's policies, how can we change or get rid of them? Two-and-one-half millenia ago, political speculation became more sophisticated in the Greek city-state system as political philosophers began spending considerable amounts of time creating formulas for successful governments. We've been at it ever since, and, along the way, we've experimented with a variety of governmental forms.

We are still trying to get it right. Some governments have been more successful than others; quite a few have indulged in inhumane practices. Clearly, many governments have caused a great deal more harm than good. Just as clearly, we have yet to achieve a perfect form of government that guarantees justice and prosperity for every member of society. People still debate whether government is supposed to guarantee either, or whether it even has that capability.

This chapter surveys some of the more interesting formulas for government. New communications technologies, unforeseen conflicts among various segments of citizenries, and evolving degrees of cultural autonomy in political jurisdictions will present government with both new opportunities and new challenges. Government and the political processes that determine who governs and through what kinds of institutions will continue to change and undergo refinement; we are far from through developing new forms of government.

THE CLASSICAL SENSE OF GOOD GOVERNMENT

As just mentioned, speculation about the means and ends of government became historically noticeable in a few of the ancient city-states of Greece. Why people began to consider proper governance as a serious profession in Greece is uncertain. A reasonable explanation is that in some of the city-states, the overall culture encouraged inquiry into a wide variety of subjects—physics, biology, mathematics, and philosophy among them. Greece twenty-five hundred years ago experienced an explosion of knowledge, yielding results so universal we still find ourselves studying, debating, and evaluating them.

Ironically, one of the first meaningful statements of good government was authored by Plato (427–347 B.C.), a political philosopher who possessed a very substantial dislike of and contempt for politics. Plato did not believe that the free play of politics actually produced useful results or resolved disputes. In politics, he argued, the decision-making process is frequently based less on reason than on what seems to be a good idea at the moment. Moreover, the problem with politics, its give and take, inconclusive ends, and unavoidable passions, has much to do with what politics does ultimately produce—namely unpredictable and therefore dangerous change.

Plato feared and hated change in great part because he was aware that other disciplines, such as mathematics, for example, are quite orderly and predictable. The correct sum of two numbers added together *never* changes. The fact that such a discipline is changeless, orderly, and predictable led Plato to conclude that the same sort of view ought to be applied to human society.[1]

Plato was a reluctant realist, and he preferred a harmonious society that would find no reason to change. He recognized that the creation of such a community would be a massive undertaking, but he firmly believed it was worth the cost. The end result would be an entity in which citizens would have responsibilities that were both necessary and would appeal to their talents. The key was to implement the proper definition of justice.

Justice in Plato's most famous work, *The Republic*, consisted of each citizen doing what he or she does best by natural talent. The health (Plato was fond of using medical terms and analogies) of the Republic was maintained by a citizenry divided into three classes, as table 2.1 summarizes. The guardians or philosophers of the Republic are analogous to the head of the body, the auxil-

---

[1] This preference for exactitude was carried to its logical conclusion when Plato calculated 5,040 as the perfect number of citizens for a well-adjusted commonwealth.

TABLE 2.1   Classes and Souls in Plato's Republic

Class	Area of the Body	Soul or Character
Guardian	Head	Thinks and directs
Auxiliary	Chest	Executes directions from the guardians; thinks less and acts more
Common	Stomach	Is acquisitive and materially productive in a variety of necessary occupations

iaries to the chest, and the rest of the society, the majority, to below the chest (the stomach or abdomen area). Most people, Plato believed, are appetitive— that is, they are motivated more by and think more with their stomachs and guts than with their heads and brains. Plato cautions that appetitive people are neither unimportant nor stupid. All three classes perform essential tasks.

Plato is very clear that all three classes are absolutely essential to the well-being of the state. No class would do well or even survive without the others. Guardians are dependent upon auxiliaries to carry out instructions and protect the society, and on the common mass for their very sustenance. Auxiliaries need direction from the guardians. The artisans and craftsmen, who are incapable of providing a just commonwealth by or for themselves, require the other two classes to resolve their disputes (the guardians) and protect them (the auxiliaries).

The guardians were the class Plato obviously favored and who reflected his own preference that society be in the care of philosophers. Many of us would find Plato's requirements for entrance into this class intimidating and unappealing: the guardians were not to own property, establish families, or pursue financially rewarding careers. The craftsmen and artisans would care for the guardians' needs. The guardians would spend their time pursuing knowledge. On occasions that required resolutions of disputes within *The Republic,* the guardians' accumulated wisdom would insure the proper application of justice.

The guardians would lead a communist life-style. Communism, for Plato, was a privilege meant only for those who don't require material wealth in the first place since they are supposed to be above the need to possess property. Socrates, Plato's teacher, argues in *The Republic* that a guardian should not possess "any property of his own beyond what is absolutely necessary."[2] Should the guardians ever give in to the temptation of becoming like artisans and craftsmen, who prefer money to virtue

> *they will become housekeepers and husbandmen instead of guardians, enemies and tyrants instead of allies of other citizens; hating and being hated, plotting and being plotted against, they will pass their whole life in much greater terror of*

---

[2] *The Republic,* Book III, p. 305.

internal than of external enemies, and the hour of ruin, both to themselves and to the rest of the State, will be at hand.[3]

Once settled into an ascetic existence, these wise men and women would make it unnecessary for the society to establish a legal system or to hold elections. Plato was no democrat, believing in the ability and right of the people to govern. Instead, he believed that democracy allowed people without the necessary talent, aptitude, or intelligence to govern badly. His argument was basically that we would not allow someone without expertise to declare him or herself an engineer and build a bridge. Why, then, should we tolerate a real estate agent who wants to become a governor? Plato also held Athenian democracy responsible for the death of his hero and teacher, Socrates.[4] He took his revenge by bringing Socrates back to life as the leading figure in *The Republic* who carefully maps out the perfect society.

However else *The Republic* may come across to the late twentieth-century reader, certain aspects of it are remarkably modern. In at least two ways, Plato makes the point that he is departing from much that was taken for granted in the ancient world, including its most progressive area, Greece. For one thing, *The Republic* is probably the first description of any society to include mention of gender equality, though its mention was restricted to the guardian class. Female guardians were not meant to simply stay at home and rear families. (In fact, they weren't to have any families to rear.)[5] They would pursue, along with their male counterparts, the very demanding physical and intellectual training that would enable them to become the best possible caretakers of *The Republic.*

There is a certain irony to the Platonic scheme described in *The Republic.* The society of *The Republic* must get its start at some point. It is unlikely that Plato had any knowledge of the Bible, but seven centuries before his own, the Hebrew tribes that had fled Egypt in the Exodus wandered for forty years in the Sinai wilderness so that a fresh generation with no memory of slavery could enter the Promised Land.

The Republic is Plato's promised land, and to enter it requires the elimination of the views of a previous generation. Plato counted on a new, very young (and therefore impressionable) generation (under ten years of age) to realize his goals. What, then, are the under tens supposed to believe? Pure and simple, they are to believe a lie, or, to be less crude, a "noble lie." And they *will* believe it. Even ten-year-olds can be skeptical, but Plato reasoned that if a generation grows to adulthood constantly exposed to a particular point of view, the mem-

---

[3] Ibid., p. 306.

[4] Socrates was condemned for corrupting the morals of Athenian youths. At seventy years of age, he was given the unhappy choice of exile from the city he loved, or death. He chose to drink poison.

[5] By this time, you may be asking yourself how successive generations of guardians would be produced. Plato addresses this issue in *The Republic* by suggesting an annual festival. The children that resulted from the "festivities" would be reared in common. For guardian parents to know who their children were would result in favoritism, a distraction from the pursuit of knowledge Plato thought this class needed to avoid at all costs.

TABLE 2.2   Myth and Structure of Plato's Republic

Class	Metal	Activities
Guardians	Gold	Pursuit of ideas and knowledge
Auxiliaries	Silver	Military and administrative activities
Artisans and craftsmen	Bronze	Production of material necessities for all classes

bers of that generation will accept the view as their own and will be reluctant to believe anything to the contrary. Plato was an early believer in the power of propaganda.

The noble lie, as summarized in table 2.2, goes something like this: each of the three classes are descended from metals that differ in strength and value. In *The Republic*, it is important to know one's place.

Aristotle

Early in his most famous work, *Politics*, Aristotle wrote that

> *Every state is as we see a sort of partnership, and every partnership is formed with a view to some good (since all the actions of all mankind are done with a view to what they think to be good).*[6]

Of course, Aristotle believed that the state the partnership created would be one in which the population was relatively homogeneous; he did not foresee the ethnic and cultural diversity that characterizes most modern states. But he did fully understand that any state has to be a reflection of common interests and is the natural outcome of human association—and a necessary one, at that.[7]

Aristotle viewed the **polis,** or city-state, as the highest stage of human social and political development, allowing its citizens to find and live the good life.[8] For Aristotle, the polis is the only place where the good life is possible, the only place where the individual can make a good life for her or himself. Since "the city-state is prior in nature to the household and to each of us individually," and since "the whole must necessarily be prior to the part," we are "either low in the scale of humanity or above it . . ."[9] In other words, Aristotle believed, no self-respecting member of the human community would consider living any-where else but within the confines of political society. Aristotle assumed that we are basically a gregarious species "and so even when men have no need of assis-tance from each other they nonetheless desire to live together."[10]

---

[6] *Politics* (Cambridge, Massachusetts: Harvard University Press, 1972), p. 3.

[7] Ibid., p. 9.

[8] Ibid.

[9] Ibid., pp. 9 and 11.

[10] Ibid., p. 201.

Once one is within the confines of the state, the critical question is how the best quality of life can be achieved. Aristotle's formula for political and social success has been imitated by numerous societies through the ages. People and political systems, he argued, enjoy long and productive lives as long as they avoid extremes. And a healthy polis requires healthy constituents. Each of us should know how much is too much to be good for us:

> *The man who runs away from everything in fear and never endures anything becomes a coward; the man who fears nothing whatsoever but encounters everything becomes rash.*[11]

In other words, neither yellowbellies nor swashbucklers can govern successful states. It is those who are moderate, who yield to no ideological or political extreme, and who may come across as dull and boring, who are actually best fit to govern and be governed.

Extremes of wealth and poverty, Aristotle believed (and modern societies can attest) are probably inevitable but should be kept minimal. He recommended a large and broadly based middle class as a recipe for political stability. The middle class society is in place in most of the western world. It has been instrumental, as Aristotle predicted, in creating successful political democracies that tend to follow moderate and sane economic and social policies. Flirtations with extremes of the political **left** and **right** have more often than not led to disaster. (See the box for a discussion of the terms *left* and *right*.)

Aristotle further believed that moderation has another value: it is an excellent preservative of the status quo. Aristotle, like Plato, feared change. Unlike Plato, Aristotle understood that some change is inevitable, but he sought to minimize its effects. In particular, he dreaded revolution, the political phenomenon that can completely upset the status quo. Constant vigilance is required to avoid the destruction that even gradual change brings. Aristotle believed it is dangerous, for example, when a government decides to "give up one of the details of the constitution" since "afterwards they also make another slightly bigger change more readily, until they alter the whole system."[12]

Change, then, is a terrifying if subtle political activity that, Aristotle was convinced, can lead to no good. In this respect he had no argument with Plato; we have already noted how Plato made his dread of change apparent throughout *The Republic*, advocating a society practically frozen in a single time period. In reality, of course, change is impossible to prevent. In advocating a totally unchanging society, Aristotle violated his own conviction that extremes are evils to always be avoided.

Aristotle's influence is still vibrant. The founders of the United States, for example, met him halfway. They had not only read his works; they applied a good many of his political principles. And they also were apprehensive about the prospect of change, and they intentionally made it very difficult to amend

---

[11] *Nichomachean Ethics*, p. 77.

[12] Ibid., p. 19.

A NOTE ON THE TERMS *LEFT* AND *RIGHT*

These terms, which apparently originated in the immediate aftermath of the French Revolution of 1789, will come up in other contexts in this text. When the French monarchy was overthrown, some of the more radical revolutionaries, who happened to be sitting on the left side of the newly constituted legislative chamber, advocated such measures as cancellation of all debts, the creation of a classless society, and disenfranchising the Catholic Church. The more moderate legislators, who happened to be sitting on the right side of the chamber, preferred greater democracy than the monarchy had ever allowed, but still preferred to retain traditional values, free markets, and perhaps the creation of a constitutional monarchy.

The United States also experienced an interesting division as a result of its revolution. The drafters of the Declaration of Independence were probably much more radical than those who drafted the Constitution eleven years later. Very few participated at both conventions. After the United States won its independence, the first assemblage, led by Thomas Jefferson, sympathized with the French revolutionaries, while those who supported ratification of the Constitution, led by Alexander Hamilton, leaned toward a more conservative Britain.

the United States Constitution. More than two centuries after ratification, the Constitution has been amended only twenty-seven times.

The Stoics

Aristotle's lifetime coincided with the collapse of the city-state system, an event he seemed oblivious to. He was well acquainted with and in favor of the system and sought to perpetuate its existence, but the city-states could not resist the strength of the empires that gradually absorbed them. By the time the Roman Empire was fully established two to three centuries later, it was becoming increasingly obvious that political philosophy must now take into account a huge political entity that, unlike the polis, included a heterogenous population numbering in the tens of millions. Making sense of a society that was bigger, more dangerous, and more impersonal (a society that in many ways resembles our own) was a complicated task.

While Stoicism was a philosophy developed by pre-Christian thinkers, it had a great deal in common with early Christianity. Each viewed the universe as a place that was not always friendly. More to the point, each viewed society as dominated by a combination of human stupidity and unjustified arrogance. Stoicism viewed the world as torn between virtue and vice; Christianity saw it as torn between salvation and sin. Both considered the world a difficult and disorderly place where personal security and happiness was infrequent and fleeting.

Stoicism offered reason as an escape route out of daily turmoil, whereas Christianity offered faith. Ultimately, the promise of a heavenly and eternal reward after a difficult and often painful life in this world had a greater appeal than a plea to do the best we can without any guarantee of benefits beyond the grave. Even today, the competition between the tradition of reason and the tradition of faith continues: many Christians write the world off as lost and prepare for the next, while those who cling to reason continue to believe that fools threaten civilization more than sinners do.

Stoics understandably preferred order to disorder, but this preference carried an element of fatalism. Everyone could be essentially equal to everyone else, since social or political rank is arbitrary and temporary, and often even a matter of luck. But this also meant one should accept one's status, whether high or low, and do the best one could in the role one was assigned.

The same principle applies to government and governing. If it is one's destiny to govern, one should do so without complaint, but obviously, it is easier to accept the role of king than of slave. For this reason, Stoicism did not appeal beyond the educated and relatively well-off classes. But Stoicism did provide a prescription for proper governance: a ruler should reject all temptations to pursue or enhance personal glory and wealth. Rather, the purpose of rulership is to provide service for the benefit of the entire society. This was certainly a noble principle of governing, though a frequently ignored one. Yet, the principle itself has been bequeathed to successive generations. Politicians are still allowed to further their own ambitions if people believe they are also serving the public good.

For the next millenium, political philosophy was in great part submerged by theology. Then, in the sixteenth century, Nicolo Machiavelli (1469–1522) produced *The Prince*. This slim volume took a radical departure from traditional political thought. Plato and Aristotle had suggested what they believed political society *should be*; Machiavelli explained how political science really *is* and how it actually functions. He argued that no leader worth his salt could do well by being morally good. To secure his own leadership, for example, a prince shouldn't hesitate to wipe out both his opponent and his opponent's family, since children who are fond of their parents may seek revenge later. Goodness would be fully exploited by those who aren't good and have no intention of being good.

The Prince, claimed Machiavelli, should uphold morality, but not take it too seriously himself. For example, the Prince should attend a house of worship because it looks good to do so, but he should not take the sermon seriously. Political morality, in other words, is separate from private morality. Machiavelli also believed a prince must be prepared to do what is necessary to uphold both his power and the security of the state. Hesitating to be ruthless when ruthlessness was required would make the prince both politically immoral and a political failure. Successful politicians were already following this advice, which explains why *The Prince* has been continuously in print for nearly five centuries.

Thomas Hobbes

The expansion of a central government's authority is dependent upon a widespread acceptance of sovereignty. The basic feature of sovereignty is indivisibility: everyone must accept one location where political power is concentrated in any political system. But establishing this type of sovereignty has always been easier said than done. Political philosophers Thomas Hobbes (1588–1679) and John Locke (1632–1704), who were close to the political notables of their times, felt compelled to develop prescriptions for the proper place of sovereignty and limitations on sovereigns.

Hobbes began by describing what he referred to as the *state of nature*. In the state of nature, Hobbes argued, each person can do anything he or she wants. Unfortunately, everyone else also has the same right. The state of nature is, in fact, stateless: every member of our species is alone and responsible for her or his own physical security in such an arrangement. The world, without order, would be a place of fear where life for everyone is "solitary, poor, nasty, brutish, and short." It would be an unfortunate place where war is perpetual and pits "every man against every man." The state of nature, in short, is a formula for a decidedly miserable existence that no one would desire or enjoy.

Hobbes proposed an effective if less than pleasant solution in his most remembered and quoted work, *Leviathan*. He had witnessed the English civil war of the 1640s that culminated in the execution of Charles I. The breakdown of order during this period distressed Hobbes. Not unlike urban Americans watching the steady increase of violent crime degrade their neighborhoods, Hobbes viewed turmoil and chaos as the breakdown not only of the legal system but of civil society itself. Whether criminal behavior or political rebellion poses the threat, Hobbes understood the threat to the maintenance of order was so severe that the end result could only be regression to the state of nature: exactly the place we all had escaped from and to which none of us would wish to return.

Hobbes proposed the creation of a sovereign power that would exercise unquestioned authority. In the dreaded state of nature, people possessed individual liberty. Since everyone had maximum liberty, complete equality prevailed. But in this state, human society could not avoid being violent—with everyone equal to everyone else, no authority could possibly exist. While everyone enjoyed equal liberty and equality, everyone was also equally threatened.

Agreeing on a sovereign authority was an act of survival. Hobbes believed that humans are a species at once argumentive and belligerent, both self-motivated and self-serving. "The object of any appetite or desire . . . a man calleth the good; the object of his aversion, evil; for these words . . . are ever used with relation to the person that useth them. . . ."[13] The sovereign must be cognizant of this very human characteristic and be both fair and firm in the administration of justice. Civil society could endure and prosper only when the largest number of its members were convinced that by obeying reasonable laws everyone's self-interest is served. (Deciding which laws are both appealing and reasonable is an issue we will discuss in a later chapter.)

---

[13] *Leviathan*, XI, p. 23.

For Hobbes, sovereign authority must be indisputable and unequivocal. A citizenry is first and foremost concerned about the physical security of life and possessions, and a sovereign must take responsibility for these concerns. Hobbes believed that many, perhaps most, people are willing and even eager to cede authority over their lives in exchange for guarantees that safeguard their persons, families, and material possessions. In fact, we do this whenever we pay our taxes, accept military conscription, and stop our vehicles at red traffic lights.

The **social contract** Hobbes advocates is not between ruler and ruled. It is a contract between those the sovereign rules. The ruled and their descendants agree "to confer all their power and strength upon one man, or upon one assembly of men."[14] Indeed, Hobbes was not particular what form the sovereign assumed. All that mattered was whether the sovereign was doing the job. Even if the sovereign wasn't performing perfectly, the people would have no recourse. Hobbes was emphatic that even a less than fully competent sovereign was better than the alternative—chaos and violence.

There is no choice in the matter, Hobbes argues. Though he preferred a sovereign that modeled its administration on the basis of justice, Hobbes believed no one should rebel against even inept or tyrannical sovereigns. Revolution is far worse, in this point of view, because it destroys any hope of maintaining the contract that provides for social order.

John Locke

Like Hobbes, John Locke saw enough civil violence in his time—in 1649, when he was seventeen years old, he personally witnessed the beheading of King Charles I—to attempt a political formula that would ensure domestic peace. Unlike Hobbes, Locke believed there was room for tolerating dissent and occasional justification for revolution. Revolution, though, would be unnecessary if the sovereign never broke the laws that applied to everyone else. Locke's theory of government was published in 1691 as *Treatises on Government*. Nearly a century later, the founders of the United States enthusiastically employed its contents to justify the American Revolution in the Declaration of Independence. A decade later, they incorporated Locke's notion of separation of powers into the United States Constitution.[15]

They did so for good reason. Locke's stateless state of nature was somewhat more benign than Hobbes's. His creation of sovereign authority provided for physical security, but it was mainly formulated for the sake of convenience. Locke's state of nature lacked any authority to make an objective decision

---

[14] Ibid., XVII, p. 89.

[15] Locke considered only the legislature and monarchy in his concept of separation of powers. Americans added the judiciary as another wedge preventing any one branch of government from becoming too powerful.

John Locke (1632–1704) was an English political philosopher.

when a controversy as mundane as a property line dispute arose. In this state of nature, Locke said, we make a contract with one another.

In fact, that is why we create government in the first place—for "the great and chief end"[16] of preserving and protecting private property. Locke argued that most of us are fairly reasonable creatures who ask simply to get on with our lives with a minimum of interference. Private property becomes both an incentive and a reward for our efforts. Government, then, is just and fair as long as it fulfills its primary obligation of protecting property through laws, courts, and, when necessary, military action. In return, government can expect the obedience of its citizenry.

Society then selects an authority to administer the laws that society imposes on itself. Keep in mind that the seventeenth century was a very autocratic time nearly everywhere. Toleration was not yet a political virtue. In this context, Locke exhibited a remarkably modern and democratic sentiment. The social contract does not give sovereignty to a monarch or anyone else in particular. Rather, the members of society are sovereign. Through voting and/or through legislators (Locke was an early advocate of parliamentary supremacy), citizens select political officers to execute and apply laws.

But governments, like citizens, are obliged to obey laws as well as avoid oppressive legislation. Government cannot appropriate property without just cause or apply unwarranted taxes (which often amounts to the same thing). If it does, "the people are absolved from obedience when illegal attempts are made upon their liberties and properties."[17]

Perhaps the most striking feature of Locke's treatment is his emphasis of the individual over the state. State power is at all times viewed within the context of the individual's chronological and ethical precedence:

> *To understand political power aright, and derive from its original, we must consider what state all men are naturally in, and that is a state of perfect freedom to order their actions and dispose of their possessions and person as they see fit, within the bounds of the law of nature, without asking leave, or depending upon the will of any other man. A state also of equality, wherein all the power and jurisdiction is reciprocal, no one having more than another.*[18]

---

[16] *Second Treatise*, No. 124.

[17] John Locke, *Second Treatise*, No. 28.

[18] John Locke, "An Essay Concerning the True Origin, Extent and End of Civil Government," in Edwin A. Butt, ed., *The English Philosophers from Bacon to Mill* (New York: Modern Library, 1939), p. 404.

This is strong stuff. Locke is arguing very democratically that no member of society who behaves within the boundaries of natural law—showing respect for the property and lives of others, for instance—should have to worry about the state's interference.

Locke's goal had been to restrict the powers of the executive branch, the one he considered most prone to regress into tyranny. His influence was persuasive. The British monarchy watched its authority gradually, and, for the most part, peacefully, diminish as it was transformed into its current ceremonial role. The real head of government, the prime minister, can serve only as long as he or she enjoys the support of a parliamentary majority.

Locke helped to create institutionalized distrust of the executive. The distrust was transplanted: in colonial America, colonial assemblies relentlessly watched over governors. Even after independence, states placed term limitations on their executives. Many states still impose one- or two-term limitations on their governors. With the ratification of the Twenty-second Amendment in 1951, a two-term limitation was imposed on presidents.

Locke's influence went beyond his own time and country in other ways as well. Baron de Montesquieu in his *Spirit of the Laws* agreed with Locke that separation of powers offered the best hope of avoiding tyrannical government. Both Locke and Montesquieu envisioned the legislative and executive branches keeping an eye on one another. The American political formulation complemented the formula by adding the judiciary as a coequal branch of government to fully ensure that no political dictatorship would become practical or likely.

CONSERVATISM AND LIBERALISM

Probably no other terms in the political lexicon have been as variously interpreted as *conservatism* and *liberalism*. Part of the explanation for this comes from the fact that both ideologies are descended from nineteenth-century *liberalism*, which developed in the aftermath of the French Revolution and Napoleonic wars (1789–1815). Prior to this period, a social order that evolved during the Middle Ages had prevailed in Europe. It was in many respects a simpler time: most of the class structure was based on a predominantly agricultural economy and social system in which a landed aristocracy controlled most of the wealth and all of the political institutions, while a vast peasantry was legally tied to the land.

Rapid urbanization, industrial revolution, relentlessly advancing technology, and the accumulation of unprecedented wealth—events that began in and forever changed the West and are now spreading to East and South Asia, Latin America, and parts of the Middle East—created new roles and opportunities for government. Conservatives and liberals formulated their differences around a debate over the role of government. Conservatives today adhere to the Jeffersonian notion that the less government (and, therefore, the less taxation) the better, while liberals believe that government has a responsibility to provide comfort and security for those who cannot provide for themselves (and to levy taxes to the extent necessary to guarantee adequate social services).

There are numerous manifestations of liberalism, including the classical type associated with John Locke. We cannot really do justice to the several excellent contributions to nineteenth-century liberal thought, including contributions by thinkers who today would be considered conservative or even libertarian.[19] Locke is only one of a multitude of thinkers who could be called or have called themselves liberal. Generally speaking, liberalism began as an ideology that encouraged the individual realization of human potential unfettered by political and social hindrances. Liberals in the twentieth century increasingly advocated a positive role for government in making the lives of the citizenry better and more secure.

It was the beginnings of the industrial revolution that began to undermine the mostly static social system in the sixteenth century as increasing wealth (much of it from gold and silver mines in North and South America) was transferred to growing urban areas.[20] Table 2.3 compares contemporary conservativism and liberalism.

The debate between conservatism and liberalism is based on different emphases and on different interpretations of human nature. Conservatives, for example, consider individual liberty an important and natural social condition. Equality for them, on the other hand, is neither natural nor feasible—members of society, in their view, are naturally and inevitably unequal. Conservatives argue that this is nothing to be embarassed about, but simply a fact. The only way to have equality is to enforce it.

Conservatives assume that in every generation individuals surface as the result of the special talents they possess and that these individuals are obligated to utilize their talents on behalf of the entire community. Talented individuals inevitably assume leadership roles, forming an **elite** within society. Most liberals do not deny that some people are more talented than others. They do believe, however, that talented people who are members of ethnic, racial, or religious minorities may be denied the opportunity to fully realize their talents. Liberals argue that government has the obligation to correct this injustice. The liberal idea is to level the playing field so that each person can maximize individual potential.

The divisions between conservatism and liberalism are serious and complicated in most democratic societies. Conservatives insist that government should leave people alone to pursue their lives as they see fit, but many conservatives also believe that a pregnant woman should not have the option of having an abortion. Liberals argue that government should obligate itself to help people, but they immediately run into the problem of what "help" means: the U.S. welfare system was created with the best of intentions, but even liberals now believe welfare may create more problems than it solves.

Both conservatives and liberals are content to operate within the political boundaries of democratic systems. While their philosophical disagreements are

---

[19] For an excellent summary see D. J. Manning, *Liberalism* (New York: St. Martin's Press, 1976).

[20] London became the first city in the western world in modern times to hit the million mark in population; it did so shortly before the year 1800.

....
TABLE 2.3　　A Comparison of Conservative and Liberal Beliefs

Topic	Liberal	Conservative
1. Government		
Primary focus	Individual	Community
Preferred government	National	State and local
Direction of sentiment	Internationalist	Nationalist
Method of government influence	Direct	Indirect
Accountability of government	To Man	To God
Rate/type of change	Faster/utopian	Slower/prescriptive
Relative importance	Equality	Liberty
Justice achieved by	Governmental reform	Spiritual regeneration
2. Economy		
Source of authority	Central government	Markets
Growth sector	Public	Private
Government function	Regulation	Competition
Tendency	Socialism	Capitalism
3. Cultural and Religious Values		
Ultimate source of knowledge	Reason	Nature/Bible
Biblical interpretation	More symbolic	More literal
Moral standards	Relative/situational	Absolute/orthodox
Relative emphasis	Humanity	God
Moral emphasis	Social	Personal
Relative importance to humanity	Rights	Responsibilities
Origin of evil	Unjust social systems	Original sin

From Charles Dunn and J. David Woodard, *The Conservative Tradition in America* (Lanhurn, Maryland: Rowman & Littlefield Publishers, 1996).

substantial, they also have a great deal in common. American conservatives and liberals both understood by the 1990s, for example, that the national welfare system was expensive, wasteful, and in need of reform. What they could not readily agree upon was how much reform it needed and where budget cuts could be made. Moreover, liberals are often concerned with preserving the dignity of welfare recipients (preferring to provide food stamps rather than set up soup kitchens), while conservatives are more interested in saving money[21] to ensure a responsible political economy and, they hope, a balanced budget.

AUTHORITARIANISM AND TOTALITARIANISM

For most of political history, people have enjoyed little access to the formulation of decisions that influence (and in some cases, even threaten) their lives. They lived under dictatorships that were largely aloof from the populations

---

[21] See Charles Murray, *In Pursuit of Happiness and Good Government* (New York: Simon & Schuster, 1988).

they governed and constituted a special segment of society that maintained a physical or even spiritual distance from them. Dictators themselves were not necessarily evil or insensitive to the needs of the people; some dictators are actually remembered for positive achievements. Four millenia ago, for example, a Babylonian king, Hammurabi, boasted of the prosperity and orderliness his long reign (from 2123 to 2081 B.C.) had brought his people:

> *I heaped up piles of grain, I provided unfailing water for the lands. . . . The scattered people I gathered; with pasturage and water I provided them; I pastured them with abundance, and settled them in peaceful dwellings.*[22]

Hammurabi bragged with some reason. His most remembered and enduring accomplishment was the Hammurabic Code, an arrangement of 285 laws that governed such familiar issues as property rights and marital relationships.[23] Like numerous other leaders in dictatorial regimes, Hammurabi secured his legitimacy through what amounts to **divine right:** he perceived his role as one of selfless devotion to the public good because the gods wanted this for him and for the people.

Unfortunately, Hammurabi is an exception to the rule of mostly brutal tyrants. Most authoritarian dictatorships are completely unconcerned with laws except in using them for self-advantage. Today's run-of-the-mill dictator does not worry much about caring for the people in his or her charge. Most are more concerned about how much money they can store away in Swiss bank accounts before they are abruptly removed from power, usually by someone just as brutal and greedy.

Ferdinand Marcos and his wife Imelda ruled (or misruled) the Philippines for the twenty years from 1966 to 1986, an ample amount of time to send hundreds of millions or, according to some sources, billions of dollars to overseas investments and banks. The Duvalier family in Haiti did much the same thing around the same time (1959–1986) before being overthrown and forced to live in comfortable exile in Paris. Mrs. Marcos and the former Mrs. Duvalier reputedly spent millions of dollars in exile refurbishing their wardrobes.[24] Many dictators and their families display such greed.

Some dictators—the Samozas in Nicaragua (1936–1979), Saddam Hussein in Iraq, the Saud dynasty in Saudi Arabia, and the Kims of North Korea—try to ensure their political longevity by placing close relations in key positions and designating their children their political heirs. **Nepotism** is a basic pillar of authoritarian dictatorship. It is

> *patronage within the family circle . . . a natural way for anybody in power, or aspiring to it, to strengthen his support in a society where other institutions are*

---

[22] Quoted in Will Durant, *The Story of Civilization,* vol. 1, p. 221.

[23] This is one of the first documents in history that insists on the physical protection of women from abusive husbands. Ibid., p. 220.

[24] "Not-So-Pampered in Exile," *The Economist,* October 22, 1995, p. 56.

TABLE 2.4   Saddam Hussein's Political Family Tree

Minister of Industry: Hussein Kamal al-Majid, son-in-law
Chief of Party Intelligence (domestic spying): Ibrahim Sibawi,
half-brother
Chief of Military Intelligence: Wadbane Ibrahim, half-brother
Ministers without Portfolio: a cousin and two sons
Another cousin was selected to be governor of Kuwait, but this
appointment was short-lived after the allied coalition led by
the United States ousted Iraqi forces from Kuwait in early
1991.

From "The House that Saddam Built," *The Economist*, September 29,
1990, p. 43.

*weak or nonexistent, or where the destruction of existing institutions forms part of
the power-grabber's intentions.*[25]

For rather obvious reasons, dictators frequently appoint brothers or sons as
their (sometimes incompetent) top army commanders. They understandably
lack confidence in those who aren't related by blood or marriage. A case study
is illustrated in table 2.4. Saddam Hussein is a firm believer in nepotism and
has appointed many of his near relatives to positions of substantial power.

The most successful and long-running family dictatorship is clearly the one
established by North Korean ruler Kim Il Sung. His success is based on both
longetivity—Kim came to power in 1945 and reigned for nearly a half century
until his death in 1994—and relentless ruthlessness—he eliminated all opposition quickly and thoroughly after taking power by arranging for the early re-
tirement of political enemies to concentration camps. By the 1950s, Kim had
placed thirty or so relatives in top positions. Their descendents remain in
power today. Kim's older son, Kim Jong Il, succeeded his father as president,
and Kim Jong Il's younger brother, Kim Yong Ju, is vice president.[26]

Nepotism is regularly practiced in all kinds of political systems. Military as well
as communist dictatorships seem to have enough megalomaniacs around to consider political succession (if they consider it all) the prerogative of their progeny.

Theocracies

Religious toleration is a recent phenomenon. The assumption that loyal citizenship includes the correct religious affiliation has been in evidence for most
of political history. In western societies, at least, both Catholics and Protestants
considered religious toleration a mortal sin for generations after the Reformation. After the Treaty of Westphalia ended the Thirty Years' War in 1648,

---

[25] "Nepotism," *The Economist*, December 24, 1994–January 6, 1995, p. 47.

[26] "Nepotism," p. 46.

Saddam Hussein (sitting) and some of his family.

the modern nation-state system in Europe began to take a form that looks familiar to the late twentieth-century student of political geography. Nationalism began to supplant religion as the primary test of citizen loyalty.

Religious conflict would continue in Europe into modern times. Residues of this conflict lingered into the closing years of the twentieth century. The "time of troubles" in Northern Ireland erupted between 1969 and 1994 as Catholics and Protestants resumed murdering one another, a practice they had engaged in off and on for over three hundred years. In southeastern Europe, Bosnian Catholics, Orthodox, and Muslims still insisted on relating political loyalty to religious affiliation.

Religious issues still adopt political features. Debates over abortion, the death penalty, and public school prayers in the United States, divorce in Italy, and contraception in the Republic of Ireland show how strong religious convictions can influence the political and judicial processes and even the outcomes of democratic elections. For the most part, though, political democracies have successfully institutionalized religious toleration. Strong fundamentalist movements, such as the Christian Coalition in the United States, must be prepared to compete with other interest groups to influence public policy.

But religious toleration is still far from a sure thing in a good part of the world. Iran, for example, in the aftermath of the 1979 revolution, created a modern **theocracy** in which both secular law and personal behavior are expected to conform to the **Sharia**, the Islamic religious law. Its advocates consider the Sharia to possess both spiritual and practical qualities. It gives the Islamic faith tangible qualities for the believer and provides guidelines for proper daily behavior. In Islamic societies such as Iran, for example, women are expected to thoroughly veil themselves, allowing only their faces and hands to show in public. The government is expected to support such guidelines and impose penalties on those who flaunt them.[27]

In this sense, government becomes the primary agent for exemplifying and enforcing a purist form of behavior. The concept of separation of church and state is both alien and immoral. One fundamentalist Muslim put it this way:

We believe the rules and teachings of Islam to be comprehensive, to include the people's affairs in the world and the hereafter. . . . Islam is an ideology and a faith, a home and a nationality, a religion and a state, a spirit and work, a book and a sword.[28]

Muslims are certainly not the only ones to offer a total life-style based on religious precepts with the enforcement of the state available when necessary. A popular movement in India, the Bharatiya Janata Party, combines nationalism with Hinduism. In Israel, fundamentalists frequently remind the (mostly secularized) government to enforce dietary laws and support the establishment of Jewish settlements in the West Bank—a place referred to by its biblical names, Judea and Samaria.[29]

We must bear in mind that no two theological regimes are exactly identical. For example, we could say that fundamentalist Islamic regimes govern both Iran and Saudi Arabia. Both countries are indeed administered by regimes that follow Islamic principles. Yet Iran holds regular elections, while no such thing exists in Saudi Arabia; and Iranian women are denied fewer rights than their Saudi counterparts.[30]

Theological regimes do enjoy an overall degree of popular support, and they serve several needs, because they

1. offer a refuge to those who fear and resent westernization and secularism—the twin representatives of corruption, criminal violence, and lax morality;

2. provide a reassuring and all-encompassing code of personal behavior to those who fear the threat that modernity brings to a traditional way of life;

---

[27] Nora Boustany, "In Iran, the Chador Cloaks a Growing Mood of Unrest," *The Washington Post National Weekly Edition*, November 2–8, 1992, p. 18.

[28] Abd al-Moneir Said and Manfred W. Wenner, "Modern Islamic Reform Movements: The Muslim Brotherhood in Contemporary Egypt," *Middle East Journal*, vol. 36, no. 3 (Summer 1982), p. 340.

[29] A valuable analysis of this issue is found in Ian S. Lustick, *For the Land and the Lord: Jewish Fundamentalism in Israel* (New York: Council on Foreign Relations Press, 1988).

[30] "Living with Islam," *The Economist*, April 4, 1992, p. 11. Iranian women are allowed to drive cars. Saudi women aren't, and they risk arrest and possible job loss if they try it. They must also apply to their husbands or fathers to secure written permission to travel (see "Silent Revolution," *The Economist*, February 4, 1995, pp. 39–40). In both Iran and Saudi Arabia, the religious police are charged with rigorously enforcing Islamic standards for women.

3. offer security to those who feel overwhelmed by the uncertainties that accompany technological change, the breakdown of the family as a social unit, and urbanization; and

4. allow the countless millions of people whose prospects for a good job, nice home, and overall pleasant life-style are remote at best, to have hopes for their children's future in terms of firm morality and minimal violent crime.

Communism

At the end of 1917, communists came to power in Russia. The regime they established endured until the end of 1991. Karl Marx and Frederick Engels capsulized the theory of communism when they published *The Communist Manifesto* in 1848. For its time, the *Manifesto* was a radical document, calling for such innovations as free public education and ten-hour (rather than longer) work days.

In later writings, Marx and Engels spelled out in detail both the desirability and inevitability of establishing communism. Their motivations were sincere: both had witnessed the more deplorable elements of the industrial revolution in Germany and later in England, where Marx eventually settled. Workers, including women and young children, were inhumanely exploited by a capitalist class that owned the means of economic production, controlled the judicial and political systems, and were motivated only by the lure of ever-increasing profits. The capitalist class was uninterested in the welfare of the workers, or **proletariat,** who, Marx and Engels held, made the profits possible.

Marx viewed the conflict between the proletariat and the capitalist class as a natural consequence of history. He developed a notion referred to as **dialectical materialism.** All history, according to the dialectic, is characterized by a conflict between social and economic classes. Through the ages, the conflict proceeds to more and more advanced economic and technological levels. Table 2.5 illustrates a simplified version of this process.

Marx and Engels were unsure whether a violent revolution would be necessary to establish what they called the **dictatorship of the proletariat.** In this system, social class distinctions would be abolished and all producers would enjoy the fruits of their labor.

Vladimir Ilyich Lenin had no such doubts. Lenin (1870–1924) firmly believed that no entrenched elite ever gives up power peacefully or voluntarily. He led the communist takeover in Russia in 1917 and quickly eliminated all po-

TABLE 2.5 Marx's Dialectical Materialism

Historical Period	Exploitive Class	Exploited Class
Ancient	Masters	Slaves
Medieval	Landed aristocracy	Serfs
Industrial	Capitalists	Proletariat

POLITICAL
BIOGRAPHY

Joseph Stalin

Joseph Stalin was a man with many natural talents and obvious leadership abilities; during his political career, he was known as the "man of steel." When he was a young man, Stalin's mother tried to influence her son to enter the priesthood. At first, he acquiesced. But after studying in a seminary for a period, Stalin left to join the communist party. Eventually, after taking control of the Soviet Union in the 1920s, he strayed far enough from his religious origins to murder an untold number of Soviet citizens.

Robert Conquest's *The Great Terror* explains why Stalin was ultimately responsible for the deaths of tens of millions of Soviet citizens through execution, starvation, and exposure in Siberian labor camps. Stalin's personality was characterized by a strong streak of paranoia; he was often suspicious of even his closest colleagues and supporters. Most of them ended up in front of firing squads, even though they scrupulously followed Stalin's orders to try to avoid just such an end. Many more people died as a result of Stalin's harsh, oppressive policies.

Not all Russians have bad memories of Stalin, however. Some consider him the architect of the Soviet victory over Germany in World War II. Stalin also led the Soviet Union to become an industrialized country and laid the groundwork for it to become a nuclear power, eventually forging a nation so strong in international politics that the United States felt compelled to treat the Soviets as equals. Many intense Russian nationalists also remember that under Stalin, Russian influence extended into the eastern half of Europe.

Stalin created the first and most durable totalitarian state in modern history. His power was absolute. The territories his armies occupied allowed Russia to realize the age-old Tsarist dream—commanding an empire that included warm water ports, had expanded into much of Europe and Asia, and had established itself as a major world power. Yet he also created a collectivized and stagnant economy, and the millions of non-Russians trapped in a modern version of the Russian Empire in the end were too much for the Soviet Union to control. Later Soviet dictators lacked Stalin's ruthlessness and were unable to prevent the implosion that came in 1991, less than four decades after Stalin's death.

litical opposition. His successor, Joseph Stalin (see the box), went further, inaugurating the "great terror" that forced people to relinquish property to the state and eliminated real or imagined opposition through political purges. In a sense, communist ideology was to blame for the excesses of its advocates. The ideology insisted that only the communist party represented the true interests of workers, and only the workers' class really mattered because they were the people in society who actually were productive. Managers and owners were parasites who enriched themselves on the backs of laborers and therefore could have no place in a communist society.

The Soviet form of communism was the cornerstone of the most durable totalitarian system in the twentieth century. It ultimately failed because of the inherent contradictions in an overcentralized control of a national economy solidly closed to criticism, innovation, imagination, and experiment. By the

Joseph Stalin (1879–1953).

end, the Soviet leadership was less interested in the ideals of communism than in retaining power; they were more willing to tolerate economic stagnation than to risk the political uncertainties of reform.

Fascism

Communists usually believed that their ideology represented the highest form of democracy, establishing complete social and economic equality. In this sense, they could claim to be within the western political tradition. Fascism, on the other hand, was a candid repudiation of democracy. Fascist movements came to power in Europe during the two decades between the end of World War I in 1918 and the beginning of World War II in 1939 in Italy (1922), Germany (1933), and Spain (1939). The first two of these regimes were destroyed by the end of World War II in 1945. The military-dominated government of Japan in the 1930s and early 1940s has also been referred to as fascist but also did not survive World War II. The Spanish form of fascism dissipated after the passing of its founder, Francisco Franco, in 1976. Since the end of the Franco period, Spain has gradually transformed into a democracy.

While Soviet communism basically imploded almost peacefully, fascism was destroyed in a titanic global military effort. Italy, Germany, and Japan were all devastated by the end of World War II, and the allied occupation forces completely eliminated their fascist regimes. As they were on the rise in the 1920s and 1930s, however, all three countries' governments urged their populations to think of their nations as something special: Benito Mussolini encouraged Italians to restore the Roman Empire throughout the Mediterranean region; Adolf Hitler entreated Germans to assume their natural role as masters of Europe because of their racial superiority; and the Japanese believed their destiny was to build an empire in East and Southeast Asia that would supply the natural resources and cheap labor required to ensure Japan's continued greatness.

European fascism never really developed a systematic ideology. It was a hodge-podge of anti-semitism, racism, and extreme **ethnocentrism.** Racial destiny was an ideological fixture for fascist regimes. This was bad news for ethnic or religious minorities, whom the majority regarded as an alien presence in a society insistent on purifying itself. Even if they weren't living in the midst of the purification effort, they could still be in trouble: one of the main goals of German Nazism, for instance, was to secure more living space by expanding into the territories of other countries whose populations they considered suitable for slavery or extermination.

Germany during the National Socialist (Nazi) era of 1933–1945 instituted the most heinous form of fascism. The Nazis persecuted or systematically murdered at least 12 million people in concentration camps. The Nazi party represented some of the worst elements in German society (one of Hitler's closest aides, Martin Bormann, was a convicted murderer), and it boldly planned extermination programs for European Jews, gypsies, and other "undesirable" minorities under German military control during the occupation of much of Europe from 1939 to 1945.

The excesses of fascism completely discredited the movement in world opinion as well as in the countries where fascism surfaced. Within a few years after the destruction of their fascist regimes, Germany, Italy, and Japan became firmly democratic. This is not to say that many current regimes don't behave badly enough to exhibit characteristics of fascism. Some, like Iraq's, have even committed genocidal acts against ethnic or religious minorities. However, unlike the case in the 1930s and 1940s, no government in any *major* developed nation has adopted foreign or domestic policies that we would consider fascist.

WHERE DOES ALL OF THIS LEAVE US?

As we shall see in an upcoming chapter, democracy has become the most creditable sort of political process. Democracies have defeated fascism and outlasted communism. Of course, plenty of individual fascists and communists remain, but they don't currently pose a serious threat to democracy. Democracy, however, was not the preferred alternative for most political philosophers. Plato and Aristotle distrusted it. Later thinkers, such as John Locke, believed in responsible and legal rulership, but they did not assume that democracy necessarily or exclusively produced it.

Every major political thinker has agreed that we are better off living within a political state, but the state is an unfinished experiment in human social development. Some of us need the state more than others; some of us want the state to do more, others want it to do less. The debate will continue. Advances in communications and transportation technologies imply new roles for the state, some with no precedent. For thousands of years, the state had no rival when it came to controlling its citizenry. National boundaries now mean less as information is exchanged over thousands of miles instantaneously and almost effortlessly.

Perhaps one reason democracy has survived and has gained so many defenders is that, unlike other governmental forms, it does not seek to avoid or suppress change. Most political philosophers (Plato being a notable exception) recognized the inevitability of change, but few before the late twentieth century understood or foresaw how rapidly change might come. Change is challenging more traditionalist societies, in some cases more severely than democratic ones. In the next chapter, we will see how culture in general and political culture in particular influences how well a government responds to social and economic changes.

SUMMARY

1. Plato's *The Republic* highlighted the concept that government could be a force for good if wise and unselfish rulers governed. In Plato's view, every citizen would assume only those tasks he or she is suited for by natural talent and intelligence. This would enhance justice and make laws unnecessary.

2. Aristotle understood the political community to be the pinnacle of human social development. For the sake of political and social stability, he argued for moderation in all things, including the establishment of a broad middle class and the avoidance of excessive wealth and poverty.

3. Stoicism offered a philosophy that tried to make sense of a world many believed to be chaotic. Stoics implored people to accept their roles in life and do their best to excel in those roles. This advice was particularly incumbent upon rulers; Stoics called on them to govern on behalf of the entire society and not in their own self-interest.

4. Thomas Hobbes argued that humans began their existence in the stateless state of nature, found its violence unacceptable, and agreed in a social contract to submit to a sovereign power. The primary responsibility of this sovereign is to provide the physical security individuals lack in the state of nature. In exchange for this security, people surrender a substantial proportion of their individual freedom.

5. John Locke adopted a milder view of the state of nature. He agreed it is in the common interest to establish a sovereign power, but he believed the sovereign must also be a party to the social contract and must obey the same generally approved laws as any citizen in the commonwealth.

6. Conservatives and liberals both believe in the intrinsic worth of every individual human being. Conservatives, however, strongly support the traditions and moral foundations of civil society, while liberals argue on behalf of nontraditional social equality and moral relativism.

7. Most governments throughout political history have been authoritarian dictatorships, and most have demonstrated few qualms about employing brutality to remain in power and control the population. Another less violent feature of authoritarianism that helps the dictator to secure power is the practice of nepotism.

8. Theocratic regimes by definition are uninterested in tolerating political dissension. Because theocratic regimes combine church and state, political opponents are also sinners. Legal systems are based on moral codes.

9. Communism is a failed system of government that endured for more than seven decades in the Soviet Union. During that period, the centralized economy created havoc, and the bureaucratization of nearly all social and political behaviors practically destroyed individual innovation and cost millions of lives.

10. Fascism is characterized by strong ingredients of ethnocentrism and racism. The fascist regimes that most seriously threatened western democracy were destroyed in World War II.

GLOSSARY

dialectical materialism   The Marxist notion of history as a series of class struggles culminating in a classless society of workers.

dictatorship of the proletariat   In Marxist theory, a condition occurring at the end of history, in which the actual producers in society seize control of the apparatus of the state, abolishing class distinctions and allowing producers to enjoy the fruit of their labors.

divine right The idea that monarchs are set in place by divine sanction and that to rebel against them is wrong because it is an act of rebellion against God's will.

elite A privileged minority in society, usually composed of no more than 10 percent of the population, that controls the political decision-making process.

ethnocentrism A population's almost paranoid aversion to "foreign" minorities and their commitment to a special destiny that justifies maltreatment of other nations.

left A common reference to ideologies that tend to be liberal or socialist in nature.

nepotism The practice of appointing one's close relatives to high political office to ensure maximum support and loyalty.

polis The city-state form of government that Plato and Aristotle regarded as the optimal political arrangement for conducting human affairs.

proletariat The class of workers who produce goods and, therefore, profits.

right A common reference to ideologies that tend to be conservative in nature.

Sharia Islamic law that provides a code of rules for correct moral behavior.

social contract An arrangement Thomas Hobbes and John Locke proposed for the establishment of a civil society under a sovereign government.

theocracy A society in which separation of church and state is forbidden, and the secular legal codes are obligated to enforce religious principles.

Political Culture

A country's political culture is rooted in the ways society's members think about and react to government and politics. This thinking, in turn, is based in great part on the country's political and social history. In this chapter, we will review how political culture influences the kind of government a society's members either choose for themselves or have imposed on them. We will also examine how a country's political culture and institutions relate to one another and what can occur in the absence of consensual political norms and values.

POLITICAL CULTURE AND POLITICAL PRACTICES

A great deal of a country's political culture is actually articulated in its constitution, especially in democracies. Although they closely resemble one another in political form, democracies have evolved under distinct circumstances. The French, for example, settled on a chief executive with more substantial powers than his or her American counterpart. The French president can assume "emergency powers"[1] that would amount to impeachable offenses if an American president attempted to exercise them. But the French political culture, as reflected in its constitution, sanctions such expansive powers. The French have determined after numerous experiments that an especially strong but popularly chosen executive is desirable.

In the United Kingdom, the House of Commons, the lower house of parliament, can call or postpone elections as long as they occur within a five-year statutory limit. In certain situations, that limit may be set aside. Because of the emergency conditions of World War II, for example, the British held no national elections between 1935 and 1945. The United States, in contrast, was constitutionally obligated to hold elections on schedule in 1942 and 1944, and neither government officials nor rank-and-file citizens seriously contemplated their delay. The British could suspend the rules of the political game with public support when an extraordinary situation justified doing so; the U.S. Constitution prohibits such an act.

---

[1] Article 16 of the French Constitution.

Political culture is often derived from the overall culture the great majority of a society's members affiliate with. In an overall culture, widely shared and accepted values provide a cohesiveness that helps keep the society intact. Ideally, a political culture does the same thing in the political sphere: contending interests understand and accept the basic political structure and obey the generally agreed upon rules of the political game. In the United States and other democracies, for example, society regards the principles of free speech, unhindered competition in the marketplace of ideas, and peaceful acceptance of electoral outcomes as necessary for political well-being. Conservatives and liberals, Democrats, Republicans, and independents agree on these principles, though they differ considerably on the degree to which they should be applied. Democratic societies believe that the political process should function in as free and unfettered a manner as practical.

Nondemocratic societies are usually characterized by a conspicuous lack of these same principles. Developing a consensual political culture in such a society usually takes a long time and normally requires generations, if not centuries, to mature. Some countries may never develop one. In fact, their citizenries may not even share a desire to establish one. Worse yet, in attempting to establish a political culture, a society may degenerate into civil war. It is one thing for a society to divide over issues: Americans, for example, are deeply divided over issues such as abortion and the death penalty. But serious division over issues does not in itself threaten the stability of a political system. Democratic societies tend to accept their institutions of government as legitimate and use the legal and political processes available to work out their differences.

In democracies, **legitimacy,** or the perceived right to govern, is conferred by a widely accepted and renewable mandate for elected leaders. Authoritarian regimes are frequently devoid of discernible ideology, but some are eager to legitimize their existence with intense nationalism, myths, or a combination of the two. Shah Reza Pahlavi of Iran (1954–1979), who claimed to speak regularly with divine authority, is an instructive example. Desirous of making his country a regional power in the Middle East, the Shah in 1971 proclaimed the twenty-five-hundredth anniversary of the founding of the Persian Empire by Cyrus the Great. This was a futile attempt to link Iran with its glorious ancient past and the Shah with one of the more accomplished empire builders in history. After the collapse of the monarchy in 1979, the Iranian political culture became intimately linked with the theocratic tendencies of a fundamentalist regime. This regime disavowed a good deal of its non-Islamic past and sought political legitimacy in religious orthodoxy.

The development of a political culture is usually a lengthy process for most societies. Many countries never really achieve a coherent political culture because the divisions within the society are so strong and persistent that they preclude its development. It is much easier on a nation's political nervous system to endure ideological divisions and debates over critical issues than to survive a fractious political culture.

INDUCTION INTO THE POLITICAL CULTURE

Political Socialization

Most people take a serious interest in and derive great pleasure from knowing who they are. It makes us feel better. Similarly, the political culture requires a relentless process of induction; each new generation must learn the particular values and norms of the society it belongs to and, it is hoped, develop a lasting affection for them. This process begins in early childhood. "Political socialization, in the broadest sense, refers to the way society transmits its political culture from generation to generation."[2] This is done through a variety of agencies that "include such environmental categories as the family, peer group, school, adult organizations, and the mass media."[3]

The importance of the process of political socialization should not be underestimated. It is essential to the survival of the political system itself.[4] The ultimate goal of political socialization is to secure voluntary and widespread support for the norms and values of the political culture. Dictatorships as well as democracies prefer that their policies enjoy popular endorsement, and both prefer it for the same reason: it makes governing much easier. Political socialization, then, enhances and helps to guarantee the legitimacy of political institutions.

Every political system, regardless of its nature and ideology, naturally wants to survive. For this reason, each regime makes an effort to emphasize the socialization process with children. Democracies such as the United States teach values such as individual freedoms and toleration of diversity as early as the primary grades. Schools also extol the more redeeming characteristics of previous political leaders. Presidents George Washington and Abraham Lincoln, for example, are frequently mentioned to young schoolchildren as models of personal as well as political honesty and integrity.

Dictatorships have a serious problem when it comes to political socialization. A typical authoritarian dictatorship revolves around the personality of the dictator. Rank-and-file citizens must be convinced that he is invincible and infallible and that they are really fortunate to have him around. Saddam Hussein, for example, has at different times proclaimed himself a pan-Arab leader, an Islamic fundamentalist, and an intense Iraqi nationalist in efforts to sustain his regime with whatever idea was popular at the moment. His is a typical political socialization process in a dictatorship, where huge pictures of the smiling supreme leader appear everywhere, especially in every school classroom.

Iraqi schools, like the mosques and the family, are critical agents of political socialization. The school may actually be the most critical agent of all, since

---

[2] Kenneth P. Langton, *Political Socialization* (New York and London: Oxford University Press, 1969), p. 4.

[3] Ibid., p. 5.

[4] Ibid., p. 6.

any regime immediately understands that its continuance depends on acquiring the loyalty and confidence of the youngest members of the political society. In a country such as Iraq, of course, the citizen has very few political norms and values to learn: he or she simply adheres to and believes in whatever the leader is quoted as saying at the moment.

This doesn't always work, though. In pluralist and democratic societies *who* we are matters, while in nondemocratic societies *what* we are may matter more than anything else. For example, the political loyalty of a citizen of Bosnia depends on whether one is classified as a Serb, Croat, or Muslim. Based upon a single criterion, ethnicity, one may be judged either a model citizen or someone who richly deserves a bullet in the head.[5]

Political socialization was (or at least seemed) simpler during the Cold War era (1945–1990). During this time, the political socialization process was clear. One was indoctrinated into the political culture of France, Germany, or the United States. A person would learn that he or she belonged to the French or German or American nation and was a citizen in the French or German or American state. This view, however, may very well be a western conceit.

The nation-state system more or less orginated in the West, and it has not caught on substantially in other regions. A political socialization process also exists in these countries, but not in the sense that most westerners understand it. One scholar has suggested that large communities of people outside of the West have more restricted political loyalties.[6] In the Arab world, for example, there is a widespread notion "that national sovereignty alone was an empty sham" and that it was necessary to turn to fundamentalist Islam and restore "holy law."[7]

Thus, analyzing and understanding political socialization may require more relevant and accurate interpretations. Few states "clearly qualify as nation-states."[8] Most people are socialized to retain only tribal and clannish loyalties and lack a full comprehension of, let alone a loyalty to, the nation-state.

These local loyalties are so durable that they can decisively contribute to the collapse of a superpower. One of the critical reasons usually offered to explain the implosion of the Soviet Union in 1991 relates to the conflicts among the approximately one hundred nationalities within the Soviet federation. Often the conflicts were simultaneously between nationalities and between various nationalities and the central government. Most of them genuinely felt coerced into the Soviet system and were alienated by a regime they were convinced exploited and brutalized them.

---

[5] Ted Robert Gurr, "Peoples Against States: Ethnopolitical Conflict and the Changing World System," *International Studies Quarterly*, vol. 38 (1994), pp. 347–77.

[6] Samuel Huntington, *The Clash of Civilizations: The Debate* (New York: Council on Foreign Relations, 1993).

[7] Bernard Lewis, *Islam and the West* (New York and Oxford: Oxford University Press, 1993), p. 139.

[8] Walker Connor, "A Nation Is a Nation, Is a State, Is an Ethnic Group, Is a . . ." *Ethnic and Racial Studies*, I (October, 1978), p. 86.

The Soviet regime tried unsuccessfully for decades to create a political culture that emphasized a new economic and political species, the unselfish and hard-working "Soviet man" and "Soviet woman" dedicated to the socialist principles of equality and devoted to "building communism." It is suspected that, in the end, not even the Soviet leadership believed communism was a worthwhile prospect. Most Soviet citizens gradually recognized that the regime was simply a successor state to the Russian Empire that the communists had destroyed in 1917. For the non-Russian half of the population, the Soviet-inspired political culture was, at best, an unrealizable myth and, at worst, a clever device to enable a Russian political elite to continue to exploit non-Russians.

Liberty Versus Equality

No two political cultures are exactly alike. Even democratic systems, which have a great deal in common, exhibit important differences. The differences are not stark enough to cause conflict between democracies. As a rule, democracies don't fight wars against one another, but they are distinguishable from one another in important ways.

Nor are political cultures static. The countries of western Europe and North America are stable industrialized democracies, at least for the most part. But like all other societies, they are undergoing social changes that are the result of or impact upon political culture. After 1945, the Germans had to reconstruct their political culture to rid it of Nazi influences and create a durable and plausible democratic system. The West Germans in 1949 promulgated their Basic Law (which served as their constitution until East and West Germany reunited in 1989). One of the Basic Law's provisions allows the federal courts to ban political parties judged to advocate un- or antidemocratic programs and ideologies. The United States Constitution contains no such provision; in fact, in view of the Bill of Rights, it cannot do so. More importantly, it doesn't have to. The United States did not lose a world war and did not install and live under a Nazi regime. Therefore, the United States did not find it necessary to rebuild a political culture by stipulating the exclusion of antidemocratic elements.

Immigrants are also responsible for changing political cultures and are most keenly felt in political democracies. Some facts we discussed in chapter 1 suggest the implications that face several democratic societies: the United States now has the fifth-largest Spanish-speaking population in the world; Germany's capital city, Berlin, is home to the third-largest Turkish community in the world; and one out of every five police officers in London is from Africa or the West Indies.[9] Most of the reactions to the newest immigrants have been positive (or at least noncommittal), but some of the reactions (such as neo-Nazi skinheads in Germany beating up immigrant workers) have been unpleasant, even violent, and probably will continue to be until the political culture can adjust.

---

[9] David C. Gordon, *Images of the West: Third World Perspectives* (London and New York: Rowman & Littlefield Publishers, 1989), pp. 40–41.

Democracy is governance by the governed. A democratic political culture involves competition between competing expressions of ideological values. Much of the time we are ideological without really noticing. Americans are prone, for example, to label one another as conservative or liberal, prolife or prochoice, or affiliates of the "religious right" or the "incompetent left."[10]

As indicated in the previous chapter, the terms *left* and *right* are frequently used to describe the ideological positions of political parties, interest groups, and individuals. Over the years, these terms have undergone substantial modifications and quite a bit of abuse. They have each had some interesting adjectives tacked onto them in recent times: the "loony" left, the "radical" right; and both left and right have been described as "extreme," "totalitarian," or "moderate." In the United States, Americans use these terms rather freely. When they are being politically polite, they tend to label others as liberals or conservatives. Each, however, sometimes refers to the other by uttering the "l" or "c" word with a sneer of contempt.

IS IDEOLOGY ON THE DECLINE?

Ideology probably is on the decline. We can at least determine with some confidence that certain ideologies are definitely discredited. By the early 1990s, communism had been swept away in Eastern Europe and the Soviet Union because of the widespread recognition of its economic and political failures. Fascism quickly went out of style after its defeat in World War II. But ideology does not necessarily disappear once it has been discredited. In the case of communism, for example, it simply modified. To gain respectability and to survive in free elections, communist parties in both Western and Eastern Europe have in many cases changed their names and reappeared as parties on the democratic left. Some, ironically, have experienced substantial electoral success. Even revived (but unreformed) fascism has done modestly well in Italian elections.

Nothing changed in places where communism was already a bankrupt ideology. There had never been more than a token amount of support for communist parties in the English-speaking countries and in the former West Germany. The political cultures of these countries had long excluded the communist ideology as politically illegitimate or simply as an unreasonable totalitarian relic in a democratic society. Communism was regarded as a political pariah and an unbeatable formula for permanent economic misery.

Nearly all ideologies by definition try to freeze society into a preferred scenario. Once having established a totalitarian system, Soviet communist leaders had little incentive to tolerate change and attempted to deny its existence. In short, communist leaders confused stagnation with perfection. The communist ideology also legitimized their monopoly on power. In fact, the ideology was the only legitimizer.

---

[10] Senator Arlen Spector used this last set of terms in announcing his candidacy for the Republican nomination for president in 1996. C-SPAN, March 31, 1995.

With the collapse of communism in most countries with communist-controlled governments,[11] a widespread assumption developed that most of the world was becoming "de-ideologized." Several signs that encouraged this point of view. Even in the Middle East, where ideological clashes between Zionists, religious radicals, Arab socialists, and intense nationalists were frequent, optimists appeared for the first time in generations to applaud the progress of a peace process that sprung from a 1993 agreement between Israel and the Palestine Liberation Organization. Pragmatism seemed in this case to replace ideological fanaticism.[12]

However, ideology is far from finished. An ideology can facilitate the legitimization of both a political regime and political culture. This is especially the case in nondemocratic societies. After all, in the absence of free elections, authoritarian governments must still try to legitimize their presence and provide a rationale for their actions. We tend to become more aware of the threat an ideology may pose when substantial arsenals reinforce it.

A telling example was the Soviet Union itself. After the communists came to power in Russia in 1917, they immediately singled out the western developed capitalist countries as the "evil" enemy.[13] The United States reciprocated, and by the late 1970s was referring to the Soviet Union as the "evil empire," a label that became especially popular during the early years of the Reagan Administration (1981–1989). Each side perceived the other as a mortal threat. By the 1950s, both nations possessed nuclear weapons capable of destroying hundreds of targets. The mutual recognition that each could completely destroy the other (and all life on this planet) certainly helped to contain full ideological expressions.

According to distinguished historian Arthur Schlesinger, Jr., the reason the Cold War between the United States and the Soviet Union did not become "hot" was the fact that both were very sensibly frightened of using nuclear weapons. Ideology apparently does have its limits: better to live with "evil" than be utterly destroyed along with it. If nuclear weapons had never been invented, the two sides might well have been tempted to opt for conventional warfare to settle their ideological disputes. Schlesinger supports the suggestion "that the Nobel Peace Prize should have gone to the atomic bomb."[14]

But nuclear destruction is not necessarily an ultimate limitation to the pursuit of ideological goals. Several "rogue" countries, such as Iraq, Iran, North

---

[11] Communism continues to destroy the economies of North Korea, Cuba, Vietnam, and Cambodia, although even in these hard-core communist states the free market is slowly gaining a foothold.

[12] See, for example, M. Al-Sayyid, "Slow Thaw in the Arab World," *World Policy Journal* (Fall, 1991), pp. 711–35, and Thomas Friedman, "Baker Sees Arab 'New Thinking' and Urges Israel to Reciprocate," *The New York Times*, March 12, 1991.

[13] For an excellent treatment of this perspective, see John Mueller, "Quiet Cataclysm: Some Afterthoughts on World War III," in Michael J. Hogan, ed., *The End of the Cold War: Its Meaning and Implications* (New York: Cambridge University Press, 1992), pp. 39–52.

[14] Schlesinger, "Lessons from the Cold War," in Hogan, p. 54.

Korea, and Libya, are attempting to either purchase or build nuclear weapons. The nuclear quests of at least two, Iran and North Korea, are partially motivated by strong ideological agendas. Of course, deciding to acquire nuclear weapons and deciding to use them are very different processes. It remains to be seen whether ideological inspirations will have their limitations in these countries as well.

THE LIMITS OF TOLERATION

Individual freedoms are most often found and most often enjoy guarantees in political democracies. However, while democracies maximize the toleration of diverse points of view and life-styles, frequently subtle and occasionally glaring differences exist between them. The United States, for example, probably offers the greatest freedom of the press in the world. It is even more substantial than Britain's, which actually has tougher libel laws on the books and is more protective of personal privacy than the American legal system.[15]

Singapore offers one of the most disciplined democracies. Consider the fact that the city-state has legally banned chewing gum as part of the government's obsessive effort to keep the country as clean as possible. Singapore's citizens have accepted without much reaction a rule most Americans would be outraged over. Nor is Singapore a democracy whose government quietly accepts criticism from the press: an article in the *International Herald Tribune* charging that the government uses a "compliant judiciary to bankrupt opposition politicians" by filing lawsuits against them caused the judiciary to fine the newspaper more than $14,000.[16] The other side of this argument, though, suggests that greater social discipline provides greater individual freedom and security. Singapore does provide a good deal less individual freedom than the United States, but Singapore also is a place in which violent crime is rare, the streets are safer, and drive-by shootings almost never occur.

Toleration ceases to be a civic virtue when it contributes to an uncivil society. Religious fundamentalists not only in theocracies such as Iran but in democracies such as India, Israel, and the United States suggest this. Fundamentalists believe it is morally wrong to tolerate "deviant" life-styles. A government is only responsible when it is moral as well as effective. "State laws, policies, and institutions must rest on a religious foundation. . . . Schools and courts must restore moral values to the community."[17] Government institutions

> *must cleanse the community of modern vices: premarital sex, pornography, abortion, homosexuality, drug addiction, gambling, and alcoholism. Public schools*

---

[15] Edwin M. Yoder, Jr., "Why Trash This Symbol of Civility?" *International Herald Tribune,* December 2, 1992.

[16] *The Economist,* January 21, 1995, p. 36.

[17] Charles F. Andrain and David E. Apter, *Political Protest and Social Change: Analyzing Politics* (Washington Square, New York: New York University Press, 1995), p. 52.

must conduct orthodox prayers and teach traditional religious values. Courts should enforce religious law based on a literal interpretation of sacred scripture, which contains only one unchanging meaning for all time.[18]

The concern that toleration may not always be an unmixed blessing is not restricted to religious fundamentalists. As we have mentioned, democracies are not all the same when it comes to the expression of individual freedoms. The United States is well known for tolerating more violence than other industrial democracies. Japan, on the other hand, is known as the "safest industrialized society in the world."[19] Criminals in Japan are socially ostracized; even their families want nothing to do with them because they have brought great shame and humiliation to their relatives. Criminals who have served prison sentences are shunned after they return to society. Moreover, the National Rifle Association would deplore the fact that there are a total of 49 legal handguns in Japan in contrast to 200 million in the United States.[20]

There is not a single recorded public protest against handgun regulations in Japan. Apparently, the Japanese are far more tolerant of restrictions on individual freedoms than Americans are. Ownership of personal firearms is almost an article of faith among many in the United States; Japan banned personal ownership of weapons in 1588. The ban has retained popular support through the last half century of democratization.

POLITICAL SELF-RIGHTEOUSNESS

Political self-righteousness is a term that helps describe regimes that refuse to submit their programs to either public criticism or a meaningful election. Dictatorial regimes rarely feel the need or desire to consult the governed about policies. A small, closed political elite controls and manipulates the political culture in such a country for the elite's advantage. The government purports to know what is best for people without asking them and rules over them without their consent.

Several chapters in this text stress the importance of ideology in the political process. This chapter is no exception. Ideology is the cornerstone of political self-righteousness because it firmly adheres to the notion "that everything is relevant to government and that the task of government is to reconstruct society according to the goals of an ideology."[21]

Since an ideology cannot be "wrong" and since it proposes answers to political problems, a government that operates by ideology can justify nearly any act, even the most outrageous and violent. Political self-righteousness is evident

---

[18] Ibid.

[19] Nicholas D. Kristol, "Social Pressure, Gun Laws Keep Crime Down in Japan," *The New York Times*, May 27, 1995.

[20] Ibid.

[21] Bernard Crick, *In Defense of Politics* (Baltimore, Maryland: Penguin Books, 1962), p. 34.

in most political settings. It is even occasionally found in democracies, although constitutional restraints limit it.

Every ideology comes equipped with a self-appointed priesthood or "keepers of the faith." They can assure their political legitimacy if they are able to convince the rest of the population of their infallibility. The communist party functioned this way in a dozen or more countries during the Cold War. The party saw no need to hold free elections, admit dissent, or allow political opposition to function freely because of their monopoly on the "truth." Most ideologies do not allow for or lend themselves to compromise. Ideological self-righteousness means never having to say you're wrong.

POLITICAL LEGITIMACY

By what right do a few govern—or establish rules of behavior—for the many? In Plato's fictional Republic, political legitimacy, as we have seen, was vested in a small cadre of philosophers who governed on the basis of their accumulated wisdom. Unfortunately, governance by wisdom has rarely surfaced in any actual political system. Yet the question of political legitimacy is ancient. Nearly every ruler and government, even the most tyrannical, have thought it necessary to somehow justify their power. If a ruler is widely considered legitimate, he or she can exercise power by making important decisions, including those that involve life and death, and expect the people to accept them without question or, at least, without serious resistance. In rather rough form, we can outline the four most traveled roads toward political legitimacy in chronological fashion:

1. The surest road to political legitimacy for rulers thousands of years ago was the divine one. Nearly six thousand years ago in Egypt, the ruling pharoahs were able to establish the notion that they were gods who had consented for a period of time to live among mere mortals. The will of the pharoah was therefore a divine commandment that was undeniable and completely enforceable as law. Egyptians by and large believed this notion for millenia—only rarely were insurrections recorded during Egypt's long pharoanic age (about 3400 to 30 B.C.). Legitimacy in this case was based on the prerogatives of a godhead.

2. Later ages produced more modest rulers. From medieval times and well into the eighteenth century, several European monarchs insisted that, while far from divine themselves, they were authorized and supported by **divine right.** This theory was based on the assumption that power is ordained by divine authority. Thus, to rebel against a monarch's rulership was not only an act of political treason, it was a mortal sin. The prophet Samuel, after all, had anointed the first two kings of ancient Israel, according to the Bible's Old Testament. Divine right fell from acceptance as a society became more educated and economically advanced. By 1649 in England and 1793 in France, monarchs who insisted they were accountable to no earthly power were overthrown and beheaded by popular movements that did not accept divine right as a viable doctrine or as a practical form of government in modernizing societies.

Hitler was one of the Nazi leaders telling German people how mentally and physically superior they were compared to non-Nordic nations.

3. In the twentieth century, legitimacy based on ideology became a crucial cornerstone of totalitarian society. The Nazis in Germany (1933–1945) and the communists in the Soviet Union (1917–1991) quickly learned how to use ideology to create popular support for their regimes. Nazi leaders consistently told the German people how mentally and physically superior they were to non-Nordic nations. To emphasize the point, government agencies referred to "inferior" peoples (Slavs, Jews, Africans, gypsies, and others) as subhuman. The Soviets stressed the economic and moral superiority of communist society. They taught Soviet citizens that communism represented the most modern form of society, a form that supported human potential more than the corrupt and decadent capitalist societies that encouraged personal greed and selfishness. Months before the Chinese communist government assumed control of Hong Kong in 1997, it announced it would not tolerate political parties or public demonstrations. A totalitarian state sees no reason to tolerate either.

4. In democratic societies, an experiment in electoral political legitimacy began in the nineteenth century and is still in progress. Democracies are distinct from the previously described political models because they base rulership on regular elections, peaceful acceptance of their outcomes, stipulated terms of office, and orderly transfers of power from an incumbent government to the opposition. In the next chapter, we will examine both democracy and democratization in some detail. For now, keep in mind that democracy is still in the experimental stages. Only recently have democracies become a firmly embraced political process in more than a few dozen European and North American countries. Over the last two centuries, we have seen democracies expand and contract in number. In the 1990s, they were in an expansionist phase. Since previous expansionist phases have yielded to contractions, a contraction may follow the current expansion.[22] Democracy has yet to prevail in a majority of the world's countries.

Even the collapse of totalitarian systems does not necessarily guarantee a bright future for the democratic process. The majority of countries in the world in the middle 1990s were governed by autocratic regimes that exhibited varying degrees of brutality. Authoritarianism, a form of government that does not bother to base its power on any form of legitimacy unless one

---

[22] On this subject see the intriguing essay by Samuel Huntington, "Democracy's Third Wave."

considers brute force legitimate, still limits and challenges the expansion of democracy.

There is a darker side to legitimacy, however. A government, especially one misguidedly following an ideology such as communism or fascism, may regard a portion of its own citizenry as illegitimate. Even worse, the ideology may consider this portion completely beyond redemption. As we have mentioned previously, Jews in Nazi Germany, Shiites in Iraq, or capitalists in the Soviet Union were liable to be executed, worked to death, or bombarded with chemical weapons. Ethnicity, religious identity, and social class origins are critical considerations to ideologically guided regimes. These characteristics can doom an often defenseless minority to punishments ranging from second-class citizenship to wholesale physical extermination.

POLITICAL CULTURE AND POLITICAL TRAUMA

A political culture is characterized by established norms and values. Americans, for example, take tremendous pride in their individualism and in the opportunities a country with abundant resources makes available. Any country that survives for long must occasionally face drastic cultural and political alterations, which may arise either suddenly or gradually. We can call these episodes **political traumas.** The term *trauma* signifies serious injury. A drastic national trauma such as a war can seriously wound or injure the political system and require extensive "reconstructive surgery." The wound need not be fatal, however, and the healing process can produce a stronger and more durable system.

As fortunate as the United States has been through most of its history, America has not been totally immune to political trauma. In fact, we've experienced several traumas with lasting effects: the Civil War (1861–1865) and the consequent social readjustments imposed on the South during Reconstruction (1865–1877); the Great Depression of the 1930s; and the national division and unrest over U.S. involvement in Vietnam (roughly 1965–1975). National traumas arise over issues that challenge the viability of a country's political institutions.

Each trauma has impacted on political culture in dramatic ways. A third of the country in 1861, for example, determined that it could no longer work within the political system and that, in fact, the system itself was detrimental to regional interests. The Civil War and Reconstruction, as difficult as they were, may well have produced both a more unified and more democratic country. The Great Depression helped usher in social programs designed to guarantee Americans some degree of economic security and persuade most of them to accept an expanded role for the national government. And Vietnam made the United States, for better or worse, much more reluctant to become involved in military activities abroad; it also made us aware that American power is not unlimited.

Other countries, democratic and nondemocratic, have experienced their own traumas, as table 3.1 summarizes. Some, like Russia, are currently going through a national trauma. Traumas themselves are not always cataclysmic, nor

Hiroshima, Japan, after the nuclear bombing in August 1945—the world's only nuclear war.

TABLE 3.1   Political Culture and Political Trauma

Country	Trauma(s)	Result
United States	Great Depression (1930s)	Unprecedented government regulation of the economy
Soviet Union (USSR); now Russia and smaller republics)	World War II invasion (1940s); economic collapse and hardline coup (1991)	Distrust of the West; breakup of USSR and democratization
Germany	Military occupation after losing World War II	Democratization
Japan	Nuclear bombing and military occupation after losing World War II	Democratization
France	Collapse of colonial empire and near civil war (1946–1958)	Strengthened executive
United Kingdom	Declining economic and political power (about 1945–1970)	Acceptance of United States as replacement world power
Canada	Bifurcation into two national communities, English- and French-speaking (ongoing)	As yet undetermined; possible separatism

must they be violent. Canada, for example, has discussed for decades whether Quebec should remain a part of the country. If Quebec does decide to secede, Canadians would expect the secession to be peaceful.

Future traumas in many areas of the world will probably redraw national boundary lines and could have implications for international security. New states are regularly appearing as smaller societies secede from older and larger ones. Successful secession is traumatic but can undergo a successful recovery. After the 1989 collapse of communism in Czechoslovakia, the Czechs reestablished a democratic form of government. A few years later, however, the Slovak third of the country peacefully seceded. In a separation fondly referred to as a "velvet divorce," Czechoslovakia divided into the Czech Republic and Slovakia.

The concept of states dividing (or even redividing) developed recently but may be around for a while. Between 1990 and 1995, twenty new states appeared on world political maps. It is almost certain that more will appear as the next century begins. Most will be the offspring of secessions, but it is far from certain that all secessions will be as peaceful as Slovakia's.

Two important factors may reduce the effects of something as traumatic as a country splitting in two. First, if the split occurs in a democracy, as it might in Canada and already has in Czechoslovakia, the secession process will most likely be peaceful; and second, the economic integration being achieved in Europe and North America will actually encourage ethnic communities seeking autonomy to secede with a minimum of economic dislocation.[23] Traumas in democratic societies since 1945 seem to be increasingly mild: no democracy has experienced a life-and-death struggle with a hostile power or an economic setback that threatened extreme solutions.

Sometimes a trauma can be so severe that a regime collapses. Such an event usually means the political culture was not very viable in the first place. A depressing example of a failed culture and a destructive trauma is the violent disintegration of the federated republic of Yugoslavia. The country imploded during the early 1990s, revealing a political culture fragile in the extreme, particularly in Bosnia-Herzegovina, one of the federation's member republics. This region dissolved into three ethnic-religious communities of Orthodox Serbs, Catholic Croatians, and Muslim Bosnians, but not without horrendous violence.

Between 1945 and 1990, constitutional devices and the charisma of Yugoslav leader Josef Broz Tito (born to a Serb father and Croat mother) were able to temporarily neutralize ancient hatreds. However, the ethnic and religious strains within Yugoslav society eventually proved too severe for the country to hold together. After Tito died in 1980, the federation began to unravel, and by the 1990s, it had collapsed into full-scale civil war. Despite the regime's best efforts, it wasn't possible to create a persuasive political culture of mutually accepted norms and values that would retain the loyalty of an extremely divided population.

---

[23] "A Wealth of Nations," *The Economist*, April 29, 1995, p. 90.

SECULARISM VERSUS SACRALIZATION

Religious values often form the basis of political cultures, especially in traditionalist societies. They exert much less influence in modern societies where secularism prevails. A secular society is one in which

> *Individuals gain greater autonomy from community controls. Tolerance for 'deviant' life-styles grows along with the pluralism of worldviews. . . . Through reason, technology, and the experimental sciences, individuals can understand and control not only the material world but also the social environment.*[24]

Sacralization is the opposite of secularization; its advocates want to restore traditional values to a society they believe has misplaced or ignored its spiritual heritage in the pursuit of material goals. Often, they do not reject the benefits of modern technology—many religious fundamentalists in the United States, for example, take full advantage of the electronic media to advertise their message. Instead, sacralizationists view technology as a tool they can use to convince fellow citizens to order their lives in accordance with time-tested social mores. In this sense, toleration, considered a virtue in secular societies, is a vice in sacralized societies. The sacralized society is often modeled on and adheres to a holy writ. Since values are considered divinely inspired, there is no reason to tolerate opinions and life-styles that don't conform to those spelled out in scripture. At best, such deviations are wrong; at worst, they are sinful. In a sacralized society, either type of deviation may deserve severe punishment. Table 3.2 summarizes the distinction between a secular and a sacralized society.

Even in modern western societies, not everyone is happy or satisfied with a secularized culture. Religious fundamentalist movements, for example, sometimes react to what they regard as excessive secularization. Such movements attempt with mixed success to *resacralize* both the political and overall cultures by extolling the virtues of ancient customs and particular religious practices. Orthodox Muslims in Iran, for example, have attempted since 1979 to restore the Sharia, or Islamic sacred law, as a code of conduct for daily behavior. In Algeria, the Islamic Salvation Front spouts the slogan, "No law, no constitution, only the laws of God and the Koran."[25]

In Somalia, local authorities strictly enforce proper personal conduct, doling out legal punishments for moral infractions most westerners would find medieval (see table 3.3). This isn't surprising—the punishments *are* medieval, having been formulated twelve or thirteen centuries ago. Such a "legal system" takes precedence over and often replaces all modern law. The government becomes morally obligated to enforce religious doctrine.

At times, sacralization can go to extremes. Iran and Sudan, for example, are countries governed rather strictly by the Sharia. Legal punishments for crimes

---

[24] Charles F. Andrain and David E. Apter, *Political Protest and Social Change: Analyzing Politics* (Washington Square, New York: New York University Press, 1995), p. 63.

[25] "Islamism: Should the U.S. Fear a Green Peril?" *ACCESS: A Security Information Service*, vol. VIII, No. 10 (September 1994).

TABLE 3.2   Characteristics of Secularized and Sacralized Political Cultures

	Secularized	Sacralized
Church and state	Separate	Together and often indistinguishable
Legal system	Mixture of custom and contemporary concepts	Based on holy scripture
Toleration	Maximized on behalf of diverse preferences and life-styles	Equated with sinful failure to condemn nonscriptural behaviors
Morality	Minimally acknowledged	Strictly enforced
Men and women	Gender equality	Women often considered inferior and subservient to men

include amputation of a limb for thievery and stoning to death for adultery. In the United States and many West European countries, crime rates are high and rising. This is the result, say some observers, of too much leniency shown to criminals in the courts and of the breakdown of the family unit—perhaps forms of secularization.

To be sure, secular societies sometimes reveal rather strong residues of a sacralized sentiment. The breakdown of social order in western and western-ized countries has frightened a great many Christians and Jews. One reaction in the United States is the Christian Coalition; in Israel, the *Gush Emunim* ("block of the faithful") fulfill a similar role, and in India a strong brand of Hindu fundamentalism has gained prominence. In all cases, these religious fundamental-ists are thoroughly politicized and exploit the latest technological developments in mass communication to reach as wide an audience as possible. There is little doubt that even political cultures generally considered overwhelmingly secular-ized will continue to experience serious challenges from sacralizers.

TABLE 3.3   Crime, Sin, and Punishment in Somalia

Crime/Sin	Punishment
Eating in public during Ramadan	Public flogging—35 lashes
Robbery	A hand cut off with a sword
Armed robbery	A hand and a foot cut off with a sword
Murder	Execution; body left outside for three days
Adultery	If married, death by stoning; if unmarried, 100 lashes
Public kissing	30 lashes
Married men caught in a homosexual act	Death by stoning
Unmarried men caught in a homosexual act	100 lashes
Making love to a goat	100 lashes

Source: William Finnegan, "A World of Dust," *The New Yorker*, p. 74.

POLITICAL AND SOCIAL FRAGMENTATION

Unfortunately, the subject of political culture is rarely easy to understand. In great part, this is because political culture itself is difficult to create and sustain, and this difficulty may increase rather than diminish over the next few decades. This text has already alluded to the resurgence of the ethnic conflict and religious radicalism that pose challenges for most political systems. Why are such challenges growing in number and severity?

These phenomena are surfacing because the most hospitable habitat for a consensual political culture, a stable society, is no longer taken for granted even in well-established democracies. The notion of "declining governability"[26] is applied to the United States because of the "incapacity of our political institutions to resolve or even mitigate the complex economic and social problems that face us."[27] What this means in a practical sense is uncertain. Apparently, though, the American political culture is changing because the norms and values of the overall culture are changing.

No political culture is static. A national trauma, such as any of those suggested earlier in this chapter, can produce sudden and irrevocable alterations in society. More often than not, though, a political culture changes gradually, sometimes imperceptibly. For example, despite unprecedented economic prosperity, a growing number of Americans sense things are not going well; others, especially ethnic minorities, do not feel they belong to the pluralist society American schoolchildren are taught to believe in. Instead, these groups feel a "coercive conformity" to become "Americanized."[28]

Another school of thought holds that tolerance, long an accepted value within the American political culture, has become excessive. Advocates of this point of view argue that tolerance may be desirable, but not at the expense of social discipline. The town of Raritan, New Jersey, for example, passed a city ordinance prohibiting "rude language."[29] Whether government has the legal right to force people to speak courteously is an open matter—one that will probably be argued rather loudly under the auspices of the First Amendment.

A political culture may also be less substantive than generally thought. Political scientists have long believed the United States to possess a coherent and fairly universal political culture. But how accurate is this perception? The April 19, 1995 bombing of a federal office building in Oklahoma City suggests that a number of people in this country do not accept a political culture that includes any meaningful presence of the national government. Even if we assume that only a handful of people are willing to resort to violence, the American political culture is still experiencing severe strain. One credible commentator has gone so far as to

---

[26] Bruce D. Porter, "Can American Democracy Survive?" *Commentary*, November 1993, p. 38.

[27] Ibid.

[28] Benjamin Schwartz, "The Diversity Myth: America's Leading Export," *The Atlantic Monthly*, May 1995, p. 62.

[29] "In the Front Line of the Politeness War," *The Economist*, February 18, 1995, p. 22.

The bombing of a federal office building in Oklahoma City is evidence some people in the country do not accept the prevailing political culture.

suggest that Americans are currently witnessing "a sort of Colombianization of the United States, in which failing political institutions become increasingly marginal in an ungovernable, criminalized, and endemically violent society."[30]

France has long been regarded as a country with a political culture supportive of the democratic process. During the presidential election in France in May 1995, however, candidates representing the (decidedly undemocratic) extremes of the left and the right together drew the support of almost three out of every eight voters. With an unemployment rate of 12 percent and nearly 4 million North African immigrants (to whom many unemployed French workers attribute their problems), voters in a free election demonstrated an interest in supporting extremist and explicitly nondemocratic policies.[31]

France is a major democracy and a West European powerhouse, possessing the second largest economy on the continent (after Germany) and the fourth largest in the world. Even so, the extremist vote in 1995 revealed a political culture not fully developed along democratic lines. France still has a coherent political culture, even with its cleavages. The less-than-democratic elements remain willing to work within the established political process.

In some developing countries, fragmentation rather than cohesion is the rule. Indigenous peoples in the western hemisphere, for example, still resent the intrusion of white Europeans. For South American Indians, the coca plant possesses religious sanctity, but in North American cities, police and health workers despise and fear it as the source of the addictive and destructive drug, cocaine.[32] In Peru, celebrations of the Spanish discovery of America aroused the indigenous peoples to express their desire to end "five hundred years of European dominance."[33] This dominance includes the U.S. threat to eradicate the coca crop, despite the practices of indigenous peoples in Bolivia and Peru. These people consume coca by chewing its leaves, believing it has both religious significance

---

[30] John Grey, *The New York Times Review of Books*, January 22, 1995.

[31] For example, the right wing National Front candidate, Jean Marie Le Pen, got 15 percent of the vote in part by advocating the expulsion of Muslims from France, even if they were French citizens. Expulsion of Muslims would mean an exile of nearly 8 percent of the country's population.

[32] Andrew Weil, "The New Politics of Coca," *The New Yorker*, May 15, 1995, p. 71.

[33] Ibid.

TABLE 3.4   Characteristics of Emerging Localized Political Cultures

1. Central government activities are replaced by local jurisdictions
2. National political institutions are eliminated or ignored
3. Social services are either suspended or administered by private (often religious) agencies
4. Popular perceptions of the central government change; the government is either completely discredited, viewed as an enemy, or viewed as incompetent and corrupt
5. Overall form of de facto government develops based either on warlordism or on a clergy extolling a religious value system

and health benefits. After a half millenium, then, Peru retains an uncertain political culture with a society still fragmented along European and indigenous lines.

Many, perhaps most, states in the world are unable to create a viable political culture. This is primarily because most overall cultures themselves are hardly functioning. Because of primitive communications technologies, the central government is often far removed from the bulk of the population in most developing countries. If it is not far removed, as in Iraq, many wish it was because of its brutality.

The centralized structures in many countries are being "replaced by a jagged-glass pattern of city-states, shanty-states, nebulous and anarchic region-alising."[34] Political cultures now and in the future may increasingly represent simple local subcultures, and the authority of the central government may not remain a part of the political culture. Such authority may actually cease to exist as it withdraws from or simply disintegrates in regions and city neighborhoods within developing countries. Fundamentalist religious organizations are taking on new authority, providing social services—schools, health clinics, even police protection and courts—that the government either can no longer afford or never provided in the first place. Table 3.4 summarizes these changes.

Political scientists have analyzed the theme of political culture rather thoroughly over the last several decades. New analyses may be necessary as national borders become unstable, as governments continue to relinquish control over segments of their populations, and as primary political loyalties draw in embrace clans and regions rather than nation-states. In such systems, the values a religious doctrine or a local warlord espouse supersede other allegiances. This concern is not alarmist—several developing countries have already deteriorated to the point where a national government is mostly ineffective or, in extreme cases such as Somalia, practically nonexistent.

Clearly, political cultures have developed unevenly in different societies. They cannot be taken for granted in even the most stable democracies. In fact, as we shall investigate in the following chapter, in democracies, political culture is perhaps most subject to challenge and change.

---

[34] Robert Kaplan, "The Coming Anarchy," *The Atlantic Monthly*, February 1994, pp. 12–27.

SUMMARY

1. Political culture is a part of a society's overall culture. It includes the political norms and values generally accepted by the overwhelming part of the citizenry.

2. Political legitimacy is a requirement for effective governance. Every regime must at least appear to be legitimate on the basis of such devices as free elections, ideology, or divine right.

3. Political socialization is the process that inducts each generation of citizens into their political culture. Agents of political socialization include peers, schools, the electronic and print media, and the family.

4. The collapse of fascism in 1945 and Soviet communism in 1991 suggests that extreme ideological convictions and lethal practices are in decline. However, some developing countries such as Iran (with its Islamic fundamentalism) and North Korea (still a Stalinist state) have domestic and foreign policies strongly motivated by ideology.

5. Toleration is not always considered a political virtue. Democracies differ because of the limits each applies to toleration. Some democracies place a greater emphasis on personal security than on maximizing expressions of individual freedom.

6. Political cultures are not engraved in stone; they change over time. Occasionally they change dramatically and suddenly because of a national political trauma.

7. Modern or modernizing societies emphasize secularization, advocating features such as toleration, pluralism, and individual autonomy. The opposite process of sacralization emphasizes a traditional heritage, religious values, and absolute ideals.

8. Very few political societies are completely united. Most constantly experience situations in which certain segments of the population, often ethnic and/or religious minorities, wish to separate or at least distinguish themselves from the rest of society. Subcultures with their own value systems and occasionally their own political agendas frequently result.

9. Many governments, some of them democratic, encourage a preferred political culture through an official or unofficial policy of "coercive conformity."

10. Because of an almost total lack of central authority or cultural cohesion, an increasing number of countries will be characterized by multiple local political cultures.

GLOSSARY

divine right   A monarch's assumption that he or she has spiritual justification for exercising complete power, with minimal or no constitutional restraints.

legitimacy   The determination through one or more means—by divine right, or through electoral or ideological processes—that a regime has the right to govern for a precise or indefinite period of time.

political trauma   A severe or devastating shock to a national society as the result of war, unprecedented economic hardship, accelerated and violent civil strife, or a combination of these factors.

Political Democracy and Authoritarian Government

It is important to remember that democracy is far from universally accepted. Tens of millions of Russians have seen their living standards plummet and their job and old age security guarantees evaporate since democracy was introduced to their country in the early 1990s. Hundreds of millions of religious fundamentalists in the developing world as well as within democracies themselves see toleration, the empowerment of women, and individualist expressions as challenges to an absolutist and spiritual authority. And scores of regimes believe, sincerely or otherwise, that enabling their citizenries to make decisions about their own political destinies is impractical and dangerous to social order.

In the established democracies, some raise occasional but very serious concerns over whether individual freedoms can be taken too far and whether social permissiveness equates with a lack of discipline and stability. The process of democracy itself is a mixed blessing. Electoral majorities can be especially unpleasant in their treatment of minorities.[1] Still, it seems safe to conclude that political democracy is a viable process that has survived severe challenges from fascism and communism. Democracy is also a process both incomplete and still evolving. Democracies tend to survive better than totalitarian regimes because democracies accept and even encourage change. In this chapter, we will pursue our understanding of democracy in terms of its current status, future prospects, and new directions.

Our study will explore both democracy and the process of democratization—both complicated subjects. Democracy has been more successful in some places than others, frequently for unanticipated reasons. In this chapter, we will explore the cultural, historical, and social motivations that either produce or proscribe democratic political systems.

---

[1] Popular majorities can be politically brutal towards individual expressions that the majority considers disagreeable. See the classic treatment of this issue in Jacob Talmon, *The Origins of Totalitarian Democracy* (London: Secker and Warburg, 1952).

TEN THOUSAND YEARS OF POLITICAL AUTHORITARIANISM

In the introductory chapter, we mentioned that institutionalized government is at most about ten thousand years old. Government evolved because the permanent human settlements that accompanied the advent of agriculture made order and security necessary. Throughout most of history, government's activities were few but critical to the success of civil society: people needed to be assured that their persons, families, and property would be secure, and government tried to offer this security. It would be difficult in the extreme for individuals to provide security for themselves on their own.

The deal struck between rulers and the ruled seemed Hobbesian: the ruled would receive protection and guarantees of security for themselves, their families, and their property; in return, they would pay taxes (to support the army that protected them) and obey laws that maximized social order. Just one other rule prevailed: keep your political thoughts to yourself. Authoritarian regimes apparently believed too much individual speculation and questioning of authority would detract both from social order and from the political power required to maintain it.

This arrangement certainly had advantages. Authoritarian government developed first in isolated societies. In a world full of predators ready to pounce on defenseless individuals and their possessions at a moment's notice, it was worth almost any price to protect oneself. Even if the government was not interested in individual rights, at least it was effective in providing security. After all, the niceties of human rights would not mean much if society itself was torn asunder by some ruthless invader.

Actually, the means to pursue the goal of security were often brutal—and in many societies still are—but they seemed to have at least tacit popular support, if only because the alternative was violent anarchy. For a long time, the term *democracy* was nearly synonymous with disorder and mob rule. At the Congress of Vienna in 1815, the major European powers agreed to keep the world safe *from* democracy. More than a century later, most of these powers and the United States at the Versailles Conference following World War I vowed to make the world safe *for* democracy.

Yet democracy is not a recent innovation. In its experimental form, it is about twenty-five hundred years old. The first people to try it gave us the term itself: *demos* is a Greek word for people and *kratos* is Greek for rule. The most successful early experiment in democracy took place in Athens during the fifth century B.C. The democracy was incomplete because it was restricted to only a small portion of the Athenian citizenry and a smaller element of the total population: to fully participate, it was necessary to be an adult free male. Women, resident aliens, and slaves were not part of the political system. In short, the majority of the population enjoyed no more than minimal human rights. At least this was a start.[2]

---

[2] For a readable analysis of the times and the experiment, see Donald Kagan, *Pericles of Athens and the Birth of Democracy* (New York: The Free Press, 1991).

The Athenian democratic experiment and its imitators in some of the smaller Greek cities did not last long. The city-state system gave way, first to the Macedonian and later to the Roman empires. Some democratic processes appeared from time to time in various locations, but they usually yielded to one form of authoritarianism or another. By the closing decades of the twentieth century, however, authoritarian forms of government appeared unattractive to growing numbers of people.

This happened not only because authoritarian governments could be extremely brutal, but because so few could claim economic success. South Korea, one of the exceptions, had become an economic success story by the 1980s, as had Chile. Both countries had experienced military governments of long duration, and these governments had not been reluctant to depress political opposition, sometimes violently. But they had also managed to encourage a substantial degree of economic prosperity and a growing middle class.

Ironically, it may have been prosperity that prompted mass demonstrations, particularly in South Korea. Protesters demanded political reform, fair and free elections, and other rights granted by democratic systems. During the 1980s, democracies began to replace authoritarian regimes in much of Latin America and, selectively, in East Asia.

One scholar, Francis Fukuyama, was encouraged by the outbreak of democratic regimes. He suggested we may be witnessing "the end of history," when the liberal democracy practiced and endorsed by Western Europe and the United States will undergo "universalization."[3] In the absence of natural enemies, democracy, according to this thesis, is destined at some point to cover the entire globe. The argument on behalf of democratic inevitability seemed to be bolstered by the collapse of totalitarian communism in Eastern Europe and the Soviet Union. Within the span of half a century, democracy had vanquished the two greatest threats to its existence, fascism and communism. Even better, once democracy was universally established, global peace would prevail. Democracies, after all, tend to refrain from engaging in wars with one another.[4]

No one can predict whether worldwide democracy is ultimately feasible. Determining democracy's staying power is of more immediate concern. Optimists enthusiastically embrace Fukuyama's thesis that democracy is inevitable. Others suggest that, while democracy has made headway over the last few decades, its final victory is far from certain. Nor is it a given that democracy as a political process will survive, even in the countries where it has recently appeared. It is perfectly possible that non- or antidemocratic governmental forms may outlast even the most significant surge of democracy history has known.

Some suggest that chaos is more likely to succeed authoritarianism than democracy. Even authoritarian forms of government may be weak or incompetent when it comes to maintaining themselves. As Somalia in the early 1990s

---

[3] Francis Fukuyama, "The End of History?" *The National Interest*, no. 16 (Summer 1989), pp. 3–19.

[4] "Democracies and War," *The Economist*, April 1, 1995.

suggested, the complete absence of a political infrastructure reduces a society to a situation reminiscent of the Middle Ages. As old political structures break down, local **warlords** replace them. These warlords may be worse for the establishment of political stability than more traditional authoritarianism since the warlords usually control fewer people and less territory, are constantly at war with one another, and provide little if any social stability.[5]

THE FEAR OF MODERNITY

It would be almost impossible to imagine living in any society that did not possess a set of widely accepted traditions the overwhelming part of the population subscribes to. Traditions survive because they make us feel better about who we are and what values we prefer. Traditions help tie us comfortably to the past and provide some basis of hope for the future—or at least, that is what they are supposed to do. But not all traditions are desirable: slavery, for example, is an ancient institution that would shame any society that practiced it today.

Traditions are found in democracies as well as in any other system. Open and pluralist societies value their traditions as much as any other. But numerous societies view democracy suspiciously, seeing it as a challenge to and perhaps a destroyer of tradition. A lot of countries associate democracy with a social permissiveness destructive of a society's fundamental values. On the other hand, traditional nondemocratic societies do not usually reject modernity per se.

Traditionalists understandably enjoy the conveniences electricity and indoor plumbing provide. Islamic, Christian, Jewish, and Hindu radicals may wish society's moral behavior to conform to holy writ, but like the rest of us, they don't object to air conditioning and central heating systems. Fear and resentment of modernization is directed mostly toward cultural expressions—"modern" music, fashion, cosmetics, and often, as we shall discuss shortly, gender equality and family planning.

Of course, societies often use modernization techniques to preserve traditions. Radio, television, electronic mail, and fax machines, not to mention sophisticated military weapons systems, have reached an expanded audience for traditionalist movements. Ironically, traditionalists may use modern technology to transmit a message condemning modernized life-styles.

Men's and Women's Roles

Perhaps no single social change in history has been as encompassing as the revision of relationships between men and women in both democratic and nondemocratic societies. While it is true that democracies were the first to recognize and guarantee women's rights, many refrained from doing so in their

---

[5] Robert Kaplan, "The Coming Anarchy," *The Atlantic Monthly*, February, 1994.

Pakistan's first female Prime Minister, Benazer Bhutto.

early years. Women in the United States and in the United Kingdom, for example, gained the vote in the 1920s and 1930s, respectively. It took a few more decades for women to begin appearing in regional and national legislatures. Women didn't start voting in Switzerland (the last democratic holdout) until about 1970.

Many authoritarian societies treat men and women equally in one sense: they systematically oppress both without regard to gender. In other societies where religion is a dominant feature of the regime, discrimination is frequently official and enforced. In Pakistan, women are by law worth only one-half of a man. In Iran, women are discouraged from revealing more than their faces and hands in public (and their fingernails must not be covered with polish). In Saudi Arabia, women are forbidden by law to drive any motorized vehicle. When several tried to do so in 1991, government officials arrested them and forced their husbands to pay large fines. On the other hand, these same regimes, which most westerners condemn as medieval in their treatment of women, boast that women can venture outside of the home (with a male relative as escort) without fear of harassment or violence, a statement most westernized nations cannot make.

Even in some democratic settings, women have had a rough time. In India, girls may be killed at birth if their sex disappoints their parents. The tendency for women to outlive men in industrialized democracies is reversed in India; it is more common for women to die before age thirty-five because of exhaustion from child bearing, malnutrition, and a lack of proper health care.[6]

India is not the only culprit. Infanticide is still widely practiced in many cultures.[7] Female babies in China had a better chance to reach adulthood before the government, in its strenuous efforts to curb population growth, encouraged Chinese couples to restrict their families to one child. Apparently, many couples killed their female babies in order to try again to have a male child. Once it realized this unintended consequence of its population control policy, the government began emphasizing how delightful baby girls can be.

Most countries in Africa are depressingly impoverished, but more women than men are living in complete poverty. Women normally work twice as many

[6] Jodi Jacobson, "Women's Work," *Foreign Service Journal*, January 1993, pp. 26–29 and 31. According to Jacobson, "Male children consistently receive more and better food and health care than their sisters."

[7] "Stark Data on Women: 100 Million Are Missing," *The New York Times*, November 5, 1991.

A Bosnian Muslim woman well prepared for ethnic conflict.

hours as men, but earn only a tenth of the income[8]—which even for men is barely at subsistence level. In parts of Africa, women are still subjected to genital mutilation. Oddly enough to many westerners, some of these women celebrate this practice as a time women can be together away from male domination.[9]

The data about the world's women are not all grisly. In many countries, women have made significant advances in professions such as journalism, business, and medicine. They have also made political gains. In several democracies—including Canada, Norway, Israel, and the United Kingdom—women are or have been heads of government. They have served as leaders in the democratization process in other countries, including Sri Lanka, Pakistan (although Prime Minister Benazir Bhutto was removed from office in 1996 on charges of corruption), Nicaragua, and the Philippines.

An increasing number of countries are realizing that to disenfranchise and abuse half of the population is to retard both social and economic development. In Russia in 1996, women accounted for 75 percent of the country's unemployed,[10] but they were beginning to account for a surge in small businesses experiencing significant success.[11] Educated and healthy women, like educated

---

[8] Daphne Topouzis, "The Feminization of Poverty," *Africa Report*, July/August 1990, pp. 60–63.

[9] Howard W. French, "The Ritual: Disfiguring, Hurtful, Wildly Festive," *The New York Times*, January 31, 1997, p. A4.

[10] Sophia Kishkovsky and Elizabeth Williamson, "Second-Class Comrades No More: Women Stroke Russia's Start-Up Boom," *The Wall Street Journal*, January 30, 1997, A12.

[11] Ibid.

and healthy men, have become firm indicators of economic and technological development. Women may have more opportunities in Russia, a country that in many ways is starting from scratch, than they did under a communistic system that preached but didn't fully practice gender equality.

The Status of Modern Democracy

As mentioned earlier, democracy as a political system is of recent vintage. In an intriguing essay, Samuel Huntington outlined three waves and two reversals of democracy:[12]

1. The first wave began rather modestly in the 1820s with the expansion of the voting franchise in the United States. The Reform Acts in the United Kingdom swiftly followed, beginning in 1832. The first wave ended in 1926 with a total of twenty-six democracies in the world; between 1922 and 1942, more than half of these democracies succumbed to autocracy or military occupation by totalitarian governments, reducing the number to twelve (the first reversal).

2. The second wave ran from about 1945 to 1962, when democratically governed countries advanced in number to thirty-six. This healthy total declined slightly as the result of a second reversal between 1960 and 1975, bringing the number back down to thirty.

3. We are currently enjoying a third wave of democracy which has been in full swing since the early 1980s. It began in Latin America and expanded to parts of Eastern Europe and East Asia. Huntington speculates on whether a third reversal is lurking in the future.

The world is certainly more democratic in the 1990s than at any previous time in history. But a considerable number of newer democracies are far from secure. Many have had only two or three free elections. Russia has conducted two free parliamentary elections in the 1990s. Its second presidential election was held in 1996, and according to independent observers, was fairly conducted. Some countries have not yet experienced a peaceful turnover in government: Mexico has conducted free elections since the 1930s, but the same political party, the PRI, dominated national politics and controlled the federal government for nearly seven decades without interruption, until it lost control of Mexico City and the national legislature in the 1997 elections.

Ironically, the **free market,** the supposed handmaiden of modern political democracy, does not automatically facilitate the democratic process. The Russian economy is being privatized, but it is also being criminalized as gangsters acquire formerly state-controlled industries. One observer has pointed out, for example, that when Eastern Europeans threw off their communist regimes,

---

[12] Samuel P. Huntington, "A New Era in Democracy: Democracy's Third Wave," *Current,* September, 1990, pp. 27–39. A full treatment of Huntington's concept of democratic phases is provided in *The Third Wave: Democratization in the Late Twentieth Century* (Norman, Oklahoma: University of Oklahoma Press, 1991).

both they and we believed they would relentlessly seek democracy and that it would prevail. To some extent, that is what happened. But more people were apparently interested in the material rather than the political advantages democracy brings. "The Eastern European revolutions that seemed to arise out of concern for global democratic values quickly deteriorated into a stampede in the general direction of free markets and their ubiquitous, television-promoted shopping malls."[13]

Neither the concept nor practice of political democracy is interpreted in a uniform fashion. For example, in one of the least hospitable climates for democracy, the Middle East, some advances have been made in the area of individual rights. But these advances are not necessarily democratic and do not necessarily lead to democracy. One scholar describing the limits of democratization in Arab states explains that

1.   rulers may allow competitive elections, but they determine who participates in them;

2.   rulers retain control of the media and the agencies that oversee elections;

3.   rulers have no intention of transferring power to anyone outside the political elite, which includes a carefully defined and narrow membership; and

4.   maximized democracy allows people to express different points of view without fear of imprisonment.[14]

No Arab society yet has gotten to point 4. Most western observers don't consider any Middle Eastern country other than Israel and possibly Turkey democratic. In the more politically progressive Arab states, one of the most critical elements of democracy—the peaceful transfer of political power to the opposition after the incumbent government loses an election—is still an unknown and, for many, unacceptable tenet.

Governments willing to conduct free elections are not always willing to accept their results, often because nondemocratic political parties sometimes win. When a fundamentalist Islamic political party won a free election in Algeria, the army intervened and nullified the results, which had caused substantial violence. And, of course, Germany provides a grim historical reminder of the dangers of free elections when nondemocratic parties prevail; in 1932, the Nazis won the country's last free election until 1949. They promptly cancelled the democracy by suspending individual rights and transporting people they didn't like to concentration camps.

For the last half of the twentieth century, a dozen countries in Western Europe and North America have been unreservedly democratic with only an infrequent relapse. Nor are democracies necessarily tied to industrial economies.

---

[13] Benjamin R. Barber, "Jihad vs. McWorld," *The Atlantic*, March 1992, p. 61.

[14] Mustapha K. El Sayyid, "The Third Wave of Democratization in the Arab World," in Dan Tschirgi, ed., *The Arab World Today* (Boulder & London: Lynne Rienner Publishers, 1994), p. 183.

Costa Rica's economy is mostly agricultural and not nearly as prosperous as any in Western Europe, but the country has been steadfastly democratic since 1948,[15] making it the oldest functioning democracy in Latin America.

Democracy, then, is not the same everywhere. A country's political culture helps to determine whether democracy will flourish or barely survive. In the next few pages, we will briefly consider the political systems generally agreed to be the oldest, most secure, and most successful.

WHERE ARE THE DEMOCRACIES?

Such a question is difficult to answer, even when we look at a world map and examine the post-Cold War political geography. The established democracies are where we would expect to find them—in North America and Western Europe. Despite the demise of communism, it is still tricky to find other democracies. As table 4.1 suggests, democracy makes only a rare appearance in most of the Middle East and Africa, is still tentative in most of Eastern Europe, and is only beginning to emerge in East and South Asia. Latin America offers a more optimistic picture since, with the exception of Cuba, civilian rule tends to prevail and relatively free elections have occurred within the last several years. But most of Latin America is in the process of democratization rather than in fully functioning democratic systems. Some South American countries, such as Colombia, have freely elected governments, but they suffer from rampant corruption as officials regularly succumb to bribes that drug traffickers offer them. The term *narco-democracy* may become familiar in years to come.

We should be careful when it comes to placing countries in the democratic category. We must ask at least two questions:

1.   How many free elections have been conducted?
2.   Has there been at least one peaceful turnover in government?

Peaceful turnovers needn't happen very often for a country to be democratic. Political party control did not change in Britain from 1979 to 1997 or in Germany after 1982. Over a period of forty-three years (from 1949 to 1992), Israel changed party control only twice. Japan was governed by one political party, the Liberal Democrats, for nearly four decades. In the United States, the Democratic party, with rare intervals, controlled both houses of Congress for more than six decades, from 1931 to 1995. The 107th Congress, 1997–1998, marked the first time in seven decades that the Republican party achieved two consecutive congressional majorities. All of these countries, however, conducted national elections when they were constitutionally required to do so. When the incumbents lost, they quietly and peacefully acceded to the election results.

---

[15] In 1948, Costa Rica tried to guarantee democratic governance by abolishing its military forces and placing strict term limits on its presidents.

....

TABLE 4.1   Variations in Political Freedom Across the Globe

Combined Average Ratings of Independent Countries (1–7)

Free	Partly Free	Not Free
1	**3**	**5.5**
Australia	Nicaragua	Brunei
Austria	Panama	Burkina Faso
Barbados	Philippines	Central African Republic
Belgium	Taiwan (Rep. of China)	Djibouti
Canada	Tonga	Ghana
Costa Rica	Turkey	Guinea
Cyprus (Greek)		Guinea-Bissau
Denmark	**3.5**	Iran
Finland	Bulgaria	Lebanon
Iceland	Colombia	Lesotho
Ireland	El Salvador	Maldives
Italy	Guatemala	Mali
Japan	Paraguay	Niger
Luxembourg	Peru	Romania
Malta	Senegal	Tanzania
Netherlands	Suriname	United Arab Emirates
New Zealand		
Norway	**4**	**6**
St. Christopher-Nevis	Algeria	Cameroon
(St. Kitts-Nevis)	Gabon	Congo
Solomon Islands	Haiti	Kenya
Spain	Madagascar	Mozambique
Sweden	Mexico	Oman
Switzerland	Mongolia	Qatar
Trinidad and Tobago	Morocco	Rwanda
Tuvalu	Nepal	Seychelles
United States of America	Pakistan	Togo
	Singapore	Zaire
1.5		
Belize	**4.5**	**6.5**
Botswana	Egypt	Albania
Dominica	Guyana	Burundi
France	Malaysia	Chad
Germany	South Africa	Laos
Greece	Sri Lanka	Malawi
Kiribati	Tunisia	Mauritania
Nauru	USSR*	Saudi Arabia
Portugal	Yugoslavia	
St. Lucia		**7**
St. Vincent and the	**5**	Afghanistan
Grenadines	Bangladesh	Angola
United Kingdom	Benin	Burma (Myanmar)
Uruguay	Cape Verde	Cambodia
	Comoros	China
2	Fiji	Cuba
Argentina	Ivory Coast (Cote D'Ivoire)	Equatorial Guinea
Chile	Jordan	Ethiopia
Cyprus (Turkish)	Nigeria	Iraq

TABLE 4.1   Variations in Political Freedom Across the Globe (Continued)

Combined Average Ratings of Independent Countries (1–7)

Free	Partly Free	Not Free
Czechoslovakia	Sao Tome and Principe	Korea, North
Ecuador	Zimbabwe	Kuwait (Iraqi-occupied)*
The Gambia		Liberia
Grenada	**5.5**	Libya
Hungary	Bahrain	Somalia
Israel	Bhutan	Sudan
Jamaica	Indonesia	Syria
Mauritius	Sierra Leone	Vietnam
Poland	Swaziland	
Venezuela	Uganda	
Western Samoa	Yemen	
	Zambia	
2.5		
Antigua and Barbuda		
Bahamas		
Bolivia		
Brazil		
Dominican Republic		
Honduras		
India		
Korea, South		
Namibia		
Papua New Guinea		
Thailand		
Vanuatu		

* Ratings may have changed since 1991 due to changes in government.
Source: Freedom Review, Vol. 22, No. 1, p. 23 (New York: Freedom House, 1991).

In contrast, democratization does not guarantee a democratic political outcome. Very often, for example, a country's population will include an ethnic or religious minority that does not see itself as an integral part of the citizenry. The government may have a similar view. The three Baltic states, Estonia, Latvia, and Lithuania, provide an interesting case in point. They were the last countries forcibly annexed to the Soviet Union (1940) and the first to declare their independence from it (1989). During the half century the Balts were Soviet republics, such a large number of Russians were permanently settled within Baltic borders that the demographics were severely altered. This was particularly true in Estonia and Latvia, where Russians now make up as much as a third or more of the total population. In some regions, such as the northeastern corner of Estonia, Russians actually form the majority. Table 4.2 summarizes the demographic figures for each republic.

Do the large Russian minorities present a problem in the new democracies in the Baltic republics? If democracy means having voting rights, holding political office, and being a part of the overall decision-making process, then ethnic Russians should have all these rights, but the Baltic governments are under-

....

TABLE 4.2   Demographic Breakdown of the Three Baltic Republics*

Country	Indigenous Population	Russian Population	Others
Estonia	62	30	8
Latvia	52	34	14
Lithuania	80	9	11

* Figures are percentages based on the final Soviet census in 1989. They do not equal 100 percent because of the presence of other ethnic minority communities.
Source: Karen Dawisha and Bruce Parrott, *Russia and the New States of Eurasia: The Politics of Upheaval* (New York: Cambridge University Press, 1994), pp. 338–39.

standably wary of Russian political power. The Latvian government is disconcerted because its citizens of Russian ancestry prefer to speak the Russian language, indulge in Russian culture, live in Russian neighborhoods, and maintain loyalties to Moscow rather than the Latvian regime in the capital city of Riga. A democracy cannot force an ethnic minority to learn to speak another language or develop a new set of political loyalties unless it wants to cease being a democracy.

DEMOCRACY, DEVOLUTION, AND CULTURAL AUTONOMY

Authoritarian and democratic governments have one thing in common: a political center where the ultimate decision-making authority of the state resides. The two systems quickly part company, however, when it comes to decentralizing authority. Democratic regimes tend to distribute power broadly, keeping a few responsibilities, such as foreign policy and military force, centralized. Activities such as public education and taxation may be shared with or delegated to regional or local jurisdictions. The United States has distributed these powers since its inception.

For some countries, including several well-established democracies, greater democracy may bring more decentralization, or **devolution.** Devolution can be defined as the political process that assigns various regions within a country increasing responsibility for managing their own affairs, to the point of creating regional legislatures. In short, devolution is the decentralization of domestic policy while the central government retains control over foreign policy and national defense. Devolution occurs in democracies where regions have historical memories of political independence and usually have a desire to preserve a distinct culture.

An excellent example is the United Kingdom. Five-sixths of the country's population and almost as much territory is English, with the remainder divided into Scot, Welsh, and Northern Irish regions and population. Until paramilitary action and political terrorism rendered Northern Ireland ungovernable by the early 1970s, the Irish had in place a regional legislative assembly called the Stormont. Both the Welsh and the Scots have strong nationalist movements represented in the British House of Commons, and both have ancient memories of political independence.[16] Thus, considerable debate has developed over whether it is a good idea for each region to have its own legislature rather than being governed directly from the central government in London.[17] The amount of power vested in regional legislatures would equal the influence London would lose over local affairs.

Very often, either the political arrangements or political geography of a country does not allow for devolution strictly along the lines of geographical regions. Such arrangements are frequently based less on political formulas than on cultural divisions that follow religious, linguistic, and ethnic patterns. Sometimes all three come into play. For example, in Israel, both Arabic and Hebrew are considered official languages and are displayed everywhere from road signs to restaurant menus.

Moreover, Arabs and Jews usually belong to their own political parties. Arab Muslims administer their own school systems where the language of instruction is Arabic. India counts fifteen languages as official, Switzerland three. Canada has long had two official languages, English and French, and an unwritten requirement over the last few decades that no national politician of any party can become prime minister without fluency in both.

Whether it is politically healthy to officially recognize and encourage these divisions is debatable. It seems clear, though, that they are permanent features of several democracies, and that the acceptance of cultural preferences may enhance internal peace. In fact, even the United States, which has long prided itself on the political integration of its many minorities, now has congressional districts where an English-speaking candidate is at a disadvantage. We are not alluding only to Spanish-speaking voters; in a few districts in southern California, a candidate fluent in Korean or Chinese may have distinct advantages.

Governments, especially but not exclusively democratic governments, are becoming more sensitive to the needs of historically ignored minorities. Indigenous peoples have frequently been victimized over the last five centuries, but governments are recognizing and rectifying this in the closing years of the twentieth century. In the northern regions of Norway, eighty thousand Saami, descendants of people who arrived there ten thousand years ago, are no longer forced to learn Norwegian, and the central government encourages them to preserve their own culture. It is difficult, though, to retain one's own culture amidst an overwhelmingly larger one.

THE INDUSTRIAL DEMOCRACIES

Most of today's democracies are the products of processes that took generations to accomplish. And most current democracies are more democratic than they were generations ago. When the United States held its first national elections

---

[16] The Scots are much more emphatic about devolution than the Welsh, whose support for devolution is only around 50 percent. See "Waking the Welsh Dragon," *The Economist*, January 18, 1997, p. 58.

[17] "Bricks from Straw," *The Economist*, July 22, 1995, p. 54.

in 1788 for the presidency and House of Representatives, only about 100,000 voters were eligible to participate.[18] Women were denied the franchise (the right to vote), as were all youths under the age of twenty-one. A tenth of the population were slaves, and in some states property and religious qualifications limited voting eligibility well into the nineteenth century.

Two centuries ago, the United Kingdom, like the United States, was one of a handful of countries that had any semblance of democratic governance. Its parliament can actually be traced back to the thirteenth century. Yet it did not seriously begin to extend the franchise until 1832 with the passage of the first of several Reform Bills, a process that went on well into the twentieth century. Until then, members of parliament were frequently elected from **rotten boroughs;** that is, from districts where only the candidate possessed enough property to vote, let alone stand for office. Some rotten boroughs had neither franchised nor disenfranchised people—the districts were under water.

Industrialized democracies are sometimes described as societies that are reasonably comfortable places to live. The *Human Development Index*, published by the United Nations, ranks about 130 countries on their quality of life. The top twenty-three countries are industrialized democracies (Japan ranks first, the United States twenty-first).[19] In nearly all of these countries, the bulk of the population enjoys a recognizable middle class life-style that includes such amenities as car and home ownership, social security systems, national health care, public education through the doctoral level, and affordable entertainment. The industrialized democracies only began to exhibit these features in the twentieth century. The national wealth that the industrial and technological revolutions generated enabled quite a few people to become rich, but, more importantly, they gave an impetus to an expanding middle class that demanded more and more services and whose earnings, savings, and taxes could pay for those services.

Until the last third of twentieth century, this phenomenon was restricted to Western Europe and North America. The devastation of World War II interrupted it, but by the mid-1950s, countries such as France and Germany were back to their prewar levels of economic production. By the early 1960s, the term **economic miracle** was being applied to Germany, but it might as easily have described the French and Italian recoveries as well. Just as impressive was the growth of the Japanese economy, which rapidly accelerated in the 1960s. Less than four decades after its defeat in 1945, Japan had the second biggest economy in the world.

All of these countries had something in common besides prosperous economies—they all had democratic political institutions. Industrialization and democracy seemed to be made for each other. With the notable exception of

---

[18] The membership of the U.S. Senate was not popularly elected until 1913, when the Seventeenth Amendment was ratified.

[19] *The Economist Book of Vital Statistics*, Economist Books, Ltd. Copyright © 1990 by Economist Books, Ltd.

Japan, industrialized democracies appeared confined to the West. This is now dramatically and quickly changing.

DEMOCRATIC FRAGILITIES: IMMIGRATION

Think about it: over the last three to four generations (the last hundred years or so), the lives of hundreds of millions of people have been irrevocably transformed under the auspices of political democracy. When they were your age, your great-grandparents would have viewed your world as the stuff of imagination or science fiction stories. The average life span has increased from about forty-five to nearly eighty, and it is no longer uncommon for some to reach their hundreth birthdays. Indoor plumbing and electric service have provided a reliable and unprecedented amount of personal hygiene. Instant communication to nearly anywhere on the planet is available through telephone service, fax machines, and electronic mail.

It is no wonder that so many millions want to leave the lives they regard as dirty, boring, miserable, and without hope to find lives they regard as utopian and we take for granted. More people than ever before are on the move. One estimate suggests that by the middle 1990s, a total of 100 million people (nearly 1 out of every 57 human beings on the planet) from North Africa, Eastern Europe, the Middle East, Latin America, and South Asia were trying to immigrate to the more prosperous regions of Western Europe and North America.

Immigration has become a political issue in most of the major democracies. In at least two, the United States and France, it is an issue that decides elections. California Governor Pete Wilson won reelection in 1994 in great part because of the strong stand he took against illegal immigrants coming across the Californian-Mexican border. Jacques Chirac won election to the French presidency in 1995 by emphasizing a hard line against further immigration from former French colonies in northern Africa.

Nightmarish scenarios have been described to convince governments to either alleviate the terrible poverty in the Third World in order to lessen the desire to migrate to Western Europe or North America, or to seal the First World's borders shut against immigrants, or both. Some of the rhetoric borders on racism: the predominantly prosperous west and its 700 million mostly white and comfortable inhabitants, alarmists warn, are in danger of being overwhelmed by an influx of millions (perhaps tens of millions) of the 5 billion non-whites and having to face "Third-Worldization."[20]

The message seems clear. If western governments want immigrants to stay home, they will need to provide an incentive to do so. The West can supply this incentive in the form of substantial economic assistance, family planning, and health care. Otherwise, the world will continue to have obscenely unequal

---

[20] For perhaps the gloomiest scenario of all, see Matthew Connelly and Paul Kennedy, "Must It Be the West Against the Rest?" *The Atlantic Monthly*, December 1994, pp. 61–91.

economies, and the West and a few westernized countries will continue to get richer while the rest of the world grows poorer.

EMERGING DEMOCRACIES

Even authoritarian regimes able to create growing economies were becoming democratized by the 1980s. South Korea is a case in point. Like Japan, South Korea is an East Asian country and, like Japan, it was devastated by war. But South Korea and Taiwan, two **East Asian dragons** or **East Asian tigers,** have taught us that the road to democracy can differ from society to society. This was true in the West: while democracy progressed rather smoothly in the United States, France, and Britain during the 1920s and 1930s, it regressed in Germany, Italy, Spain, and Portugal during the same time and then made a comeback later.

The same process seems to be going on in East Asia. Both South Korea and Taiwan are strong examples of authoritarian systems undergoing democratization, but in different ways. To summarize the distinctions:

South Korea: The year 1987 was key. Demonstrations by students and a growing middle class ended the rule of the last of a series of militarily supported dictators and installed a popularly endorsed regime.

Taiwan: In 1986, the ruling party initiated democratic reforms in anticipation of rumblings among members of a growing middle class that wanted access to the political decision-making process. The reforms abolished martial law (in effect since 1949) and legalized opposition parties.

In the Huntington analysis mentioned earlier, South Korea experienced a *transplacement* "in which an authoritarian regime and a strong opposition first clash and then compromise when both realize that neither long-term repression nor revolution are feasible." Taiwan experienced a *transformation* that occurred "through management by liberalizers within the government."[21]

The East Asian tigers have more in common with each other than with the western democracies. There is no reason to expect South Korea, Taiwan, and Singapore to develop the same western economic and political precedents at the same rate because of their tremendous cultural differences. According to one highly reputable analyst, world economic competition, while no longer between capitalists and communists, is now between two distinct forms of capitalism.

One form is familiar to most of us in the West: *individualistic capitalism* characterizes the American and British version, which emphasizes intense, often ruthless aggressiveness to win short-term goals and immediate profits. Participants engage in competitive practices such as corporate raiding and extend

---

[21] Steve Chan and Cal Clark, "The Price of Economic Success: South Korea and Taiwan Sacrifice Political Development," *Harvard International Review* (Winter, 1992–1993), 24–26, 64.

minimal (if any) cooperation to either rivals or governmental agencies for the common good. The other form, *communitarian capitalism*, emphasizes the qualities frequently associated with the East Asian success stories: firm loyalty, long-term investment strategies, and policies that require teamwork, social responsibility, and a concern for sustaining growth by constantly updating and refining industrial techniques and workers' skills.[22]

Obviously, it is not impossible to locate both individualist and communitarian features in East Asian and Western societies, yet the distinctions are often crucial in understanding the economic and political processes in these societies. The East Asian democracies require and generally receive greater discipline and conformity from their citizenries than their western counterparts do. Such a requirement does not make them less democratic than those in the West: social discipline and a lack of interest in individual expression sounds suspect in the West, but East Asians also enjoy lower crime rates and less violence than western peoples.

Even if we assume that democracy is the form of government many of the world's people prefer, it does not necessarily follow that American-style democracy will prevail in the end. Nor should we insist on it doing so. Political culture, as indicated in the previous chapter, has a lot of impact in determining the kind of political regime that governs a society. It would be a mistake to assume that democracy evolves in just the same way in differing political cultures. It is likely that democracy means different things in different societies. Newer democracies will probably place less emphasis on the prerogatives of the individual than older (western) systems, as we shall see.

AUTHORITARIAN AND DEMOCRATIC BLENDS?

Why have some authoritarian regimes, such as South Korea, begun democratization processes, while others, such as Indonesia, haven't? Two reasons—economic development and the accompanying urbanization—have already been discussed. Apparently, both are necessary to democratization. A study of rapid economic growth in South Korea and Indonesia revealed that as the 1990s began, 70 percent of the South Korean population lived in towns and cities, while only 30 percent of Indonesians did.[23] With the bulk of the South Korean labor force concentrated in the cities, it was easier for workers to organize themselves and protest governmental excesses. Indonesia has a population four times that of South Korea spread out over a land area nearly twenty times as large. This makes it much more difficult to organize politically.

Moreover, Taiwan and South Korea are much more urbanized societies than Indonesia. An interesting theory suggests that democracies tend to de-

---

[22] Lester C. Thurow, "Who Owns the Twenty-First Century?" *Sloan Management Review*, Spring 1992, pp. 5–17.

[23] David Potter, "Democratization in Asia," in David Held, ed., *Prospects for Democracy: North, South, East, West* (Stanford, California: Stanford University Press, 1993), pp. 364–65.

velop faster in cities than in the countryside.[24] Cities, as centers of commerce and industry, are richer and are home to a larger middle class than rural areas. Ancient Athens, remember, was a city-state noted for commerce and, for the time, substantial wealth. Of course, plenty of countries are urbanizing without democratizing. This urbanization is going on so quickly that it may at least temporarily outpace any political development and, perhaps more ominously, any economic development as well.

Perhaps an even more compelling reason for some countries to democratize is that it is politically chic to do so. The industrial democracies command so much of the world's wealth, so much sophisticated technology, and such a preponderance of military strength that no single nondemocratic regime or combination of dictatorships can hope to challenge them. Moreover, several countries began to realize by the 1990s that to establish advantageous commercial relationships with these democracies, they would need to democratize themselves, or to at least reduce or eliminate their more brutal practices. The industrial democracy "club," in the immediate aftermath of the Soviet collapse, appreciated the fact that developing countries need economic assistance and could turn nowhere else for it.

Of course, whether all this will work out remains to be seen. Established democracies have their own problems. For a long time, western democracies have been viewed as the product of cultural and technological revolutions as much as ideological and political ones. Consider the events of western historical epochs that serve as the cornerstones of modern democracy (and, by the way, tended to begin in cities):

Renaissance (1300–1600): This period ushered in the rediscovery of ancient classical scientific learning and philosophical speculation that encouraged free inquiry, experimentation, and toleration of unorthodox ideas.

Reformation (1500s through the seventeenth century): During the Reformation, the principle of separation of church and state developed and links between citizenship and religious affiliation, began to disappear.

Enlightenment (1700s): Contradictions between science and religious faith eventually encouraged an atmosphere of freedom of inquiry during this period. This in turn helped produce beneficial technologies and a greater democratic climate.

Industrial and Technological Revolutions (1600s to present): These revolutions introduced a gradual increase in and eventual redistribution of economic wealth to enable masses of people for the first time in history to become educated, travel widely, and dismantle theories of government.

To be sure, these processes began in and were dominated by the West, and to an appreciable extent they were geographically restricted to the West. An important question remains: how successfully can democracy be transplanted to

---

[24] See "Cities," a survey published in *The Economist*, July 29, 1994.

other countries and regions? Equally important, should transplantation occur at all? It may be better to let political processes work out naturally. One argument suggests that a country probably shouldn't be forced to become democratic before it's ready to. A perhaps even more intriguing question is whether the more democracies we have, the more peaceful the world will become. Because democracies are inherently peaceful and consistently focus on economic prosperity, this theory goes, they are reluctant to fight wars with anyone, especially one another.[25]

This concept has not met with universal agreement. Some have argued, for example, that World War I (1914–1918) was fought between contenders who were fairly democratic, considering these were the early years of the twentieth century. Germany had a strong parliamentary system, as did its main antagonists, France and Britain, and, in the last two years of the war, the United States. World War I notwithstanding, democracies have not recently been inclined towards international violence. They have tried to encourage other countries to become democratic in the belief that democracy is a good system and that the more democracies there are, the safer the world will be.

This is why the United States, for example, concerns itself with postcommunist Russia. The logic is appealing: we must assist Russia economically in order to make its democratic regime credible; as Russia democratizes, it will become more stable and the world will be more peaceful. But Russia is a non-western country that missed most of the pivotal thinking of the Renaissance, Reformation, and Enlightenment. Its industrial revolution did not begin until industrialization had been well underway in the West for generations. Even at the time of the Soviet Union's collapse in 1991, more than 30 percent of the Russian labor force worked in agriculture, many times the number in western countries such as the United States, France, Germany, and the United Kingdom (where the proportions range between 3 and 8 percent).

Free elections are the most evident characteristic of political democracy. Yet Russia's elections have not been particularly encouraging. Extremist parties on the left and right have support. Some observers remind the world of the ultimate fate of Germany's precarious democracy between 1919 and 1933. A large proportion of the German electorate supported either extreme left or right political parties, until the moderate and democratic center shrank to the point where it no longer attracted enough support to maintain power. Too many Germans in 1933 were disillusioned with democracy to continue to sustain it.

Russia's democratic experiments remind political historians of Germany because of the attraction extremes have for large proportions of voters in both

---

[25] "Democracies and War," *The Economist*, April 1, 1995, p. 17. One analysis found that "of the 416 wars between sovereign powers recorded between 1816 and 1980, only 12 were even arguably wars between democracies, and most of those had extenuating factors."

nations. Of course, precise historical parallels are impossible. But concern over the popularity of undemocratic parties and leaders in a democratization process is both understandable and legitimate.

DEMOCRACY'S FUTURE

There is little point in trying to predict democracy's future. For one thing, democracy is most likely still in its beginning stages as a political system. Only seven countries in the world have been consistently democratic for at least a full century. Five are English-speaking nations. And democracy is not an easy accomplishment. No democracy is a finished story, and although democracies closely resemble one another in their constitutional and political structures, no two democracies are quite the same.

Democracy's future is also uncertain because democratization sometimes proceeds haphazardly, as we have seen, in places where it hasn't tread before. In much of Eastern Europe, Latin America, and nearly all of Africa and the Middle East, democracy is a precarious thing. Even optimists suggest that democracy inherently contains real dangers that could in the end destroy it. As pointed out earlier in this chapter, antidemocratic forces can do well in free elections and occasionally even win them.

Finally, one scholar has warned that we have to be careful not to revert to what he refers to as **tribal democracy.**[26] The earliest democracies were, understandably, tribal communities in which democracy functioned rather well, but only for those admitted to its processes as full and equal partners. For example, earlier in the chapter, we mentioned the rather restrictive democracy of the classical city-state of Athens. Modern political systems these days can actually function democratically if one overlooks the people who are refused admittance. Non-Shiite Muslims in Iran, for example, are severely discriminated against, while Shiite Muslims regularly vote in free elections.[27] The United States briefly regressed to a tribal democracy between 1942 and 1944, when the government interned citizens of Japanese descent, an obvious violation of the constitutional rights of 120,000 Americans. The dual notions that democracy has come a long way and still has a long way to go are equally reasonable assumptions.

Throughout their long histories, authoritarian regimes have varied in terms of brutality and repressiveness. It seems reasonable for democracies, as they spring up in nonwestern regions, to also vary in form and degree. Some may well remain tribal, restricting democracy to certain groups. After all, for most of their history, western democracies themselves were restrictive and discouraged full citizen participation on the basis of race, ethnicity, gender, or religion. Just as these governments progressed, however, there seems little doubt that democracy will continue to evolve as a viable political system.

---

[26] Raymond D. Gastil, "What Kind of Democracy?" *The Atlantic*, June 1990, pp. 92–94 and 96.
[27] Ibid.

Pericles.

POLITICAL
BIOGRAPHY

**Pericles,
History's
First
Democrat**

The earliest experiments in democracy began about twenty-five hundred years ago. Democracy appeared in Athens under the auspices of the city-state's leader, Pericles (495–431 BC). It might be more accurate to give Pericles credit for democratizing Athens rather than for establishing a democracy. He governed by consistently winning office for three decades, a long tenure for a democratic politician; but this was an age that did not impose term limitations on its top political leaders.

Accomplishments attributed to Pericles include employing the unemployed in public works programs (a policy that helped build the Parthenon), paying citizens for jury duty and military service, and insuring that every voter was also a legislator and could attend and deliberate in Assembly meetings. Only a minority ever did, however, since most Athenian citizens were either too far away to conveniently travel to the meeting place or had no interest in participating. Even the judiciary was democratized in a sense: hundreds of jurors could assemble to hear a case, and the outcome was based simply on majority vote. Apparently, few worried that juries could make mistakes.

Athens, of course, was an incomplete democracy. Pericles himself was referred to as *strategos autokrator,* or commander-in-chief of the army; in other words, he was an officeholder of unequalled power. This was an elected office, however; perhaps Pericles was simply a democratically chosen dictator. Ironically, one of his most controversial measures restricted Athenian citizenship. To acquire citizenship, one had to prove that both parents were Athenians. This rule was designed to prevent immigrants from becoming citizens for fear of diluting the original citizen fabric of Athens. This issue is a familiar one in most democratic societies today.

SUMMARY

1. Despite the collapse of communism in Eastern Europe and the Soviet Union, democracy is far from a sure success. While it has expanded greatly over the last decade, many people around the world still view democracy with suspicion, distrust, or hostility.

2. Authoritarian forms of government preceded and still coexist with democratic forms. In several countries over the last decade, authoritarian regimes that have presided over substantial economic growth have gradually given way to democratization.

3. Democratization is often resisted because of its association with modern morality, gender equality, and a secularized culture.

4. Samuel P. Huntington's concept of waves of democracy suggests that we are in a third (and so far, successful) wave of democratic growth. The first two waves were followed by reversals in which democracy receded, and we have no guarantee that a similar reversal won't slow the third wave.

5. Democracies are still rare in the Middle East and Africa. They are well established in Western Europe, are gaining footholds in Eastern Europe, have begun to tenuously appear in some of the former Soviet republics and East and South Asia, and are showing substantial promise in most of Latin America.

6. Firmly entrenched democracies do not require frequent changes in government. One political party may remain in control for several decades before giving up power peacefully.

7. Problems associated with severe demographic changes may influence a society's progress toward democracy. If the indigenous majority of the country is distrustful of a large ethnic minority, the majority may be tempted to deny the minority the full advantages of citizenship.

8. Several democracies or countries undergoing democratization seem destined to experiment with devolution. Many countries include regions that have long memories of political autonomy or outright independence. These regions often desire to reassert at least some degree of control over local affairs.

9. Many democracies, particularly those in close proximity to the Third World or developing countries, are encountering moral and political dilemmas as large numbers of desperate immigrants attempt to enter. Both legal and illegal immigration has become a major political issue in Western European and North American democracies.

10. Emerging democracies will democratize at their own rates and in their own ways. There is little reason to believe that future nonwestern democracies will be carbon copies of the West.

GLOSSARY

devolution   The decentralization of the roles of a national government with a gradual and usually peaceful transfer of domestic authority to regional jurisdictions.

East Asian dragons (or tigers)   The East Asian countries of South Korea, Taiwan, Singapore, and Hong Kong, whose economies and standards of living are approaching those of the West and Japan.

Other countries may be applying for membership in this club soon, including Indonesia, Malaysia, and Thailand.

economic miracle   The rapid economic recovery of a country militarily defeated and economically devastated. Germany and Japan, the defeated Axis powers in World War II, are generally regarded as case studies of countries that fully recovered both their economic importance and global standing in just a few short decades.

free market   An economic system characterized by minimal government regulation and opportunities for every member of society to acquire material wealth.

rotten boroughs   British electoral districts in which only one person owned enough land to be able to vote or stand for office. He faced no opposition and simply voted for himself in parliamentary elections.

tribal democracy   A society that is democratic but extends democracy only to citizens who possess certain ethnic or religious characteristics.

warlords   Political or military leaders who appear when national order and government break down to take control of small territories and populations.

The Institutions of Government and the Political Process

••

*T*he next four chapters emphasize the most basic features of modern political systems. Of course, as we point out throughout these chapters, some political systems are not modern. Many, for example, lack or prohibit a recognizable political party system (chapter 8). On the other hand, the legislative, executive (including bureaucracies), and judicial functions, the subjects of chapters 5, 6, and 7, respectively, are apparent in nearly all political systems. Even authoritarian systems (with some notable exceptions) evidence these three kinds of institutions, if only because they are useful to the regime. These chapters concentrate on analyses of and examples from democratic regimes, discussing the important ways they resemble one another as well as how they differ.

Legislatures

The legislature is probably the earliest and most durable political institution, one that maximized access to the decision-making processes that impact on entire societies. Legislatures can be traced back millenia: classical Greece and Rome had vibrant legislatures. Rome even had a sort of two-chamber legislature. The Roman upper house was the Senate, a term that has obviously stuck, since Italy, France, Canada, and the United States still use it. The Roman Senate's membership, referred to as the "Fathers of Rome," were primarily representatives of Roman aristocracy. For the great majority of the citizenry who lacked aristocratic credentials, the Romans created popular assemblies, the equivalent of modern-day lower legislative houses.

In the early centuries of the Roman Republic, the Senate consisted of energetic and public-minded members. It eventually deteriorated and became one of history's first "rubber stamp" legislatures, agreeing to nearly everything the Roman emperor wanted. Rubber stamp legislatures are in ample supply in dictatorships today. Although the Soviet Union is gone, its legislature, the Supreme Soviet, will probably hold the record for consistent rubber stamping for a long time, with an unbroken unanimous endorsement of all legislation submitted to it for nearly seventy years. Much the same situation currently prevails in China's National People's Congress.

Understandably, there isn't much to say about the legislative process in countries that still employ rubber stamp legislatures. Some countries have no legislatures at all. Most of these are traditionalist monarchies in the Middle East or elsewhere. Some do have **legislative councils** that act only in an advisory capacity and are dependent upon the monarch for continued service. In traditionalist monarchies such as the Kingdom of Saudi Arabia, the monarch usually relies on family members (the Saudi Arabian ruler has several hundred half-brothers) for advice on policy matters. (See table 5.1 for an outline of legislative assemblies in nondemocratic political systems.)

The collapse of the communist regimes in Eastern Europe may have ushered in a new era for national legislatures. While countries in Eastern Europe all had parliaments, during the Cold War they were ineffective. A parliament in a communist country exists primarily to endorse the policies of the executive, which in turn is dominated by the Communist party. In the 1990s, former com-

TABLE 5.1   Legislative Assemblies in Nondemocratic Political Systems*

Country	Legislature	Main Features
Brunei	Legislative Council	Members appointed by the Sultan
China	National People's Congress	All 2,976 seats controlled by communist party
Iran	Islamic Consultative Assembly	Membership elected by several religious factions
Democratic People's Republic of North Korea	Supreme People's Assembly	All 687 seats controlled by communist party
Iraq	National Assembly	Four ethnic/religious communities represented (Christians, Kurds, Shiite Muslims, Sunni Muslims), all guided by doctrines of Ba'ath party

* Not all nondemocratic regimes have equally undemocratic legislatures. Iran does have relatively free elections, but it is very difficult for any candidate who does not subscribe to a fairly stringent religious agenda to win a seat.

munist countries elected legislators in competitive elections, but few candidates had any legislative experience. Those who did were former communist legislators who, understandably, were still inexperienced in the political art of compromise and negotiated legislation. One scholar has written that

> New members in new parliaments are not well-equipped to face their new tasks. The members are inexperienced. Depending upon the duration of the dictatorship, few persons in society will themselves have any personal experience of democratic procedures. They will be asked to make new decisions on new problems without guidance or experience in the open expression of disagreements.[1]

The future success of political democracy in Eastern European countries may well depend upon the ability of new legislators to learn fast.

Democratic systems usually have viable legislatures. No political democracy, in fact, functions without a representative assembly. Much of the progress of democratization in many countries is traceable to their national legislatures. The people elect a democratic legislature, and in the process they provide limited political prerogatives to their representatives for a stipulated term of office. The notion of citizen-legislator is in fact making a comeback, especially in the United States, where the idea of legislators with lifetime careers in politics is becoming increasingly unpopular. Numerous members of the United States Congress have practically placed their hands on their hearts to insist they will serve no more than three terms.

---

[1] David M. Olson, "The New Parliaments of New Democracies: The Experience of the Federal Assembly of the Czech and Slovak Federal Republic," in Attila Agh, ed., *The Emergence of East Central European Parliaments: The First Steps* (Budapest: Hungarian Centre of Democracy Studies, 1994), p. 37.

In a crunch, it would be possible for the people to make laws without a legislature. They could simply vote yea or nay in a national **referendum** on an issue. In fact, several democracies have constitutional procedures that allow the entire electorate to vote on such matters as taxation or whether to join an economic organization. One notable exception, the United States, has no provision for national referenda, though most states occasionally hold them.[2] Congress made the decision to join NAFTA (the North American Free Trade Association). Several European countries, in contrast, conducted a referendum on whether to join the European Economic Community. The referendum's outcome has the force of law.

Still, no country with the exception of Switzerland uses the referendum on a regular basis.[3] France has used it only about a half dozen times since 1958, the year the Fifth Republic was established. Many nations hold referenda on issues of critical importance or, as in France, when the executive wants to bypass the legislature. The referendum in effect makes the entire electorate a national legislature.

In this chapter, we will emphasize democratic legislatures, but carefully and selectively. While all democracies have legislatures, they differ in their powers and in their relationships to the executive branch of the government.

LEGISLATIVE BEGINNINGS

During the Greek city-state period and through the history of the Roman Republic, legislative assemblies functioned relatively well. They were responsible (as legislatures in parliamentary systems are now) for enacting laws as well as for furnishing the executive. In very small city-states, legislatures were composed of all adult male citizens, and these men made the decisions that immediately affected their own lives. If they voted to go to war, they became the soldiers; if they levied a tax, they paid it.

These assemblies were basically one-branch governments that selected, as we saw in the career of Pericles, the civilian executive and military leadership, often for clearly defined terms of office. Some assemblies could grant life tenure for certain offices during difficult times. They could also grant emergency powers and create what might be called constitutional dictatorships, and they could function as juries in trials that involved the security of the state. Probably the body with the closest contemporary resemblance to these legislatures is the New England town meeting, where all residents are free to attend and to make decisions affecting their lives by majority vote.

---

[2] The United States Supreme Court in *City of Eastlake v. Forest City Enterprises, Inc.* (1976) maintained the right of the American people to legislate by referendum. See John T. Rourke, Richard P. Hiskes, and Cyrus Ernesto Zirakzadeh, *Direct Democracy and International Politics: Deciding Issues Through Referendums* (Boulder, Colorado: Lynne Rienner Publishers, Inc., 1992), p. 155.

[3] Switzerland conducts about half of the nearly one thousand referenda held annually throughout the world.

Modern legislatures have deep roots. The British parliament, for example, has antecedents centuries old. Other European political systems are equally aged. Iceland boasts the oldest, longest functioning national legislature in the world—theirs is nearly a millennium old, established when Scandinavian settlers arrived in the tenth century.

The strong social class divisions in Europe were long reflected in national parliaments. The institutions of upper and lower houses developed because social class lines were very distinct. Membership in the upper houses, such as the House of Lords in Britain, required an aristocratic pedigree. Lower houses were filled with members of lesser social (but not necessarily financial) standing. Hence, the British House of Commons was, as the name suggests, composed of members who were commoners, not members of the aristocracy.

Even the electorate itself reflects class lines. Neither members of the House of Lords nor members of the royal family can participate as either voters or candidates for seats in the Commons. To do so requires giving up one's title, at least for the duration of one's political career. The decline of upper houses and the rise in the power of lower houses corresponded to the widening process of democratization in several Western European countries in the early nineteenth century. By the early years of the twentieth century, most democracies were increasingly relying upon the popularly elected lower houses to make laws, and many had begun to restrict the legislative prerogatives of the upper house. A few countries, like Sweden, abolished their upper houses.

As we will see in this and the following chapter, in many ways, parliamentary democracies remain one-branch governments; it is still the parliament (or, usually, the lower house of parliament) that supplies the top personnel of the executive department. The United States is actually one of a minority of democracies (France has been another since 1958) that chooses the executive independently of the legislature and that constitutionally provides for coequal and separate government branches. Germany and the United States are two of a small number of democracies that grant their upper houses substantial legislative powers.

Countries serious about representative government have concentrated tremendous powers in the legislative branch. Indeed, the legislature is often the only branch with any powers: the American system of coequal branches is not a widely emulated arrangement. Even the United States began its political existence as a one-branch government; the Continental Congress was the only governmental body for a decade (1777–1787), until the the Constitution was drafted and ratified (1787–1789), creating the familiar three-branch government.

Some observers believe that in most parliamentary democracies, political power has been transferred from the legislative to the executive. This common observation may be exaggerated. After all, parliaments can bring down governments with a vote of no confidence. Moreover, democratic parliaments do not simply rubber stamp anything the government proposes: rank-and-file parliamentary members like to be asked for their opinions and insist on being informed.

They can be unforgiving when neither occurs. When British Prime Minister Anthony Eden evaded giving a full account of a combined British and French invasion of the Suez Canal Zone in 1956, members of his own Conservative party were outraged. They might have been placated had not the United Nations forced both countries' military forces out a few weeks later through a rare cooperative effort involving the United States and the Soviet Union. Eden was forced to retire from the prime ministership by early 1957.

In some instances, parliaments may have *too much* power or, perhaps more accurately, exercise too little responsibility. During the brief career of the French Fourth Republic (1946–1958), for example, the French National Assembly got rid of governments in rather quick succession. During this period, new governments were formed on the average of every seven months. When the constitution of the Fifth Republic was drafted, it shifted power from the legislative to the executive branch. The President of the Republic was to be selected in a separate popular election (purposely held at a different time from National Assembly elections). And French presidents justifiably claim to have a mandate from the people, since they must be elected by an absolute numerical majority.

There is no doubt that the focus of power in parliamentary systems has shifted from the legislature to the executive. The executive often proposes most legislation, though in Britain, members of parliament can introduce bills that reflect particular needs in their districts. Moreover, members of parliamentary systems usually have the opportunity to ask cabinet ministers questions. "Question hour" is most beneficial to opposition members; they can get information from the executive branch, or, in many cases, embarrass the executive if it can't or won't provide information.

UPPER HOUSES

Upper houses do matter, even though most of them lack substantial legislative powers. In Britain, for example, the House of Lords reviews legislation, often passed in haste by the busier House of Commons. This is often a worthwhile process since only a fourth or so of the Lords's potential membership of about a thousand normally attend its sessions: the minority of the Lords who take their few duties seriously are generally well educated, some with degrees in law, and have the time and expertise to pay careful attention to legislation that comes to them from the House of Commons. The Lords cannot thwart or greatly change laws the House of Commons passes, but they can suggest revisions that improve upon the language and, in certain instances, the intent of the legislation.

The Lords is not and does not pretend to be the equal of the Commons. Its lack of real power helps to explain why most members don't bother to go to the sessions. Others become bored with the proceedings and can go for decades without visiting the House of Lords: inheriting a seat doesn't necessarily mean inheriting an interest in politics. If a member of the Lords does want a serious

....

TABLE 5.2   Methods of Selection for Upper House Membership

Country	Chamber	Form of Selection
France	Senate	Special electoral college of municipal councillors
Germany	Bundesrat	State governments
Italy	Senate	Mostly popular election
United Kingdom	House of Lords	Inherited or royal appointment
United States	Senate	Popular election

political career, he or she (there are now ladies in the House of Lords) can re-sign his or her peerage and stand for a seat in the House of Commons.

Memberships in many upper houses are won in rather undemocratic fash-ion (see table 5.2). In a democracy, this fact alone generally makes the upper house less powerful than the lower house. Members are normally selected by regional or state governments, special electoral colleges, or the executive. The British monarch can often recruit members by simply appointing dis-tinguished individuals (often leading politicians retiring from the House of Commons) life peers. The Senate in Italy is unusual in that most of its mem-bership is popularly elected, but it still allows the appointment of some life termers.[4]

Upper houses do matter in some political systems, and they attract very ambitious politicians. The United States Senate is an obvious example. The U.S. Senate, though, is exceptional in that it is both a powerful and a popularly elected legislative chamber. Most upper houses, whether they have political significance or not, are filled with people who have either inherited their seats or have arrived at them without bothering with a popular election. For in-stance, a huge electoral college of over 80,000 members, most of them munici-pal councillors, choose the members of the French Senate, and in Germany, the federal republic's sixteen state governments select the members of the Federal Council (Bundesrat). The Bundesrat is exceptional in one sense: though its selection process is not truly democratic, it exercises real legislative authority.

With some exceptions, upper houses tend to have substantial legislative powers in federal systems, such as Germany and the United States. In these systems, states or provinces completely or largely control a great many of their own affairs, including education, health care, public transportation, and taxa-tion. Regional governments are less powerful or nonexistent in smaller and more homogeneous systems. In Germany, the Bundesrat consists of delegations of three to five members for each of the sixteen states (the exact number is

_____

[4] Former prime ministers, for example, may be elevated to one of seven appointed Senate seats. For an interesting insight into Italian politics, see Alexander Stille, "The Fall of Caesar," *The New Yorker,* September 11, 1995, pp. 68–83.

The German Federal Council, the Bundesrat.

based on the state's population). Each state government charges its delegation with advocating and protecting the state's particular interests.

The U.S. Senate and the German Bundesrat are arguably the most powerful upper houses in the industrialized democracies. Upper houses in most other democracies can at best delay legislation the lower house has passed. The power to delay legislation, however, should not be underestimated; it is often actually helpful to the legislative process. The well-educated and legal-minded members of the House of Lords, as we have seen, on occasion make very useful revisions to legislation sent to them from the Commons.

Legislative assemblies have often been rather noisy and sometimes even violent in their debates. The majority party that controls the government in the British House of Commons and the minority party, politely known as the **loyal opposition,** are separated by a "sword's length," a tradition dating back to the time when members habitually wore swords and sometimes challenged one another to a duel. Shoving and brawling are still a regular feature in some of the newer democracies in East Asia. Taiwanese and South Korean citizens watch events in their respective National Assemblies for much the same reason Americans attend hockey games: a fistfight could break out at any moment.

Upper houses usually have smaller memberships than lower chambers. Most upper houses (Britain's House of Lords is an exception) have precisely set memberships: two senators from each of the fifty states in the United States, for a total of 100; three, four, or five from each of sixteen states in the German federation, for a current total of 69.[5] The relatively smaller size allows the members to do business more efficiently—at least, most of the time. Many upper houses have delay tactics built into their parliamentary rules, although it is difficult to find one equivalent to the U.S. Senate's filibuster.

Most upper houses have limited powers because they are not popularly chosen; upper house members in nonelective systems cannot claim a popular mandate. In a democracy, this means that political power in most instances must reside in the lower house. This is especially true in parliamentary systems, where the lower house supplies the personnel for the executive.

LOWER HOUSES

With a few important exceptions, most legislative business in a democratic political system is conducted in the lower house. In parliamentary systems, the same political party controls both the lower house and the executive. The opposition may actually control the upper house, but, as we have seen, its power may be limited. For example, the Conservative party in Britain is in perpetual control of the House of Lords, but it influences legislation only in innocuous ways. In presidential systems, the executive and legislature are chosen in separate elections. Since January 1993, for example, a Democrat has occupied the American presidency; since January 1995, a Republican majority has held both houses of Congress.

From 1979 until 1997, the Conservative party held the majority in the British House of Commons and therefore chose the executive leadership. The British prime minister and the rest of the cabinet ministers hold seats in the Commons and are expected to attend its sessions. There is no division of powers in Britain, as there is in the United States. This **parliamentary majority,** the party controlling both the House of Commons and the executive, is crucial to the passage of legislation. (Table 5.3 points out other distinctions between the lower houses in the United States and Great Britain.)

Parliamentary majorities are essential if a government is to be formed and to endure. In a parliamentary system, if a government proposes a piece of legislation and loses the vote on it, the government can collapse; the prime minister is ousted and a new majority may take over. To put it succinctly: no parliamen-

---

[5] Before the reunification with East Germany, the Federal Republic of (West) Germany's upper house had a membership of forty-five from ten states.

The British House of Commons looks congested because there are only two-thirds of seats as there are representatives.

tary government can survive without a guarantee of majority support for its policies. In the mid-1990s in the British House of Commons, the Conservative party controlled more seats than all other parties combined (even though it secured less than a majority of the popular vote, an issue we will examine in a later chapter). The Conservatives therefore controlled the government. However, in May 1997, the Labour party gained control. Labour's leader, Tony Blair, became the new prime minister.

To form a legislative majority, however, may sometimes require a coalition of two or more parties. The parliamentary democracy of Israel, for example, has produced government by coalitions since its establishment; no one party

TABLE 5.3   Some Distinctions Between the U.S. House of Representatives and the British House of Commons

Feature	U.S.	British
Term limitations	Three terms (6 years) in several states	none
Length of term	2 years	up to 5 years
Size of constituency	average of 560,000	under 100,000
Nominating process	mostly primaries*; possible run-off	interview by leadership of local party

* In some states, a party caucus or convention rather than a primary election is held to select candidates.

can seem to win a majority of votes. In such a situation, the executive must be carefully selected to represent all the parties in the coalition and all their political points of view.

The executive branch of government in a parliamentary system does seem to get most of its legislation passed. But it is also true that it carefully considers proposed legislation. After all, majority support is required, or the party may lose power; legislative proposals must be carefully crafted to secure the endorsement of rank-and-file members. Usually, **party whips** act as liaisons between the party leadership and rank-and-file members, helping to get proposed legislation in shape and then persuading party members to be present and voting when the legislation reaches the house floor. There seems to be a correlation between the size of a ruling party's majority and its leadership's respect for rank-and-file opinions. The more narrow the majority, the more influence rank-and-file members have on legislation.

Party discipline, the efforts parties make to ensure that the parliamentary members support the official position on legislation, is normally exerted during the legislative process. Party discipline is stronger in some systems than in others. American presidents, for example, expect little party discipline and even a fair amount of defiance from members of the same party in Congress. In parliamentary systems, however, parties require strong discipline not only to pass legislation, but to retain control of the government. Presidents can lose votes in Congress and even see Congress override a veto and still remain in office; prime ministers have no such advantage.

Party discipline has two complementary aspects. First, it is crucial to accomplishing legislative business. Both the government and the opposition need to know how many votes they can count on to either formulate or oppose legislation. Second, representatives need to be faithful to party policies if they want the party's support during the next campaign. In most democracies, citizens tend to cast their ballots more for party than for candidate.

Both the voters and the party leadership in a parliamentary system are horrified should a member of parliament defy the party line. A maverick parliamentarian has on occasion survived the displeasure of the party establishment, but consistent defiance is usually a sure-fire method of political suicide. The local party leadership will simply replace the delinquent parliamentarian with another candidate in time for the next election.

Breaks from party discipline in a parliamentary system can occur but are remarkably infrequent. After all, parliamentarians with similar ideological convictions naturally tend to vote together. Moreover, rank-and-file politicians tend to owe their careers to the party. It is very unusual for aspiring politicians to be elected to public office because of celebrity status or because they have enough money to finance their own campaigns. They generally are elected (or defeated) on the basis of their party label. Political life rarely exists outside the party in a parliamentary system.

Even when party discipline is weak, as it is in the United States, there is usually no question as to who has the ultimate authority to decide which legislation to try to enact into law. Legislative roles differ from one system to another, however. The **Speaker of the House,** for example, has different powers in the U.S. Congress than the British parliament. While the American Speaker is expected to be partisan in advocating or opposing legislative programs, the British Speaker is expected to be completely nonpartisan, regardless of her previous political experience. The American Speaker always comes from the majority party, while the Commons Speaker, once installed in office, no longer belongs to any party and usually stays in office for a lengthy period of time regardless of which party controls a parliamentary majority.

The United States Senate may present at least a partial exception to most notions of party discipline or institutional control of party members. A U.S. Senator normally has his or her own base of support that only modestly relies on the national party organization. Some U.S. senators, especially from more populous states, are also nurturing presidential and vice-presidential ambitions. One or two of them have even been former vice presidents.[6]

All of this suggests that parliamentary systems are smooth-running affairs compared to systems that don't enforce strong party discipline. But this is not necessarily true. Challenges to the party leadership are far from unknown in parliaments—they simply come from the opposition party. In a typical parliament, cabinet ministers are also legislators and are therefore subject to scrutiny from the opposition. Opposing legislators seek every opportunity to ask embarrassing questions of a minister whose department is having trouble providing public services or who is suspected of corruption.

In fact, it is part of the loyal opposition's job to keep the majority on its toes. It often spends most of its time challenging government-sponsored legislation. Considering that the government controls a parliamentary majority and is nearly certain to win any vote, one might ask why the opposition bothers. The answer is simple. By stating in a public forum its ideological position on a piece of legislation, the loyal opposition reveals what it would do if it became the majority party after the next election. This enables it to offer an alternative to the electorate.

In some instances, a **minority government** forms as the result of an indecisive parliamentary election. For example, the February 1974 national elections for the House of Commons yielded no party with an absolute majority of seats. The Labour party had a plurality of seats, however, and was able to join forces with the small Liberal party in an unofficial coalition. The arrangement was short-lived, as minority governments usually are, and another election was held eight months later that provided Labour with a small but workable majority.

---

[6] The only example of a former American president returning to the Senate after leaving the presidency is Andrew Johnson. His tenure was brief, however. Johnson died several months after arriving at the Senate in 1875. Hubert Humphrey, vice president from 1965 to 1969, returned to the United States Senate in 1971 and remained there until his death in 1978. He had previously served in the Senate from 1949 to 1964. John Quincy Adams, America's sixth president (1825–1829), is the only former chief executive to pursue a career in the House of Representatives. His career in the House (1831–1848) was long and distinguished.

Minority governments are understandably weak and usually of brief duration. The executive in such a situation tends to lose power to the legislature. The parliament, after all, has a majority of seats the government doesn't control. The government's best chance for survival is if the opposition is divided, as it frequently is in a legislature populated by several political parties. One other consideration may also provide a reprieve for a minority government: legislators may not want to risk their seats again soon after an election and may cooperate with the government (at least to an extent) in an effort to avoid another electoral contest.

Occasionally, legislative proposals are neither partisan in origin nor require the imposition of party discipline when it comes to a vote. For instance, the question of whether to impose capital punishment on convicted murderers in Britain is a moral issue. In such matters, each individual parliamentary member is left to vote his or her conscience.

At first glance, a parliamentary system seems much more efficient than the congressional-executive system in the United States and most other countries in the western hemisphere. This is because the lower house in a parliamentary government, because of party discipline, tends to approve nearly all legislation the government submits to it. Also, since there is no separation of powers in such a system, law, once approved, remains law unless the lower house repeals its own legislation. This is unlikely to happen unless the legislation sponsor— usually the government—agrees. With the government in effective control of a parliamentary majority, an "elective dictatorship"[7] can prevail.

The only hope of blunting any lower house excesses may rest with the unelected upper house. In Britain, for example, the House of Lords raised a hue and cry over the Police Bill the House of Commons passed, a bill that would allow law enforcement agencies to "break into anyone's home or office in secret, carry out searches and plant eavesdropping devices."[8] In this matter, the Lords practically condemned the bill as an affront to individual rights. The public concurred, and the Commons was moved to reconsider the legislation.[9]

THE LEGISLATURE AND REPRESENTATIVE GOVERNMENT

The ideal of popular selection of legislators is generally regarded as admirable. Yet the selection process does not always permit the widest possible choices, even in democratic systems. From the time it gained its independence from France in 1943 to its collapse in civil war in 1975 and 1976, Lebanon functioned as the most democratic state in the Arab world. However, Lebanon's political system rested rather nervously on arrangements that reflected its sectarian character. Its numerous religious sects had to be politically accomo-

---

[7] Anthony Lewis, "Champions of Liberty," *The New York Times*, January 31, 1997, A19.

[8] Ibid.

[9] Ibid.

If upper houses do not have much real political significance in the legislative process, then why do they exist? Many countries have either eliminated upper houses or never had one in the first place. Because of their diversity, federal systems such as Canada and the United States usually find it convenient to establish upper houses to represent geographical units. Smaller and relatively homogeneous countries often get along nicely with a single legislative chamber. (Notable exceptions include countries such as Denmark and Norway, which, for historical reasons, have retained bicameral legislatures.)

Most unicameral legislatures, like most of the countries they are located in, are relatively small. Costa Rica, Israel, and Lebanon, for example, are countries with populations around or under 5 million. Their national legislatures have only 60, 120, and 99 members, respectively. Sweden, with a population of nearly 9 million, is one of the larger countries with a unicameral legislature; its chamber has 349 members. Legislation is not necessarily more efficient in countries with unicameral systems. As we have seen, most countries assign limited roles to their upper chambers anyway. Moreover, a single chamber might very well be unable to handle the workload many legislatures increasingly confront.

dated to avoid violence. Though ethnically and linguistically an Arab country, Lebanon's population is divided into a variety of Islamic and Christian communities. The ninety-nine National Assembly seats are distributed proportionally among seventeen officially recognized *religious constituencies* (four Orthodox Christian, seven Uniate Christian, five Islam, and one Jewish). The seventeen sects doubled as political parties at election time. Even the executive is determined by sect: the president must always be a Maronite Christian, the prime minister a Sunni Muslim.

Prior to its civil war, the distribution of power in Lebanon was based on the population of each sect. That sounds fair until one learns that the last census was taken in 1932, when Christians were the majority. They aren't any longer; the Islamic sects are now the most likely majority, and they are understandably urging a a redistribution of political power.

The arrangement in Lebanon was precarious and clumsy, but it was also a formula for civil peace that endured for a third of a century. It may now be in the process of renewal. Moreover, Lebanon's example had its emulators. Some congressional districts in the United States have been drawn, sometimes rather bizarrely, to purposely include African-American majorities with the assumption that such districts would elect African-Americans to Congress. Decades ago, some district lines were drawn, sometimes rather bizarrely, to guarantee white majorities.

Democracies attempt to guarantee representation for the major segments of the population. Legislatures are therefore expected to reflect the electorate's major components and preferences. They rarely do so completely. In the United States, for example, only about a tenth of 535 members of Congress are women. In Norway, women occupy about half of the parliamentary seats. (Norway also has a female prime minister). This makes it one of a handful of countries to achieve gender equality.

If some groups are underrepresented, others must be overrepresented. In the English-speaking democracies, elections are decided in a winner-take-all system: whichever candidate receives a plurality of the votes wins the seat. Such an electoral process frequently means that a large minority or even a majority cast ballots for candidates who do not gain legislative seats. Some parliamentary systems are sensitive to this problem—they allow smaller parties that receive as little as 5 percent of the total vote (or less, in some countries) to earn seats. This more equitable arrangement, though, creates other problems that we will examine in a later chapter.

POWERS AND LIMITATIONS OF THE LEGISLATURE

Legislative Selection of the Executive

Legislatures do more than pass laws. One of their important functions is to perform as an electoral college. The **parliamentary parties** in the British House of Commons, for example, choose their party leaders knowing those leaders may become prime minister. When Margaret Thatcher resigned the prime ministership in 1990, the Conservative party selected John Major as her successor. When the majority party chooses its leader, it is actually choosing the next prime minister. The queen asks the majority party leader to form a government (a request that is never refused), and no one is surprised at the result.

In Germany, the chancellor is chosen directly by the Bundestag in a vote taken as a new session opens following a national election. The vote generally follows party lines. Thus, the leader of the party or parties that control a majority of Bundestag seats becomes chancellor.

In the United States, the House of Representatives, under the rare circumstance that no candidate for president secures the required majority in the electoral college, can select the president. While this has happened in only two elections, 1800 and 1824, it has come close to happening on several other occasions. In the 1948, 1968, 1992, and 1996 elections, third party candidates nearly prevented any candidate from securing an electoral college majority, and in all cases they did prevent the new president from winning an absolute popular majority. (See table 5.4 for a summary of how different legislatures select the head of government.)

Since the ratification of the Twenty-fifth Amendment in 1967, the U.S. Congress can also vote on a replacement, nominated by the president, if the vice-presidential office becomes vacant through resignation or death. When a vacancy occurred in 1973 because of a resignation, both houses confirmed Gerald Ford, President Richard Nixon's choice, as vice president. The next year, after Ford became president, Congress confirmed his choice of Nelson Rockefeller as vice president.

TABLE 5.4   Legislative Selection of the Head of Government

Federal Republic of Germany: Chancellor is chosen by a majority vote of the membership of the Bundestag.

France: No legislative influence; presidents are popularly elected, but the National Assembly confirms the president's choice of prime minister.

Japan: Prime Minister is chosen by a majority vote of the House of Representatives.

United Kingdom: Monarch asks leader of the majority party to form a government.

United States: If no presidential candidate secures an electoral college majority, the House of Representatives can choose the president.

Because of their composition and powers, legislatures only infrequently initiate legislation. The government introduces most of the bills in parliament. In a nonparliamentary system such as the United States, members of the legislature submit much legislation individually or collaboratively. The American president, however, is the "chief legislator" in one sense: any of his supporters in Congress can introduce legislation the administration formulates. The president rarely gets everything he wants, even if his party is the congressional majority. Members of the president's party tend to pay close attention to preferences of their own constituencies, which may not be in concert with those of the administration.

Legislatures in both parliamentary and congressional-presidential systems do possess ultimate controls on the executive. In a parliamentary system, the government must at all times have the support of the legislative body. Should the government lose a **vote of confidence,** it usually has to leave office. The tenure of presidents is somewhat safer, as we shall see in greater detail in the following chapter. The American president, for example, serves a four-year term regardless of how many legislative battles he loses with Congress. The French president is assured of a seven-year term even if his party loses control of the National Assembly.

Nevertheless, an unhappy legislature can usually remove a president in certain cases. **Impeachment** allows the legislature to make serious charges against a president and to remove him or her if found guilty of wrongdoing. In the United States, the House can accuse a president of "high crimes and misdemeanors," and the Senate then tries the case. (The Senate actually receives the charges of impeachment from the House and then acts as a jury.) To be constitutional, there must be good reason to believe the president has broken the law. Only once in American history has a president faced impeachment proceedings: Andrew Johnson was charged in 1867 and was acquitted. Another president, Richard M. Nixon, resigned from the presidency in 1974 to avoid certain impeachment and likely conviction.

Impeachment suggests that Congress has a judicial role. The U. S. House of Representative can bring impeachment charges not only against presidents but against federal judges. This has happened at least five times. Ironically, in the most recent impeachment case, the Senate convicted federal judge Alcee L.

Hastings in 1989; Judge Hastings was removed from the judiciary but returned to public life after winning a seat in the House of Representatives in 1992. Hastings made history by being the first person impeached by the House to later be elected to it.

Recruitment of the Executive

In parliamentary systems, it is nearly unheard of for the prime minister or a cabinet member to arrive in their positions without legislative experience. This stands in stark contrast to the American system. In the United States, serving in Congress before running for president may now be a disadvantage—of the four presidents who have served since 1977, only one, George Bush, had congressional experience, and Bush had only served two terms in the House.

It is customary in parliamentary systems for cabinet ministers to rise through the ranks and establish seniority before securing a position in the executive branch. The typical cabinet minister can serve a couple of decades as an MP (member of parliament) before rising to the executive, usually as a junior minister. Legislative experience enhances the opportunities of the politically ambitious in a parliamentary system, while in the United States, too much time in the capital makes one a suspected "insider."

But parliamentary politics has its own problems. Most members of Congress don't anticipate or even hope for cabinet posts; they prefer the comfort of a reliable constituency. However, failing to attain a cabinet position is a major disappointment for most parliamentary members. The British House of Commons is a case in point:

> *Politics has become a profession, with a well-understood career structure. By this standard, most MPs are doomed to fail; at any one time, only around 14 percent of them are members of the government. The consequences are obvious. In the Commons bars and offices lurk many bored, soured souls. A few are dim-witted drones, but most are talented, frustrated, wasted people. The still-ambitious ones (often career politicians who have had no other job) are voting-fodder, humiliatingly dependent on the goodwill of the party bosses and whips.*[10]

In parliamentary systems, the legislature also depends upon the executive to determine the next election date. Rank-and-file members of parliament (MPs) can easily become nervous wrecks since they may not know the next election date much sooner than the public does. Everyone knows when by law an election must take place: in parliamentary systems, national elections are scheduled to occur from three to five years apart. A government in danger of losing the next election will let the clock run out. In 1964 and 1997, British Conservative governments, in trouble in the polls, waited until the last minute before the five-year limit ran out to set a date for elections. (Even so, the Labour party managed to take control both times.) However, as we shall see in the next chapter,

---

[10] "Bagehot," *The Economist,* August 3, 1991, p. 58.

the prime minister can decide to dissolve parliament and call new elections before the scheduled term ends. In sum, a prime minister calls for an election when he or she believes the party has the best chance to win it.

At least MPs don't have to worry about term limits. Parliamentary systems have not seriously considered term limits and is not a political issue for them. MPs can serve for indefinite periods as long as their party leadership—especially the leadership at the local district level—is happy with them and as long as they can win elections in their constituencies. These are not always easy tasks. New candidates for parliamentary seats may have to campaign in districts that have not elected anyone from their party to parliament in decades.

In congressional-presidential systems, terms of office for both the legislature and the executive are comparatively firm. In the United States, for example, members of the House of Representatives serve two-year terms. The House doesn't have to worry that the executive will dissolve it and call for new elections. By the early 1990s, though, many representatives were subject to term limits imposed by their state legislatures.

Sometimes House members impose term limits on themselves, pledging not to serve more than a set number of terms, even without the prodding of their state legislatures. Politicians both in and out of Congress have suggested a constitutional amendment to place a limit on terms in both the House and the Senate. In American legislative politics, an excellent way to get elected to Congress is to promise to leave it quickly.

LEGISLATIVE TASKS

National legislators have earned inconsistent evaluations from their constituencies. In the United States, for example, members of Congress are not considered much more trustworthy than used car dealers. Of course, too much cynicism can pose a danger to democracy. For every member of Congress who is accused in the media or actually brought to trial for some type of wrongdoing, many more steadfastly do their jobs and labor to benefit their home districts or states.

There is good reason to believe that the memberships of parliaments and congresses tend to represent both the moods and the demographics of their constituents. In almost every democracy, for instance, legislators must pay increasing attention to their elderly constituents. As the people over age 65 become the fastest growing demographic group (except for those over 85), their Congressional representatives must respond to their concerns about health care, pensions, and living standards.

Despite the transfer of power to the executive, national legislatures in democracies perform tasks critical to the political process:

1. They are in constant communication with their constituents and are therefore one of the few political organizations consistently aware of changing opinions on issues. Legislative members in all industrialized democracies have become accustomed to receiving volumes of mail, telegrams, phone calls, and

BOX 5.2

A Note on
Legislature
Size

Legislatures may be unwieldy if their memberships grow excessively large. It's hard to determine an optimal size for a legislature that both allows it to represent the various interests in society and to complete its work efficiently. Consider, for example, some of the numbers: the British House of Commons includes 650 members, the French National Assembly 577, the American House of Representatives 435, and the Italian Chamber of Deputies 630. There is nothing magical about any number, and all of these numbers have changed from time to time.

Legislatures that become much larger than 600 members do seem to have difficulty conducting business. During the last decades of the Soviet Union, each chamber of the Supreme Soviet counted around 1500 members. Some of the Supreme Soviet's committees were as big as entire houses in several western democracies. This huge membership made it almost impossible

for various factions to form, as they do in democratic legislatures. Large size was most likely intended to make sure that divisions never occurred or would not matter if they did. All votes taken were by design unanimous.

Predictably, upper houses are normally much smaller (the British House of Lords is a notable exception) and sometimes, though certainly not always, more efficient. The American, French, and Italian Senates have 100, 317, and 315 members respectively. One of the most powerful upper houses in the world is the German Bundesrat (Federal Council) with only 69 members. Only the American Senate is a popularly elected body, and its powers are substantial. The United States Senate is perhaps the only upper house in a democracy that includes members who frequently challenge executive authority, perhaps partially because several senators may be eyeing the presidency at any given time.[11]

fax and e-mail messages on a regular basis. Their constituents consistently instruct them on what stands to take on the issues, how to vote, and, overall, how best to do their job.

2.   Legislators in many countries have the responsibility of choosing the executive leaders. The German Bundestag, for example, elects the chancellor. (The vote, of course, is always in favor of the leader who controls a majority of seats in the Bundestag.) Both the Bundestag and Bundesrat choose the German president. Japan chooses its prime minister in a similar fashion, and in Israel, the parliament chooses the president. In the United States, Congress can choose a president if no candidate receives a majority of the electoral college

---

[11] Most of these senators are not successful in their quest to become president. The last sitting senator to be elected president was John F. Kennedy in 1960, and no president since Richard M. Nixon (1969–1974) has served in the Senate. Still, these facts did not discourage at least four senators from seeking the Republican presidential nomination in 1996, including the eventual nominee. Robert Dole resigned his seat as the senior senator from Kansas to run as the Republican candidate for president.

BOX 5.3

A Note on
the European
Parliament

*O*ver the last several decades, some legislative authority has been gradually transferred to the executive in some systems. The amount of transfer varies by country and, to some extent, by the popularity and persuasive appeal of the executive. In the United States, a series of relatively weak one-term presidents, with the exceptions of Ronald Reagan (1981–1989) and Bill Clinton (1993–2001), made few inroads on lessening the prerogatives of Congress. During the 1970s, for example, Congress was instrumental in forcing Richard Nixon to resign the presidency and effectively appointing his successor, Gerald Ford. Legislatures in almost every democratic political system continue to serve as the recruiting ground for future members of the executive branch.

Yet legislatures in democratic societies are far from finished products. In parliamentary systems, governments still depend on the national legislature to provide crucial support for their programs. Moreover, legislatures can have regional importance that goes beyond national borders. The European Parliament is a legislative (some would say quasi-legislative) body that includes 567 members elected from twelve West European countries. These countries belong to the European Union, a primarily economic organization. The Parliament's functions are still being clarified.

In a sense, the European Parliament is a legislature that doesn't legislate. It is unfair to simply refer to the EC as a debating society. It does examine and evaluate the policies of the European Commission, a quasi-executive body. The most important aspect of the European Parliament is probably its potential. Its membership represents nearly 350 million West Europeans, and in all likelihood, countries in the eastern half of the continent will eventually join the European Union and elect representatives to the European Parliament (several have submitted applications). The Parliament may one day be regarded as one of the first critical steps toward political integration on a continental scale.

vote (though this has never happened in modern times).[12] With the ratification of the Twenty-fifth Amendment in 1967, Congress gained the additional constitutional responsibility to confirm a presidential nomination to fill a vice-presidential vacancy.

3. National legislatures govern themselves and can govern the executive. Prestige and authority go along with being a national legislator; so does a great deal of responsibility. As we have seen, the House of Commons forced Anthony Eden out of the prime ministership because he refused to be forthcoming about British involvement in a military attack on the Suez Canal Zone. Several years

---

[12] Congress has done this twice, in 1800 and 1824, and came close to it in 1948 and 1968 when third-party candidates threatened to secure enough electoral votes to deny a majority to either the Democratic or Republican candidates.

later, a minister of defense was forced to resign because he lied on the House of Commons floor about his romantic liaison with a call girl who also enjoyed the attentions of a Soviet military attache. In 1995 in the United States, a senator and a representative, both embroiled in charges of sexual harassment, were threatened with expulsion from Congress if they refused to resign. They resigned. Under drastic circumstances, Congress can also impeach or threaten to impeach high-ranking federal authorities, including the president.

4.   Finally and most obviously, legislatures draft, propose, debate, and pass legislation into law. In this sense, the executive and the legislature share the obligation of making laws. Individual members of parliament tend to have more to say if they belong to a narrow majority. The government that controls a majority of only a few seats must be concerned that a few defections, resignations, deaths, or independent-minded members could not only defeat government-sponsored legislation but could bring the government itself down. As we will see in the following chapter, a democracy tends to induce an intimate and sometimes noisy relationship between the executive and legislative branches. As we will also see, though, this relationship can vary in significant ways between parliamentary and presidential systems.

SUMMARY

1. Legislatures are an ancient political institution. They trace back to classical Greece twenty-five hundred years ago, when the first legislative assemblies began to meet in Athens.

2. Many modern legislatures have upper and lower houses that formed along the social class lines that characterized European societies hundreds of years ago. In most modern legislatures, the lower house has more real political power.

3. In a parliamentary legislative system, the lower house furnishes the executive from its own membership and at any time can withdraw support for the government.

4. Members of most upper houses are not chosen democratically and have little real power. However, they can help draft legislation and help revise legislation passed by the lower house.

5. Parliamentary systems differ from presidential systems such as the United States because parliamentary systems have no division of powers between the various branches of government.

6. Party discipline is a requirement in parliamentary systems. It ensures a productive legislative process and furthers the business of the government.

7. Representative assemblies only rarely represent all of the various social groups and are often disproportionate when it comes to representing gender, ethnic, and religious communities.

8. An important function of some national legislatures is to select the head of government. Some legislatures can, when circumstances dictate, remove him or her from office.

GLOSSARY

impeachment   The process in place in presidential systems that allows legislatures to charge officeholders with wrongdoing and remove them from office if they are found guilty.

legislative councils   Advisory bodies that monarchs in Persian Gulf states and other traditionalist regimes choose and maintain.

loyal opposition   In democratic regimes, the "loyal opposition" is usually the minority party in the legislature. The minority will challenge the government on various issues while awaiting the opportunity to become the majority in the next election.

minority government   Occurs in a parliamentary system when no party or coalition of parties can secure a numerical majority of legislative seats; a minority government functions only until a new election, which often occurs within several months.

parliamentary majority   The majority party in a parliamentary system. The executive must receive consistent support from a numerical majority of legislators to continue in office and to secure the passage of its legislative program.

parliamentary party   Those in a parliamentary system who have been elected to seats in the national legislature, who affiliate with a particular political party, and who normally decide on a party leader.

party discipline   The efforts political parties make to get their own legislators to support the party line on various issues, to guarantee both party solidarity and party support for the individual members at election time.

party whips   Legislators who work between the party leadership and the rank-and-file members; whips must ensure that on any parliamentary issue, all members will be present and voting, and they must try to persuade members to support the party's position.

referendum   A provision allowing the entire electorate in a region or a country to vote on an issue. The outcome becomes law without requiring legislative action.

Speaker of the House   The presiding leader of the lower legislative chamber. The Speaker has substantial powers when it comes to setting legislative agendas, recognizing members, and maintaining order.

vote of confidence   A device often the legislative opposition in a parliamentary system can use to embarrass or bring down the government. The government must win every vote of confidence; if it doesn't, it no longer controls the legislative majority, and a new government is formed.

6

The Executive: Presidential and Parliamentary Government

The national leaders nearly everyone in a country can identify are the **head of government** and **head of state.** The former holds real power, while the latter may only perform ceremonial roles and activities. Americans have it easy in this respect: the two heads are combined into one office, the presidency. In the United States, however, the vice president (like a head of state) often doesn't have enough to do; recent occupants of the office have gratefully received meaningful assignments from the president.

In democracies, it is unusual for either head to be chosen by popular election. (France is a noteworthy exception to this rule and one we will examine in some detail shortly.) Yet the head of government must be able to secure wide support for his or her policies to be effective. This normally happens through an election—if not a popular election, then election by a parliamentary majority.

A national executive personifies her or his country and is, fairly or not, held responsible for how well the country is doing. The executive makes decisions that influence millions of lives. The quality of these decisions and the chances they will be successfully implemented are determined by the level of cooperation the executive receives from the bureaucracy.

In this chapter, we will survey the various dimensions of the executive office, including selection procedures and the extent and variety of executive powers. We will emphasize the executive in democracies, but we will also touch on the diversity of executive offices and roles in nondemocratic systems. We will also continue to use the U.S. political system as a comparative backdrop when appropriate. Most national executives have more power today than they have ever had; at the same time, they probably face more constraints. We shall focus on how effectively they use their powers to respond to their constraints.

PRESIDENTIAL AND PRIME MINISTERIAL GOVERNMENT

The American Presidential System

A political executive is, as the term implies, someone who executes government policy. In a democracy, the legislative and executive branches collaborate to both formulate and implement policy. In parliamentary systems, the executive (in this case, the cabinet) can be realistically considered a kind of senior legislative committee composed primarily of the leadership from the party that controls a majority of seats within the legislature. In the nonparliamentary democracies, though, power is often less concentrated. A president, for example, has less freedom of action than a prime minister when it comes to making policy. A president usually has to negotiate policy, often in a bipartisan fashion, with legislators who as often as not are members of the opposition party.

Although he is the leader of the most powerful country in the world, the U.S. president is remarkably frail in several ways. Unlike a great many other democratic executives, the American president faces term limits and a frequently hostile legislative majority. Also, the public tends to become dissatisfied with their chief executive rather quickly. Since World War II, only two presidents, both Republicans, have been elected to and have served out two complete four-year terms. If he serves as president through his entire term, President Clinton will be the first Democrat to be elected to and complete two consecutive terms since Franklin Roosevelt (1933–1945), and only the fifth president in the twentieth century to do so.

Even with these limitations, however, the American public still expects much from the office of the presidency. And successful occupants usually thoroughly enjoy the considerable prerogatives and powers the office provides. Teddy Roosevelt viewed his presidency (1901–1909) as a chance to use a "bully pulpit" and believed that presidents ought to be presidential: "My belief was that it was not [the president's] right but his duty to do anything that the needs of the nation demanded, unless such action was forbidden by the Constitution or the laws."[1]

The American presidency has evolved into a carefully watched political phenomenon. While Americans seem to quickly grow to dislike presidents and often limit them to one four-year term, they still adulate and respect the office. It's no wonder: the American president is simultaneously head of state, chief executive of the world's only current superpower, diplomatic leader, commander-in-chief of the most powerful armed forces in the world, principal legislative leader (though the influence of this role diminishes when the president faces a congressional majority from the opposition party), and leader of his party.

United States presidents tend to represent the American political mainstream, which is usually slightly to the left or right of the ideological center. Would-be presidents who stray too far from the center or try to push the elec-

---

[1] Arthur B. Tourtellot, *Presidents on the Presidency* (Garden City, N.Y.: Doubleday, 1964), pp. 55–56.

torate too far to the left or right often come to unrewarding ends. Both the Democrat and Republican parties learned valuable lessons when each nominated presidential candidates from extremist wings. In 1964, Republican candidate Barry Goldwater and in 1972, Democratic candidate George McGovern ensured landslide victories for their opponents by offering programs with little popular appeal. Goldwater suggested the repeal of the Social Security Act of 1935, and McGovern proposed the government provide a miminum guaranteed income for every American family. Each suggestion horrified and repelled huge segments of the electorate.

The American presidency has not only grown in stature and power. It is an office that requires its occupant to either sleep very little or be able to delegate tasks to cabinet secretaries, the White House office staff, and to such agencies as the Office of Management and Budget (OMB) and Council of Economic Advisors (CEA). Calvin Coolidge (1923–1929) was most likely the last American president to be able to sleep twelve hours a day as well as brag about doing so.

When the first president met with his first cabinet, the scene stood in stark contrast to what goes on more than two centuries later. George Washington's cabinet consisted of the Secretaries of State and Treasury and the Attorney General. This cozy government was small, because government in those days wasn't capable of performing more than a few basic tasks. As the economy industrialized and became more prosperous, government could do and was often asked to do more.

Modern presidents, probably beginning with the Eisenhower Administration (1953–1961), have provided vice presidents access to high-level meetings and substantive roles in policy formulation. Vice-presidential involvement is important if only because several modern vice presidents have become presidents themselves, either because of a sudden vacancy created by assassination or resignation or by election in their own right. Over the last half century, current or former vice presidents have generally been well prepared to succeed to the presidential office. This contrasts with their often less-carefully-selected predecessors, most of whom, as the observation goes, were individuals no one would have supported for president.

The modern American presidency is often beset with crises, and public opinion polls and voters evaluate how successfully he responds. President Franklin Roosevelt (1933–1945), for example, rallied the full powers of the office and his own considerable persuasive abilities to lead the United States out of the Great Depression. He was also the American leader in World War II, a conflict that challenged the very survival of western democracy.

Recent presidents have not dealt with such momentous events, but neither have they been able to avoid severe national strains. The Vietnam conflict, periodic economic recessions, technological changes, and the arrogance that power encourages produced new challenges and occasional discomforts. Two presidents in succession, Lyndon Johnson (1963–1969) and Richard M. Nixon (1969–1974) were driven from office, even though both had won overwhelming election victories. Johnson's pursuit of the Vietnam War dissatisfied so many people that he chose not to run in 1968. Nixon's disregard of the law during the Watergate scandal would have resulted in impeachment had he not resigned.

Despite these setbacks, the presidential office remains vibrant. For example, Congress may have declared war for the last time (in December 1941, against Germany, Italy, and Japan). The president can now dispatch American soldiers anywhere he can justify their presence. President Reagan ordered an invasion of Grenada, and President Bush ordered troops into Panama and sent a half million troops to the Persian Gulf in 1990 and 1991 to deal with the menace Saddam Hussein posed to the industrial world. When President Clinton offered to send 20,000 American troops to Bosnia in 1996, the offer met with little criticism from Congress.

In one sense, American presidents who face no severe crises almost have a more difficult time. President Clinton, for example, saw his domestic policy agenda thwarted during his first term, especially after the Republican party achieved majorities in both houses of Congress in the 1994 elections. He turned to the foreign policy arena (which most of his critics and supporters maintained he had little interest in) to demonstrate presidential success. Israeli and Palestinian leaders signed two important accords at the White House in September 1993 and September 1995. An obviously pleased president sat between them, hoping to receive some credit as a peace broker.

When it was created, the presidency was a unique office—no other country in the 1790s had anything quite like it. The American presidency became a model for other political systems, particularly in the western hemisphere. Nearly all of the Latin American countries have adopted a presidential form of government. Like the United States, quite a few have imposed term limits: by law, the Mexican president may serve only one six-year term, and Costa Rica has limited its presidents to a single four-year term since 1948. An important difference is that Latin American presidencies are strictly decided by popular election, without an electoral college.

The United States president is probably the most watched and studied political figure in the world. The electronic and print media observe his every move. His words have the potential to make millions of listeners happy or depressed. The outcome of his annual medical checkup is awaited with great anticipation; a presidential illness—even a mild one—can cause jitters in the stock and currency markets.[2]

As we will see, national leaders in other countries are also carefully observed. Interestingly, though, they sometimes seem to have more extensive powers than their American counterpart. They also tend to last longer. Even

---

[2] The public is not always informed when the president has a health problem. For example, Grover Cleveland (1893–1897) had cancer during his second administration, though the public did not know it. See Robert H. Ferrell, *Ill-Advised: Presidential Health and Public Trust* (Columbia and London: University of Missouri Press, 1992). Woodrow Wilson suffered a stroke and Dwight Eisenhower a series of heart attacks, and the public was informed in these instances.

democratically chosen executives can be quite distinct from one another when it comes to acquiring and exercising political power.

Prime Ministerial Government—The United Kingdom

An interesting characteristic of the American presidential system is that quite frequently American presidents seem to arrive at the White House without much national political experience. Popular generals such as Ulysses S. Grant and Dwight Eisenhower served in no public office before their elevation to the presidency. Colin Powell, a former Armed Forces Chief of Staff and hero of the Persian Gulf conflict, was considered a strong presidential possibility in 1996 despite (or perhaps because of) the fact he had never ventured into politics. Warren Harding was governor of Ohio when he was elected president in 1920, but he was almost unknown outside his state. Harding may have received the Republican nomination for president, some believe, because he "looked presidential." Bill Clinton was an obscure governor of a small state. Steve Forbes became a candidate for the 1996 Republican presidential nomination with no prior political experience, but equipped with $25 million dollars of his own money to spend on his campaign.

Prime ministers don't achieve office this way in most parliamentary systems. Candidates for the prime ministership are almost never war heroes or billionaires (although multimillionaires aren't uncommon). The typical ascension for British heads of government is to work up through the ranks, starting in the House of Commons and working up to a top cabinet position: backbencher, junior minister, senior minister. Consider, for example, the qualifications a prospective prime minister's resume typically includes. He or she must

1. have long-time service in the lower (elective) house,
2. have previous Cabinet experience that includes such powerful ministries as foreign affairs, defense, or finance,
3. be leader of the majority party in parliament, and
4. be unrelated to the royal family.

In Britain, as in the United States, the party leader is usually from the party's center but is at least minimally acceptable to the various ideological wings within the party.

Although this section of the chapter is entitled "Prime Ministerial Government," it is as convenient and probably as accurate to apply the term **cabinet government** to a parliamentary system. In many respects, the cabinet is more critical than in the American system because of its membership. American presidents usually choose cabinet secretaries whose names are unfamiliar to the American public. Cabinet secretaries are often recruited from the ranks of career civil servants or from major corporations in the private sector. In some cases, they come out of an academic setting, as did Secretary of State Henry Kissinger (1973–1977).

Former British Prime Minister Margaret Thatcher (1979–1990).

In contrast, parliamentary systems such as the United Kingdom's produce cabinets filled with well-known and ambitious political personages, at least at the top levels. It is likely that one or more of them will eventually go on to become prime minister. The cabinet is viewed as preparatory training for the top job. However, it isn't unheard of for a former prime minister to occupy a cabinet position.

Another rather critical difference exists between American and British cabinets. When the prime minister makes his cabinet selections, he or she must be mindful of at least two interrelated considerations. First, the cabinet should reflect an ideological balance between the various wings of the political party. The prime minister himself is usually the product of a hard or soft ideological emphasis. If he comes from the more moderate elements within, say, the Conservative party, the prime minister will probably bring into the cabinet a representation of the right wing. Second, the prime minister must acquiesce to the political fact that all or most of the top cabinet positions will be filled by people who want his or her job. Usually, some are political allies or protégés willing to wait patiently for their turn until the prime minister retires. Others may not be so patient and are prepared to take full advantage of any opportunity to create a vacancy in the party leadership. Such individuals often represent various factions within the party who may believe the prime minister is taking the party in the wrong ideological direction.

The fact that senior-level cabinet appointments are more political than practical can, of course, detract from a minister's impact. He or she can easily serve in several ministries during a career, but may only infrequently serve in one long enough to fully understand or significantly influence the effectiveness of an individual ministry. A minister is expected to take full responsibility for his or her department's problems, even though ministers are shifted around a lot or occasionally dropped from the cabinet, usually for political reasons.

Most of the time, however, cabinet members offer at least a facade of political loyalty. Governments in the British and other parliamentary systems stand or fall together. This solidarity demonstrates **collective responsibility.** Before the government makes a decision, there can be (and usually is, if the decision is controversial) a great deal of debate at cabinet meetings. However, once a decision is finally made, the debate is over. Cabinet members are expected to present a united front to the public at large and, especially, in parliament. They unanimously defend the policy the government has formulated and decided to implement. A cabinet minister who for any reason simply cannot go along with the decision is expected to resign from the government though he or she retains his or her parliamentary seat.

Finally, the prime minister and his or her colleagues in the cabinet are members of the House of Commons. They must regularly respond to questions and charges from other members, who often word their challenges to create maximum embarrassment and discomfort for the government. Unlike their somewhat luckier American counterparts, who appear only infrequently in Congress and can often get away without appearing at all, senior British ministers are constantly on the firing line.

Ceremonial Heads of State

The American president is both head of government and head of state. Parliamentary democracies separate the two offices. The British, for example, have enjoyed the institution of the monarchy for a millennium. The only interruption came in 1649, when Charles I was executed. It took only a dozen years, though, for remorseful subjects to restore his son to the throne. The people had grown weary of the puritanical government that ruled England in the interim.

The British monarchy survived over the next three and one-half centuries by gradually agreeing to give up political powers to popularly elected assemblies. Monarchies in other European countries that didn't accept their declining roles were ended, often in violence. For a monarchy to survive in a democratizing country, it needed to become relatively powerless. The less power a monarch possessed, the more public popularity he or she earned.

Monarchies became symbols of national unity and enjoyed widespread respect and affection because they no longer participated in policy making. Unlike her prime ministers, Queen Elizabeth II of England consistently draws cheers and applause whenever she appears on public occasions. (This is not true of her children, however, whose occasional scandalous behavior has damaged the monarchy's prestige.) In most democratic societies where they still exist, royal family members aren't even allowed to cast ballots in national elections—one of the only things they have in common with convicted felons.

A goodly number of countries have dispensed with their monarchies. Italy did after World War II, and France broke with monarchy after 1870. Others, such as Spain, have abolished a monarchical institution, missed it, and restored it. In fact, exiled royal family members are usually available to be restored. No sooner had the communist regime of the Soviet Union dissolved than many Russians expressed a preference to reestablish the Russian monarchy. They wanted to return the Romanov family, which had ruled Russia from 1613 to 1917, when the last Russian Tsar and his immediate family were shot, to the throne.

Many countries without monarchies have heads of state who are effective national symbols. Some systems, such as Israel, Italy, Germany, and Austria, have presidents. While the Austrian president is popularly elected, most aren't; instead, one or both parliamentary houses chooses them. Without a popular mandate, there is little danger that a ceremonial president could actually become an influential political force.

A ceremonial president usually has a record of distinguished service, often having established a noteworthy career outside of politics. A ceremonial president can be a career politician, of course, but usually not one who has been successful enough to become a head of government. A prime minister, by contrast, has often made a good share of enemies on the way to the top and has been a partisan politician for decades. Former prime ministers normally retire to write their memoirs without expecting to serve in public office again.

What is the purpose of having a ceremonial head of state? They basically serve very few but still important functions:

1.   As mentioned previously, a head of state is a symbol of national unification. He or she regularly appears at important events, lending a degree of dignity to them. The head of state also receives high-ranking personages visiting from other countries, including other heads of state, and travels abroad on goodwill visits to other countries.

2.   After every election, the head of state asks the leader of the party (or coalition of parties) with a parliamentary majority to form a government. Most of the time, this is a pro-formal act since the head of state cannot act to contradict the results of a free election. On occasion, though, an election result is extremely close and may even be in dispute. At such a time, the head of state can exercise, usually within carefully specified constitutional limits, an independent choice.

3.   The head of state is the personification of political legitimacy. In most parliamentary systems, he or she appoints the head of government. In a clear-cut electoral outcome, as just mentioned, this appointment is fairly automatic. Yet, because, Queen Elizabeth II, for example, represents a thousand years of political traditions and institutions, she almost "anoints" a prime minister and confers legal authority on that person. In other words, she selects someone to safeguard British interests for four or five years.

4.   The head of state provides stability in unstable or rapidly changing political situations. A long reigning monarch (Queen Elizabeth II, for instance, came to the throne in 1952) will normally outlast several prime ministers, but even a presidential head of state can serve a term as long as seven years. In a country such as Italy, where there have been fifty governments in the half century since 1945, a long-serving and familiar head of state offers a reassuring presence that comforts a population that has an understandably difficult time keeping up with changes in government.

Some heads of state, especially the comparatively few who are popularly elected, have more authority than others. By and large, though, their powers are ultimately constrained by an electorate that makes its political preferences clear at the polls. Heads of state, therefore, only rarely challenge or disagree with the heads of government.

SELECTION OF THE EXECUTIVE

In nondemocratic systems, national leaders are self-selected. As we shall see, a national leader in an authoritarian system will frequently seize power through a coup or a rigged election. Often a rigged election will follow a coup to insure at least the appearance of legitimacy. Perhaps the easiest way to become and remain a national leader is through an inherited monarchy, another aspect of authoritarianism we will soon investigate.

However, in this section of the chapter, we will survey the selection of the chief executive in three industrialized democracies. Table 6.1 demonstrates that not all are chosen in a completely democratic manner. The table also shows that the distinct peculiarities of a political system and culture are instrumental in shaping the selection process.

France

The most democratic process for choosing an executive is through a direct popular election that requires an absolute majority of the electorate to officially endorse a particular candidate. In 1965, the French dispensed with an electoral college to enable the president of the republic to come to office with a popular mandate. In effect, the French have a two-stage election for the presidency. The first ballot is the rough equivalent of a national primary as voters choose from any number of candidates. Only three or four are serious candidates, who come equipped with the support of major party organizations, substantial expe-

TABLE 6.1   Direct and Indirect Ways of Selecting a Chief Executive

Direct Selection	Indirect Selection	
French president	American president	British prime minister
	Electoral college	Majority party
Electorate	Electorate	Electorate

POLITICAL BIOGRAPHY

Charles de Gaulle

The founder and first president of the Fifth Republic, Charles de Gaulle (1958–1969) reasoned that the French had spent a good deal of their history and blood trying to make up their minds between a republic and a monarchy. He also understood that the French had rarely been a united people. De Gaulle once asked how it was possible to govern a country that produced two hundred different kinds of cheese!

The compromise was a seven-year presidency secured by an indisputably popular mandate. The president of the republic would be able to govern because the electorate had chosen him. He could also function as head of state because he would choose a prime minister and other cabinet officials to carry out the daily business of government and take the blame for anything that went wrong with the economy.

De Gaulle, who was primarily responsible for drafting a new constitution in 1958, also gave the president the authority to call for a national referendum. The French electorate may vote yes or no on any issue the president puts to them. The referendum is an excellent technique for bypassing the legislative branch and insuring a direct link between president and people. De Gaulle had little respect for the National Assembly, which he considered divisive and inefficient.

Much of de Gaulle's political design seems to be working. When de Gaulle took power, France was on the brink of civil war. De Gaulle reasoned, apparently with justification, that the French people required strong but popularly chosen leadership with somewhat more authority than counterparts in most other democracies. The Fifth Republic has survived its founder by several decades and seems, unlike previous regimes, to have the confidence of the bulk of the French nation.

rience, and name recognition. Unless one of them wins an outright majority (which has not happened in the six presidential elections since 1965), a second election or run-off ballot between the two top vote getters occurs two weeks later. One will secure an absolute majority and a mandate for a seven-year term of office.

A plurality winner on the first ballot may not end up the majority winner on the second. For example, two conservative candidates may compete on the first ballot, with a socialist candidate opposing them, as happened in 1995. The socialist came in first. The strongest conservative candidate then overwhelmed his socialist rival, drawing support on the second ballot from those who voted for the losing conservative on the first.

Seven years is a long time, and only one Fifth Republic president, Francois Mitterand (1981–1995), has won election to and survived two full terms. One of his three predecessors resigned in mid-term, a second died in office, and a third lost to Mitterand in a bid for reelection. On the other hand, Mitterand himself had lost in two previous attempts for the presidency. His successor, Jacques Chirac, also tried without success on two occasions before finally succeeding in 1995. Both Chirac and Mitterand had made it a lifetime ambition to become president. Each began presidential politics in his forties and achieved the ultimate prize when he was in his sixties.

Colin Powell, American military hero and possible presidential candidate in 2000.

Unlike the American and several Latin American presidencies, the French presidency does not have the constraint of term limits. The French believe their executive is entitled to serve as long as a popular mandate is retained. The insistence on a popular majority eliminates the possibility of a **minority president,** or a president who wins office without a majority or a plurality of popular votes. (U.S. presidents can be minority presidents.)

Should a president leave office for any reason before the completion of his term, the French simply have another election for a full seven-year term. During the few weeks between the vacancy and the new election, the President of the Senate functions as interim president. There is no vice president who automatically fills out the remainder of the term. The French consider this another important democratic feature. Unlike the United States, France never has an **accidental president,** or a president who suddenly and unexpectedly steps up to fill a vacancy without direct election to the office.

There is a debate as to whether the term of office is itself an undemocratic feature of the French presidential system. A seven-year renewable term is the longest mandate for a chief executive in the western democracies. A new president may begin his term with substantial popularity only to see it dissolve after one or two years. (Seven months after taking office, Jacques Chirac had a popularity rating of 11 percent, a record low for any French presidency.) He can also make a comeback, as Mitterand did in the last stages of his first term, and secure reelection in the process. The French may be more patient with their chief executives than Americans, who are liable to get rid of their presidents after only one four-year term.

In a peculiar blend of presidential and parliamentary features, the French president appoints the prime minister and other members of the cabinet. Unlike a strictly parliamentary system, the French system forbids cabinet members to simultaneously hold legislative seats. They have no mandate of their own. If the economy sours, for example, a French president may simply allow the prime minister and/or other cabinet ministers to take the blame. It is not unusual for the president to go through two or three prime ministers in a single term of office.

It isn't surprising that many French prime ministers who remain in office for a respectable length of time and escape the onus of serious scandal desire to become president. Three of France's five Fifth Republic presidents were previous prime ministers. Chirac himself was a prime minister under two different presidents. The prime minister therefore has an especially important stake in the success of the government that holds the key to his or her own political future.

The president tries to remain politically aloof as the head of state and allow his prime minister to deal with the day-to-day workings of the government. This goal does not always meet with success, though. Within weeks of his ascension to the presidency in April 1995, Jacques Chirac announced that France would carry out a series of nuclear tests in its South Pacific possessions. The timing could not have been worse: the announcement came on the fiftieth anniversary of the atomic bombings of Hiroshima and Nagasaki. Neighboring countries around the possessions were outraged. In protest, the governments of Chile and New Zealand recalled their ambassadors from Paris, and Australia's prime minister called France's nuclear testing "an act of stupidity."[3] At least on the international level, the French president cannot escape responsibility for the policies of his or her government.

A French president must also assume responsibility for the direction of domestic policy. Chirac's "honeymoon period" was probably the shortest in French presidential history. Within a few months, he was being blamed for a 12 percent unemployment rate and for changing his mind too often on what to do about it.[4] Fortunately for him, Chirac had another six years to demonstrate effectiveness.

The United States

Choosing an American president is an expensive and time-consuming matter. It is also a process watched avidly by most of the rest of the world. For the party out of power, the event begins as much as a year and a half before the national

---

[3] "Test and Shout," *The Economist*, September 9, 1995, p. 50.

[4] France Strikes Against Chirac," *The Economist*, October 14, 1995, pp. 57–59.

election. If an incumbent president is finishing a second term, even the party in power begins early to consider several candidates for the succession.

The 1996 election began early in 1995 as one candidate after another declared his candidacy for the Republican party nomination. By late summer, 1995, ten individuals had declared; by early fall, three had announced their withdrawal from the race. Of course, only a few of these candidates had a real chance for the nomination. Usually, such candidates have a combination of name recognition and money—lots of money. An American presidential campaign can easily cost a total of $200 million for all candidates.

Not even a multimillionaire or a billionaire can guarantee victory, however. Ross Perot, an independent candidate in 1992, received 19 percent of the popular vote—the best showing for a minor or third-party candidate in modern political history—but he carried no states. He received only 8 percent in 1996, but this was still enough to deny President Clinton a popular vote majority. Similarly, multimillionaire Steve Forbes offered himself for the 1996 Republican nomination. He announced his willingness to spend $25 million of his own money, but ultimately got nowhere.

Glory may matter as much as money in American politics. Successful generals with no political experience such as Ulysses S. Grant (1869–1877) or Dwight David Eisenhower (1953–1961) can be so popular that their names and reputations can carry them to the nomination and to electoral victory. In fact, by the late 1970s, it was becoming increasingly fashionable to attempt to win political office by posing as someone with modest or no political experience. Presenting oneself as a "Washington outsider" and a "fresh face" was considered to be an excellent campaign strategy. This is why the former Chief of the Armed Services and hero of the Persian Gulf conflict, Colin Powell, appeared to be a serious contender for the Republican nomination before he announced he would not be a candidate in 1996.

There is actually no sure route to the American presidency. Political leaders in other democracies customarily work their way up through the ranks into party leadership positions and high-level cabinet posts. In contrast, an American president need not have held any previous political office, or may have held an office in a small state—Governors Carter and Clinton, for example, were unknown outside of their home states before they achieved success in the Democratic party primaries. No cabinet official has become president since the 1920s. No sitting vice president between 1837 and 1988 won a presidential election.

If a candidate survives the primaries and goes on to win the national election, he or she may not even then be assured of a popular mandate. Voter turnout is miserably low in the United States and, because of the electoral college, a candidate can win the popular vote and still lose the election. While this hasn't happened since 1888, the potential is clearly there, especially if a strong third-party candidate runs.

It is only in the electoral college that a majority matters. Becoming president requires the support of a minimum of 270 electors out of a total of 538. Only on two occasions, in 1800 and 1824, has no presidential candidate achieved an electoral college majority. When a majority is lacking, the House of Representatives is constitutionally obligated to decide the outcome. A strong third-party movement may not be able to overcome Democrat and Republican dominance, but it has on several occasions threatened to throw the election to the House.

Some have suggested that the electoral college be abolished or reformed to reflect the proportions of the popular vote. The chances are slim that either will happen. Doing anything to the electoral college would require a constitutional amendment. Besides, there is a general satisfaction with the college, especially among the larger states, which have large electoral blocks. California, for example, has 54 electoral votes, one-fifth of the total needed to win. If a presidential candidate can carry the eleven largest states, he or she will win the election even if an opponent wins the other thirty-nine. The electoral college also seems to provide a certain peace of mind—the electorate knows they can count on it to secure a final and usually indisputable election result.

Several presidents have actually been minority presidents, coming to the office with less than 50 percent of the popular vote. Bill Clinton won the 1992 election with only 43 percent and the 1996 contest with only 49 percent of all ballots cast. He has a lot of company: Harry Truman in 1948, John Kennedy in 1960, and Richard Nixon in 1968 all won close elections with under 50 percent of the popular vote.

In some cases, it is possible to become president without any popular or electoral college votes. American presidents have a high mortality rate. Between 1841 and 1963, no fewer than seven presidents were either assassinated or died in office. An eighth, Richard Nixon, resigned in 1974. In all of these instances, the vice president assumed the office. Several other presidents, including Ronald Reagan in 1981, have survived assassination attempts.

Accidental presidents may have successful administrations. Then again, they may not: how well remembered are the accomplishments, for example, of President Millard Fillmore, Zachary Taylor's vice president, during 1851–1852? Vice presidents who suddenly become presidents have no mandate beyond the constitutional one. Fortunately, recent vice presidents have been much better prepared to assume the presidential office. This is because modern presidents, beginning with Eisenhower, have invited vice presidents to cabinet meetings and generally kept them well-informed. Some, like Walter Mondale during the Carter Administration (1977–1981) have worked very closely with their presidents. A vice president is still selected by and must at all times be loyal to the president, but at least he or she is no longer an unknown or inexperienced novice.

The United Kingdom

The British prime minister, as is typical in parliamentary systems, is the leader of the majority party in the lower house. He or she must remain party leader in order to remain prime minister. The support of the House is forthcoming as long as the government's policies are generally acceptable, cabinet level scandals are infrequent, and the party's parliamentary majority is maintained.

Whether prime minister or not, the party leader is dependent upon and requires the continual support of the party's parliamentary members. If a sudden vacancy occurs in the party leadership, there is no automatic successor. Both of Britain's major parties are restrictive when it comes to choosing their respective leaders.

There is no popular election except at the local level: a party leader, like the other 649 members of the House of Commons, is elected from a single-member constituency of about 100,000 people. He or she becomes party leader by securing the support of the party organization and, in particular, of the majority of party MPs. As in other democracies, the public opinion polls influence the status of party leader and prime minister. John Major, for example, saw his leadership seriously threatened in July 1995 by John Redwood, an aspiring Conservative politician. Redwood understood that the polls indicated a general dissatisfaction with Major. (The dissatisfaction was confirmed in May 1997, when the Conservatives lost decisively to Labour.)

Redwood was correct, but Major rode out the 1995 storm and for some instructive reasons. Most British Conservative party leaders tend to represent the ideological center of their party. That is where the bulk of any party's supporters are, and that is also where a good part of the British electorate is found. The Conservative party has a strong right wing, which Redwood drew his support from, but the party tends to stay with moderate policies and leadership.

This was not historically true of the Labour party, as we will see in chapter 7. The Labour party lost four consecutive national elections between 1979 and 1992, in great part because of its proclivity to produce leadership too closely associated with its extreme left wing. Younger and more moderate leaders reversed this feature[5] in 1995, electing Tony Blair as party leader.

Of course, whether a party leader becomes prime minister (or remains as party leader) is determined by how well the party does at election time. A typical party leader will get two or three chances to gain a parliamentary majority and form a government. Some are rather successful at doing this: Margaret Thatcher became the longest serving British prime minister and Conservative party leader in modern times by winning three consecutive national elections and remaining head of government for eleven years (1979–1990). She had become the Conservative leader four years earlier, in 1975. During the same sixteen-year period, Labour went through no fewer than five party leaders.

Becoming party leader requires a great deal of persistence and patience. These requirements were especially in evidence in the Conservative party during the past few decades. The Labour party in the 1990s began choosing younger leaders. Their new prime minister, Tony Blair, was still in his late thirties when he assumed Labour's leadership in 1995. Successful party leaders in

---

[5] "Portillo's Complaint," *The Economist*, October 22, 1995, p. 63.

Britain, as in most of the industrialized democracies, usually emerge from moderate elements.

The ultimate selection of a prime minister also depends on the public perception of political personalities. Like occasional American presidents, British prime ministers have sometimes been accused of being "wimps." No such charge was ever leveled at Margaret Thatcher: she was affectionately known as the "iron lady." Presidents Jimmy Carter and George Bush had the "wimp" problem. So did former Prime Minister John Major, Thatcher's successor, despite the fact that he repulsed numerous intra-party efforts to get rid of him.

Personality does seem to play a part. British prime ministers tend to remain in power in great part because of their perceived or real strength of character. Winston Churchill, Britain's prime minister during World War II, was often characterized by both friends and critics as a bulldog in his relentless refusal to give in to an enemy he personally despised. Margaret Thatcher's nickname attests to her strong personal stubbornness and her forceful political style. When the British imprisoned Irish Republican Army agents in Belfast as common criminals and murderers in the 1980's, the prisoners threatened a hunger strike unless they were reclassified as political prisoners. Prime Minister Thatcher suggested they were free to starve themselves to death (a few did) and argued they at least had a choice they didn't allow their victims.

After a national election, the leader of the majority party or, in rare circumstances, the plurality party, in the House of Commons is expected to form a government by invitation of the Queen. The leader becomes Her Majesty's first or prime minister. In reality, of course, the government is already in place. The interview with the queen is a pro-formal act. However, this pro-formalism does give a prospective prime minister's political legitimacy a boost. Queen Elizabeth II is, after all, the head of state. She confers the authority of the state to her government when she names a prime minister and requests her or him to form a cabinet.

Self-Selected Executives

Most of the world's government leaders are not popularly chosen through regular and honest elections. Nondemocratic regimes regularly display varying degrees of disregard for basic human rights. Some "honest" dictators sincerely desire to do what is best for their countries. Most dictators, however, are rather mindless of and insensitive to the suffering they cause their own citizens.

One extreme case is Saddam Hussein, the president of Iraq. His dictatorship enhanced its legitimacy in October 1995, when 8.4 million Iraqi voters participated in a national referendum to renew President Hussein's tenure for an additional seven years. He received 99.96 percent of the votes in a record voter turnout of 99.47 percent of the eligible electorate. Approximately thirty-three hundred Iraqis were courageous enough (or foolish enough) to vote No.[6]

---

[6] "King of a Sad Castle," *The Economist*, October 21, 1995, p. 45.

What makes the result suspicious is not just the overwhelming endorsement, but the idea that in a country where 30 percent of children under age five are malnourished[7] President Hussein could be so universally loved.

The regime of Saddam Hussein is typical of perhaps five dozen countries governed by a frequently despised but feared dictator. In these countries, the political system exhibits several or all of the following characteristics:

1. The principal constituency is the military hierarchy. The dictator is often a military leader and sees the officer corps, many of whom he knows personally and who secured his power, as the means by which he can retain and expand power.

2. The dictatorship relies on secret police. Because a dictatorship cannot rely on voluntary citizen support, a secret police force, often run by a near relative of the dictator, reports and punishes any sign of dissent or opposition. For example, the Iraqi secret police might be expected to try to figure out the identities of the few thousand voters who had the nerve to cast "No" ballots against Saddam Hussein. In some dictatorships, several versions of the secret police actually spy on one another as well as on the general citizenry.

3. Power is vested in the dictator's close associates. Family members and/or retainers from a particular region or tribe are placed in positions of authority because the dictator does not have the luxury of choosing people on the basis of merit. This practice often leads to governmental incompetence, since totally unsuited people may be placed in high office. It also can encourage rampant corruption, since political leaders may feel they have a license to enrich themselves while they can, until the day the regime is overthrown.

4. The dictator is installed for life, or until he is overthrown. Unless the dictator is also a monarch, little or no provision is made for political succession. Thus, when a dictator is overthrown or dies after several decades in power, national turmoil may ensue. Dictatorships are rarely succeeded by democratic regimes. A country may wind up sincerely mourning the passing of a dictator when the alternative is chaos or civil war that will end only when another, perhaps even more brutal, dictatorship is established.

5. The dictatorship is especially oppressive to select groups. A dictatorship may be especially desirous of making life miserable for an ethnic or religious minority that has sought to establish political autonomy or to gain outright independence. This feature is a main characteristic of Nigeria, where the military regime is very fond of hanging dissidents based on both their opposition to government policy and on their tribal associations.

Many political democracies are also described as **constitutional monarchies.** Britain's Queen Elizabeth, for example, is a constitutional monarch. A constitutional monarchy is not a dictatorship because the monarch is usually stripped of real political power. This contrasts with the rulers in **absolute**

---

[7] Ibid.

monarchies, who are certainly masters of their countries. Some of them, like the Saud family of Saudi Arabia, will not even hear of a popularly elected legislature. Others, such as Algeria, may tolerate one but are quick to cancel or nullify elections if the result does not meet with their approval.

Monarchs come to power quietly and usually peacefully through inheritance. Unlike military dictators, monarchs rarely have to kill people to gain power. Currently, monarchies seem to be more powerful in the Middle East than in any other region. This is especially noticeable in the Persian Gulf, where several countries are traditionalist monarchies; the same royal house has been in power for several generations and is accustomed to having things its own way.

Some absolute monarchies may be losing their absolutism. In Jordan, King Hussein has permitted free elections, although he still retains ultimate control over the country's armed forces. Unlike military dictators, monarchs are usually more relaxed about their positions. Even King Hussein, who has been the target of innumerable assassination plots, is noted not only for his strong governing style but for his toleration of occasional dissent. Of course, outright opposition to the institution of the monarchy is not allowed.

EXECUTIVE POWERS

The powers of the head of government vary from system to system. Democracies have a great deal in common, but they are distinct from one another in significant ways. Consider, for example, what a French president can do in comparison to his or her American counterpart:

- serve as many terms as he or she can win (U.S. presidents are limited to two four-year terms)
- govern unilaterally, without the national legislature, during a state of emergency (which he can unilaterally declare) for up to six months
- dissolve the lower house of the national legislature (but no more than once in a twelve-month period)
- announce a national referendum, the result of which has the force of law

The British prime minister also has some helpful advantages an American president can only envy; specifically, the prime minister can:

- ensure that a parliamentary majority equipped with party discipline will pass his or her legislative proposals
- choose the time of the next national election, as long as the date is within five years from the most recent election
- normally rely on a majority of his or her party's MPs in the House of Commons to ensure his or her position
- work without facing the restriction of term limits

CONSTITUTIONAL RESTRAINTS

Every democratic system places serious limitations on the powers of its government. Most have a constitution that guarantees the civil rights of the citizenry. As we shall see in the next chapter, such guarantees often form the relationship between government and the governed.

Restrictions on the powers of the executive are especially pronounced in most democratic processes. In most of the presidential systems in the western hemisphere, the chief executive is limited to a precise number of terms, often just one for a set number of years. In several of the Latin American democracies, dictators proclaiming themselves presidents for life is a disconcertingly recent memory. Several of these countries have constitutions that not only limit incumbents to one or two terms but prohibit immediate family members from succeeding to power.

The United States is a recent convert to term limits. The Twenty-second Amendment, ratified in 1951, limits American presidents to a total of two four-year terms, or a total of ten years if a vice president takes over for a president and then is elected him or herself. A comparative summary of term restrictions appear in table 6.2.

Some presidential systems are more restrictive than others. The French president is probably the most powerful. He or she faces no term limits, is elected by an absolute popular majority, and has emergency powers that can be invoked when the president thinks they are needed. Article 16 of the French Constitution states that

> *When the institutions of the Republic, the independence of the nation, the integrity of its territory or the fulfillment of its international commitments are threatened in a grave and immediate manner and when the regular functioning of the constitutional governmental authorities is interrupted, the president of the Republic shall take measures commanded by these circumstances . . .*

The president can determine when "a grave and immediate manner" exists, but the emergency powers themselves have limitations: the president is obligated to apply emergency measures with the cooperation of the prime minister and the presidents of the Senate and National Assembly.

Finally, government leaders, including presidents, are constitutionally required to obey the same laws as everyone else. They cannot bribe their way

---

TABLE 6.2   Presidential Term Limits in Selected Countries

Country	Length of Term	Renewable?
Costa Rica	4 years	No
France	7 years	Yes
Mexico	6 years	No
United States	4 years	Once

New Socialist cabinet ministers walking to their offices after the 1997 French National Assembly elections.

to power, rig elections, or arbitrarily repeal laws they don't like although the latter becomes excusable and perhaps even justified in national emergencies. Lincoln, for example, suspended the writ of *habeus corpus*, which allows a citizen to challenge the government for imprisoning him or her without due process of law, during the Civil War, from 1861 to 1865. This was clearly an impeachable offense, but a Congress dominated by Lincoln's party and determined to retain the Union's sovereignty ignored it. Eighty years later, the U.S. government detained 120,000 Americans of Japanese descent, confiscating property from many, during World War II. No president could get away with such a disregard of the law in peacetime.

In most democratic systems, restraints on executive power are both constitutionally required and voluntarily self-imposed. In Britain, for example, there is basically nothing to thwart or delay a parliamentary act. National elections are required at least once every five years, but from 1935 to 1945, elections were not held because of the emergency of World War II. The prime minister simply refrained from asking the king to dissolve parliament. The leaders of the political parties, already bound together in national unity, agreed that elections would be held immediately after the end of the war in Europe. They were.

When no restraints are imposed on government in general and on the executive in particular, government is usually ineffective or worse. Many authoritarian dictators are too busy maintaining power and building expensive (and often tasteless) monuments to themselves to be bothered about the needs of their people. While North Korea's economy was deteriorating and causing much human suffering, the country's leader, Kim Il Sung, constructed a statue of himself bigger than any building in the country. Saddam Hussein, while decrying the economic sanctions the international community imposed on his country, was still able to scrape $1.5 billion together to build a total of seventy-eight luxury palaces for his family and himself. Even worse, an authoritarian leader only reluctantly thinks about the long-term interests of his or her country, such as political succession. Restraints on power help a government work effectively for long-term good.

BUREAUCRACY

It is difficult to imagine modern or modernizing societies attempting to deliver public services to an ever-demanding citizenry without a bureaucracy. Ideally, **bureaucracies** assist the executive in providing at least those basic services, such as police and fire protection, that make our lives more secure and comfortable, as well as implementing policy for the executive branch. The rapid growth of technology has enabled the bureaucracy to deliver more services efficiently at an affordable cost. Because technology is often a double-edged sword, bureaucracy may also be perceived as increasingly intrusive in the private lives of individuals. Moreover, depending on the system, bureaucracies can be beneficial, but they can also be murderous. In this section, we will briefly examine how bureaucracies work in various political systems.

The Executive and the Bureaucracy

Most civil servants (the more polite term for "bureaucrats") perform important activities. Assuring even minimal services to an industrial society of millions of people is a daunting task. It isn't as though bureaucrats haven't been at it for a long time. Sumerian kings and Egyptian pharaohs relied on a professional civil service four millennia ago to make sure taxes were collected, roads were built, armies were paid, and the pyramids were constructed.

Until modern times, few bureaucracies thought much about training or developing skills. France has been a pioneer in this effort, developing the *grandes écoles*, special schools dedicated to preparing civil servants to serve the public interest. One French president, Valery Giscard d'Estaing (1974–1981), was a *grand école* graduate.

Most countries, including the United States, have no equivalent to the *grandes écoles*. This is a pity, since the schools not only train civil servants, but can increase or decrease the number of students they admit. This is an excellent way to ensure that the bureaucracy does not become top-heavy.

Occasionally, bureaucracies forget their reason for being. They exist to help rather than hinder people. At the same time, citizens demanding services need to remember that their taxes pay for the services bureaucracies provide, and when they want more services, bureaucracies will grow and become more costly. If, for example, we want breathable air, a governmental agency is probably going to have to ensure that industry complies with antipollution standards. Of course, breathing healthy air will then cost us more in taxes.

In a democracy, a bureaucracy is supposed to serve rather than control. (The latter, as we will shortly see, is in ample supply in nondemocratic systems.) Even a bureaucracy with good intentions and substantial resources may not find it easy to provide public services. As urban areas have expanded and as national borders, particularly in Western Europe and increasingly in North America, have partially broken down as the result of economic integration, bureaucratic jurisdictions have become complicated and confused.

In both Germany and the United States, for example, it is common for an individual to work in one city (or state) and live in another. He may receive services where he works but pay taxes only where he lives.[8] In several European countries and in North America, city boundaries are even beginning to flow over national frontiers. There is little doubt that in the near future, bureaucracies from a variety of national and local jurisdictions will have to cooperate to serve the needs of distinct populations that impact upon one another.

Clearly, bureaucracies must constantly reform and revise policy as demands change and grow and as resources become less dependable. Local and national bureaucracies may be unprepared for demographic shifts. In the United States, for example, the bureaucratic structure of the public school system has been unprepared to cope with dramatic increases in numbers and in ethnic diversity.[9] Citizenries in democracies tend to evaluate governments on the basis of their comfort level. Bureaucracies will therefore not go away, nor should we expect to see them significantly reduced.

Governments that have tried to drastically reduce the role of bureaucracies have not been especially successful. In a modern industrial society, it is probably futile to try to reduce the role of the bureaucracy in any substantial fashion. A population that is rapidly aging—a feature particularly apparent in countries such as France, Germany, and Japan—and that is increasingly dependent on medical care funded by the public sector and concerned about the relationship between monthly social security checks and the inflation rate is going to make increasing, not diminishing, demands.

Moreover, bureaucracies must sometimes deliver services to people who haven't paid for them. New York City officials, for example, get annoyed at the great number of people who derive their livelihoods in the city but live and pay their taxes in another jurisdiction. As metropolitan areas spill over and across national borders, as they are between the United States and Mexico, bureaucracies may have to pool resources and combine certain services. In sum, bureaucracies are liable to grow rather than shrink in the years ahead. It has become increasingly evident in recent years that we like the services bureaucracies provide. What we don't like is paying for them.

Bad and Ineffective Bureaucracies

A bad bureaucracy and a bureaucracy that is ineffective are not necessarily the same. Governments implement policy through various bureaucratic agencies. The political traditions of responsible government strongly suggest that policies be geared to protect and help people. Too often, though, a government can cause a great deal of harm to its own citizenry and sometimes to other nations.

---

[8] "Federal Jigsaw," *The Economist*, June 2, 1990, p. 51.

[9] "Next Population Bulge Shows Its Might," *The Wall Street Journal*, February 3, 1997, pp. B1 and B5.

A government can formulate and a bureaucracy pursue policies that intentionally hurt or destroy entire communities.

Several governments, such as the Soviet Union under Stalin (1924–1953), China under Mao Tse-tung (1949–1976), and Germany under Hitler (1933–1945), have exhibited frightening lethality. Tens of millions of people under the control of these regimes perished because of inhuman conditions that bureaucratic agencies planned, created, and maintained. A bureaucracy is supposed to do what a government tells it to. In some political regimes, the careers of bureaucrats are determined by how efficiently they carry out their assigned tasks.

Adolf Eichmann (1906–1962) provides an example of the negative nature a bureaucracy can take on. Eichmann was part of the Nazi regime in Germany. He was placed in charge of transporting Jewish and other victims across Europe to concentration camps, where most of them died from exposure, disease, or hunger, or perished in gas chambers. After his capture by Israeli agents and during his subsequent trial, Eichmann insisted it was his job to pack people into cattle cars and ensure that they arrived at their destinations on schedule. What happened to them after that was not his concern. One observer at the trial suggested that Eichmann would have had his own father executed if he had been ordered to do so.[10] In the sense of carrying out state-mandated policy, Eichmann was a "good" bureaucrat.

Unfortunately for their victims, neither the Nazi nor Soviet bureaucracies were inefficient. Obviously, efficiency can have its darker side. However, many national bureaucracies are inept to the point of tragedy. The ineptness is not always the bureaucrats' fault. At times, they simply may not have enough resources to accomplish much. For example, the typical Egyptian bureaucrat puts in only twenty-seven minutes a day at work.[11] It is unlikely that the short work day can be attributed to sheer laziness. More likely, the Egyptian bureaucrat, like most of his Third World counterparts, has plenty to do but few resources to do it with.

The Egyptian capital city, Cairo, has a population of perhaps 16 million. No one is sure of the exact number. One of every four Egyptians lives in a city with a bureaucratic infrastructure geared to provide services for about a third of the current population. Each day, Cairo adds a thousand new people to its population. There is no way the bureaucracy can even begin to provide the most basic public services.

The trend in Egypt and other Third World countries is clear: most have more civil servants than they know what to do with. The government hires college graduates because the private sector cannot yet provide enough jobs for white collar workers. The government jobs unfortunately involve little real work.

---

[10] Hannah Arendt, *Eichmann in Jerusalem* (New York: Viking Press, 1963).

[11] Mary Anne Weaver, "The Novelist and the Sheikh," *The New Yorker*, January 30, 1995.

There are limits to the services bureaucracies can provide and the powers they hold. In many cases, the limits are too weak to protect people from abuse; in others, the bureaucracy lacks the resources to do much. In either case, it is hard for the executive branch of a government to achieve its goals without a viable bureaucracy.

SUMMARY

1. National political leaders are generally *heads of government*, the people whose parties win elections or who appoint themselves in dictatorships. Heads of state, in contrast, are not politically powerful, but they do provide a symbolic legitimacy for the government and unity for the nation.

2. The American presidency is the world's single most powerful political office. However, it is an office subject to constitutional limitations and restraints other strong democratic executives do not have to face.

3. In parliamentary systems such as the United Kingdom, the prime minister is invariably an individual who has worked his or her way up the party hierarchy. American presidents can have a power base separate from the national party hierarchy.

4. The cabinet in a parliamentary system stands or falls together. It is composed of the top leaders of the majority party.

5. Ceremonial heads of state are useful symbols of national unity and political legitimacy in great part because they lack significant political power.

6. Democratic executives are not always chosen in the most democratic process; they may be selected in indirect fashion, as in the United States. In several Latin American countries and in France, the chief executive must be elected by an absolute popular majority.

7. Self-selected executives often install themselves following a military coup, which may or may not have been violent.

8. Constitutional restraints on executive powers vary from democracy to democracy. They may also increase or decrease depending on whether a severe national crisis crops up.

9. In a democracy, the bureaucracy is supposed to implement executive policy. In nondemocratic systems, the policies may be inhumane and even criminal.

GLOSSARY

absolute monarchy   A system in which the chief executive holds all significant political powers and transfers power to his or her heirs.

accidental president   A phenomenon in American politics: the sudden and unexpected ascension of a vice president to the presidency.

bureaucracy   The machinery of government that carries out the policies that the executive and legislative branches have formulated.

cabinet government   In a parliamentary system, the cabinet is composed of party leaders who stand or fall together, creating a cabinet government. Cabinet members must publicly agree and must maintain a parliamentary majority to retain power.

collective responsibility   Once a policy is formulated, all the cabinet ministers in a parliamentary system assume responsibility for its defense and implementation.

constitutional monarchy   A system in which a nondemocratic institution, the monarchy, is preserved by transferring any substantive decision-making power from the monarch to the parliament.

head of government   The top government officer who exercises actual political power.

head of state   The ceremonial leader who symbolizes national sovereignty and political legitimacy.

minority president   A phenomenon that characterizes American presidential politics: a candidate can win an election without acquiring either a majority or plurality of popular votes.

The Law and the Judiciary

A body of laws or legal system is required for social coherence. Laws can come from a variety of sources or simply from a single source. They are usually based somewhat on the customs and traditions that characterize a particular society. Whatever their origins, **laws** are essentially rules that identify, formalize, and reinforce patterns of social behavior that the overwhelming majority of society's members consider acceptable and beneficial.

Laws serve complementary functions: they are intended to protect each of us from the predatory actions of others and from outrageous acts the government may commit. Simply put by political thinkers from Aristotle to Thomas Aquinas to John Locke, without constant adherence to law, any government is liable to become arbitrary and tyrannical. Locke, for example, argued that

> *whosoever in authority exceeds the power given him by the law, and makes use of the force he has under his command to compass that upon the subject which the law allows not, ceases in that to be a magistrate, and acting without authority may be opposed, as any other man who by force invades the right of another.*[1]

This basically means that without law, society is either chaotic or autocratic. In effect, Locke concludes that if a political authority violates or ignores the law, the authority itself is illegal. We have both the obligation and the right to rebel if that is what it takes to establish a political authority that behaves lawfully. Locke provided the argument against a disreputable government that the American Revolutionaries adopted a century later. As this chapter will emphasize, laws must not only exist, they must possess integrity. Unless both ruler and ruled voluntarily and steadfastly accept and obey them, laws are meaningless.

In this chapter, we will examine notions of law and the various formulations laws take as well as the relationship between law and justice. This examination will also consider where laws come from and how they relate to particular cultures. Finally, the chapter will review the place of the judiciary in the legal system.

---

[1] John Locke, *Second Treatise on Civil Government*, XVIII, pp. 199 and 202.

WHERE LAWS COME FROM AND WHAT THEY ARE FOR

The Reasons for Laws

Crime has always been present in human society, yet both the nature of some crimes and the motivations behind them change over time. Laws must therefore also be flexible and be prepared for change. As we shall see, this is a difficult challenge; since laws enforced over time acquire a degree of respect, society is often reluctant to change them. Criminals, however, often invent new reasons for committing crimes.

Take bank robbery in the United States, for example. Bank robberies have increased dramatically since the 1960s (even though bank robbers are, after kidnappers, the most likely to be caught).[2] Bank robbers in the 1990s, however, are often motivated by more than the desire to get rich quick. Many are now inspired by political ideology: two bank robbers arrested in Ohio in January 1996, for example, had studied racist and other extremist literature published by the Aryan Nations and the Freemen. The two criminals hoped to acquire funds to help support the organizations' political activities and to purchase weapons.[3]

Laws need to be revisited from time to time. A society must bring them up to date, if only because of rapid technological progress. Sometimes entire legal systems must be revamped. On other occasions, a legal system can survive longer than the political institutions that created it. When they formed the United States, the founders retained many legal traditions inherited from Britain. Though they were fighting the British for independence, they respected Britain's legal system—they simply believed the British government was violating its own laws.

When the Soviet regime collapsed in 1991, the Soviet legal system largely survived, at least in the immediate aftermath. This legal system, though, was part of a discredited regime and economy. Much that had been illegal now became legal. Private businesses, for instance, now opened, new political parties formed, and publications critical of government policy sprang up without breaking the law.

Laws and legal codes appeared because human society requires at least a minimum of order and discipline. Plato's Republic, remember, was a vision of society without laws. In fact, Plato's view was that laws were unnecessary since nearly omniscient philosopher-kings could preside over justice. Yet even Plato gave up on this ideal and wrote a sequel to *The Republic* appropriately entitled *Laws*. Neither in Plato's time nor in ours are philosopher-kings commonly available.

The idea that a person's word is his or her bond was a reality for much of human history. Societies were usually small populations made up of people

---

[2] "The Santa Gang," *The Economist*, February 3, 1996, pp. 21–22.

[3] Ibid. These bank robbers and their colleagues were responsible for a series of bank robberies throughout the midwest. They often "disguised" themselves in Santa Claus costumes.

The Nuremberg Trials in 1946 involved the prosecution of Nazi war criminals.

who knew and trusted one another. In such a situation, lawyers were rarely needed. A modern society, though, may be composed of tens or hundreds of millions of people who have complicated business and political dealings with each other but never meet. Lawyers in modern society have become abundant, though not always loved. In the United States, where two-thirds of the world's lawyers practice their profession, "Opinion surveys measuring the public's trust in various professions generally find lawyers ranked just below plumbers (and journalists) and just above taxi drivers, car salesmen, and politicians."[4]

The regulation of human activities by laws rather than the personal whims of an all-powerful (and perhaps pathological) government is a notion that has taken root in numerous countries. Laws that are more or less equally applied to all citizens, including those who govern, do seem to create an environment that the great majority of people have confidence in and will therefore support.

Generally speaking, crimes of violence are universally condemned. No government, even one that commits violence itself, can tolerate individual acts

---

[4] "The Plummeting Price of Justice," *The Economist*, August 10, 1991, p. 53.

of violence. To do so, as Hobbes pointed out three and a half centuries ago, would create chaos and drastically reduce public confidence in government.

However, definitions of criminal acts are not always the same in every country because legal systems are never exactly the same. In the United States, for instance, there is no legal requirement to work. While it is necessary for most of us to pursue careers spanning four decades or more, the wealthy few can cheerfully live off the income from their investments without fear of punitive action on the part of the government. In the Soviet Union, on the other hand, it was against the law not to work. This law made sense in a communist society: those who don't work have no place in a workers' paradise. **Antiparasite laws** thus insured that every able-bodied member of Soviet society fulfilled his or her obligations to labor toward building communism.

Lawgivers and Law Codifiers

It is far from accidental that some of the most memorable political personalities in history were individuals who took a substantial interest in or were authors of the legal system in the countries they governed. We have already referred to Hammurabi in an earlier chapter as the first leader in recorded history to codify laws. The biblical Moses is another example of an early leader who combined political and legal leadership. Moses, of course, was a lawgiver. To a large extent, though, the Mosaic law that evolved over several centuries was both a codification of existing customs and habits and a detailed arrangement for the conduct of daily life. Both the Hammurabic Code and the Mosaic law paid close attention to details of personal behavior. Neither separated the secular from the spiritual.

The history of a society or even a civilization can be characterized by its legal traditions. Ancient Sparta, known for the harsh regimen it imposed on its citizen-soldiers, became a rigid and stern system only after a perhaps mythical law codifier, Lycurgus, admonished Spartans to distrust foreigners, ignore the arts, and devote themselves solely to military training and civic duty. Thus, the term *Spartan* came to mean someone who lives simply and submits to harsh physical discipline. Another Greek law codifier was Draco—an Athenian—who for good reason inspired the term *Draconian legislation*. Draco's code emphasized not the law itself, but what would today be regarded as inhuman punishment for breaking the law.

Lawgivers and law codifiers have left a strong imprint on legal systems. They have also caused considerable debate. Many people assume that laws, especially those with a moral content, are absolutely binding on any generation, regardless of how far removed in time it might be from the original. The ancient legal codes are, to varying extents, still in force. They are applied where laws and punishments against the more heinous crimes of murder and rape have their origins. Most of the ancient lawgivers and codifiers, including those previously named, claimed to be legislating with a divine purpose. As the world has (unevenly) moved into more modern times, though, the authority to make laws has become increasingly secular and more flexible, as we shall see.

In modern societies, it is especially difficult to escape debate on issues that some regard as sacrosanct and others see as reactionary or nonsensical. Natural law and divine law are two concepts that tend to supplement one another. Both assume that a law divinely revealed or reasonably thought out is absolute everywhere, throughout time. An opposing school of thought, known as **positive law,** suggests that absolutism simply doesn't work: change is constantly occurring, and laws cannot remain immutable. Moreover, while different societies undergo change at different paces, they nevertheless remain distinct from one another. Laws that protect one form of behavior in one society may not be found in another society where that particular behavior is patently illegal. Law is a complicated matter.

Law and Morality

Legal systems almost always include some moral values that a society has cherished for generations, sometimes for centuries. Murder was most likely considered immoral long before it became illegal. As one scholar has asserted,

> *It is of course clear (and one of the oldest insights of political theory) that society could not exist without a morality which mirrored and supplemented the law's proscription of conduct injurious to others.*[5]

At the same time, however, the state's physical enforcement of a particular morality is usually self-defeating. While most people would agree we are probably better off adhering to standards of moral conduct, most would also be more likely to adhere to moral standards arrived at through reasoned argument and persuasion.[6]

Laws formalize customs and traditions that have existed for generations. A law works well when:

1. Everyone without exception is obligated to obey it. Laws lose credibility if they don't apply equally to everyone.

2. Compliance is voluntary and nearly universal. A bad or silly law is quickly found out when large segments of the population oppose or simply ignore it. When the United States attempted, through the Constitution's Eighteenth Amendment, to prohibit the sale and consumption of alcoholic beverages in the 1920s, the experiment failed and the constitutional amendment was repealed (the Twenty-first Amendment) because so many people refused to obey a law they regarded as either unnecessary or absurd.

---

[5] H. L. A. Hart, *Law, Liberty, and Morality* (Stanford, California: Stanford University Press, 1963), p. 16.

[6] Ibid., p. 45.

3.   It is enforceable. While most people will obey a reasonable law, a few won't. The state must be prepared to ensure compliance by pursuing the alternatives of incarceration and/or financial penalties.

Morality has always underpinned the law. As one scholar succinctly expressed it, in both civil and criminal cases, the law's "function is simply to enforce a moral principle and nothing else."[7] This seems an easy principle to follow until we remember that morality is supposed to be absolute—that is, never changing—while the law must be flexible.

Laws and Obedience

Most of us generally obey the law because it is almost always in our mutual self-interest to do so. We believe that the law requiring us to stop our cars at red lights, for example, is an excellent idea, and we consistently obey it. In fact, it is difficult to think of one good reason not to do so.

Laws are relatively painless to obey when they make sense. Most laws do make sense most of the time, but it is sometimes questionable whether the punishment for breaking a law is sensible. For example, several western democracies have engaged in a serious debate about drug laws. Is it reasonable to imprison people who commit nonviolent criminal acts such as smoking marijuana? Should a person who uses marijuana to alleviate the discomfort associated with multiple sclerosis be considered guilty of possession of an illegal drug? According to Florida law, such a person is destined to go to prison—and in fact, one has.[8] In another case, a law-abiding dentist who had unwittingly lent money to someone running marijuana was convicted for conspiracy to distribute illegal drugs.[9] Laws that aren't sensible can be expensive; it costs between \$25,000 and \$30,000 annually to imprison one person in the United States.

Still, we are required to obey laws even when we disagree with them. This principle may sound peculiar, but people adhere to it in many cultures and nations, particularly in the democracies. Most laws that result from democratic processes and institutions enjoy nearly universal compliance because of the procedures by which they are adopted and implemented.[10] Moreover, people in democracies know they can resort to the same processes and institutions to change laws they disagree with.

In an increasingly global society, it may be a good idea to have laws that make sense to anyone. With occasional exceptions, Americans find it easy to obey laws in other democracies, for example. Although they encounter some

---

[7] Patrick Devlin, "Morals and the Criminal Law," in David Spitz, ed., *On Liberty, John Stuart Mill* (New York and London: W. W. Norton, 1975), p. 179.

[8] Anthony Lewis, "First, Do Less Harm," *The New York Times*, March 1, 1996, p. A15.

[9] Ibid.

[10] R. A. Dahl, "Political Opposition in Western Democracies," in R. A. Dahl, ed., *Political Opposition in Western Democracies* (New Haven: Yale University Press, 1965), p. 390.

The abortion debate: little room for compromise.

unaccustomed inconveniences in nondemocratic systems, such as restrictions on personal travel, the inconveniences are modest compared to those the permanent residents of these countries usually endure.

Nearly all legal systems contain numerous common features. This is hardly surprising, since all members of these societies are human. The fact that we all experience similar needs and apprehensions suggests that a universal legal system might apply to everyone.

Throughout the western democracies, an independent judiciary has been instrumental in protecting individual rights. Many democracies, particularly the English-speaking ones, build on the judicial outcomes of cases. Courts do not explicitly make law—that task belongs to the legislatures—but they do interpret laws. The result is **case law.** The courts often make meaningful changes in existing laws by interpreting the law in new ways.

As an example, the United States Supreme Court legalized abortion in January 1973 in *Roe v. Wade.* This one decision forced several states to revise their abortion laws because any Supreme Court decision becomes the law of the land. The Court would have to reverse its decision or Congress would have to pass a constitutional amendment (which two-thirds of the states would then have to ratify) for the United States to again outlaw abortion.

Why did the Court issue its 1973 opinion legalizing abortion? No previous Court had done so mainly because neither its members nor the public was ready to accept such an outcome. The Court was aware of changing public sentiment and a growing women's movement, and they changed the law to reflect those trends. This is not to say that abortion became any less controverisal after *Roe v. Wade;* quite the contrary. Nevertheless, this example shows how case law reflects changing social and technological circumstances—abortion became more acceptable as a growing number of women argued that their bodies were their own domain and no one else's, and as the medical profession became better able to develop safe procedures.

CASE LAW AND CODE LAW

In modern societies, the law for several generations has appeared to lag behind social and technological developments. For example, in 1900, the average life span in the United States was 48 for men and 51 for women. By the late 1990s, these numbers had increased to 73 and 80, respectively. Congress enacted new laws against age discrimination and developed new programs for health care, social security, and welfare. Legal systems and judicial interpretations of the law undergo change because society is not static. Case law has demonstrated its usefulness as judges face new social, economic, and technological conditions and render decisions accordingly.

While the English-speaking democracies have relied heavily on case law, most other democracies, especially on the European continent, rely on **code law.** For Americans unfamiliar with code law, its most remarkable and perhaps most frightening aspect is the absence of an automatic presumption of innocence in a criminal case. Still, an accused individual is far from unprotected. A code of laws gives as much opportunity to someone charged with a crime to demonstrate innocence as it gives a prosecutor to demonstrate guilt. A trial judge in a code law system can and usually does take a more participatory role than his or her counterpart in a case law system. For example, the judge does not hesitate to question witnesses.

In the English-speaking democracies, it is difficult to imagine a trial without a jury. Justice appears to be better served when a panel of jurors evaluates a defendant's plea of innocence—jurors who have been carefully screened by both the defense and prosecution to ensure fairness. Nevertheless, jurors come from all walks of life, and few are extremely familiar with the law. For obvious reasons, such jurors may or may not follow the letter of the law in rendering a decision.

Countries that have long relied on judges or tribunals are slowly adopting the jury system in selected categories of cases. Spain, for example, has turned to jury trials for fraud cases. However, some cases are so complex that jurors are understandably unable to reach a verdict. The details of a 1994 murder trial in the United Kingdom were so intricate that several jurors used a *oujia* board in an attempt to consult one of the murder victims![11] Their eventual guilty verdict was later reversed for that reason.

Case law is an evolving set of legal principles whose origins trace back to English **common law.** Common law is also based on judicial decisions, some of which go back to the Middle Ages. By the seventeenth century, the English began collecting and systematizing these decisions into a body of law. **Statute law,** law enacted by a parliament or other legislative body, came later; it supplements and supersedes case law.

Modern code law goes back two centuries to the **Napoleonic Code,** named after Napoleon, founder of the first French Empire (1804–1815). The Napoleonic Code evolved in early nineteenth-century France and was adopted (sometimes in revised form) by Belgium, Italy, the Netherlands, Portugal, and Spain. A century later, the German Civil Code became the model of codification for Germany's Scandanavian neighbors.

As the French armies conquered and occupied much of Western Europe

---

[11] "A Mystery," *The Economist*, January 27, 1996, p. 51.

during the early 1800s, the French government under Napoleon found the various legal systems archaic. Moreover, because Napoleon intended his empire to endure long after his demise, it was reasonable to conclude that these laws would need to be standardized. Ironically, the Napoleonic Code has long survived the empire and may be the most useful part of its legacy. The Code was instrumental in modernizing European law, first in France and eventually in much of Western Europe. Unlike Britain, France had not developed a tradition of common law. The Code enabled the French to standardize their laws, many of which go all the way back to Roman times.

More than two millenia ago, the Romans developed a very practical legal system after they had conquered the Mediterranean world. As long as local legal systems did not interfere with or pose a challenge to the Roman state's authority, the Romans left the local systems alone. At the same time, though, Rome appreciated *ius naturale*, or natural law. Natural law is law that is universal and absolute: it applies to and prevails over all peoples throughout time.

In nearly all societies, murder is considered the most heinous crime. Other "wrongs" such as thievery, fraud, and rape are severely punishable offenses wherever they occur. These "intrinsically" wrong activities can never be right regardless of circumstances. We know they are wrong because no reasonable mind would doubt their wrongness.

Put another way: some activities are genuinely evil, and they cannot under *any* circumstances be used for good. To emphasize this last point, one sixteenth-century natural law theorist, Hugo Grotius, invoked divine authority as final proof just in case reason doesn't totally convince. Grotius argued that evil is evil and good is good. It is impossible for either to become the other; not even God can make evil into good. As Grotius put it,

> *Just as even God, then, cannot cause that two times two should not make four, so he cannot cause that which is intrinsically evil to be not evil.*[12]

RELIGIOUS LAW

Presumably as rational beings we discern natural law through our ability to reason. For many, however, reason is not an entirely reliable basis. For some, reason can even lead to wrong conclusions, and not everyone entirely trusts reason. On what other basis do people decide right and wrong in order to create laws?

Hundreds of millions of people rely on religious law because they believe it is indisputable. Religious law is, they argue, divinely revealed; it cannot be challenged or appealed. Secular law must therefore be subservient to and consistent with religious morality. Since a criminal act constitutes sin, penalties for sin are

---

[12] Grotius, De jure belli ac pacis, quoted in George H. Sabine and Thomas L. Thorson, eds., *A History of Political Theory*, 4th ed. (Hinsdale, Illinois: Dryden Press, 1973), p. 394.

prescribed in holy writ and the secular authorities implement punishment accordingly. In such a system, usually referred to as a **theocracy,** religious considerations dominate the legal and judicial process.

Generally, religious law neither acknowledges nor condones the western concept of separation of church and state. If, for example, a citizen in a theocracy refuses to respect the Sabbath, the state executes a punishment for sin, whether it be a flogging or a fine. Western society is certainly not without experience in this type of government. The authorities in the earliest American colonies insisted on punctual church attendance. Even today "blue laws" in many American communities require drinking establishments and places of entertainment to close on Sundays.

The judges in theocracies receive training entirely in religious law. They are less free, therefore, to evaluate a case on the basis of their own interpretations. In many instances, they have no discretion at all. Divine law as revealed in holy writ is interpreted literally.

In many political systems, religious law and secular law often conflict. In theocracies, this conflict is minimized because religious law automatically takes precedence over any other legal system. In secular societies, especially those that include substantial religious diversity, certain religious practices that seem perfectly reasonable to the practitioners may violate secular law.

In the early 1990s, France's Muslims represented the largest Islamic community in Western Europe and the second largest denomination in France. Muslim men may marry more than one wife at a time (though this isn't a religious requirement).[13] While this custom is acceptable within Islamic tradition, it violates French law. This presents an unresolved controversy in France and may introduce one into other western countries where Muslim communities have formed.[14]

Different societies, though, encounter different problems. In the United Kingdom, the state must support religious schools—at least Christian and Jewish schools—as well as the regular school system; this practice is considered unconstitutional in the United States. However, the growing Islamic population in Britain is now seeking to gain state support for their school system.[15] Some of the public fears that Muslims would not teach the usual academic subjects but instead would emphasize religious indoctrination, and they are questioning whether the government should support these schools. Of course, some Christian and Jewish educational facilities probably emphasize religious doctrine over traditional academics as well.

---

[13] Muslim men are allowed to take up to four wives as long as they can fully support their wives.

[14] *The New York Times,* January 26, 1996, pp. A1 and A6. It also isn't necessary for a husband to inform his current wife or wives that he is about to marry again, although he is expected to do so out of simple courtesy. Ibid.

[15] *The Economist,* April 20, 1996.

LAW IN NONDEMOCRATIC STATES

Citizens in western democratic societies are accustomed to seeking the protection of law, and they assume that the state will apply the law fairly and equally. They also expect the law to prevent the state itself from making unwarranted intrusions into their lives and property. Most democratic constitutions include substantial lists of individual protections such as the Bill of Rights (in the American Constitution) or the Rights of Man (in the French).

Other systems have protections, but they are not as formalized. Britain, for example, pioneered such concepts as *habeas corpus* as well as the right of trial by jury, but it has yet to draft a permanent written consititution.[16] Israel, like Britain, also lacks a written constitution. Unlike the Anglo-American systems of justice, however, Israel has refrained from instituting trial by jury, preferring to rely instead on panels of judges.

It is difficult to understate the status of individual rights in nondemocratic states. Put bluntly, the security and welfare of the state takes precedence at all times over individual concerns. Often a regime's leader does not distinguish between his or her desires and law. A dictator only infrequently believes that the rule of law is preferable to his or her personal whim and is usually aghast at the notion that laws should apply to the ruler him or herself.

This is not to say that nondemocratic systems have no legal systems at all. On some levels, there are bodies of laws that actually work. Rigidly totalitarian systems such as Nazi Germany or the Soviet Union retained the usual laws against thievery, for example: these laws would at least be recognizable to citizens in western democracies (though the penalties for such a crime would almost certainly be more harsh than in the West). However, dictatorial regimes are much more concerned with what they regard as **political crimes.** These normally include any demonstration of opposition to the regime's policies or irksome clamoring for the regime to change its ways and guarantee human rights. Such regimes characteristically formulate and enforce laws that violate both human decency and common sense.

Because of a nearly universal respect for the principle of state sovereignty—the jursidiction a regime retains over the internal workings of the country it governs—governments can literally get away with murder if they are willing to ignore world public opinion, the condemnation of human rights organizations, and, at worst, economic sanctions. Most are willing to ignore these external voices, but some do revise or abolish laws the world considers injurious to human welfare. South Africa, for instance, began in the late 1980s to repeal the decades-old apartheid laws that ensured race separation and preserved the economic and political privileges of the white minority. These laws were repugnant to most of the world community. A combination of global displeasure and

---

16 Alexander MacLeod, "Britain's Constitutional Question," *The Christian Science Monitor*, March 3, 1992, p. 12.

economic sanctions seemed to at least accelerate the reforms that led to the establishment of more democratic institutions.

An important distinction between democratic and nondemocratic legal systems has to do with ideology. Racial purification laws in Nazi Germany and economic demands in the Soviet Union are cases in point. During the Nazi regime, Germans were legally forbidden to marry non-Aryans or employ non-Aryan physicians and lawyers (Aryans were whites of Nordic heritage). Some laws were both annoying and insulting: German Jews were legally forbidden to have private vegetable gardens or use public swimming pools. The Nazi ideology held Aryans to be a "superior race," and the laws reflected this thinking.

In the Soviet Union, antiparasite laws asserted that every adult member of a socialist society had a responsibility to work. Since everyone was legally required to work in the Soviet Union, the country technically experienced no unemployment problems. The Soviet and other communist systems stressed **economic rights** in their constitutions—the right of every worker to a pension and free medical treatment. Such a focus stands in stark contrast to the legal and political rights normally guaranteed in western democratic constitutions. In the United States, for example, a citizen has a constitutionally protected right to vote, but not a right or, for that matter, an obligation, to hold a job.

Totalitarian legal systems often attempt to enforce a particular form of human behavior. Article 10 of the 1977 Soviet Constitution, for example, explicitly denied the right of an individual to be selfish. While such a requirement may strike a westerner as bizarre, in the Soviet Union, the legal and judicial systems cooperated with the political and ideological institutions to define acceptable human conduct. In a commonwealth of workers, all laboring for the welfare of the whole, no one had the right to be self-serving.

It may not come as a surprise to learn that the judiciary in a dictatorial system views its mission as protecting state and society *against* the individual. Defense lawyers are state employees. In fact, in the Soviet and Chinese communist systems, it was not unusual for a defense lawyer to occasionally denounce the defendant, particularly if the defendant was accused of heinous "crimes against the state." During the purge trials under Stalin in the Soviet Union during the 1930s, even the defendant might denounce him or herself (usually as a result of torture or threat) and beg the court for punishment (usually by execution). The court rarely turned down such a plea. Defendants who cooperated in enthusiastically condemning themselves were assured that their families would be spared.

Communist ideology became the standard of Soviet law: every able adult was required to work because the ideology insisted upon a society with maximum productivity and with no one benefiting unduly from the labor of others. In sum, many laws in totalitarian society are never revised or updated because the ideology they are based on is itself inflexible. This system works quite well on the state's behalf but is often to the individual's detriment. That, after all, is the intention of the legal system in a communist system: the collective takes both legal and political precedent over the individual members of the society.

The Chinese political system offers a more current case in point. China is still a totalitarian state with a communist party dictatorship firmly in control of the government and the (increasingly capitalist) economy. To continue its rapid economic development, China must keep technologically up to date. Yet the more technology the Chinese adopt, the more legal dilemmas crop up for the state. The regime understands the critical need for information but wants to control its availability. By early 1996, for example, the government published new laws regarding the regulation of the Internet in China.[17] These laws require that a government channel be used for making international connections, overall supervision by the Ministry of Electronics, and the banning of any production, retrieval, or duplication of information considered harmful to state security.[18] The Internet is now apparently emerging as the greatest challenge to totalitarian government.

There is little evidence thus far that China's rapidly expanding economy is helping to democratize its political system. Nor does the legal system seem to be awakening to human rights. China still executes more people annually than the rest of the world's countries combined.[19] Some evidence shows that the situation is actually getting worse: in 1980, twenty-one crimes were punishable by the death penalty; by 1995, this number had risen to eighty.[20]

Governments that are unrepentant about safeguarding basic individual rights are often difficult for westerners to deal with. During the period when the international community began imposing economic boycotts on South Africa, the United States had to decide how to deal with the most prosperous country on the African continent—a country that was also severely violating human rights.

A similar dilemma currently involves the Southeast Asian country of Myanmar (formerly Burma). Some large American companies, such as Levi Strauss, have withdrawn from Myanmar because of the government's miserable human rights record. Pepsico, on the other hand, is steadily increasing its presence.[21] At the same time, the United States Congress is considering imposing economic boycotts on Myanmar, a country with a rapidly growing economy.[22]

Legal and moral arguments trip over each other in such a situation: Levi Strauss has argued that Myanmar's human rights record must improve before it will consider returning. Pepsico, on the other hand, argues that Myanmar will inevitably democratize after its economy grows, and Pepsico will help it economically. They also maintain that, in any case, it isn't up to American corpora-

---

17 Seth Faison, "Chinese Cruise Internet, Wary of Watchdogs," *The New York Times*, February 5, 1996, p. A1.

18 Ibid., p. A3.

19 "China's Arbitrary State," *The Economist*, March 23, 1996, pp. 31–32.

20 Ibid. In 1996, at least two thieves were shot for stealing cows.

21 Seth Mydans, "Pepsi Courts Myanmar, Preferring Sales to Politics," *The New York Times*, February 22, 1996, p. C6.

22 Ibid.

TABLE 7.1   The Federal Court System of the United States

Court	Original Jurisdiction	Appellate Jurisdiction	Caseload (per year)
Supreme **1 Court** **9 Justices**	1. Lawsuits between two or more states 2. Lawsuits between the United States and a state 3. Cases involving foreign ambassadors and other diplomats 4. Lawsuits between a state and a citizen of a different state (if begun by the state)	1. Lower federal courts 2. Highest state court	1. Approximately 130 signed opinions 2. Approximately 4,500 petitions and appeals 3. Fewer than ten cases of original jurisdiction
Appeals **12 Courts** **135 Judges**		1. Federal district courts 2. U.S. regulatory commissions 3. Certain other federal courts	1. Approximately 41,000 cases
District **94 Courts** **515 Judges**	1. Federal crimes 2. Civil suits under federal law 3. Civil suits between citizens of different states when the amount exceeds $50,000 4. Admiralty and maritime cases 5. Bankruptcy cases 6. Review of actions of certain federal administrative agencies 7. Other matters assigned by Congress	(No appellate jurisdiction)	1. Approximately 49,000 criminal cases 2. Approximately 218,000 civil cases

Sources: Annual Report of the Director of the Administrative Office of the United States Courts (Washington, D.C.: Government Printing Office, 1990); Harold W. Stanley and Richard G. Niemi, *Vital Statistics on American Politics*, 2d ed. (Washington, D.C.: Congressional Quarterly Press, 1990); Bureau of the Census, *Statistical Abstract of the United States, 1990* (Washington, D.C.: U.S. Government Printing Office, 1990).

tions to interfere with or dictate foreign policy.[23] Obviously, there is no easy answer. But it is apparent that issues such as human rights under different systems of law will continue to affect the global economy as well as the relationships between democracies and nondemocratic regimes.

JUDICIARIES

Judicial systems are not unlike their executive and legislative counterparts in terms of organization; the higher an agency is in the hierarchy, the greater the prerogatives of the agency. The American federal court system, for example, is arranged as outlined in table 7.1. In addition to the national court system, of

---

[23] Ibid.

course, there are also regional or state and local systems. Even nondemocratic systems seem to generally follow the pattern of higher and lower courts.

The powers and prerogatives of judicial bodies vary from country to country; even democracies differ substantially. The American federal judiciary, for example, long ago established the principle of **judicial review,** or a court's ability to declare an act of the executive or the legislature unconstitutional. Other democratic systems have constitutionally mandated judicial review but limited its application. France's Constitutional Council has been able to decide on the constitutionality of a legislative bill only since 1974. The German Federal Republic's Constitutional Court is specifically charged with protecting individual rights. Interestingly, the Constitutional Court can ban an extremist political party if it concludes that the party's program is potentially injurious to these rights.

The United States places a strong emphasis on separation of the judiciary from the other two branches of the federal government, as well as from the vagaries of public opinion. In a democracy, a judiciary must function beyond the influence or control of other political institutions to maintain impartiality. However, the judiciary in most democracies is not a coequal branch of government. In Britain, for example, no high court can declare a law that parliament has passed unconstitutional. In most parliamentary systems, the parliament's decisions supersede court decisions. Only parliament can reverse, revise, or abolish the laws it enacts.

Other systems have judiciaries that can exert powerful influence but that also reflect the peculiar political cultures of their countries. In Costa Rica, one of the oldest and most stable democracies in Latin America, a special judicial body, called the Supreme Electoral Tribunal oversees and monitors elections to watch for any voting irregularities. The Tribunal can order the results of an election void if it finds evidence of fraud. Many countries, including the United States, do not have an equivalent body, although the normal judicial processes seem to adequately cope with election fraud. Costa Rica, however, does not take the protection of the normal processes for granted.

Judiciaries in most societies are limited in scope. This is true for many of the same reasons that even authoritarian governments are limited in power. The rule of law remains tentative in much of the world, where communication and transportation systems are either primitive or nonexistent. In such places, traditional customs and cultural values underlie much of the legal system, and the people themselves enforce these traditions in an almost religious fashion. To again use our frequent example of Saddam Hussein's regime in Iraq:

> *In 1994, two of his sons-in-law fled with valuable information from Iraq to Jordan. In February 1995 they decided to return. Saddam publically forgave them, but they were quickly killed along with their father and a third brother by a mob in their home town. Their crime had been to embarrass their clan with what was generally perceived to be treason.*

Clan dignity and honor superceded any protections the law or government might offer. It is unlikely that any judicial body in Iraq will have either the desire or the courage to prosecute anyone in this episode. In the Iraqi view, justice was simply meted out to those who had disgraced their clan. In this sense, justice was more important than legality.

Judiciaries have modest authority in parts of the world that either lack or question governmental authority. The relentless advance of technology in modern and modernizing society has created huge gaps in the application of the law. In effect, judicial bodies are often being asked to make determinations where the law may be unclear or may not yet exist. Of course, in many societies formal judicial bodies may not even exist. Justice may simply be left to local village elders or even to public opinion when it comes to crimes that are an affront to the religious or social sensitivities of the population.

Judiciaries in modern societies, in contrast, are practically under seige to increasingly decide what is legitimate privacy and how much of it can or should be protected. The European democracies are somewhat more conscientious about this issue than the American one. In October, 1995 most western European countries jointly established "a comprehensive set of data protection guidelines." Privacy in Europe is protected somewhat more than in the United States where there has been no federal legislation on this issue since 1974. In the quarter century since then much has happened. With the advent of greater access to computer technology it is rather easy to compile dossiers on every American who uses a credit card or a phone. Databases contain an ever growing bank of information on our buying habits, hobbies, the size of our bank accounts and stock portfolios, what we read, and the movies we watch. The databases are found in both government agencies and marketing organizations in the private sector.

In contrast to the United Kingdom, though, the United States is far ahead in its protection of individual rights. Britain does have a Bill of Rights which really tends to emphasize parliamentary prerogatives and it doesn't have a constitution even though four fifths of the population believe that drafting one is a good idea. As discussed in the previous chapter, a law passed by the British parliament cannot be declared unconstitutional by any court. Eventually, either the Congress or the federal judiciary will have to decide to what extent privacy and should protect privacy. Most likely, the judiciary will play the larger role. In the United States, the judiciary has traditionally been the ultimate source for interpreting what the Constitution says and what that means.

The judiciary in most democratic countries simply does not enjoy the relationship with the legislative and executive branches the federal courts in the United States have been designed to enjoy. In particular, the judiciary usually lacks judicial review and the power to overturn executive and legislative decisions. However, the French have a limited form of judicial review in their Constitutional Council. Since 1974, the Council has had the authority, which it infrequently uses, to decide on the constitutionality of a legislative bill. Council members, unlike their U.S. Supreme Court counterparts, do not receive life tenure. The presidents of the Republic, National Assembly, and Senate each choose three justices for nine-year nonrewable terms of office. Thus, it is likely that the justices will represent a variety of viewpoints since the three presidents can come from different political backgrounds.

The German courts also have a form of judicial review. Because of the American occupation of Germany in the immediate years following World War II (1945–1949), a strong American constitutional influence exists. Moreover, both Germany and the United States, unlike the British and French systems, are federal republics with histories of disputes between the state and federal governments. Accordingly, the Germans also have a close approximation of judicial review that tends to emphasize protection of individual rights. In the German version, the executive is completely removed from the selection of justices. Each of the two legislative houses chooses eight justices. The sixteen justices divide their labor: half deal with conflicts between the federal and state governments, while the other half concentrates on individual civil liberties.[24]

The legal process is rarely simple or uncontroversial. The seemingly relentless march of technology has forced all branches of government to deal with legal questions that simply did not arise earlier. The inalienable right to life is in many societies the primary natural right of every citizen. In western societies, citizens are now also grappling with the question of whether every person also has a right to die at a time and place of his or her choosing. Is it legal for a physician, trained to support and sustain life, to ignore state prohibitions against "assisted suicide"? The American courts have not yet made a final ruling on whether assisted suicide is illegal,[25] but the Supreme Court may yet take on the issue.

Independent judiciaries understandably dread court cases that involve strong doses of morality. Life-and-death issues such as abortion, capital punishment, and euthanasia are rarely resolved in the public mind, even after a court decision is made. These issues are constantly revisited because any judicial decision on such a matter usually dissatisfies a large proportion of the citizenry. It may be that when all is said and done, we expect too much of our judicial system precisely because we have placed so much authority for determining right and wrong in its hands.

SUMMARY

1. Nearly every society has instituted some sort of legal system that most of its citizens voluntarily obey. Laws are useful devices that help us understand what constitutes socially acceptable behavior.

2. Ancient legal systems often came from mystical lawgivers who usually claimed that their laws were divinely inspired or sanctioned.

3. Many laws in both ancient and modern societies have their basis in universal moral values that prohibit such actions as murder.

4. Laws also may arise from custom and tradition. A society usually accepts such laws easily.

5. In the end, even in nondemocratic societies, people obey the laws only if they are willing to do so. Laws that make no sense or seem

---

[24] For a succinct summary discussion of the German Constitutional Court, see David P. Conradt, *The German Polity*, 3d ed. (New York and London: Longman, 1986), pp. 204–6.

[25] "Dr. Death Walks," *The Economist*, March 16, 1996, pp. 34–35.

out of step with the times are either ignored or challenged.

6. Case law has evolved primarily in the English-speaking democracies; its origins trace back at least a millenium. Code law usually prevails in the continental European countries.

7. Countries that apply religious law are rarely democratic. Regimes employing religious law in effect do not distinguish between church and state. Instead, they invoke the precepts of a particular faith to govern the society and to attempt to control elements of daily human behavior.

8. Other kinds of nondemocratic systems apply laws in a discriminatory fashion; these laws are often based on the personal whim of a dictator, or emphasize the ideology the regime has adopted.

9. Judiciaries are not always independent from or uninfluenced by the government, especially in dictatorial regimes. In democratic systems, judiciaries usually have the opportunity to make independent decisions and to affect the political process itself.

10. With the relentless advance of technology, judiciaries may be asked to resolve questions beyond the expertise and interests of the judges.

GLOSSARY

antiparasite laws   Instituted by the Soviet government, these laws discouraged laziness by requiring all members of Soviet society to work.

case law   Law based on judicial interpretations of existing laws and statutes. Court decisions become law themselves.

code law   Law based on written codes that give judges little leeway in interpreting established laws.

common law   Law based on judicial decisions that trace back to the Middle Ages in Britain. Common law is the antecedent of case law.

economic rights   The right to a pension and guaranteed medical treatment, earned by each able-bodied individual who fulfills his or her duty to work in a socialist or communist system.

judicial review   A court's ability to declare an act of the executive or the legislature unconstitutional, whether on the state or national level.

laws   Rules that formalize and reinforce patterns of social behavior that the overwhelming majority of society's members consider acceptable and beneficial.

political crimes   Acts that demonstrate opposition to a regime's policies or that clamor for change.

positive law   The philosophy that law is what a particular society decides it is for itself alone, not an absolute.

statute law   Law based on parliamentary or congressional legislation.

Political Parties and Electoral Systems

This chapter has two goals. The first is to examine the purpose of political parties, different kinds of political party systems, the relationship between parties and interest groups, and the impact of party politics on government formation. The second goal is to review the various kinds of electoral systems and how they influence and even shape the outcomes of elections. Particularly in the democracies, the character of the electoral system can determine in great part how parties operate and how successfully they compete.

THE PURPOSE OF POLITICAL PARTIES

Political parties are present in all democratic and most nondemocratic systems. In democracies, a political party is interested in two main activities: winning elections (and increasing the number of its members holding public office), and exercising political power to advocate or oppose different pieces of economic and social legislation. Most parties tend to be pragmatic rather than ideological: they prefer to win elections rather than consistently go down to defeat while preserving a purist ideology that irritates most voters. Finally, parties in democracies regularly participate in constitutionally guaranteed elections.

A party in a nondemocratic system is another thing. It is often the creation and/or the tool of a dictator who uses the party to retain and expand his power. Such a party is uninterested in holding, let alone participating in, regular and free elections. Since such parties usually ban political opposition, there isn't much point to elections, anyway. As we shall see, though, a single-party system occasionally does find elections useful. Its candidates can't lose, and even an election that is obviously rigged provides a small degree of legitimacy for the regime.

In yet another arrangement, a nonparty system, all parties are banned as a public nuisance. Absolute monarchies such as Saudi Arabia and Brunei have never allowed parties to function in any modern sense. These regimes equate political parties—not entirely incorrectly—with political opposition and factionalism, which they in turn equate with treason.

In this chapter, we will concentrate mostly on political systems that include parties. One-party systems, of course, are not competitive, although intraparty competition may flare up between factions that represent a spectrum of ideological viewpoints or interpretations. In a one-party system, personalities also matter; competition between claimants to party leadership can become strident. This often occurs when a founding leader such as V. I. Lenin in the Soviet Union or Mao Tse-Tung in China die (in 1924 and 1976, respectively) and potential successors fight to inherit the mantle of leadership.

In a single-party system, the party serves a quite different purpose than its counterparts in multiparty political systems, where several parties submit their programs to an electorate on a regular basis. The party is less concerned with elections than it is with retaining and expanding the party elite's control. The Soviet Union, for example, was often referred to as a party-state because the party created and used the state to carry out the party's ideological programs and to preserve the elite's privileges.

Finally, intensely nationalist and theocratic political parties are currently functioning in several developing countries that are in the process of becoming political democracies. We can briefly mention two examples in this space: the Islamic Welfare Party in Turkey and the BJP in India. Both parties have done very well in free elections, are in power in several states and regions, and have achieved national electoral success. Both advocate a rigorously religious lifestyle for the citizenry, insisting on strict adherence to religious holidays, dietary laws and standards of feminine modesty, and supporting morality with the full strength of the state.

POLITICAL PARTIES

Party Recruitment: Leaders and Followers

It is difficult to imagine a functioning democracy without a competitive political party system. Yet parties arose in the more mature democracies as an afterthought, and people often distrusted them, believing them to be sources of social division. In several cases, parties were instead the *result* of social division. In retrospect, political parties seem to be a natural development in almost any democracy: like-minded people tend to associate with one another in a political organization to pursue agreed-upon political goals.

Political parties certainly seemed to develop as an outgrowth of the democratic process. As the franchise (right to vote) was extended in the democracies during the nineteenth century, parties evolved as vehicles for winning elections. Parties were unnecessary before voters and elections existed; officeholders who were appointed to or inherited their positions had little need to form political organizations, preferring instead to develop and rely on personal followings.

With the advance of democracy in North America and Western Europe, political leaders realized they needed to organize to win elections and remain in office. In fact, this lesson has not been lost on leaders in nondemocratic systems. In single-party states such as Iraq, party organization is important not for campaigning but for mobilizing masses of people to appear "spontaneously" at strategic times to support and celebrate the political leadership. The sight of hundreds of thousands or millions of people surging down a capital city's main avenues chanting their leader's name can be impressive to an outsider and, even more importantly, to the participants themselves.

In authoritarian systems, parties also can provide the means for getting ahead politically. A substantial proportion of the adult population normally join the only legally sanctioned party because of the benefits membership can bring: better housing and food, educational facilities, and health care and, for those at the upper rungs, a car and perhaps travel abroad. Party members are genuinely loyal to and work hard on behalf of the regime since they have an important stake in its survival.

The politically ambitious in democratic societies quickly learn that they will get nowhere without the support and label of a political party. It is rare for anyone in the United States or the United Kingdom, for example, to be elected to office without a party endorsement. One of the rare exceptions is Strom Thurmond of South Carolina, who was elected to the United States Senate on a write-in vote as an independent in 1954. No one else in modern times has been able to equal that feat. Even nationally known or popular figures such as Sony Bono, a comedian-singer who was elected to Congress in 1994, require a party label to have any realistic hope of success.

Of course, some party systems are less strict than others when it comes to recruiting leadership. In the parliamentary systems of East Asia and Western Europe, an aspiring officeholder is expected to work her or his way through the ranks. In Britain, for example, a young man or woman who aspires to eventually become a cabinet minister usually starts out in one of the 650 single-member districts as one of several potential party candidates. Once the party selects him or her, this young politician is expected to tow the party line in her or his constituency even if this guarantees electoral defeat. Defeat in this sort of situation may actually benefit a candidate; local party selection committees see the candidate as dependable. The reward for party loyalty frequently is an opportunity to stand for a seat in a "safe" district the party has traditionally done well in.

Primary elections in parliamentary systems are rare. The local district party organization—not the voters—interviews applicants and then chooses the party candidate. Once a parliamentary seat is secured, its holder is still obligated to submit to party authority: vote the party line, he or she is told, and refrain from speaking during parliamentary sessions unless the leadership requests your comments. A young party member may then gain opportunities to move from the back to the front benches if he or she holds the seat in reelection campaigns and as vacancies in junior ministries become available. A noncooperative individual or political maverick has little chance to rise in the party hierarchy in a parliamentary system. Few people get to parliament without passing the party leaders' careful screening.

Britain's Prime Minister Tony Blair and Cherie, his wife.

Sometimes, the process is put on the fast track in times of desperation. When Britain's Labour party chose Tony Blair as party leader, he was still in his late thirties. The party was desperate to revive its electoral fortunes; between 1979 and 1992, Labour had lost four consecutive elections. This was enough to induce both the party leadership and rank-and-file members to move the younger generation up on the fast track. When Blair became prime minister in 1997, he also became the youngest British head of government in the twentieth century.

The United States is an unusual political system because it is possible to achieve the highest political offices without moving through the party ranks. Only infrequently does one move directly, say, from the Congress to the presidency. In fact, this hasn't happened since the 1960 election placed Senator John Kennedy in the White House.

Dwight Eisenhower, a national military hero, became president without holding any prior political office or even belonging to any political party. Yet Eisenhower is an exception. Despite the lip-service given to the notion of "citizen-politicians" the experienced politician equipped with a long record of service to his or her state, country, and party, usually becomes a candidate for president. The two major party candidates for president in 1996, for example, had both political longevity and party service. The Republican candidate, Bob Dole, rose through the ranks of his party during his long tenure in Congress (1961–1996). The Democratic candidate, Bill Clinton, had served six terms as governor of Arkansas before moving into the White House in 1993.

One-party systems are far more exclusive. No matter how well known or popular a military or sports hero may be, he or she has no political standing unless a member of the party organization. In one-party systems, membership in the only legal party makes one a member of the political elite. The former communist systems of Eastern Europe and the current ones in China and Cuba offer excellent examples of this.

To attain political greatness in a communist system, one must begin early, usually by joining the communist youth league. In the former Soviet Union, a child could start the process by joining the preadolescent Young Octoberists. The party carefully screened promising youths who applied for party membership to insure they would be loyal to the leadership and ideology. Admittance to full party membership in the typical communist system included a probationary period of one to two years.

Absolute loyalty to party doctrine and the pronouncements of the leaders was required. Once accepted, the communist party member remained a member for life unless he or she became the victim of a purge. During the dictatorship of Joseph Stalin (1923–1953), an atmosphere of paranoia pervaded both the Soviet state and the communist party. Millions of party members were expelled, thousands were put on trial for counterrevolutionary activities, and most of them were executed or sent off, sometimes with their families, to Siberian labor camps—which usually amounted to a death sentence.

From the 1960s through the end of the communist regime in 1991, the 6 to 8 percent of the adult population that belonged to the Soviet communist party became a privileged class in a theoretically classless society. Recruiters began to focus on the children of party members in good standing. In the end, the Soviet communist party was the most corrupt political institution in the country. It also was apparently the most incompetent. As the Soviet economy deteriorated and verged on collapse, the party hierarchy, the *apparatchiks*, were obsessed with retaining their privileges. In the last years, they were hopelessly out of touch with the needs of the citizenry, tied to an outmoded and dated ideology, and helpless or unwilling to implement desperately needed reforms.

While the Soviet example may be extreme, there is little doubt that one-party systems are, at best, inefficiently responsive to the country's citizenry. Recruitment of both leaders and rank-and-file members tends to become incestuous. Eventually, the more qualified people in society are excluded from recruitment and governance. The party gradually loses its effectiveness and loses the confidence and respect of the governed.

Political Parties and Interest Groups

Interest groups are fixtures in every political system and are very visible in democratic politics. In fact, it is as difficult to imagine a democracy without active interest groups as it is to imagine a democracy with no political parties. An interest group is an organization of individuals who seek to influence the outcome of government policies on issues of special concern to them. Prolife and prochoice organizations, for example, are especially interested in legislation that determines abortion policy. To have its way, an interest group may raise money on behalf of a candidate sympathetic to its point of view and mobilize volunteers to work on behalf of that candidate in a political campaign.

Depending upon their resources and expertise, an interest group can provide a great deal of help to a candidate who has a shortage of both. Better endowed organizations such as the American Medical Association and the National Rifle Association can generate letter-writing campaigns to people already in office as well as raise much needed and often substantial sums of money for the candidate's campaign. The arrival of large numbers of faxes, telegrams, letters, and electronic messages can be very persuasive to an officeholder soon to seek reelection or a candidate hoping to win political office.

Interest groups frequently exercise influence beyond their numbers on both parties and government, but their influence is usually consistent with their resources. Some kinds of interest groups may represent an overwhelming number of members of an organization; this is especially true of **professional interest groups,** which exert influence on behalf of members of certain professions. Most practicing attorneys in the United States, for example, belong to the American Bar Association (ABA). The ABA regularly assumes it speaks for all lawyers by protecting what it views as the interests of the profession.

Interest groups are also called (usually by their critics) lobbying or pressure groups. Whichever term is applied, their function is the same: to advance the cause of a group's political agenda, which is usually centered around a position on a particular issue or a small set of similar issues. Interest groups tend to be single-minded. Some consider their cause of such overriding importance that their support for or opposition to a party or a candidate depends solely upon the position the candidate has taken on the relevant issue.

Interest groups are frequently at odds with and in competition with one another. The competition seems to be especially severe in the case of **single-issue interest groups,** or groups that seek to shape policy on one particular issue. Legislation considered favorable to one interest group can be viewed as detrimental to another. Animal rights' activists, for example, have encountered unexpected opposition from AIDS activists.[1] The animal rights' groups don't want animals used for medical and scientific experimentation that is often painful and lethal to the animals. AIDS activists argue that while it is unfortunate that medical research may result in pain and death to animals, the experiments are conducted to relieve human suffering and save human lives. The lives of human beings, they argue, are more important than those of animals, and experimentation is needed if AIDS is to be cured or a preventative innoculation is to be developed.

Such dilemmas are not uncommon. Few causes are, after all, devoid of controversy. Even consumer and health groups whose efforts have tremendous popular support occasionally encounter organizations such as the American Civil Liberties Union, whose lawyers worry whether a ban on television commercials for tobacco products may be an abridgement of the First Amendment's freedom of speech clause.

Interest groups in democracies often link their prospects for success with a political party that suits their ideological needs. The British Labour party, for example, in part grew out of the trade union movement it has been closely associated with throughout its history. Unions are the most vocal and largest support base for many democratic socialist parties throughout Western Europe, while business, commercial, and professional organizations tend to align with parties to the moderate right of center. Britain's Conservative party, Germany's and Italy's Christian Democratic parties, and the United States's Republican party are all noteworthy examples.

Larger parties understandably enjoy and depend upon the support of numerous interest groups. Occasionally, though, a large national party may become too closely associated with a particular interest group for its own good. One of the misfortunes to befall the British Labour party during the 1980s was the public perception that the large trade union bosses almost completely controlled Labour's organization and parliamentary members. Regardless of whether the perception was the reality, it was strong enough to convince sub-

---

[1] "Weekend Edition," NPR, June 23, 1996.

stantial numbers of voters that Labour was not a national political party so much as a vehicle functioning expressly to serve the demands of trade unions.

There is little doubt that interest groups are both important and powerful (though their power should not be overestimated). Many have the ability to raise the huge amounts of money candidates and parties require to run their campaigns and maintain their organizations between campaigns. American politics is especially susceptible to interest group influence because many candidates for Congress tend to be on their own and can often expect little or no support from the party organization. If they aren't independently wealthy, congressional candidates need and depend upon contributions from interest groups.

This is in substantial contrast to the European democracies, where party discipline is so strong that interest groups are hard put to exert influence on individual members of parliament. No member of a typical European parliament, for example, can afford to offend his or her party leadership; to do so risks political disaster. The decision to choose between party loyalty and interest group pressure doesn't require a great deal of thought. "Whatever an interest group might threaten to do to a deputy who doesn't vote as it wants, it is nothing compared with what the party will do if the deputy doesn't vote as *it* wants."[2]

In contrast, American candidates for political office can be very accommodating to well-heeled interest groups, perhaps because they feel they have little choice. Consider the expense of running a campaign for the U. S. House of Representatives or the Senate in 1996: the average expenditures of $1 million for a House seat and $8 million for a Senate seat[3] can be very compelling arguments to a candidate considering accepting an interest group donation.

It's safe to say that while nearly every political society has interest groups, sometimes thousands of them,[4] interest groups have more freedom to operate and are a lot more active and independent in the democracies. They also exist and compete, however, in nondemocratic societies, and they often have goals similar to those of their democratic counterparts. Ultimately, any interest group serves its own interests. During the Soviet Union's final years, its most powerful interest group, the *nomenklatura* (the top 250,000 or so communist party bureaucrats and their families) fought desperately to preserve its own prerogatives, including access to luxurious housing and cars and quality food and medical care unavailable or unaffordable to the rest of the society.

In the average authoritarian system, the most powerful interest group may be the military and/or a landed aristocracy, as many Latin American countries have demonstrated for most of the twentieth century. Even a single family with numerous retainers may become the most influential group. A few hundred

---

[2] Michael Gallagher, Michael Laver, Peter Mair, *Representative Government in Western Europe* (New York: McGraw-Hill, 1992), p. 134.

[3] "All Things Considered," NPR, June 4, 1996.

[4] By the early 1990s, the United States had an official count of nearly 4,200 Political Action Committees (PACs). Each one represents an interest group with a political concern.

princes of the house of Saud control Saudi Arabia. In Iraq, control ultimately rests in the hands of a single clan from the town of Tikrit—Saddam Hussein, his immediate family, and dozens of lesser relatives.

Types of Party Systems in Democracies

Democratic party systems tend to fall into two general categories: strong two-party systems and multiparty systems. Many of the English-speaking democracies favor two parties. However, a significant and permanent third party exists in the United Kingdom, and occasional third parties, and, in some cases, fourth and fifth parties, arise from time to time in Canada, Australia, and the United States. The Western European countries usually have institutionalized multiparty systems. Newer democracies such as India and Japan also enjoy the benefits and disadvantages of multiparty systems.

In the United States, the Democratic and Republican parties over time created a duopoly that emphatically discourages the rise of third parties. Third-party movements or individual candidacies have sprung up at the national level with varying degrees of success. Substantial third-party efforts were mounted in the modern presidential races of 1948, 1968, 1980, 1992, and 1996. At the local level, though, third-party movements have been regularly squeezed out of the electoral process for lack of funding and an ability to secure even a modest core of popular support.[5] The Republican party, founded in 1854, is the only successful third-party movement in American history. Within a few years of its founding, the Republican party overtook and replaced the fading Whig party.[6]

The two-party system suggests in theory that two major political organizations control the policy process. Keep in mind, though, that a two-party system frequently means one or the other party is politically dominant for decades or even generations at a time. Table 8.1 summarizes some major examples of party dominance in different democratic systems. Whether a long epoch of one-party dominance is healthy or desirable for political democracy is debatable. But regardless of one's position on this issue, the dominance is the result of regularly held free elections.

The two-party system usually creates a clear winner—though not always. Some fundamentally two-party systems include permanent third parties that occasionally win enough parliamentary seats to prevent either major party from securing a majority. Two important examples include the Liberal party in the United Kingdom and the Free Democratic party in Germany. Both parties suffer from severe electoral disadvantages, as we will soon see; yet both cause the major parties to look over their shoulders. None of the major parties in either the United Kingdom or Germany has won a majority of the popular vote since the 1950s.

---

[5] *The Economist*, May 18, 1996, pp. 23, 25

[6] The Whig party seemed doomed, anyway. During its entire history, the Whigs were able to elect only two presidents, both of whom died in office. One of them died thirty days after inauguration.

TABLE 8.1   Party Dominance in Some Major Democracies

Country	Political Party	Period of Time
Germany	Christian Democratic	1949–1969 and 1982–present
Israel	Labor	1949–1977
Japan	Liberal Democratic	1947–1993
United Kingdom	Conservative	1951–1964 and 1979–1997
United States	Democratic	1933–1993*

* This sixty-year period reflects a Democratic-dominated Congress interrupted infrequently and briefly by a Republican majority in one or both houses.

In a parliamentary democracy, a political party participates in a national election in hopes of securing control of both the legislative and executive branches in one effort, or at least of winning enough parliamentary seats to help form a coalition government with one of the other parties. The majority party leader or the leader of a block of parties with a parliamentary majority takes control of the government and becomes prime minister. A vote for the party of choice is in effect a vote for a head of government.

The United States presents a major exception to this rule. Because it is a presidential rather than a parliamentary system, the American system is often characterized by divided government or, less politely, gridlock. Republican President George Bush, for example, faced a Democratic congressional majority during his term (1989–1993), while his successor, Democratic President Bill Clinton, was confronted with a Republican congressional majority halfway through his first term (1993–1997). A more durable episode of gridlock occurred from 1969 to 1993, when the Republicans controlled the presidency (except during the Carter years, 1977–1981), but never controlled both houses of Congress.

Multiparty Systems

Multiparty systems are more common than two-party systems. Many of the smaller parties in a multiparty systems tend to resemble **single-issue interest groups,** forming around one issue and attempting to make policy on it. During the 1950s, the West German Federal Republic system included the Refugees Party. The Refugees succeeded in securing parliamentary seats but eventually dissolved since their concern—getting ample government assistance for East German refugees—was satisfied as the refugees integrated into the growing West German economy. During the same period, the Poujadist party in France achieved temporary success simply by calling for an abolition of most taxes. It was, in effect, an antitax party.

Other small parties have substantial staying power. **Regional** or **separatist political parties** have appeared in several Western European democracies. In Italy, for instance, the Lombard League seeks to detach the northern half of the country from the remainder or—what amounts to the same thing—throw the southern portion out of the Italian state. The Lombard League is convinced that the south is a drag on an otherwise prosperous economy. In Britain, the Plaid Cymru, or Welsh Nationalist party, and the Scot Nationalist party (generally and affectionately referred to in Britain as the Welshnats and Scotnats) draw a respectable segment of the vote, usually between 20 and 30 percent in their respective regions. Both desire separation from, or at least greater autonomy in, an English-dominated United Kingdom. These parties contribute to the weakness of the two-party system and even hint at the rise of a multiparty system, at least in their respective regions, since both the Welshnats and Scotnats regularly win parliamentary seats.

In some multiparty systems, such as India and Israel, **religious parties** have consistently done well at the polls. In 1996, both countries held national elections that brought these parties unprecedented successes. While the religious parties in both countries received only about a fifth of the popular vote, this is a very significant proportion in a multiparty system and normally cinches their inclusion in a coalition government.

Extremist parties, parties with radical viewpoints on the left and the right, can also do well in multiparty systems and can even threaten the larger parties' dominance. Since the 1980s, the National Front in France has regularly drawn support from 15 to 20 percent of the electorate in national elections. The Front has done even better on the local level and controls the municipal governments in several large cities. The National Front's political program is basically anti-immigrant and antisemitic.

Communist parties have traditionally represented the extreme left in most parliamentary systems. In some parliamentary systems of Western Europe, they have attracted rather sizable followings, and in France, they are the junior partners in a coalition government with the Socialists. The Italian communist party was the most successful, often winning as much as 30 percent of the popular vote in national elections. Italian communists did even better in local elections and won mayorships and municipal council majorities in several Italian cities. For a time, the Italian party was the largest communist party in Europe and the second largest party in Italy. The end of the Cold War significantly reduced the electoral hopes of communists and all but wiped the party out in some countries. It has occasionally resurfaced under another name, such as the Party of Democratic Socialism in Germany, professing a less doctrinaire political program.

Mainstream parties are usually the biggest and most successful players in a multiparty system. A mainstream party normally receives a fourth to a third of the total vote. It is rare but not unheard of for such a party to win a majority; the Liberal Democratic party in Japan did so for decades. Most of the time, though, a multiparty system has a strong party slightly to the left of center and one to the right. The leftist party usually is called the Socialist, Social Democratic, or Labor party, while the rightist one is the Conservative or Christian Democratic party. Whatever they are called, these parties tend to be centrist and moderate though they also come equipped with hardline wings on either the left or the right—or, on occasion, both.

These are the parties that are the principal opponents in national elections and the ones that lead in the formation of coalition governments. Typically, a large party with the greatest electoral support attempts to form a government by combining forces with one or several of the smaller parties. This is not always an easy feat. Smaller parties invited to join the government are expected to be ideologically compatible, willing to accept ministerial posts in proportion to their parliamentary numbers, and committed to remaining in the government for the term of office. As one might guess, it doesn't always work out quite that way.

With some justification, multiparty systems can claim to be more democratic than two-party systems. In a multiparty system, every constituency of any significant size in an electorate can usually find a political vehicle to express its point of view. Consider, for example, the names of some of the parties found in multiparty systems: the Women's Rights party, the Agrarian or Farmers', the Veterans', the Green or Environmentalist, and the Refugees. Some of these parties sound rather exotic to American voters unless they realize that we have had parties that called themselves the Vegetarians and the Prohibitionists. Of course, interest groups operating in two-party systems are perfectly capable of articulating their point of view within one or both of the parties; in this sense, one could argue that interest groups make two-party systems more democratic.

One group of parties in multiparty systems is in reality composed of interest groups, since such parties are normally concerned only with a particular issue they consider to be of paramount importance. The Green party that has earned uneven electoral success since the 1980s in Germany is an example. Greens often pursue with relentless dedication a narrow platform that their followers regard as all-consuming. Most of these parties understandably appeal to a hard-core constituency that only infrequently expands into a broader base, but they frequently possess the electoral ability to win parliamentary seats and can hold the balance of power when a larger party is attempting to form a coalition government.

A second group of parties tend to be characterized by strong ideological statements with long histories. The socialist parties active in Western European politics since the beginning of the twentieth century provide the best example. Their platforms tend to be strongly ideological. Many of them, however, have mellowed over the last few decades—perhaps because mellowing has become a requirement for political survival. Many West European Socialist parties met little electoral success during recent decades. They have had to seriously modify their programs and subscribe to the advantages of a strong free market to appeal to a growing middle-class electorate. Once they make this move to the center, socialists then find themselves less socialist and more electorally successful. By the mid-1990s, nine out of fifteen members of the European Union had left-of-center governments.

A third kind of party in a multiparty system is one that emerges with enough strength to dominate the government without the need for coalition partners. This is unusual, but it has occurred in a number of countries. Until recently, the Liberal Democratic Party in Japan and the Congress party in India won elections so resoundingly that the several opposition parties combined did hold as many parliamentary seats.

A fourth situation in a multiparty system is a transitional system that is in the process of becoming more streamlined. When Germany's sovereignty was restored after World War II in 1949, a dozen or so parties competed in the first parliamentary elections. Most of them won seats. By the late 1950s, the number of parties capable of winning seats had been reduced to three, and Germany appeared headed for a two-party system. In recent years, however, the number of viable parties increased to five, in part because of the new political constellation produced by East Germany's unification with the Federal Republic in 1990. It now appears that Germany is reverting to a multiparty system.

The results of the 1994 elections to the German lower house, the Bundestag, are instructive (table 8.2). Members can earn seats in either local or national elections. Only two parties, the Christian Democrats and Social Democrats, have the ability to win races in districts that elect just one member from all candidates. The other parties all rely on winning at least 5 percent of the national popular vote, and thus earning that portion of seats. Occasionally, a small party may be strong enough regionally to win seats directly in a few districts where it may have a regional stronghold. The only party to do this in recent elections is the Party of Democratic Socialism, which received only 4.4 per-cent nationally but won in four districts, all of them in the old communist party stronghold of eastern Germany. The party therefore gained some Bundestag seats.[7]

More extremist parties are usually ignored when it comes to forming a coalition government because their agendas are unacceptable to other potential coalition partners. Of course, some parties generally considered extreme can do so well in elections that it is politically impossible to shut them out. Parliamentary results in the world's largest democracy, India, provide a case in point. One political party, the Bharatiya Janata Party (BJP) stands for strong Hindu nationalism and is widely regarded as oppositional to the interests of non-Hindus (about 15 percent of the population, or close to 150 million people). One of its political goals was to advocate the destruction of an Islamic mosque built on the site of an ancient Hindu temple, enabling the construction of a new Hindu temple. Despite its extreme position, the BJP won more seats in the May 1996 elections—194 out of 534—than any other party.

Of course, not all religiously oriented parties are extremist, nor are all extremists successful at the polls. In some countries, such as Israel, a hard core of religious enthusiasts can usually guarantee a steady turnout at the polls. In the most recent elections (May 1996), religious parties achieved their traditional goal of insuring that neither of the major parties would be able to secure a majority of seats. One would have to outbid (or perhaps outbribe) the other to win the support of the religious party leadership in order to form a government.

---

[7] *Fact Sheet*, October 18, 1994, p. 2.

TABLE 8.2   1994 Bundestag Election Results

Political Party	Percent of Popular Vote	Number of Seats
Christian Democrats*	41.5	294
Christian Democratic Union	[34.2]	[244]
Christian Socialist Union	[7.3]	[50]
Free Democrats	6.9	47
Social Democrats	36.4	252
Alliance/Greens	7.3	49
Party of Democratic Socialism**	4.4	17

Source: Fact Sheet, October 18, 1994, German Information Center, pp. 1–2.
* Combines the national Christian Democratic Union and the Bavarian Christian Socialist Union.
** The Party of Democratic Socialism is led and supported by former members of the East German communist party and is based primarily in the former communist territory.

In more secular systems, such as Germany's, both major parties may be denied outright majorities in one parliamentary election after another because of a third party, in Germany's case, the Free Democrats. Since 1949, the Free Democrats have been the junior partner in every German government, except the one ruling from 1966 to 1969, even though they consistently receive less than 10 percent of the popular vote.

We can draw a few general conclusions regarding smaller but viable political parties. They can

1. be confident they will be decisive in determining which of the larger parties forms the government;

2. hold the balance of power and earn inclusion in any new government, usually with a disproportionately large number of cabinet ministries; and

3. exert power over their larger coalition partner(s) by threatening to leave the government, thereby reducing or eliminating the government's parliamentary majority, unless their policy preferences are at least partially placated.

Two-Party Systems

A two-party system is not always as simple as it sounds. Two-party systems are rarely pristine. Third parties frequently appear and can seriously challenge one or both major parties and, on infrequent occasions, even replace a major party. The American two-party system has been remarkably durable: the modern Democratic party goes back at least to the early 1830s or, in the opinion of some, earlier still to the Jefferson presidency (1801–1809), while the Republican party was founded in 1854. The British two-party system is about as old. But in both systems, third parties have risen and faded at different times.

The two major parties in a two-party system are also prone to be divided houses. The Republican party in 1992 and 1996 faced a challenge from its hard right or more populist wing, led by Pat Buchanan. This wing was adamant in its refusal to compromise on abortion, arguing that the procedure is wrong under

An Algeria experiment in political democracy as voters cast ballots in 1997.

any circumstances. It took equally extreme views on immigration (favoring severe limitations); exhibited deep suspicion of the American role in the global economy, preferring a strong program of economic protectionism; and disliked the 1990s emphasis in foreign policy, preferring nationalism to internationalism. Mainstream Democrats had their own problems with an uncompromising left wing that vocally supported affirmative action, homosexual rights, and multiculturalism.

Major parties in the two-party systems occasionally find themselves in serious trouble. Political obituaries have been written for most major parties from time to time. Yet the major parties tend to survive and have demonstrated remarkable resilience. Over the last century, either the Democrats or the Republicans were expected to collapse on several occasions. Their supposedly imminent demises are briefly summarized in Table 8.3.

TABLE 8.3   A History of Near Party Collapse in the United States

Times of Democrat "Collapse"	Reason
1890s	Rise and serious challenges of Populist Party
1972	Disastrous presidential election result after party's left wing provided candidate and platform

Times of Republican "Collapse"	Reason
1929 and 1930s	Stock market plunge and Great Depression
1964	Disastrous presidential election result after party's right wing provided candidate and platform

In all of these cases, the major party recovered and eventually went on to prosper. Democrats and Republicans have also withstood challenges in presidential races that threatened to deny either of the major candidates an outright victory in the electoral college and to throw the race into the House of Representatives. Over the last half-century, this threat loomed seriously in the elections of 1948, 1968, 1980, and 1992. In all four races, the winning Democrat or Republican was denied an absolute popular majority.

Much the same could be (and in fact, was) said regarding the British Labour party during the 1980s and 90s. The Labour party during this period was barely able to secure a third of the electorate's votes in national elections. A major party in a two-party system is surely in trouble if it is consistently unable to win at least 40 percent of the vote. Nor have the Conservatives escaped expectations of political death. In 1996, numerous prognosticators predicted disaster for the Conservatives at the next parliamentary elections; in 1997, their predictions were at least partially proved true when Labour handily won the elections and formed a new government.

The Democratic party in 1972 and the Republican party in 1964 were humiliated in the presidential elections, as each barely received 40 percent of the popular vote. In both of these cases, the party faced electoral disaster because it had veered much too far from the political mainstream for its own good. The Republican candidate in 1964, Barry Goldwater, frightened voters with what seemed at the time an extremist right-wing platform, while the Democratic candidate in 1972, George McGovern, did the same with a platform produced and dominated by the left wing of the party.

In Britain, Labour annoyed middle-class voters in the 1970s and 1980s by its apparent subservience to the trade union movement. The more moderate Labourites understood that the perception to some extent agreed with reality. It is impossible for a political party to win national elections in a democracy by restricting its appeal to a segment of the electorate. In this case, the segment was the working class, which was gradually diminishing in numbers as more and more Britons became better educated and moved into the middle class. By the middle 1990s, Labour had succeeded in positioning itself as a centrist party no longer in the hands of union leaders or tied to a socialist ideology with minimal popular appeal. Shortly thereafter, it succeeded in taking over the government.

There are few two-party systems in the purest sense. The American system probably comes the closest, since in a typical year the two major parties can expect to win the votes of 95 to 98 percent of the electorate. As we have seen, though, plenty of atypical election years crop up. Most two-party systems can be considered modified multiparty systems in which the larger parties tend to draw various ideological points of view into their ranks. The Republican party, for example, contains both prolife and prochoice supporters, both crucial to any hope of electoral victory. In contrast, multiparty systems may include two, three, or, infrequently, four large parties, none of which has much of a chance of winning a parliamentary majority, and numerous smaller ones.

Are There One-and-a-Half-Party Systems?

In established democracies, there is an assumption that the major parties alternate in power. Generally speaking they do, but not as frequently as one might expect. In the United States, for example, the Republican party dominated the presidency from 1861 to 1933 with occasional exceptions (1885–1889, 1893–1897, and 1913–1921), while the Democrats remained the majority party in Congress for more than sixty years (1933–1995). The British Conservative party controlled the government for eighteen uninterrupted years (1979–1997). Germany's Christian Democratic party (with help from the Free Democrats) has controlled the government since 1982.

Several other systems have more recently applied the democratic process. One party may dominate without rival for decades or even generations. The Labor party in Israel controlled the country's coalition governments for twenty-eight consecutive years, from 1949 to 1977, without a break. The Liberal Democrats in Japan held power for more than four decades after the country regained sovereignty in 1947.

One-party dominant systems normally exist in countries that are not full-fledged democracies, most of them in the developing world. Such a party tends to evidence the following characteristics:

1.   The political leaders are also the founders of the state; the first generation of leadership is often venerated for leading the country to independence from a colonial status.

2.   The party is so closely associated with state institutions that it is difficult to imagine the party and state distinct from one another.

3.   Party workers and supporters fill most political offices and effectively discourage opposition parties in seeking to win national and most local elections.

4.   After around two generations in power, the founding party becomes increasingly sensitive to opposition, which by this time is usually attracting popular support as public discontent with the corruption and conspicuous arrogance of the ruling party grows.

There is always a danger these traits will appear if a party stays in power too long, even if it submits to regular free elections. A founding party often earns or renews the electorate's support only after being in power for a twenty- or thirty-year period and then decisively loses a national election. If it accepts defeat gracefully—as did Labor in Israel, the Liberal Democrats in Japan, and the Congress party in India—it eventually makes a comeback.

The *Partido Revolucionario Institucional* party (PRI) in Mexico has yet to do either. The PRI has governed Mexico since the late 1920s. It has never lost a national election (although critics contend that the PRI won the1988 and 1994 presidential elections with fraudulent ballots). However, time is probably running out for the PRI. It has lost several state elections to parties on its left and its right. Once the PRI finally does lose a presidential election and leaves power peacefully, observers believe Mexico will advance to a more mature and more stable democracy.

In such party systems, which include a legal but underdeveloped opposition, people may experience a high degree of frustration with the political process. However, they may also evidence a great deal of patience. In the examples just discussed, opposition parties patiently waited for decades (and some are still waiting) to achieve power, repeatedly contesting elections and accepting defeat peacefully. The ability of such parties to remain peacefully but actively in the political wilderness for a lengthy period of time gives a great deal of credence to the claim that democratic institutions are working.

One-Party Systems

A one-party system is another matter entirely. Such a system is often referred to as a **party-state,** since it is often the party that determines the nature of the government and of the political institutions. The former Soviet Union was an excellent example of a party-state. In a one-party system, the party dominates all state institutions. The state is simply an agency of the party and is in place only to implement party programs and agendas. Opposition political organizations are banned and, ideologically speaking, for good reason: in a communist system, the ruling party is the only legal party because it is the only party that represents and advocates on behalf of the working class, and working class members are the only people who matter because workers are a society's only productive members.

Under such a system, other political parties, by definition, are both unnecessary and wrong. Communist systems, like one-party systems everywhere, have a very pronounced tendency toward self-righteousness. During the last decades of the Soviet regime, it was not only wrong but indicative of clinical insanity to oppose the party and be unhappy with all the party was doing to improve society. Opponents were sometimes institutionalized in mental asylums until "restored to sanity," usually with electric shock treatments. Since such people supposedly detract from and may be injurious to the cause of the working classes, they cannot be allowed to function freely in a proletarian paradise.

All of this may sound as if the average person in a one-party state would have little to do with politics. One would think the absence of competitive elections would result in a disinterested citizenry. Yet the last thing any self-respecting totalitarian regime wants is political apathy among its people. In fact, the citizen has no legal right to be apathetic. Not only must a good citizen accept without reservation the party's interpretations of ideology, but he or she must do so enthusiastically and must help fulfill these interpretations.

Drumming up enthusiasm is not easy in a one-party state, but most one-party systems attempt to do so. The German Nazis, Italian Fascists, and Soviet Communists all put substantial resources into youth organizations, for example, intending to produce a new generation of selfless, disciplined, and obedient citizens whose first loyalty would be to the regime and the party that was inseparable from it. Professional organizations, labor unions, the media, and even the military were laced with party agents who ensured that every organization's members were thorough in their devotion to the goals of the party.

Enough of the adult population—say, 6 to 8 percent—belonged to the party in these systems to guarantee that the party's continuance and effective control would not diminish over time. In these one-party systems, party members became the most powerful interest group. Those who gained membership were envied by their fellow citizens, for the honor of membership meant joining society's political elite. It also meant, as we've already discussed, great privileges.

Privileges aside, membership also meant a lot of hard work. Party workers were expected to mobilize the masses to turn out for an election or referendum (to endorse the party's choices) or for a national holiday's parades (to illustrate the near-hysterical happiness that accompanies the good fortune of living in a perfect society). More ominously, party members were also expected to keep their eyes open for any hint of discontent with or hostility toward the regime.

There may be a fatal flaw in one-party systems that doom them to self-destruction. Without competition, meaningful elections, or any reason to know about—let alone respond to—public opinion, the state may eventually succumb to institutionalized corruption, until the party becomes incapable of telling the difference between protecting its own interests and those of the country. In the end, the loss of public confidence becomes so great that repair is impossible. Because the party and the state are politically inseparable, they can both collapse at the same moment. This is certainly what happened in the Soviet Union in 1991.

ELECTIONS AND ELECTORAL SYSTEMS

There are still some countries in the world that do not hold any elections, free or otherwise. All democratic and a good number of nondemocratic countries hold elections, but for different reasons. In democracies, elections are usually constitutionally mandated, and the political culture has induced the citizenry to expect and even look forward to participating in them at regular intervals.

The Point of Holding Elections

Elections in democracies provide the most important and widespread manifestation of popular political participation. They are the essence of what makes a political system democratic: the electorate decides who will govern and what policies will be enacted. While elections are commonplace in the democracies, electoral systems differ somewhat from country to country. Voter registration requirements such as age and residency may differ slightly, for example. Overall, though, universal suffrage has been achieved in every full-blown democracy. In some democracies—the United States is an exception—even convicted felons can vote.

Voter turnout of the eligible electorate can be very high. Some countries come close to getting 90 percent of their people to the polls; a few, the United States being the most blatant example, do well to see 50 percent cast ballots (see table 8.4). Americans are notorious for exercising their democratic right not to vote.

The dismal voter turnouts in the United States are a source of frustration for political scientists (who, after all, deserve a little sympathy). They have suggested several reasons why American turnouts are so low compared to voter turnouts in other democracies:

1.   American elections are always held on Tuesdays, although nobody seems to know why. Tuesday is a workday and a school day; this makes it difficult for voters to vote. European elections are usually held on Sundays, a non-working day for most voters.

2.   American elections are seemingly endless. There are off- (presidential) year elections and even off-off-year elections. The primaries precede the general election campaign, consuming media attention for months at a time and leaving many voters bored and exhausted. We have more elections than most democracies and longer campaign seasons than any. The 1996 national election campaign began in the snows of Iowa and New Hampshire in February and went on until election day, November 5, mercifully ended media coverage. National election campaigns nearly everywhere else are much shorter in duration, perhaps six weeks at the most. They may occur at five-, six-, or even seven-year intervals.

3.   The European systems tend to have more partisan voters. Up to 40 percent of American voters classify themselves as Independents. Neither Republicans nor Democrats can win an election without substantial support from voters who consider themselves unaffiliated with any political party.

As table 8.4 illustrates, voting Americans may be an endangered species. Only the Swiss have a lower turnout among the established democracies. Perhaps this isn't entirely negative, though. Not voting is one's choice in a democracy, and

TABLE 8.4   Electoral Turnout in Recent Elections in Selected Countries

Country	Percent Turnout
Australia	94
Belgium	85
Canada	69
France	69
Germany	77
Israel	77
Japan	73
Norway	76
Switzerland	46
United Kingdom	78
United States	53

Source: Adopted from Russell J. Dalton, *Citizens Politics*, 2d ed. (Chatham, New Jersey: Chatham House Publishers, 1996), p. 45.

millions who make this choice have intelligent reasons. Many of the 50 million Americans who could vote and don't are making a conscious decision because of their displeasure with the available choices.

Moreover, as we just suggested, Americans understandably become worn out from the relentless frequency of elections. Most of those who do vote visit the polling places more often than their counterparts in other nations:

> *No country can approach the United States in the frequency and variety of elections, and thus in the amount of electing. No other country elects its lower house as often as every two years, or its president as frequently as every four years. No other country popularly elects its state governors and town mayors, or has as wide a variety of nonrepresentative offices (judges, sheriffs, attorneys general, city treasurers, and so on) subject to election. Only one other country (Switzerland) can compete in the number and variety of local referendums, and only two (Belgium and Turkey) hold party "primaries" in most parts of the country.*[8]

No matter how many elections or how often elections are held, it is critical that the campaign and election themselves are conducted fairly, that voting activity is free of intimidation, and that both winners and losers accept the election outcome peacefully. These conditions are very important in any effort to promote the efficacy of a democracy. Any election in a democracy is an indication that the system is working and that, regardless of whether people are satisfied with prevailing economic and social conditions, they still have confidence in the overall political process.

None of this means, however, that even fair and punctual elections always yield the best possible results. The Nazi party was the largest recipient of the popular vote in the 1932 German elections. As a result, the Nazis took power in early 1933 and almost immediately began to suspend democratic processes; the Germans had to wait seventeen years and lose World War II before voting in their next free elections.

Still, people are better off with than without elections. Some parties and politicians will always want to win elections only to end them. But freely and fairly conducted elections provide the following advantages:

1.　An entire electoral population gets an opportunity at regular intervals (normally between two and five years) to evaluate and choose new or veteran political leadership.

2.　The policy debates that surround elections enable electors to decide, with (it is hoped) objective information, which economic and political policies they want the government to adopt.

3.　Popular support is mobilized on behalf of a position or candidate. For all of its clumsiness, a political rally (even one with planned "spontaneity") suggests a degree of popular endorsement.

---

[8] Ivor Crewe, "Electoral Participation," *Democracy at the Polls*, ed. David Butler, et al. (Washington, D.C.: American Enterprise Institute, 1981), p. 262.

4.   Finally, elections renew the contract between the government and the governed and illustrate the people's commitment to the political system.

Nondemocratic systems also find reasons to have elections. The communist states held elections on a fairly regular basis. True, communist candidates for political office ran unopposed, and one-candidate elections do not excite the electorate. Voters were still expected to cast ballots, though, and they were encouraged to exercise the limited choice available to them: they could vote for the candidate or vote against him or her by striking his or her name out. This happened often enough to embarrass the party in the Soviet Union.

Types of Electoral Systems

Two general electoral systems are widely used: **single-member (SM) district** systems are found mostly but not exclusively in the English-speaking countries. As the term suggests, in SM systems, the country is divided into electoral districts roughly similar in population, and each one furnishes one member to the legislature. This is a winner-take-all system. Normally, a candidate is required to capture a **plurality** of the vote—the largest number of votes cast, even if less than 50 percent—to secure the seat.

The other and more popular electoral system is **proportional representation** (PR). In a parliamentary election, a political party receives representation in the national legislature *in proportion to* the percentage of popular votes the party receives in an election. Ten percent of the popular vote normally provides a party with 10 percent of the parliamentary seats.

Variations and combinations of both of these systems exist. Until 1996, for example, Japanese elections were conducted in **multimember districts** that elect three, four, or five candidates to parliamentary seats. Both Germany and Japan now use both SM and PR.

SM works well in the United States, where it is common for either a Democrat or a Republican to receive an absolute majority of votes in a district. Absolute majorities are far from common in the United Kingdom, however, where

---

ELECTORAL SYSTEMS	**Reasons for SM Systems**	**Reasons for PR Systems**
	1. Single-member systems promote efficient and decisive electoral outcomes, usually placing a single majority party in control of the government.	1. Proportional representation systems allow for numerous minority constituencies to elect representatives to parliament.
	2. SM systems encourage two large parties to be pragmatic and moderate in their policies by coopting issues of concern to smaller parties.	2. PR systems encourage a coalition government that represents a variety of opinions and ideologies.

THE ISRAELI ELECTORAL SYSTEM

For electoral simplicity, it is difficult to beat the Israeli system for the following reasons:

1.   The entire country is treated as a single constituency.

2.   A voter casts one ballot on behalf of the party list of her or his choice.

3.   The list can include up to 120 names for 120 parliamentary seats.

4.   A party receives a total number of seats in proportion to the number of votes it receives in the national election.

there are often at least three serious candidates contesting a seat. The Liberals, the long-time third party of British politics, can win as many as a fourth or even a third of the votes in many single-member districts and have won a fifth or more of the total vote in national elections. Even such a respectable proportion does the Liberals little good; they are usually edged out by one or the other major parties and have to make do with winning only 30 or 40 seats of 650 in the House of Commons. A glance at table 8.5 demonstrates why Liberals would prefer a revision of the current electoral system to proportional representation. The same glance explains why the Labourites might prefer the current system.

The SM system does not necessarily sentence a third political party to permanent minority status. The Liberals could certainly make better use of their electoral base of 20 percent if their supporters were concentrated in one region of the country. A regional proportion of 30 to 40 percent would make the Liberals a serious contender for parity with the Conservatives and Labourites. Of course, there is no humane or sensible way to group all Liberal voters in one region.

The SM system tends to produce a government controlled by a single political party. This is not to say that PR systems can't produce stable governments with several parties sharing control; successful coalition governments form all the time. In fact, coalition governments may be more successful than single-party governments, if only because they often have a broader base of popular support.

On the other hand, some PR systems can get out of control. The 1996 Italian election is a case in point: the 628 seats of the Chamber of Deputies ended up divided among no fewer than twenty-six parties and parliamentary groups.[9] The largest of these parties, the Progressives, carried only a fourth of these seats. The two largest parties together accounted for only about 43 percent of the total vote. Forming a coalition government in these conditions is a political nightmare. It is also a partial explanation as to why Italy has had fifty governments over the last half-century.

The most obvious compromise in any debate over the relative merits of SM and PR is to offer an electoral system that uses both. Germany, for exam-

---

[9] "Mess Continues," *The Economist*, January 20, 1996, p. 49.

TABLE 8.5   Popular Vote and Seat Distribution in the British House of Commons

Political Party	Percent Popular Vote	Percent of Seats	Actual Number of Seats Won	Number of Seats if PR Were Used
Conservative	30.7	24.0	165	200
Labour	43.2	64.5	419	281
Liberal Democrat	16.8	7.1	46	109
Others	9.3	4.4	20	60

Source: Data from the 1997 parliamentary elections, obtained from the '97 Election Home Page.

ple, has done so since 1949. Each German voter casts two ballots, one for a general party list and one for a favorite candidate in the voter's district. In the German lower house, the Bundestag, half of the 656 seats are determined by each type of vote.

The two larger parties, the Christian Democrats and Social Democrats, usually win all of the SM seats between them. A smaller party that can manage a constitutionally required **threshold** of 5 percent receives seats in the general election proportional to the total vote. With one notable exception (1966–1969), every German government since the late 1950s has been a coalition between one of the largest parties and the Free Democrats. The objective of applying both SM and PR systems is to insure representation in the Bundestag for any party that receives a respectable showing on election day, while avoiding any serious possibility that the government would be immobilized by and fragmented between too many parties.

DEMOCRACY AND EFFICIENCY

As table 8.5 suggests, the British after the 1997 elections had a party that controlled an absolute majority of seats in the House of Commons but had won fewer than 44 percent of all votes. If the British had had a PR system in 1997 or in most previous elections, a coalition government would have formed. Most likely, the Liberal party would have become the junior coalition partner to either the Conservative or Labour party. The coalition government would then have the endorsement of a majority of the voting population.

A coalition government, though, almost always means that none of the parties in the coalition can pursue their policies without compromising with their partners. In contrast, a two-party system allows the majority party to pursue its political agenda without much interference. Governing becomes much more efficient. It may also be less democratic, though, because the majority need not consider other points of view.

Since politics is the art of compromise, there may be a compromise between the choices of more democracy and greater efficiency. A coalition government of only two or three like-minded parties may actually represent the interests of a broad-based constituency while remaining streamlined enough to avoid the turmoil that a coalition of half a dozen or more parties can bring. In the end, of course, the choice lies with the electorate.

Referendums

The public is active in determining policy through such devices as referendums. In a referendum, the public (or, more realistically, interest groups concerned with a particular issue) petition to allow the electorate to decide on a legislative action in a ballot box.

In a real sense, every election is a referendum since voters determine whether to retain one government's policies or replace them with alternatives. Most democracies also have a provision for a formal referendum to implement or reject a proposed policy on the basis of popular will. (French presidents have used their ability to call for national referendums on six occasions since 1958, usually when they simply wanted to circumvent or ignore the national legislature.) In a referendum, the voters might decide, for example, whether their taxes should be raised or lowered. If a simple majority passes a referendum, it generally has the force of law, and the legislature cannot override it.

American presidents do not possess the power to authorize referendums, nor are they likely to acquire it. Congress is certainly not about to lessen its authority by allowing a president to bypass its prerogatives and appeal directly to the electorate. However, referendums are legal and frequently held on the state and local levels in the United States. In fact, about half of the 900 or so referendums held each year in the world occur in the United States. American voters are increasingly asked to vote on referendums that involve social and moral issues, such as homosexual rights, at the state and local levels. Problems are sometimes inherent in this sort of a referendum when constitutional issues are involved. Even a referendum passed by an enthusiastic majority will not ultimately become law if any part of it violates a constitutional provision.

In a modern society with tens or hundreds of millions of people, a referendum may be as close as it is possible to come to direct democracy. Moreover, in the age of rapidly advancing computer technology, an **electronic democracy** may actually be feasible. This possibility was first advocated during Ross Perot's 1992 presidential run, when televised national "town meetings" became part of the campaign. Universal voting on national issues could be handled through electronic voting, with the entire electorate participating through devices such as e-mail and fax machines.

As a rule, political parties don't have much affection for referendums since they tend to lose control of the legislative process if the electorate can directly resolve an issue. Electronic democracy could make public officials more responsive to and perhaps more knowledgeable about the public will. They could test their proposals for public approval or disapproval before making them law. On the other hand, public officials could also become confused since the public often changes its mind. In any case, it is unlikely that political parties will become obsolete in the face of electronic democracy. Candidates will still need party organizations to raise money, recruit supporters, and mobilize voter turnout.

SUMMARY

1. Political parties exist in both democratic and nondemocratic political systems. In the democracies they seek to win elections, whereas in nondemocratic systems they are more interested in extending the power and control of the party leadership.

2. In democracies, a political party is usually critical to the success of an aspiring politician since one is expected to work his or her way up through the ranks. The United States is an exception; here, a popular nonpolitician can occasionally win political office.

3. Interest groups have a pervasive influence over political parties; in some cases, they even become political parties. At the same time, a political party must be careful not to become associated too closely in the public mind with a particularly influential interest group.

4. Party systems are generally classified as either two- or multiparty. Multiparty systems may be just as stable as two-party systems, even when a coalition government forms. One-party systems are usually dictatorships. Nonparty systems also exist in authoritarian regimes.

5. Extremist parties often do well in free elections. Their electoral prosperity usually rises when bad economic times or other causes of social unrest crop up. Within their own regions, separatist parties can often effectively compete with larger parties.

6. Electoral systems are usually based on either single-member districts or on proportional representation. In some instances, combinations of the two are available.

7. A referendum enables an electorate to either petition a legislature on an issue or, in some cases, to override the legislature altogether.

GLOSSARY

electronic democracy   An electoral system in which each participant or voter can register direct approval or disapproval on issues through a computer or other electronic device.

extremist political party   A political organization on the radical left or right that espouses an ideological viewpoint that usually (but not always) lacks popular support at election time.

mainstream political party   A political organization that strives to win elections by appealing to moderate, centrist voters and, when necessary, playing down its ideological bases by emphasizing pragmatism and flexibility.

multimember districts   A region in which the constituency elects two or more representatives who may or may not be from the same political party.

plurality   Simply the largest number of votes, which need not be a majority, for a candidate in an election.

professional interest group   An organization that strives to lobby for and reflect the values and preferences of a career professionals such as lawyers or physicians.

proportional representation   An electoral system that allots legislative seats to political parties on the basis of each party's percentage of the total popular vote.

regional or **separatist political party**   A political movement with an appeal in a precise geographical part of the country or to a particular segment of the national population.

religious party   A political organization with a religious agenda that calls for laws and life-styles to be consistent with a scriptural doctrine.

single-issue interest group   An organization that seeks to influence policy according to a usually uncompromising point of view on a particular issue, such as abortion or capital punishment.

single-member district   A region in which the constituency elects one representative, usually the individual who receives a plurality of the votes cast.

threshold   A requirement that a political party receive a minimal percentage of the popular votes cast in order to receive parliamentary seats. In Germany, the threshold is 5 percent; in other countries, such as Israel, the percentage can be lower.

Ingredients of International Politics

he fast-changing world necessitates these three chapters (9, 10, and 11) on political economy, political geography, and political violence. The 1990s has been a decade that has seen unprecedented economic growth across the planet (between 1972 and 1997 China's economy quadrupled), but has also seen economic disparities accelerate. Economic growth or the lack of it impacts on both the hopes for political democracy and the sustaining or establishing political stability. What ensures a country's stability, longevity, and perhaps even its survival? Its physical location, the quality and quantity of its population, and the behavior of its closest political neighbors are all important determinants. States have been known to disappear. Some have disappeared and reappeared. Finally, political violence, despite, and in some cases because of, the advance of democracy, has characterized a good part of our century through world war to terrorism. It is often political violence that makes states appear or disappear.

The Global Political Economy

One important reason the Cold War wound down during the late 1980s was the increasingly undeniable realization that the industrialized and technologically proficient countries were leaving the Soviet Union and other communist societies behind. Given its antiquated and bureaucratically impaired economy, there was not much that the Soviet system (or its imitators) could do to remedy this. No longer was the world divided simply by the ideological contrast between communism and democracy; now an economic rift divided the two as well.

In the immediate aftermath of World War II, most of the industrialized powers needed to rebuild their shattered economies. The war's destruction in Europe and Asia was devastating to many countries. The American economy, unlike many of the others, had actually expanded. The United States was the only major participant that had not been repeatedly bombed, militarily occupied, or both. As the war ended, the American economy made up nearly half of the globe's overall economy, an unnatural and even undesirable situation that couldn't be sustained. It wasn't, of course, and while the United States still had the world's largest economy fifty years later, its proportion had diminished to a still impressive quarter of the total. The planet had changed in other dramatic ways that seemed irreversible; the population had more than doubled from 2.6 billion to 5.8 billion, and both overall global wealth and regional poverty had grown substantially.

In this chapter, we will explore the global economy, examining how governments and economies interact and produce both benefits and negative effects. We will consider the growing impact of the global economy on the lives of countries and individuals. Moreover, we will discuss how the world is splintering into more and more countries even as, paradoxically, entire regions of the world integrate economically.

Never before has the world seen such a prosperous life-style as we have in the industrialized nations at the close of the twentieth century. One indication is the automobile. Researchers have noted that while the world's population more than doubled during the half-century from 1945 to 1995, the total number of automobiles has increased 1000 percent, from 50 million to 500 million.[1]

---

[1] "Living with the Car," *The Economist*, June 22, 1996, p. 3.

To this total one could add another quarter billion trucks and motorbikes.[2] The globalization of the internal combustible engine—its accessibility to hundreds of millions of people in the 1990s—suggests unprecedented and increasingly widespread wealth.

Yet unprecedented poverty also remains. At least a billion people on this planet live in an extremely impoverished state, and they have little or no prospect of ever escaping this condition. Their misery is a mystery to many economists who wonder why countries with substantial natural resources remain poor.[3] On the bright side, many societies that seemed hopelessly poor thirty or forty years ago are vibrant today: South Korea was an economic backwater in the 1950s, but by 1992 it had the fifteenth largest economy in the world, and by 2020 it is expected to rise to seventh (which would put it ahead of France, Italy, and the United Kingdom).[4]

Because politics and economics are frequently intertwined, we will explore both the connection and its implications in this chapter. The relationship is critical for political stability; it seems that democracies cannot thrive in poor societies, while brutal dictatorships seem to manage quite well with an impoverished populace. However, this observation can sometimes be simplistic: the largest economy in the world by 2020 could be China's, a country not currently a sterling example of democratic tendencies. Thus, we will also need to explore the tantalizing question of whether economic growth softens some nondemocratic regimes.

SOME BASIC PRINCIPLES

The last quarter-century has seen dramatic changes in the world's economy. Many people are indeed getting richer, at least on paper. In 1974, for example, the capitalization of all the world's stockmarkets was about $900 billion. By 1994, this figure had grown to $15 trillion in constant dollars.[5] The world has never before seen such a rapid or widespread growth in wealth. Most of this remarkable increase came in western economies and indicated the growing gap between the West and the communist sphere as well as the developing countries. But recently, the most impressive advances have been in East Asian countries, where

> the incomes of many of their citizens have doubled in a decade: their people also eat better, drink cleaner water and live longer, and more of their children survive early illnesses, get a better education and can find a job at the end of it.[6]

---

[2] Ibid.

[3] "The Poor and the Rich," *The Economist*, May 25, 1996, p. 25.

[4] "The Global Economy," *The Economist*, October 1, 1994, p. 4.

[5] "Cities," *The Economist*, July 29, 1995, p. 4.

[6] "A Global Poverty Trap," *The Economist*, July 20, 1996, p. 34.

That is certainly the good news. Th bad news is that many other people are not getting any richer and may be getting poorer. According to the United Nations Development Programme (UNDP), people in 70 countries have lower average incomes than they did in 1980, and those in an alarming 43 are even poorer than they were in 1970.[7] If one takes the long (and optimistic) view, the quality of life for most national populations has improved. Even in Africa, where poverty is endemic in some countries, living standards have improved by 21 percent overall since 1980. But while averages are up, those who lost ground are even poorer than they were two decades ago.

As most of Africa suggests, progress can be painfully slow. An annual economic growth rate of 2 to 3 percent is not inconsiderable over the long term, but populations may wait decades before they experience a noticeable improvement in the quality of life. Moreover, there is no guarantee that progress is either inevitable or sustainable.

Some economies can actually regress, often rather quickly. This happens most vividly when the political system itself collapses. The Eastern European and former Soviet republics (FSRs) had stagnated for years before their communist regimes imploded. Reformers wanted to establish free market economies in a hurry, so they implemented **shock therapy**—dismantling the collectivized state-controlled system and replacing it with a free market. The reforms produced mixed results as national economies disintegrated and were characterized by frighteningly rapid declines in gross domestic products (GDPs), ot total goods produced. Millions of people in the FSRs had become accustomed to a social system that provided for their basic needs, though the provisions were often primitive. These citizens suddenly confronted the disappearance of subsidized (if often inadequate) foodstuffs, rampant inflation (officially nonexistent in the Soviet Union), and the dismantling of an extensive state welfare system (especially disconcerting to older people dependent on government pensions).

During the Cold War, it was convenient, if not completely accurate, to divide the world's countries into the following three groups:

First World—the democratic and economically advanced countries of western Europe, North America, Japan, and a few westernized societies such as Australia and Israel. The bulk of the population in these regions enjoy the highest living standards and quality of life in the world. Welfare programs at least partially alleviate the substantial pockets of poverty that exist.

Second World—the communist countries of the Soviet Union and Eastern Europe, where the economy was industrializing but, as we now know, not advancing appreciably and lagging behind the First World. Compared to the First World, the standard of living in these countries was abysmal. Communist systems achieved the distinction of equalizing poverty, making it easily available to the entire society with the exception of the party hierarchy. The average

---

[7] Ibid.

citizen had to wait years before getting a telephone and had little hope of owning a personal car (though public transportation was usually more than adequate).

Third World—most of the rest of the world in the "underdeveloped" regions of Asia, Middle East, Africa, and Latin America. The economy in many of these countries was characterized by extremes of wealth and poverty with a decidedly underdeveloped middle class. Several countries were considered Third World only in a nominal or geographical sense. The populations of the East Asian "tigers" (or "dragons") enjoy rising living standards that are increasingly similar to First World countries, and Chile, though part of Latin America, is quickly developing a modern economy equipped with an expanding middle class.

Well before the Cold War ended, this three-world model ceased to make sense. We still use the terms, however, because we haven't found substitutes that are much better. The term *Third World* is perhaps the most misleading because this group contains so much diversity and represents many times the population of the first two combined. The "Third World" is a vast place with three-fourths of the human race. The differences between rates of economic development and political democratization in these countries are so gaping that it makes little sense to classify them together. As one observer has explained,

> *Today, two new forces are finishing off the tattered Third World idea. The first is the West's victory in the cold war. There are no longer two competing "worlds" with which to contrast a "third." Leaders can't play one superpower off the other, or advertise their misguided policies as alternative to "equally inappropriate" communism and capitalism. The second is rapid growth in many once poor countries.*[8]

Besides, many so-called Third World countries have long demonstrated a strong resemblance to First World countries, achieving and sustaining remarkable levels of economic growth. Several are also in the process of democratizing.

While it is helpful to use what we hope are appropriate terms, placing Sierra Leone, Sri Lanka, and Bolivia together in a category such as "Third World" is not very informative. Third World societies are distinct from one another in history, culture, and economic development. Moreover, even within a developing country, some regions are almost certainly more advanced than others. In the state of Bihar in India, poverty is endemic for the usual reasons: illiteracy, malnutrition, overpopulation, and miserable sanitary conditions. Perhaps most telling of all, 90 percent of Bohr adult women are illiterate (and in some parts of the state, the percentage rises to 98).[9] At the same time, India's middle

---

[8] Charles Lane, "Let's Abolish the Third World," *Newsweek*, April 27, 1992.

[9] "India Survey," *The Economist*, May 4, 1991, 8.

class is growing, and its democracy has worked well since the country achieved independence in 1947.

To be more accurate about the global economy, we can try to describe some basic demographics:

1. Well-established, high living standards among the great majority of the population are currently limited to Western Europe, North America, Australia, New Zealand, Israel, Japan, and the "little tigers" of East Asia—South Korea, Singapore, and Taiwan. These regions account for only a seventh of the world's population of nearly 6 billion but together create two-thirds of the global economy.

2. The former "Second World" of Russia, other former Soviet republics (FSRs), and most Eastern European countries is in a state of transition. A few of these countries—the Baltic states, Czech Republic, Hungary, and Poland—seem to be developing both democratic institutions and working market economies with some success. Geographically, ideologically, and even religiously, these countries have been close to and are hopeful of rejoining the West. The majority of the FSRs are still tentatively exploring the possibilities of a non-communist world. All told, this region contains about 400 million people, about half the number in the first group.

3. A third group of slowly developing countries is defined by no single geographical region but consists of at least 100 countries scattered throughout the developing world. The Asian "tiger cubs" of Malaysia, Indonesia, and Thailand could fall into this category. So could Chile and perhaps Argentina and Mexico. India raises the biggest question; it is so huge and diverse that it could almost be treated as several countries. Some parts of India are doing well, others dismally. This group probably contains another 400 million people, which increases to 1.3 billion if India is lumped in. (China and India are such large countries that it isn't unreasonable to place each in a category by itself.)

4. Countries with valuable natural resources that enjoy global demand, such as the Persian Gulf states, could make up a fourth category. Their economies are rich, and their populations may be coddled in the sense that their overall needs are provided by the regime's largess. This policy does not, however, encourage real economic development. In many other instances, corrupt and/or incompetent governments and megalomaniac dictators keep the population relatively poor. It is difficult to be sure, but perhaps half a billion people may live in these countries.

5. Nearly a fourth of humanity lives in the least desirable places, where the life span is barely half of the life span people in the first category enjoy. Most Africans, a large proportion of South Asians, Latin Americans, and Chinese live in conditions that can only be described as abject poverty. In some cases, the country has too small an infrastructure in place to build on. Several countries, such as Somalia, Rwanda, and Burundi, have no infrastructure at all; they do not exist in any modern sense except on maps. Their governments are either nonexistent or unable to control much more than the capital city. Most

of the population is endemically poor because of relentless civil strife, political corruption, and even wholesale massacre or because of natural disasters such as desertification.

These categories demonstrate the great unevenness of economic development. Surprise upturns and downturns further complicate the picture. In the 1950s, the Philippines was the most prosperous country in East Asia. Today, it is one of the poorest. In 1980, Nigeria, the largest country in Africa, had a larger economy than South Korea, Thailand, or Malaysia. By 1990, all three had larger economies than Nigeria.[10]

Economies can and sometimes do regress. What goes wrong? Several potential problems are always on the horizon. A country can degenerate into civil war, and the war can drag on for years, decades, or even generations. A country may be ruled by a dictatorship more concerned with enriching itself than encouraging economic progress. The Philippines was moving along well until two decades of the Marcos regime (1965–1986) shattered the economy. The Marcos family and its retainers systematically robbed the national treasury.

Another problem arises when a country relies too heavily on a particular product such as oil and leaves itself at the mercy of fickle world markets, as Nigeria has done. Ironically, possessing a natural resource that the rest of the world constantly demands can hurt a country's chances to develop. It is almost better to have too few resources; then the country places greater reliance on the most valuable resource of all—the population. Countries such as Singapore, Japan, South Korea, and Israel have all been mentioned as economic success stories: none of them have attained economic modernity because of any resource other than an educated, skilled, and diligent work force.

It seems clear that an increasing number of nonwestern countries are doing well for themselves economically and are fashioning their own democratic styles. Many of these newly industrialized countries, **NICs,** are located in East Asia, but it would be wrong to assume that they are all the same. South Korea, Taiwan, and Singapore compete as much with one another as they do with the American and European economies, and they all worry about the predominance of the huge Japanese economic system and the potentially even larger Chinese economy. Japan currently possesses the second largest economy in the world, while China could have the world's largest economy in half a century.

The world economy is not yet global, but it is certainly globalizing. Perhaps if one insists on categorizing countries, it might be logical to group them into three worlds after all: the North American-West European world, where established democracies and advanced economies are taken for granted; the up-and-coming NICs in Asia and elsewhere, where advancing economies are helping provoke demands for democratic reforms with as yet uncertain success; and the remainder of the world's countries, many of which are now attempting

---

[10] Keith B. Richburg, "Why Is Africa Eating Asia's Dust?" *The Washington Post National Weekly Edition,* July 20–26, 1992, p. 11.

The stock market in Tokyo, Japan.

with varying degrees of success to find the formula for sustainable economic development.

DEMOCRACY AND CAPITALISM

Capitalism has become "the mode of production of a globalized economy,"[11] but capitalism alone doesn't guarantee democracy. While the world now has unprecedented global wealth, this wealth is concentrated in a minority of the world's countries. The fact that nearly all rich countries are democratic is meager consolation to poor places that are neither. In 1995, the seven largest economies, usually referred to as the **G7,** were all western with the single exception of Japan. Together these seven countries account for nearly half of the world economy—46 percent—though they contain only a tenth of the world's population. Moreover, while the rich in this context may not be getting richer, they aren't becoming less rich, either. The G7's proportion of the world's economy has remained fairly constant since 1960.[12]

It is true that both democracy and free markets seem to be catching on in nonwestern regions. It also seems at least partially true that some cultures remain resistant to either or both. India is the world's largest democracy, but its economic development has been stalled by its early history as an independent state and by ancient traditions that discouraged Hindus from adopting non-Indian ways. Not all Indians have followed this advice, but hundreds of millions

---

[11] Kathryn A. Manzo, *Creating Boundaries: The Politics of Race and Nation* (Boulder and London: Lynne Rienner Publishers, 1996), p. 49.

[12] "Can the G7 Ride Again?" *The Economist*, June 22, 1996, p. 76.

have. India's political elite have been wary of emulating the economic habits of those who colonized the country for centuries.

India, according to some experts, must turn its back on its own form of **autarky,** a largely discredited model of economic nationalism that emphasizes producing as much as possible within a country's own borders and avoiding foreign markets and international commerce. While economic success stories such as Singapore, Taiwan, and South Korea depend on foreign trade, India is more self-reliant.[13] It is also lagging behind in the remarkable economic growth these countries have experienced for more than a generation.

Of course, every society in the end must find its own (sometimes tortuous) path to prosperity. Obviously, some do better than others when it comes to finding the most suitable path. The factors that work well in an ethnically homogeneous and geographically compact society of 3 million people, as in Singapore, are unlikely to work in a heterogeneous and huge society of 950 million, as in India. Such a comparison can be extended: Singapore is no doubt a prosperous place, but its democracy is hardly the sort normally found in western countries. In fact, Americans would be hard put to recognize Singapore as a democracy at all. People in Singapore are well off because they work hard. They are, however, legally obligated to be neat, tidy, and industrious—whether they want to or not. To make sure,

> . . . *police keep watch from the rooftops of Singapore to catch people committing such crimes as littering or chewing gum. Parents of schoolchildren deemed to be overweight receive letters ordering them to change the family menus. The government tells people how much of their money to save.*[14]

The Asian model of development is a complicated one, assuming a particular model exists. Singapore may be self-righteously clean, but South Koreans chew gum and do worse things in their streets.[15] Moreover, at this point none of the participants in the "Asian miracle" can be considered full-fledged democracies. China, a decidedly undemocratic country, has experienced nearly unprecedented economic expansion in the 1990s based on the free market currently operating in the eastern regions of the country. India, a practitioner of democracy for the last half-century, is still reluctant to relinquish government-maintained barriers to market-based economic reforms.[16]

Obviously, some cultures possess an antimarket bias that seems to override or direct the political climate. Before communism came to power in Russia, a collective perspective prevailed in rural villages. Now, even with democratic institutions in place, many Russians are unsure of the benefits of the market economy. The outcome of the 1996 presidential elections, which presented an option to return the communists to power, suggest that a small but firm major-

---

[13] "India Survey," p. 4.

[14] T. R. Reid, "Confucius Says: Go East, Young Man," *The Washington Post Weekly Edition,* November 27–December 3, 1995, p. 21.

[15] Ibid.

[16] "Tread Carefully," *The Economist,* June 29, 1996, p. 33.

ity of voting Russians, about 53 percent, still have confidence in economic reforms that emphasize the free market.

South Korea for centuries was both poor and contemptuous of entrepreneurs, and South Koreans were deeply respectful of the Confucian-inspired scholar-bureaucrat.[17] The country had to overcome its cultural bias against making individual fortunes before it could advance economically. Once this happened, the cap on economic development was removed, probably for good.

As we have pointed out, we cannot blithely assume that free markets and democracy go hand in hand, even though it is tempting to do so. Free markets in the modern world can't be entirely free. The public sector plays a necessary role since the government is expected to engage in regulatory activities and, in deference to its traditional role, guarantee personal security. Moreover, as already indicated, some cultures are plainly more amenable to market economies *with* democratic processes than others.

What, then, does it take for a society to achieve both a prosperous economy and democratic polity? Apparently, the same sorts of conditions apply to both. An economist with international repute suggests that economist Adam Smith stated the answer quite simply nearly two-and-a-half centuries ago:

> *Little else is requisite to carry a state to the highest degrees of opulence from the lowest barbarism, but peace, easy taxes, and tolerable administration of justice.*[18]

Successful democracies contain these three elements, although they may fall somewhat short of perfection. Figure 9.1 suggests that the quality of life, as measured by the Human Development Index, is higher in democracies, though some democracies are simply more democratic than others. Singapore, for example, has a high quality of life but is far less concerned about individual rights than are the United States or the United Kingdom.

Ironically, the world's fastest growing economies in the 1990s have turned out to be in East Asia, where governments are involved in a "strategic growth" model.[19] Under this model, governments don't interfere in the free market so much as they monitor where they might help promote certain aspects of the market. This is done by bureaucrats who behave as though they are entrepreneurs, but only when no one else does. In Singapore, one of the top success stories in East Asia, when private companies "failed to respond to opportunities identified by bureaucrats, state-owned or controlled groups were often pushed to the fore . . ."[20]

There are certainly varying paths to prosperity. According to an important study published in the early 1990s, the more individual freedom government provides, the greater the economic growth.[21] This finding makes sense if we

---

[17] Michael Prowse, "Miracles Beyond the Free Market," *Financial Times*, April 26, 1993, p. 15.

[18] Quoted in Jeffrey Sachs, "Growth in Africa: It Can Be Done," *The Economist*, June 29, 1996, p. 20.

[19] Prowse, "Miracles Beyond the Free Market," p. 15.

[20] Ibid.

[21] "Democracy and Growth: Why Voting Is Good for You," *The Economist*, August 27, 1994, p. 17.

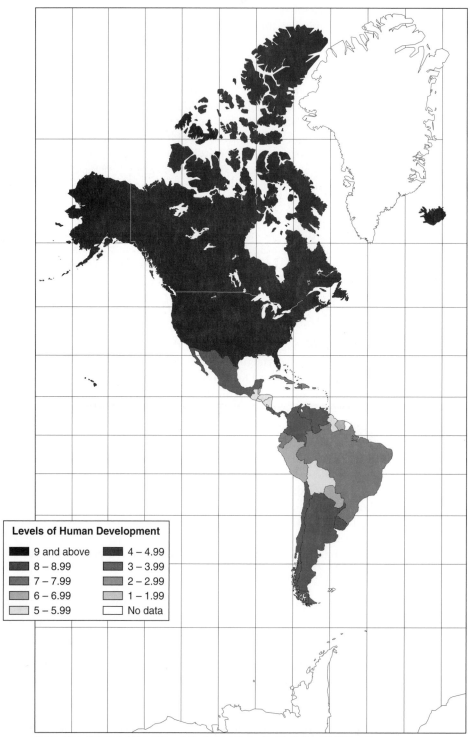

Source: John L. Allen, *Student Atlas of Economic Development*, (Boston: Dushkin, McGraw-Hill, 1997), p. 34.

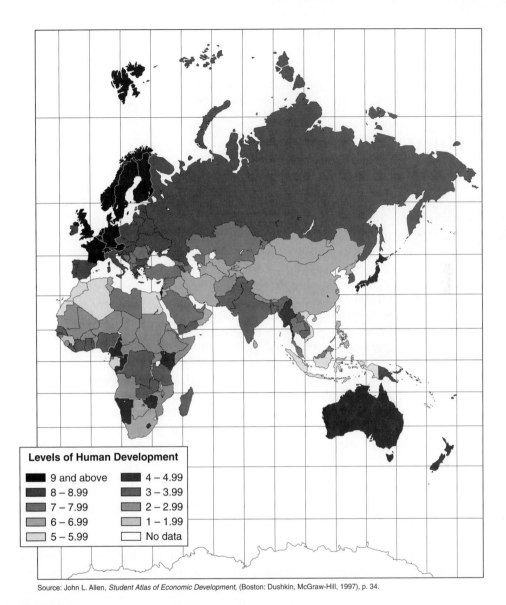

Levels of Human Development

9 and above	4 – 4.99
8 – 8.99	3 – 3.99
7 – 7.99	2 – 2.99
6 – 6.99	1 – 1.99
5 – 5.99	No data

Source: John L. Allen, *Student Atlas of Economic Development*, (Boston: Dushkin, McGraw-Hill, 1997), p. 34.

Figure 9.1
Quality of Life: The Human Development Index

simply consider the fact that under dictatorships, even those that encourage entrepreneurship, the government can arbitrarily take away anything a citizen has at any time. This hardly creates an incentive to work hard, accumulate wealth, and invest. The government must insure that contracts between parties will be honored and property secured for its owner.

THE GLOBALIZING ECONOMY

There is a certain sense in which the world's economy is really global: more than ever before, most people are living in an increasingly interdependent world economy. This interdependence is, if anything, accelerating because of new information technology and the linking and internationalization of financial markets. Simultaneously, viable economies seem to be dismissing nonviable markets, and some economies (such as the command economies) are dissolving and disappearing.

Economic prosperity and the enjoyment of a decent life-style have been exclusionary for most of modern history: they were confined for the most part to the "First World." Even there, large pockets of the population had to struggle before they gained the opportunities available to the prosperous majority. Prosperity is spreading and growing, though it is still confined to a minority of countries and peoples.

Still, prosperity is often considered a mixed blessing. It almost always means that traditional life-styles will change; some beyond recognition. For some traditionalists, prosperity is threatening because it is often associated with American traits. In fact, the global economy is frequently criticized because of its "Americanization." In part, this is because the American economy is unrivaled in its success and scope and because Americans are so good at selling their products. As the global economy expands, "American consumer goods are likely to be first choice for millions of new consumers in the Third World, who want to drink Coke, smoke Marlboro cigarettes, and watch Hollywood films."[22]

Americanization is definitely going on, but it is most noticeable in selected locations. Many people in developing nations are migrating from rural areas to quickly developing urban centers to find work and a better life. In the process, they often find poverty and unhealthy environments, too. Yet if a global economy exists or is emerging, it will most likely be found in cities, where both the advantages and disadvantages of development are most pronounced.

The growth of urban communities over the last half of the twentieth century has been relentless. In 1950, only two urban areas had populations over 10 million—London and New York. Forty-five years later, fourteen urban areas had populations that ranged from 11 million in Tianjin, China, to 26 million in Tokyo, Japan. London is off the list altogether, and thirteen of these largest

---

[22] "The Global Economy," *The Economist*, October 1, 1994, p. 38.

cities are nonwestern.[23] Clearly, economic growth focuses on urban centers regardless of culture or country.

ECONOMIC REGIONALISM

There is probably no such thing as smooth and even economic development in any country. For example, if the American South had become a separate state in 1861, it would have been at that time the wealthiest country in the world, but by 1865, its primarily agriculture-based economy was devastated. It took nearly a century for the region to again become the most prosperous area in the United States.[24] In the meantime, the northeastern and midwestern parts of the country moved rapidly ahead as industries and commercial centers expanded into world centers.

Not only can a country's geographical regions develop unevenly, but race, religion, and ethnicity may also cause uneven economic growth. In the United States, for example, African-Americans do not generally enjoy the same quality of life as white Americans. The former die sooner, are less educated, and are in poorer health than the latter. In many urban areas, economic and social decay is in ample evidence in the inner cities, while suburbs contain a thriving middle class. Whites have fled to the suburbs, taking their education, skills, and money with them, while blacks, who tend to possess none of these advantages, have been trapped in places such as Chicago's southside and New York City's Harlem.

It is a truism that young people hear all the time: staying in school and getting an education is the only way to a better life. And the truism is true: "Since 1970, the incomes of the least educated 10 percent have fallen, while those of the best educated 10 percent have surged."[25] More broadly, the gap between the rich and the poor has widened:

> *Globally, the situation isn't any better. During the middle 1960s, the poorest 20 percent of the world's people used to have 2.3 percent of the world's income but now have only 1.4 percent, while the richest 20 percent have increased their share from 70 percent to 85 percent.*[26]

To use other revealing numbers, 1.2 billion people—nearly a fourth of whom live in the United States—enjoy 85 percent of the world's income, while 4.8 billion people have to scrape by (if they can) with only 15 percent.

Development seems to get underway in a few locations and, if all goes well, spreads (or at least acts as a catalyst). In the seventeenth and eighteenth centuries, London and Paris became the financial and industrial centers of Britain and France. They remain so today, though several other urban areas have

---

23 "Cities," *The Economist*, July 29, 1996, p. 5.

24 "The American South," *The Economist*, December 10, 1994.

25 "The Impossible Dream," *The Economist*, July 13, 1996, p. 89.

26 "A Global Poverty Trap?" *The Economist*, July 20, 1996, p. 34.

established themselves as critical components of the national economy in each country. Other industrial powers, such as the United States and Germany, have economies that developed in several major urban areas, partly because both the economic and political systems were relatively decentralized.

Many developing countries lack the leisure the established economies of the First World enjoyed as they developed. Cities in Western Europe and North America grew steadily as people left their farms and small towns and moved to urban areas for a better quality of life (a pattern that reversed in the last years of the twentieth century in the United States as increasing numbers of Americans, desperate for peace and quiet, returned to smaller towns). Cities in developing countries, by contrast, are growing quickly—too quickly—as millions stream into them. Earlier urban expansion proceeded with a more or less adequate accompaniment of public service infrastructure. Today, cities such as Cairo, Mexico City, and Dacca lack the resources to cope with the rush of added residents that are overwhelming public services. Thus, while economic development can proceed at a suitable pace in some aspects such as business zones, where industries as disparate as diamond cutting and tourism provide jobs, the avalanche of people precludes the possibility of anything close to full employment.

Often, a developing country's government spends its limited resources in an often futile attempt to simply maintain order in the capital. It then faces the difficult task trying to extend its authority to the country's hinterland and build an economic infrastructure: transportation and communication systems, educational and health facilities, and guaranteed civil order.

Other serious problems are associated with developing economies. Not the least is the character of the political system. Dictatorships are not as plentiful as they were in the 1970s and 1980s, but they remain numerous, particularly in Africa and the Middle East. These regions also experience the greatest difficulties in economic development.

Even in some Middle East countries that are wealthy according to many indices, overall development may be minimal. This is because wealth is concentrated rather than dispersed. In several cases, especially in the Persian Gulf states, national wealth is typically controlled by a ruling family that uses it to sustain political domination and discourage competition. It is very difficult for a broad-based middle class to emerge. Much of the national wealth, which may be considerable, is sent overseas for safety's sake—to Swiss bank accounts, for example—or is directed away from building the infrastructure for the private pleasures of the ruling family and its retainers. Saddam Hussein and his children, for instance, spent $2.5 billion building seventy-five palaces at a time when a fourth of Iraq's children suffered from malnutrition.

A GLOBAL UNDERCLASS

A global or globalizing economy has a generally positive connotation. Its advocates tend to ignore possible negative features, such as the often destructive influence globalization has on local traditions and values. Lives are disrupted as a rapidly changing technology and marketplace force people to retrain or acquire new skills. Soon, it will be rare for an individual in any economy to remain in the same job for his or her entire working career.[27]

Social dislocations are inevitable as a truly global economy evolves. The "downsizing" large corporations have undertaken since the late 1980s in the United States and Western Europe and the stagnant standard of living millions of families in these areas have experienced are indications that global transitions do not occur without substantial difficulties. The dislocations, not surprisingly, are far more serious and widespread in the developing economies, where the infrastructure may not even have existed, let alone be capable of revision. Where poverty is extreme and widespread, there is little hope of progress: investment, transportation and communication systems, skill and education levels, are often very primitive and always inadequate. Just as importantly, political coherence is frequently absent if the government lacks the will and capability to extend its authority throughout the country.

In fact, the government's authority may be so minimal that other political agents usurp it. Some may be openly hostile to the regime. In Egypt, religious organizations such as Hamas and the Islamic Brotherhood deliver public services including health clinics, food stations, and educational facilities. These organizations have filled a void in places where governmental authority has broken down, never had a significant presence, or is viewed for all practical purposes as military occupation.

It is unclear what can be done to alleviate the conditions of the global poor. Governments, as just suggested, are often helpless to act. Much of the time they are incapable of imposing or collecting taxes from those in a position to pay them. Without an adequate tax base, a government cannot provide stimuli for economic development or even take back neighborhoods from nongovernmental organizations that provide public services.

Even if a government can acquire resources to improve upon an economic infrastructure, **corruption**—the practice of bribing officials to secure government contracts—remains an important and probably permanent problem. While corruption occurs everywhere, it is most pervasive where one would expect it be: in developing societies where laws against it are lax, nonexistent, or safely ignored because they are unenforced.

Developing democracies have little to be smug about. Competing political parties in countries as different as India and Russia have concentrated on promising giveaways to large numbers of people. (One presidential candidate in Russia promised free vodka.) When a successful party comes to power, it must make good on at least some of its promises. In doing so, it can bankrupt the state or, at a minimum, discourage foreign investment in an economy whose leaders exhibit no self-discipline.[28]

---

[27] See Ralf Dahrendorf, "Preserving Prosperity," *New Statesman and Society*, December 15–29, 1995, pp. 36–41.

[28] "Road to Ruin," *The Economist*, August 17, 1996, p. 32.

One argument holds that corruption is actually good for development: simply pay the appropriate individual to override red tape, saving money and time. Unfortunately, such a formula is actually too simple. Evidence suggests that the higher the level of corruption, the lower the rate of investment.[29] Haiti has one of the highest rates of corruption, for example, and very low investment.[30]

The gap between rich and poor is tremendous and growing. One estimate suggests that the average GDP per person in the Organization of Economic Cooperation and Development (OECD) is 55 times that of the poorest countries.[31] Rich countries are confronted with a dilemma: whether to commit substantial resources to struggling societies, or simply let them continue to flounder.

DEVELOPMENT AND DEMOGRAPHICS

Throughout this text, we have maintained that government is both a necessary and permanent fixture in our lives, usually for better, occasionally for worse. Government can do a great deal to encourage economic development. It can even encourage or discourage what is arguably the most important determinant of development: the quality and quantity of the population.

A government can encourage or discourage population growth by establishing a set of incentives or disincentives. At one extreme, for example, China's government strenuously pursues a **zero population growth (ZPG)** policy. Chinese authorities often pressure a pregnant woman to undergo an abortion if she already has one child. At the other extreme, governments can encourage population growth by prohibiting or severely restricting not only abortion, but all family planning efforts.

Government economic policy in developing societies often confronts severe demographic pressures. The most serious include a very large proportion of young people and an increasing population that is outstripping any economic progress. These are two interrelated problems, but let's consider them one at a time:

1.   In most developing countries, as much as half the population is under the age of fifteen. The under-fifteens require educational facilities as well as proper nutrition and health care if they are to become productive working adults who will make durable contributions to the economy. It is expensive to provide such services, though, and the infrastructure needed to do so is often lacking or inadequate. Millions of children reach adulthood every year without preparation for employment and become a constraint on rather than an asset to economic progress.

---

[29] Paul Blustein, "Pssst. Here's a Little Something that Seems to Slow Growth," *The Washington Post*, July 17, 1996, pp. D1 and D7.

[30] Ibid.

[31] *The Economist Book of Vital Statistics* (New York: Random House, 1990), p. 34.

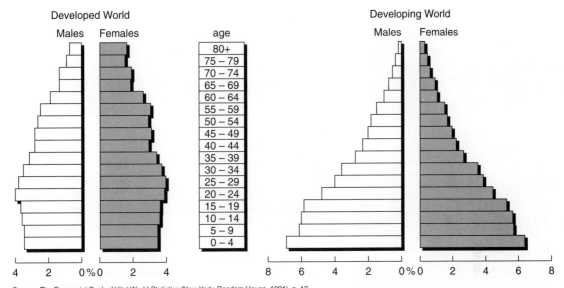

Source: *The Economist Book of Vital World Statistics* (New York: Random House, 1991), p. 13.

Figure 9.2
Percentage of Population in Different Age Groups, 1985

2. The under-fifteens, for reasons just indicated, aren't economically viable; they can't be until they possess necessary work skills. Unemployment can reach high levels, perhaps a third of the work force, and underemployment—part-time or seasonal employment—also skyrockets. Young people without jobs or prospects may become prey for political or religious extremists who offer solutions and hope. Political instability is a frequent consequence of economic underdevelopment.

Figure 9.2 suggests the problem developing societies face. Notice that First World countries have the opposite problem: a bulge of older people. There are proportionally three to four times as many older people in developed societies as in underdeveloped systems. As people live longer, a country's labor force faces the possibility of paying higher taxes to provide entitlement programs such as social security for older people. In developing economies, the labor force is too big for the number of available jobs; in established and industrialized economies, the labor force is often too small, at least as far as skilled workers, to support government programs.

In France, 20.2 percent of the population is under age fifteen, about the average of 20.5 percent for the developed economies of the OECD. The United States is slightly over the average at 21.5 percent. Contrast those numbers with Sub-Saharan Africa, where the percentage is 46.2 percent or the Middle East, where the average is 42.3 percent. The under-fifteens increase to between 48 and 52 percent in such countries as Kenya, Kuwait, Nigeria, and Yemen. Most of the young are also among the poorest members of these societies.

Posters in a shopping area in China emphasizes family planning.

Trends for the future are not especially encouraging. By 2010, the world will add at least another billion over the nearly 6 billion recorded in 1997. Almost all of the population growth will occur in the developing areas. (See the population distributions and projected trends in figure 9.3). In 1950, the developed world included about a third of the planet's total population. By 1985, this proportion was down to one-quarter, by 1995 one-fifth, and by 2025, it will be around one-sixth. Significant population growth, in other words, is occurring precisely in the parts of the world that need it least.

Of course, at some point, the world's population will level off. Estimates vary widely and range between 8 billion by the middle of the twenty-first century and 12 billion at the end of that century. Even in the fastest growing areas of Africa and the Middle East, the percentage increase is declining, though the growth in absolute numbers is still substantial. In the meantime, though, the world's population is gaining more than 90 million members annually, mostly in regions where poverty remains endemic.

PROMOTING AND SUSTAINING ECONOMIC DEVELOPMENT

Why does one country have a growing economy that benefits most of the population while another is mired in poverty? Fortunately, our task here is not to provide an answer; there is no completely satisfactory answer. It may be just as useful to suggest how government can help as well as how it can destroy economic development by doing the wrong thing or by sheer negligence:

1.   It is up to government to guarantee that the *rule of law* is fully applied. Imagine, for example, the consternation of foreign investors when, in 1995, the Chinese government disavowed the twenty-year lease it had given to McDonald's on a piece of property in Beijing because there was more money in building a $2.1 billion Oriental Plaza for commercial and residential development.[32] Unless a government can guarantee that both citizens and bureaucratic agencies will live up to contracts and respect the law, others will have little confidence in a country's long-term prospects.

2.   The first point argues persuasively for the second: we have discussed the fact that democracy and successful and prosperous economies tend to go together (though the tendency is not an absolute rule). A few dictatorships have managed to move national economies along. Chile during the Augusto Pinochet regime of 1970–1989 and China since 1979 have demonstrated that

---

[32] Orville Schell, "China—the End of an Era," *The Nation*, July 17–24, 1995, p. 85.

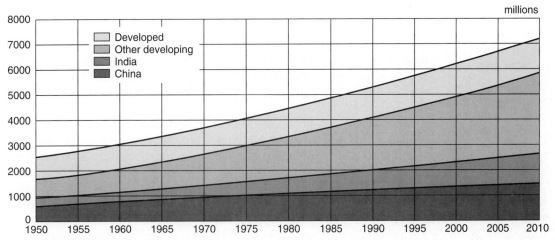

millions

Source: *The Economist Book of Vital Statistics* (New York: Random House, 1991), p. 12.

Figure 9.3
World Population, 1950–2010

both rightist and leftist governments can foster economic growth. Most dictatorships, however, destroy economic development. For every Pinochet, there are at least a dozen Duvaliers of Haiti. Investors naturally prefer to deal with governments that depend on durable legal institutions rather than political personalities who may tear up past agreements.

3. Government is the only institution that can effectively intervene in the economy, but it must do so wisely. For example, it does not benefit society to rush headlong into development with no consideration of the effect on the physical environment. The Soviet Union's economic policies ignored ecological concerns with catastrophic results. Industrialization was considered so important that lakes and rivers were terribly polluted. Nuclear waste was buried in public parks in Moscow. Leaded gasoline is still used in developing countries, including several in East Asia. All these policies have long-term negative health effects on populations that insist on achieving modernity regardless of cost to themselves or future generations.

4. Rapid modernization is often the goal of a government that feels it must move quickly to satisfy a population tired of austerity and deprivation. The rapidity frequently destroys traditional values and customs that have the sanctity of past centuries. In many developing societies, remember, amassing wealth is considered to be a vice rather than a virtue. People frown on commercial activities, preferring less development and more civility. Even the third American president, Thomas Jefferson (1801–1809), expressed doubts about those who made their livings from banking and mercantile activities and lived and worked in bustling cities whose inhabitants, Jefferson opined, led less wholesome and moral lives than their rural counterparts.

Government can't do much about changing values, especially if it is committed to promoting and encouraging modernization. The late Chinese leader, Deng Xiaoping (1904–1997), made a noncommunist remark when he proclaimed that "to get rich is glorious," perhaps the Chinese equivalent of the "greed is good" notion that developed during the 1980s in the United States. Dang's comments were also non-Confucian in stressing opportunism over obedience and harmony.[33]

China isn't the only country subject to such contradictions. Even in the very modern country of the United States, incongruities crop up. As indicated earlier, the American South at the end of the twentieth century is probably the most economically advanced region of the country. Its economic progress is most noticeable and in the "boomtown" of Atlanta. Other southern cities, such as Savannah and Charleston, have preferred to conserve their historical qualities even at the cost of curtailed economic expansion. Atlanta's local government has consistently and enthusiastically encouraged economic growth since Reconstruction in the 1860s and 1870s.[34]

5.   The size of the role government plays in economic development may be difficult to balance. We know that making government the sole coordinator of the economy is a prescription for disaster. At the same time, economic development is almost inconceivable without the presence of the public sector. Governmental agencies provide and usually help maintain an infrastructure critical for national development—public education, public health delivery systems, and public transportation systems are all essential.

6.   Government may have to intervene in delicate social issues if an economy is to move forward. This is not always easy, but on occasion a government is able to preserve tradition while still building a modern society. One of the most traditionalist societies in the world, Saudi Arabia, insists on keeping women hidden by veils and segregated from men. At the same time, though, Saudi females "are often sophisticated computer programmers, business professionals, and other educated women . . ."[35]

The Saudi government, consistent with orthodox Islam, permits and even encourages women to pursue their educations through the doctoral level and to enter the professions as long as they continue to appear in public veiled, with only their eyes showing. At workplaces, where they usually are removed from contact with any men who aren't family members, they may wear lab coats or business attire. Most westerners of both sexes would find such a social system far-fetched and intolerable, but different cultures travel different paths to modernization.

While few seriously dispute that government has a role in the economy,

---

[33] Ibid., 93.

[34] Alexander Stille, "Who Burned Atlanta: The Real Story of the All-New City," *The New Yorker,* July 29, 1996, pp. 52–58.

[35] Scott Peterson, "Women Live on Own Terms Behind the Veil," *The Christian Science Monitor,* July 31, 1996, p. 10.

The global economy in the Middle East: well-off Saudi shoppers.

public confidence has diminished that government always knows what it is doing. Every developed society has a large governmental presence and substantial social programs, but it also has increasingly severe restraints as populations age and taxes are increased to take care of the aged.[36] Ironically, the poorer societies envy these problems since they can't even dream of providing luxuries such as public housing and national health insurance. While the economies of the world may be globalizing, we are a long way from a truly integrated global economy.

SUMMARY

1. The world is increasingly becoming a global economy. This economy includes both advantages and dislocations; substantial regions of the world are extremely poor, while other countries are achieving unprecedented economic advances.

2. The trichotomy developed during the Cold War of First, Second, and Third Worlds applies far less in the 1990s, but it does

   highlight some of the more important discrepancies between countries that have and have not established viable free market economies in a democratic context.

3. Even a country fortunate enough to possess substantial natural resources may not have a developed economy that enables the growth of a strong middle class or provides most members of the society access to economic

---

[36] George Melloan, "The Welfare State Is Being Altered, Not Scrapped," *The Wall Street Journal,* July 29, 1996.

opportunities and benefits. Even in progressing countries, economic development rarely occurs evenly or smoothly across the society.

4. The relationship between free market economies and political democracy seems inevitable, but there are important exceptions. In some cases, economic development has stimulated a desire on the part of a rising middle class to gain access to the political process.

5. The world economy is still in the process of globalizing. As prosperity increases, large elements within traditionalist societies perceive modernization as a mixed blessing.

6. A global underclass may be developing as dozens of poor countries lag farther and farther behind the countries that have taken off economically. In the poor regions, government may have minimal authority or may even be replaced by nongovernmental organizations that provide services to the populace.

7. Economic development in several countries is racing against population increases that can threaten to overwhelm both the economic and social infrastructures.

8. Government has a permanent role in promoting and sustaining economic development. The role takes on different dimensions in different societies, and governments must know when and how much to intervene in economic development.

GLOSSARY

autarky   An economic system in which a society strives to achieve economic self-sufficiency within its own borders and become independent of foreign markets and international commerce.

corruption   The practice of bribing government officials to receive contracts for economic projects. Corruption is considered a way to do business in many societies.

G7   The top seven economies of the world—the United States, Japan, Germany, France, Italy, United Kingdom, and Canada. These countries may be joined in the near future by rapidly advancing economies such as China's.

NICs   The acronym for *newly industrialized countries*, most of which are located in East Asia and Latin America.

shock therapy   The sudden and rapid dismantling of a collectivized economy and maximized state control, replaced with a free market and minimal government supervision.

zero population growth (ZPG)   A policy that promotes a controlled birth rate, encouraging no more than two offspring per set of parents. Germans and Italians, for example, are barely replacing themselves and are only modestly increasing their populations because of immigration.

Political Geography and Demography

Human beings have, in a relatively brief time, populated the entire planet and established themselves as the earth's dominant species. Human populations did not multiply substantially until the last few centuries, as the industrial revolution and the development of medical science and health care delivery systems gradually lowered infant mortality and lengthened the life span. In 1800, the world's population reached the 1 billion mark for the first time; by 1900, it crossed 2 billion; and by 2000, there will be more than 6 billion people living on the planet.

In this chapter, we will examine how geography and population affect a country's political process. Geographical location—whether a country is an island, surrounded by mountain ranges, or set in an exceptionally hot or cold climate—is important because it helps determine a country's political history and culture. We will also study what impact the quality and quantity of a population have on a country's domestic and foreign policies. We will consider various demographic features, including the impact of ethnic and racial minorities, and examine how geographical setting, location, and natural resources combine with demographics to influence a country's participation in international politics.

DEMOGRAPHY, GEOGRAPHY, AND POLITICS

We can hardly overestimate the influence of demography and geography on politics. Demography's impact, though gradual, adds up to a substantial determinant: "Just as Maynard Keynes observed, the great events of history are often due to slow changes in demography, hardly noticed at the time."[1] As we will shortly see, population changes can have a drastic effect on a country's world standing, its future, and even its survival. For example, in one part of the world,

---

[1] "Ten Billion Mouths," *The Economist*, January 20, 1990, p. 14.

the West and several westernized countries, the population is "aging" because people are having smaller families, so a greater portion of the population is adult. Fewer children means more individual wealth, but it also means a smaller labor force takes on a greater burden to support people too old to work. By contrast, in nonwestern areas, economically speaking, there are too many young children; as we learned in chapter 9, a large proportion of young people means less individual wealth because a smaller portion of the population can be productive economically.

For the sake of convenience, we like to divide the world into distinct political blocks. During World War II (1939–1945), two blocks of countries, the Allies and the Axis powers, confronted one another. During the Cold War (roughly 1945–1990), the western democracies competed with the communist states for political and economic influence across the globe. Some world maps used in public high schools and libraries portrayed the communist countries in red during this period. If there was some uncertainty about a country's ideological allegiances, the country was often colored pink.

When the Castro regime was established in Cuba in 1959, and Castro declared himself to be a communist, Cuba became "red." The island is only ninety miles from Key West, Florida, a geographical fact disconcerting not only to many Americans who made their homes in southern Florida, but also to those further away who had not thought about Cuba previously. Suddenly, geography became a key factor in the Cold War.

Where we are often helps to determine our perspective on world events. During World War II, Americans on the West Coast felt that the United States should try to defeat the Japanese first. East Coast Americans were convinced it was in the national interest to concentrate on the Germans first. World events also have an effect on our knowledge of geography: few Americans could have identified Korea, Vietnam, Somalia, Bosnia, or Kuwait on a blank world map before American soldiers were sent to these countries.

Both our history and politics are determined to a great extent by our geography. Where we live is a tremendous determinant of who we are and how we view the world and our place in it. Russians, for example, see the world much differently from Americans. With the exception of the American Civil War (1861–1865), no military conflict has been fought on American soil since the republic was established (although British soldiers briefly turned up in Washington during the War of 1812 to burn down the White House and other public buildings). Surrounded by vast oceans and bordered by two countries, Canada and Mexico, incapable of and uninterested in doing harm to the United States, Americans have enjoyed peace and security through more than two centuries.

In contrast, the Russians have not been as fortunate. Sweden (then a major European power) in the early eighteenth century, France in the early nineteenth century, and Germany in the first half of the twentieth century all invaded Russia (Germany did so twice). The invasions were unsuccessful, but they caused terrible losses of life and property. The Russians remember them as examples of heroic and desperate struggles in their national history, and they find it difficult to trust countries that repeatedly invaded them.

Countries that are well-established and rich dominate the global economy. Several of these countries invited young immigrants from the Third World to join their labor forces during the 1960s, further changing world demographics. The governments of this more wealthy societies fear that a recession would make immigrants a natural target for popular resentment. Ironically, until a half-century ago, governments didn't have to worry about taking care of older people because there weren't very many, and immigrants had not become a factor in the labor force. Technology has changed and even reversed these situations. Especially in the West, the number of people over age sixty-five is increasing faster than the number of people under the age of fifteen, and governments are grappling with immigration policy.

THE POLITICAL IMPORTANCE OF SETTLED POPULATIONS

The earliest large populations settled in river valleys such as the Nile, Tigris-Euphrates, Indus, and Yangste, where fertile soil provided sufficient food for communities that sometimes numbered in the millions. The first governments most likely appeared in these areas to manage extensive agricultural systems and secure them against occasional marauders.

Baghdad on the Tigris River. Iraq is one of the world's earliest settled regions where political institution began to appear.

During these times, government took on the qualities familiar to any current resident in a political system: a central place of authority, representatives in various regions of the country, a bureaucracy to collect taxes, a judicial system to interpret laws and evaluate disputes, and a military formation to maintain order, discourage foreign invasion, and perhaps do some invading of its own.

Governments in ancient states did not provide many services to the population—they collected taxes, conscripted youths into the army, and maintained a haphazard network of roads. Even this latter activity was unnecessary in the political societies that were little more than small city-states, as during the classical period in ancient Greece. Tradition rather than government encouraged large families, but governments were grateful: large numbers of people were, until recent times, widely considered a crucial ingredient of political power. Yet the greater the population, the more governments felt the need to expand.

Population therefore became an early and critically important determinant of both economic and political power. To a substantial extent it still is, but the emphasis has changed; the *quality* of the population has become the main criterion of national success, supplanting the *quantity* of the population. Not that quantity is totally unimportant. A country with political ambitions must have enough people to be taken seriously, although the number itself will differ from region to region. A country with a population of around 30 million, for example, is almost automatically a serious regional power in the Middle East, while a similar population in western Europe or East Asia is considered modest.

Quality of population can prevail over quantity in both an economic and a military sense. Consider the two neighboring countries of Egypt and Israel. In the quarter-century between 1948 and 1973, these two countries fought four major wars with one another. Egypt's population is about ten times that of Israel's (see table 10.1), yet Israel won these wars. The real advantages were Israel's: its soldiers were better motivated (convinced they were fighting for their country's very survival), better fed, educated, trained, and equipped with a first-rate military technology. Numbers, of course, do matter. Yet, at least in the short run (Israel can't afford to fight a major conflict for more than a few weeks), quality prevailed over quantity.

Quantity of population can actually become a great disadvantage when it comes to a country's expression of political power. Robert Malthus, an eigh-

TABLE 10.1   Egypt and Israel: A Brief Demographic Comparison

	Egypt	Israel
Average life span	56 years	77 years
Literacy rate	45%	91%
Infant mortality	113 per 1,000 live births	7.8 per 1,000 live births
GDP per capita	$867	$13,000
Total population	58 million	5.8 million

Source: Adapted from information furnished by the Egyptian and Israeli embassies.

teenth-century scientist and demographer, warned that populations were out-growing the resources in most countries. It was easy to understand why he came to this conclusion: the industrial revolution was beginning to take off in central and Western Europe, and the population, especially in the urban areas, was increasing dramatically as sanitation and medical science made remarkable advances. Malthus argued that populations increase geometrically—in other words, they keep doubling every generation or so until some disaster occurs. A plague such as the Black Death that killed a third of Europe's population in the middle of the fourteenth century is certainly a memorable disaster. Yet, history strongly suggests that wars, famine, diseases, and other lethal events only briefly blunt population growth. Within a few generations after the scourge of the Black Death, Europe had more than recovered, experienced the Renaissance, and begun an economic and political domination of the globe that would not diminish until well into the twentieth century.

Malthusian fears have simply not been realized—at least, not yet. Malthus underestimated the ability of societies and technologies to care for the needs of several billion people. This is not to say that some countries aren't heeding the admonition to discourage population growth. China has a rigorously advocated if incompletely enforced one-child-per-family policy. Couples who insist on having more than one child sometimes face economic sanctions imposed on them by their own government. In other countries, particularly economically advanced ones, the government doesn't have to establish a population policy. Large numbers of children used to provide "social security" in old age—children and grandchildren provided for elderly family members. As economic prosperity has grown, so have government-sponsored old-age security plans. There is simply much less reason than there used to be to have large families.

Malthus still may prove right in some places. Populations are doubling precisely in societies where they shouldn't be. Many African countries see their populations double every twenty to twenty-five years. In true Malthusian fashion, Africa's rapid population growth has made it the world's only region to experience a decline in food production per person over the last three decades of the twentieth century.[2]

DEMOGRAPHY AND POLITICAL STABILITY

The ethnic and religious features of a population are frequently very powerful determinants of political stability and overall social harmony. A community with a history of ethnic and/or religious conflict can be severely detrimental. An already tense situation can erupt into violence when, over a few generations, it is possible for a majority to become a minority. When the "time of troubles" began in 1969 in Northern Ireland, Protestants outnumbered Catholics two to one. A quarter-century later, the proportion was reduced to three to two.

---

[2] "Sub-Saharan Africa," *The Economist*, September 7, 1996, p. 3.

Catholics, if current trends continue, could outnumber Protestants in another couple of decades. This prospect concerns many Protestants, who have long been a minority on the rest of an overwhelmingly Catholic island. Two main Protestant fears have substantially governed their political attitudes. They fear:

1. Becoming a religious minority in their own country (Northern Ireland) and suffering persecution accordingly

2. Being annexed by the Republic of Ireland and its dominant Catholic majority, and therefore becoming a small and probably permanent religious minority in a united Ireland.

Israeli Jews during the 1980s experienced similar anxieties when the Arab population of Israel began increasing at a much faster rate than the Jewish population. If Israeli Arabs combined with the Arab population of Israeli-occupied Gaza and the West Bank, Arabs could outnumber Jews in Israel in the foreseeable future. This anxiety was markedly reduced when hundreds of thousands of Russian Jews were allowed to migrate to Israel during the late 1980s and the Israeli government began to withdraw its presence in selected portions of the West Bank and all of Gaza in the middle 1990s.

The Irish and Israeli examples are only two of many we could cite. Governments have throughout history used population as a tool to change demographic features in regions and even in entire countries. China, for example, has since the 1960s systematically moved large numbers of its citizens into Tibet (which it annexed in 1958) to insure that Tibet will remain a Chinese province. Indigenous Tibetans are gradually becoming a minority in their own country. Governments who use demographics to further their political ends often cause much human suffering. The suffering or its legacy can endure for generations, causing political consequences that in themselves have significant potential for tragedy.

POLITICS, POLICY, AND POPULATION

The frequent drawing and redrawing of political boundary lines have created all manner and sizes of countries. The largest countries in the world, in terms of population, tend to include some with huge territories, but also several of relatively modest geographical size. (India, for example, has three times the population of the United States in one-third the territory.) The pressure of population growth has sometimes persuaded governments to expand their jurisdictions at the expense of their neighbors. Governments encourage large numbers of people to move for several reasons. The most important are:

1. Moving population into sparsely settled regions strengthens the claim of a government to the territories in question, an especially helpful policy if a territory is partially or wholly claimed by a neighboring country. For many years, for example, the Soviet government enticed Russians to move to western Siberia, offering all kinds of material benefits. They pursued this policy vigorously because of a not unjustified fear that China was interested in claiming parts of Siberia—parts that belonged to China for centuries before the Russians seized them in the eighteenth and nineteenth centuries. Similarly, the Israeli government has provided tempting tax advantages to motivate thousands of its citizens to establish homes in the West Bank. They reason that the more territory Israelis settle, the less territory they will have to surrender to the Palestinians in any final peace settlement.

2.   Government may sincerely desire to settle "virgin territory." During the nineteenth century, the United States government, seeking to expand to the West Coast, sold land very cheaply to Americans willing to go and settle the west. Brazil currently offers incentives to its citizens to move into the Amazon river valley, including some places where nonindigenous peoples have never gone. As they encounter indigenous populations they were previously unaware of, these Brazilians repeat history: five centuries ago, Europeans spread diseases to indigenous peoples who had built up no immunity against them, and Brazilians are doing the same today.

The expansionist tendencies of Germany, Italy, and Japan in the years leading up to and including World War II (roughly 1931–1945) were in part motivated by the desire to acquire natural resources and **living space** for their rapidly growing populations. Unlike the United States and Russia, these countries did not possess vast, untapped resources. They felt compelled to seek these resources elsewhere, and their solution was to expand across borders. Obviously, one political problem's resolution created many more. Germany's expansion into much of Europe and Japan's into Asia made a lot of enemies for

German soldiers invaded areas outside Germany's boundaries to acquire living space.

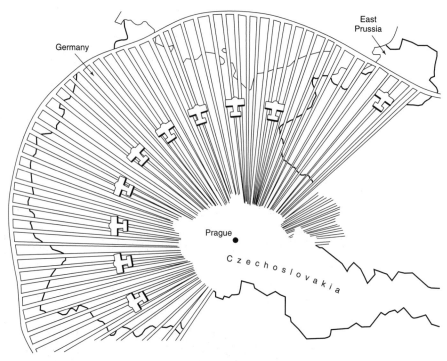

Source: J. P. Cole, *Geography of World Affairs*, sixth edition (London: Butterworths, 1983), p. 15.

Figure 10.1
German Map Showing Czechoslovakia as Threat (1930s)

both countries. Even today, neighbors still view both countries rather apprehensively, feeling they have reason to be suspicious.

A government may also implement an expansionist policy because of real or perceived threats to its sovereignty or even its continued existence. Consider, for example, a 1938 German-produced map that illustrates Germany's fear of Czechoslovakia (figure 10.1). The message was simple: if Germany did not dismember Czechoslovakia, it would have no choice but to live in the shadow of attack by a Czech air force that was in theory able to strike anywhere in Germany.

How real was the Czech threat? It wasn't very real at all. Czechoslovakia's population and military forces were a sixth the size of Germany's, and its military capacity was certainly inferior. Objectively, Czechoslovakia had neither a reason nor the ability to threaten its neighbor. But even brutally aggressive states feel compelled to somehow rationalize their ambitions. They can do so, as Germany did, by portraying the intended victim as a capable predatory force with evil designs. The intended victim must therefore attack in self-defense.

Within a country, the government may exercise policies that blunt economic growth, cutting off portions of the population from participating fully in the economy. The most blatant example concerns gender. As figure 10.2 suggests, women experience severe discrimination in much of the world, especially

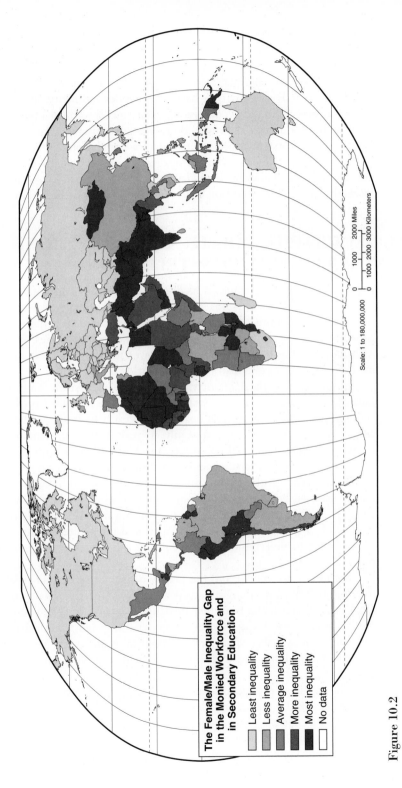

Figure 10.2
Female/Male Inequality in Education and Employment

(and ironically) in countries that need every available and qualified person to contribute. Women are often excluded from gaining access to educational facilities and training programs for skilled and well-paid jobs.

It is clear that the quality of demographics impacts substantially on economic growth. Discrimination based on gender, ethnicity, and/or religion is usually a prescription for economic disaster since a lot of people aren't allowed to be fully productive. However, there are governments that prefer economic stagnation or worse to losing control over a population. In fact, as bizarre and inhumane as it sounds, governments have been known to pursue economic policies that they know are likely to result in stagnation. Giving up control enforced by ideology or tradition is difficult for a political elite to do.

POLITICAL GEOGRAPHY, POLITICAL DISSOLUTION, AND THE INTERNATIONAL CONSTELLATION

A major power usually achieves its distinction by going through a period of expansion. The expansion is not usually terribly considerate of people who are in the way. The Empire of Japan, for example, decided to acquire territory and concomitant natural resources by pursuing military strategies. A political elite with modernizing tendencies came to power in Japan in 1868 and almost immediately set out to establish Japan as a world contender.

At times, though, a country may become excessively ambitious. Just as Japan began its expansion in East Asia during the last third of the nineteenth century, the United States was beginning to exert its influence beyond the Pacific coast of North America. Only a year before the modernizing elite launched Japan's territorial conquests, the United States acquired Alaska from Russia. American and Japanese goals in the Pacific were destined to conflict. In the closing years of the nineteenth century, the United States annexed several Pacific islands, extending American influence as far west as the Philippines, which it wrested from Spain in a three-month war in 1898. From that point on, it was only a matter of time before Japan and the United States collided with one another to determine which would be the supreme power in the Pacific region.

Both the government and the people of a country may sincerely believe in their nation's destiny. Many nineteenth-century Americans were convinced that the United States had a **manifest destiny** to expand across the continent from the Atlantic to the Pacific Ocean. The expansion led Americans into conflict with indigenous tribes that were in their way and with Mexico, which the United States eliminated as a serious rival in the Mexican-American war of 1846–1848.

The Japanese possessed a similar feeling about themselves, genuinely believing they were the natural leaders of Asia. To prove it, the Japanese for nearly half a century followed an aggressive military policy that led them to occupy Taiwan in 1895; wage a successful war against Russia in 1904 and 1905 that won the Japanese several strategic Pacific islands; colonize Korea beginning in 1910; and invade China beginning in 1931. Japan's goal was to become the greatest economic and military power in East Asia, in the process securing the natural resources and cheap (sometimes slave) labor required to maintain its great power and status. Japanese ambitions almost inevitably led them to Pearl Harbor and Hiroshima.

Almost every major country has an expansionist past. From the sixteenth through the nineteenth centuries, Britain and France, for example, established far-flung colonial empires that were global in scope. Nor did Britain and France go unchallenged. Germany and Japan were latecomers in the colonizing game, but they were still able in the late nineteenth and early twentieth centuries to acquire extensive holdings of their own. The rapacious nature of the territorial acquisitions of several countries helped produce World War I as great powers with global interests competed for the territory, population, and vast natural resources required to sustain industrial economies.

Expanding powers that eventually collide with one another provide only one example of how changing political lines and spheres of influence affect the international constellation. A **political implosion,** or total political collapse, within a country represents another. Whenever a political breakdown occurs, the impact can drastically change the entire international situation. When the Roman Empire dissolved over fifteen hundred years ago, for example, the map of the ancient world changed both drastically and irrevocably, creating opportunities for new and innovative political configurations.

More recently, the Soviet Union offers an example of what happens when a major global power first retreats from superpower status and then simply disappears as a political entity. By the end of 1991, the Soviet Union had not only ceased to exist but had been replaced by fifteen sovereign states, the former Soviet republics (FSRs). International politics, for four decades characterized by the Cold War between the Soviet Union and the United States, would now need to be described by a new paradigm. The world is likely in the process of formulating one, and we will examine some possible scenarios in a later chapter.

International politics became characterized by several complicated features after communism's collapse:

1. Instead of one Soviet nuclear superpower, four lesser ones now existed: Russia, Belorussia, Ukraine, and Kazakhstan.

2. Several of the new or renewed FSRs have themselves been in danger of dissolving as secessionist movements appeared and challenged the central government.

3. The new states have often engaged in territorial disputes—Russia and Ukraine, for example, have argued about who possesses Crimea. In 1954, then Soviet leader Nikita Khruschev "gave" Crimea to Ukraine as a gesture. This did not pose any special problem since Russia, Ukraine, and Crimea were all under the jurisdiction of the Soviet Union. While Crimea is still under Ukrainian authority, this region features a Russian majority that accounts for two-thirds of the total population. To further complicate matters, Crimea is the homeland of the Tatars, hundreds of thousands of whom Stalin exiled thousands of miles east to "Tatarstan" because he considered them untrustworthy. Many of these Tatars and their descendents want to go home to Crimea.

The collapse of one political system, even one as little lamented as the Soviet Union, can cause severe dislocations both internally and in the international arena. Public services, for example, may deteriorate or disappear completely. The Soviet health care delivery system at its best was far from equal to that of any western country, and the system grew worse after the Soviet collapse as services deteriorated. In the meantime, Russians who had grown accustomed to being a superpower now saw their empire quickly unravel. The 25 million Russians in the non-Russian FSRs were no longer a privileged elite, and non-Russian regions within the Russian federated republic itself began to question Russian sovereignty. The end of the Soviet state and the Cold War did not mean an end to friction and conflict, but simply created a new and unfamiliar international arena with its own problems. In some respects, as we will see later, it is also a more dangerous arena.

DEMOGRAPHY AND POLITICAL PARTITION

It is no secret that different kinds of people sometimes don't get along. In the same vein, some countries prefer not having to tolerate the company of those they don't like. This intolerance is frequently based on the way people look and speak, their religious convictions (whether wrong or entirely lacking), or their ethnic backgrounds. Toleration or its absence has tremendous implications for a nation's political history and culture. In literally dozens if not hundreds of current examples, diverse populations resolve their difficulties by simply drawing new boundary lines to replace those they don't like—a remedy known as **partition.**

Some partitions are *de facto* (actually, or by fact)—that is, the result of an armed conflict. Bosnia and Lebanon, for example, are partitioned into various religious communities for this reason. These separate communities may or may not be recognized by the international community, though with the passage of time they usually gain at least tacit acceptance. Other partitions are *de jure* (by right), officially arranged by the contending parties or perhaps imposed by an international organization such as the United Nations. De facto and de jure partitions have at least one feature in common: they rarely satisfy any of the parties, all of whom are convinced that someone else got the better deal.

The modern version of partition was a frequently-resorted-to solution in the aftermath of World War II, as major colonial powers withdrew from their possessions. The Middle East and South Asia had endured conflicts between such implacable foes that partition presented the only sensible way out. Thus, the British divided the Asian subcontinent in 1947 into India and Pakistan, creating states that were predominantly either Hindu or Muslim. Although the partition was not intended to hurt anyone, it caused great human suffering on both sides. As millions of people, Hindus and Muslims, moved (or were or-

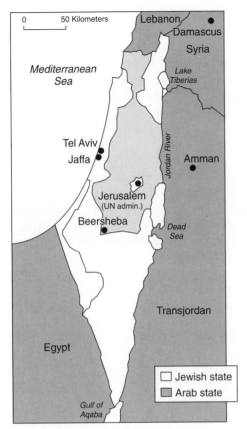

Figure 10.3
United Nations Partition Plan for Palestine, 1947

dered to move) hundreds of miles, mostly on foot, they suffered great hardship—the result of lack of adequate planning, poor sanitation, and thieves along the way. These two countries then fought several wars over disputed territory. Half a century later, Kashmir, on the border between India and Pakistan, is still the territorial prize in a dispute between the two countries.

In another region, the British became completely frustrated with their mandate in Palestine after World War II. They turned the matter over to the United Nations (UN). The UN partitioned Palestine in 1947 into Palestinian Arab and Jewish states (figure 10.3). The partition was agreeable only to the Jewish community; the Arabs refused to recognize the authority of the United Nations to impose a partition. In the resultant war, the UN partition plan was never implemented. Half a century and several wars later, the Jewish state of Israel is working out its form of partition with the Palestinians in the area of the West Bank.

The British more or less brokered the India-Pakistani partition, and the UN tried to broker one in Palestine. In both cases, an outside agent was involved in the partition process in a mostly nonmilitary fashion. In a third case, Cyprus in 1974, an outside agent with ethnic interests militarily imposed the partition. When Cyprus received independence in 1960, four-fifths of the population was Greek and the remainder was Turkish, two communities with a centuries-old tradition of hostility toward one another. The Turkish minority felt that the Greeks were exploiting and discriminating against them. In 1974, Turkey decided to come to the assistance of its kindred souls in Cyprus. Turkish soldiers invaded and occupied the northern (and more economically developed) third of the island, where they remain to insure continued Cypriot-Turkish autonomy.

Partitions aren't necessarily in place forever, of course. After World War II, Germany was partitioned into East and West. Forty-five years later, the two parts reunited as communism collapsed in Eastern Europe. Nor are partitions always violent. Occasionally two antagonists agree to what is called a "velvet divorce," the term applied to the peaceful and orderly dissolution of Czechoslovakia into the Czech Republic and Slovakia in 1993.

Unplanned and even accidental partitions also occur. Lebanon is a small country (about 4 million people in an area smaller than the state of Connecticut) with a remarkable number of religious sects. Several sects possess their own well-armed militias and have carved out their own territorial statelets. It is difficult for the official Lebanese government to exert its authority beyond the confines of the capital city of Beirut. Lebanon may be a country in name only—its inherent and historical disunity has resulted in a number of de facto "natural" partitions.

Political partitions and dissolutions are not confined to the nonwestern parts of the world. In 1996, a large proportion of Quebec's French-speaking community almost passed a referendum that would have amounted to the province's secession from Canada. Canada may still be partitioned sometime in the near future. Almost certainly, another referendum will arise and could pass, especially if more and more English-speakers leave the province and settle in other parts of Canada.

Italy may offer an even more precarious example; it is not the successfully united country it seems. A strong movement has arisen in the northern and most economically prosperous part of the country to partition Italy into two parts.[3] The Northern League's political program is innovative. The League plainly suggests that the way to end excessive taxation is to get rid of the central government and its penchant to take from the rich (north) and give to the poor (middle and south). It calls for ejecting the southern part of the country from Italy since it considers the south economically backward and overly dependent on welfare. The Northern League wants to establish a new state in the north and even has a name picked out—Pandania.

What do these partitions and potential partitions portend? Over the last decade or so, countries have been multiplying at an unprecedented rate, mostly because other countries, like the Soviet Union, have dissolved, or because competing ethnic and religious communities have separated, as in India and Pakistan.

Are more partitions on the horizon? We can't say with certainty that they aren't. Large and diverse countries such as India, Canada, and even China are all potential candidates, with substantial and disaffected minority populations concentrated in various regions. Smaller countries, though, may take the opposite tack and take the opportunity to merge rather than divide. Some neighboring countries or regions within countries have more in common with people just across the border than they do with people in other regions of the same country. Consider, for example, Estonia and Finland: their languages are almost identical (Estonians are fond of watching Finnish television) and their cultures and ethnic backgrounds are very similar. Azerbaijan and Turkey are another possible combination of countries that share similar or identical languages, religion, culture, and ethnic heritage.[4]

Even seemingly solid countries such as the United States and Canada may have regions that see natural partners across the border. Many residents of Washington state and Oregon feel a certain commonality with Canadians living in British Columbia and Alberta. By the same token, Americans along the country's southwestern border may develop an increasing economic and cul-

---

[3] Lara Santoro, "Flamboyant Politician Would March the North Out of Italy," *The Christian Science Monitor*, September 13, 1996, p. 7.

[4] "Mergers and Acquisitions," *The Economist*, August 31, 1996, p. 44.

tural overlap across the frontier with Mexico. If northern Italians feel disaffected with Rome, Quebecois with Ottawa, and Chechens with Moscow, it is not unreasonable to conclude that some Americans living in the westernmost states (or anywhere, for that matter) might have less than maximum loyalty to Washington.

This is not to say that the United States is close to unraveling—it isn't. But very few countries in the world enjoy permanent frontiers that can be traced back more than a few generations. In any event, there is no reason to believe that after centuries of constantly shifting national boundary lines, no changes are yet to come. We will briefly examine the impact partitions will have on the conduct of international politics in a later chapter.

SUMMARY

1. A country's geographical location and the size and quality of its population are crucial determinants of a society's history, culture, and political processes and institutions.

2. Political power once depended heavily upon the numerical size of a nation's population. Today, the quality of a population—its health, education, and skill level—is increasingly the most important demographic aspect.

3. Population growth is rapidly increasing in relatively poor countries. Economic development is not keeping up and in many instances may even be regressing.

4. Powerful countries usually have a history of territorial expansion. Their expansions were designed to secure additional land for a growing population, to acquire needed natural resources, or both. Expansionist countries can eventually collide, as Japan and the United States did in 1941.

5. Colonial empires built on expansionist agendas inevitably seem to collapse. The last to do so was the Russian-dominated Soviet Union.

6. Political partition is a common if less than satisfactory solution to historical conflict between communities of people. The differences that cause partition may be ethnic, religious, linguistic, and/or cultural in nature.

7. While partition is one way to resolve disputes between different communities, forging economic mergers between like-minded regions in different countries may become a new way.

GLOSSARY

living space   The German term, popularized during the 1930s, describing the goal used to justify acquiring territory in eastern Europe, removing the indigenous populations, and sending Germans to replace them—the Germans needed "living space."

manifest destiny   The term used to describe and justify the American expansion from ocean to ocean.

partition   The political remedy of dividing a territory among two or more antagonistic communities without much likelihood of satisfying any of the parties.

political implosion   The collapse of a political system from within, usually caused by a breakdown in public confidence in the economic and political institutions.

Political Violence

If one even glances at human history, it is easy to conclude that we are a species with a disposition toward violence, and perhaps escalating violence at that. The twentieth century has seen two world wars and numerous other conflicts that visited unprecedented violence on large civilian populations in meticulously planned and purposefully pursued endeavors.

The United States is a comparatively violent country, but with the exception of the Civil War, most of the violence has thus far been criminal rather than political. Not that this makes much difference to the victims of violence. Nearly all European countries (except for obvious exceptions such as war-plagued Albania and Bosnia) are less violent than the United States. Some theories about human evolution suggest we descended from violent ape-like predecessors. Perhaps, the reasoning continues, the United States is an unusually violent country because "most of the killer-apes migrated to America over the centuries."[1] Moreover, most of these killers were men, since males are much more violent than females and kill twenty times as often.[2]

There is little doubt that the United States has a great deal of crime and that much of the crime is violent.[3] Political violence is not unknown in the American or other democracies, but the fact that most people worry more about criminal than political violence is instructive. In most nondemocratic societies, political violence exceeds criminal violence. Criminals, too, can be more

---

[1] Peter C. Sederberg, *Fires Within: Political Violence and Revolutionary Change* (New York: HarperCollins, 1994), p. 103.

[2] See Richard Wrangham and Dale Peterson, *Demonic Males: Apes and the Origins of Human Violence* (Boston: Houghton Mifflin, 1996).

[3] At the end of 1995, 1.6 million Americans were in state and federal prisons. This is a high number that also represents a high proportion: one out of every 167 Americans is in prison. Each inmate costs $25,000 annually to maintain, so we spend about $40 billion on all 1.6 million prisoners. "Marketplace," National Public Radio, August 19, 1996.

afraid of a government with minimal or no concern about legal rights and processes.[4]

This chapter examines various dimensions of political violence. We will be concerned with legal as well as illegal violence, the sometimes conflictive and adversarial relationship between state and citizen, and the kinds of violence—wars, government brutality, and terrorism—that often characterize the international constellation and frequently define relations between specific states.

GOVERNMENT, PEOPLE, AND VIOLENCE

Do we as human beings really possess a genetic disposition toward violence? Most people live their lives without ever committing violent acts, and many are fortunate enough to never suffer a serious violent act committed against their persons. Other people cause others pain throughout their lives.

In western societies, most of us confine any violent expressions to officially sanctioned channels and usually express violence in a vicarious fashion—for instance, at a football game. We appreciate the fact that the opposing side is our political equal and is guaranteed the same rights we enjoy. Yet for a few hours

> . . . there is only one side that's created equal—yours. The rest are misshapen, mutant bastards, who deserve to suffer horribly because they are so ugly.[5]

Perhaps this is a slight overstatement but, except for occasional aberrations, violence is normally constrained and kept within bounds at a sporting event.

Political violence is a different matter. We who live in stable polities where government discharges its obligation to protect human rights enjoy wonderful benefits—personal security, enriched life-styles, and material comfort. Citizens in democratic states believe it is the government's responsibility to create and sustain a secure environment. Many nondemocratic governments will not guarantee such rights. Argentina during the 1970s and 1980s, for example, was ruled by a military regime that caused thousands of its own citizens to permanently disappear. We now know many of these people were political prisoners who were arrested, drugged, and pushed out of airplanes over the Atlantic Ocean.[6]

A government is, by common agreement, established to protect its citizenry from harm. The potential for harm may come from outside sources or

---

[4] Driven to desperation, normally law-abiding citizens, even in a country such as Iraq, will commit violent crimes. The government has responded with Koran-inspired amputations of the hand for thievery and automatic death sentences for especially violent robberies and murder. It blames the United States for imposing economic sanctions that have made Iraqis miserable. Neil Mac Farquhar, "After the War Blockade, Crime Frays Life in Iraq," *The New York Times*, October 18, 1996, p. A3.

[5] Bill Buford, "Un-American Activities," *The New Yorker*, July 8, 1996, p. 90.

[6] Horacio Verbitsky, *The Flight: Confessions of an Argentine Dirty Warrior*, trans., Esther Allen (New Press, 1996).

from elements within the citizenry itself. When its political authority is widely respected and accepted, a government can do a fairly solid job of providing the physical security each of us requires. A citizen need not worry about the government itself doing harm since its agents are subject to the same laws that apply to the rest of society. Governments that carry this out are usually (but not exclusively) democratic.

Some societies have decidedly undemocratic governments who nevertheless protect individuals from crime. The streets of Baghdad and Beijing are a lot safer at night than those of New York and Washington, D.C.—unless, that is, an Iraqi citizen in Baghdad is overheard making a disparaging joke about Saddam Hussein (which may earn him or her a death penalty) or a resident of Beijing suggests that competitive and free elections would be good for China. In these instances, the government infringes on rather than protects personal security.

Government all too often is the source of, rather than the resolver of, political conflict. The government monitors all other social agents for potential violence. Violence is considered legitimate only when it is applied by an authorized agency of the government (the police or a national militia, for example). This aspect of political violence, though, becomes controversial when a sizable number of citizens or the international community consider the government itself to be illegitimate. This happens when a government commits arbitrary acts of violence that are injurious to basic human rights.

Unfortunately, examples are abundant. In the Russian Federated Republic, Chechens (residents of a region called Chechnya) do not accept control from Moscow. With good reason, Kurds in northern Iraq are convinced that the central government wishes to destroy them. Indigenous tribes in southern Mexico are hostile to the central authority in Mexico City, which they feel has cheated and exploited them (probably also with good reason).

Still, while violence is always unpleasant, it may not always be legally wrong. **Legal violence** is the prerogative of the state. This means the state must apply violence in a fashion that the law sanctions and the public voluntarily supports. In democracies, legal violence is applied with restraint and, usually, only as a last resort. **Illegal violence** is violence inflicted by unauthorized agents. It is illegal violence that understandably worries most people; in the summer of 1996, 61 percent of Americans listed crime as their second concern (their first was the educational system).[7] To make matters worse, a state can commit illegal violence if the state violates its own laws.

It is occasionally difficult to separate criminal from political violence. Sometimes the two overlap, as criminal organizations become increasingly powerful while governmental authority weakens and law enforcement deteriorates or ceases to exist altogether. This happened in Somalia in the early 1990s; by the middle 1990s, Bosnia was deteriorating as criminal gangs, probably with

---

[7] Dale Russakoff, "Faces in a Crowd: Schools in New York are Running Out of Space and Tax Revenues," *The Washington Post Weekly Edition*, September 23–29, 1996, p. 31.

The skulls of Tutsis massacred by Hutus in Rwanda during the summer of 1994.

more money than any honest business, competed with one another to purchase government concessions being privatized.[8] Large parts of Bosnia were falling under gang control as different criminal organizations carved out their own fiefdoms. Needless to say, criminal gangs are not often democratically inspired. However, they can become the only source of order in a region.

Violence is normally considered illegal whenever nonstate agents commit it. Yet the state can be the greatest perpetrator of political violence. **Death squads** in several Central American countries, though not official agents of the state, have murdered people opposed to the policies of the government. During the 1980s in El Salvador, for example, off-duty police officers moonlighted by murdering civilians the government considered a threat.

This is not to say that democracies are immune from illegitimate political violence. In 1968, a police riot occurred during the Democratic Party Convention in Chicago. Officers freely swung their nightsticks at the heads of Vietnam war protesters who were calling them names and raining plastic bags of excrement on them from the upper stories of nearby buildings. Chicago was a brief and dreadful but instructive exception.

Clearly, a historical and often intimate association exists between violence and the political process. This association, though, is sporadic. Most governments are actually nonviolent most of the time. A large proportion are alto-

---

[8] Chris Hedges, "Gangs Descend to Pick Bosnia's Carcass Clean," *The New York Times*, October 7, 1996, p. A4.

gether loathe to invoke violent methods to preserve order except as a last resort.

Yet there is no denying that political violence characterizes many modern governments. Perhaps the greatest current example is in sub-Saharan Africa. Several states in this region have not experienced sustained, peaceful political change since they become independent countries in the 1950s and 1960s. African politicians are in a profession that has an incredibly high mortality rate:

> *In the past thirty years or so, Africa has averaged a couple of coups a year, and more than two dozen presidents and prime ministers have lost their lives through political violence.*[9]

The political violence that plagues Africa is at least in part related to the pronounced economic misery of most of the population. Much of the developed world has lost interest in Africa. Moreover, some countries that had an interest did the region little good. Soviet economic advisors, for example, ruined every African economy they influenced.[10] Collectivized economies worked no better in Africa than they did anywhere else. Economic despair and tribal conflicts have combined to make political violence the rule rather than the exception in many African countries.

THE PHENOMENON AND UNCERTAINTY OF STATE VIOLENCE

The ability of the state to sustain itself and its institutions is described as **enforcement violence.** The term sounds ominous, yet both democratic and nondemocratic regimes assume they must maintain order and enforce legal resolutions to social problems. Very few regimes have ever had an interest in fomenting chaos.

But in politics there are always exceptions, and some of the exceptions are critically important. In China during the Great Cultural Revolution (approximately 1966–1976), mobs of ideologically inspired youths, with the government's encouragement, became a law unto themselves as they rampaged through the streets of China's major cities and throughout the countryside. The Chinese communist leadership had reasoned that after two decades of quiet, it was necessary to renew the revolution that had brought it to power in 1949. A generation with no personal memory of pre-Revolutionary China seemed the perfect vehicle. Members of the older generation whose revolutionary fervor was considered inadequate were paraded through the streets with duncecaps on their heads. Others were exiled from the cities to rural areas to learn humility by working with their hands in open fields. Some were merely beaten, and not a few people lost their lives from mistreatment.

---

[9] "Sub-Saharan Africa," *The Economist*, September 7, 1996, p. 4.

[10] Ibid.

During this period, China demonstrated an excellent example of the dysfunctional aspects of political violence. Millions of Chinese teenagers who should have been in school learning to become engineers and scientists were instead wasting their time bullying their fellow citizens. It is difficult to be sure how much talent and productivity were lost because of this self-defeating policy. Perhaps even more frightening, though, was another lesson—how easily even a strong totalitarian government can lose control of events, even if it instigated those events itself. The violence the leadership had encouraged quickly got out of hand. In the end, the state had to call out army units in some regions to insist that the students return to their homes and schools.

It is disconcerting to realize how quickly a government can lose control of events in a territory and population it supposedly has jurisdiction over. When the government loses control or simply disappears from the scene, criminal and political violence tend to blend. Along the border between the United States and Mexico, for example, drug-trafficking gangs have acquired so much power, wealth, and organization that citizens on both sides of the border are moving away, selling their homes and ranches to representatives of the gangs at low prices.[11]

States, of course, can be exceptionally violent toward one another. Wars in the twentieth century have involved entire populations, usually as victims, but also as willing and even enthusiastic participants who feel they are fighting for their lives. (Sometimes they are.) Prior to modern times, major wars were more often confined to battlefields safely removed from civilian population centers. By the 1930s, though, armies in Europe and Asia were occupying entire countries and systematically abusing local populations. In fact, armies received a new duty: they were to help eliminate populations considered dangerous or unwanted by the occupying regime. Armed forces now became collaborators and participants in political violence rather than merely the military arm of a regime's policy.

POLITICAL VIOLENCE AS THE SIN OF OMISSION

If we return to our original role of government as the protector of individual security and property, then we have reason to assume the worst when government is insufficiently filling the role. Take the deplorable institution of slavery, for instance. Though outlawed by every government on earth, it flourishes on three continents. In the African republic of Mauritania, which in 1980 outlawed slavery for the third time, one out of every twenty residents is a "full-time" slave. Many more are "semi-free"—people who aren't allowed to marry

---

[11] William Branigin, "Drug Gangs' Terror on the Texas Border," *The Washington Post National Weekly Edition*, September 30–October 6, 1996, pp. 17–18.

or own property without the permission of those who, in effect, own their labor.[12]

Most slaves are children and women, and black Africans still furnish the greatest number of slaves. Women of all races in many countries are treated as chattel and endure a great deal of abuse. In fact, women can be bought or sold like cattle and even for cattle—in Sudan, five cows is the going rate for a young and healthy female.[13] While in the West, women tend to outlive men, the reverse is true in numerous African and Middle Eastern countries.

Some governments attempting to encourage the growth of the free market ignore certain forms of slavery. In China, young women are kidnapped and forced into slavery. An unmarried man can purchase a woman for between $250 and $500 from a kidnapper, no questions asked.[14] Enslavement is nearly unknown in the cities, but it is a familiar activity in the rural areas of China, where three-quarters of the population still lives and works[15] and where women are valued as cheap farm labor.

Slavery is not the only form of violence governments fail to quench. Sometimes a government tolerates violence because it diverts the attention of masses of people from their problems and from their dissatisfaction with the government. Two millenia ago, unknown thousands were slaughtered by wild animals or by one another in the Roman colisseum. Government employees financed and even choreographed these activities for the "amusement" of spectators. An emperor remained popular as long as he could provide imaginative and spectacular ways to kill people.

Violence is an effective political tool in a variety of ways. Secretary of State William Seward (1861–1869) advised President Abraham Lincoln at the beginning of the Civil War to ask Congress to declare war on both Britain and France as a way to unite the country and keep the North and South from one another's throats. Lincoln wisely dismissed the advice. At the time, though, the idea was not completely without merit. A foreign war against two major powers would certainly have concentrated the entire country's focus.

Mao Tse-tung, founder and longtime ruler of the People's Republic of China (1949–1976), is remembered for his statement that "political power comes out of the barrel of a gun." In his case, this was no exaggeration. Mao apparently had few qualms about using violence both before and after he came to power. Nor is this atypical. In both the Soviet Union and China, many times more people perished *after* the revolution brought totalitarian regimes to power than *during* it.

---

[12] "The Flourishing Business of Slavery," *The Economist*, September 21, 1996, p. 44.

[13] Ibid., p. 43.

[14] Seth Faison, "Women as Chattel: In China, Slavery Rises," *The New York Times*, September 6, 1995, pp. A1 and A4.

[15] Ibid.

A sick Polish survivor in the Hannover-Ahlem concentration camp receives medicine from a German Red Cross worker after liberation in 1945.

IDEOLOGICALLY DRIVEN VIOLENCE

As we saw in an earlier chapter, a fascist or communist movement usually has the capacity and the will to violently campaign for political power. Once in power, an ideologically motivated regime can become more rather than less violent. It now has, after all, an entire state apparatus—secret police, intelligence services, and the army—available for violence. Those who don't fit a regime's definition of loyal citizen often find themselves in serious trouble.

For millions of people and dozens of regimes, ideology is a convenient way to relate to the world, though not necessarily a realistic way. The trouble begins when some do not, or because of race or ethnic background cannot, subscribe to the prevailing ideology. Ideologies frequently have their own logic. Those who don't accept the ideology must be removed.

Ideologically based regimes are intent on building or returning to a golden age in which disapproved minorities have no place and no future. The Nazis wanted to create a "New Germany." The Soviet communists wanted to create the "new Soviet man." In each case, society had to be purged of those the government considered totally irredeemable. Jews and gypsies in Germany, and "counterrevolutionaries" in the Soviet Union and, later, in China, were deemed believed unfit to live in the new society each regime was about to construct.

Much the same happens with regimes that base their legitimacy on theocratic or religious pillars. In Iran and Sudan, for example, holding a religious conviction inconsistent with the government-endorsed theology, or holding no conviction at all, can draw officially sanctioned reprisals, some of them involving physical penalties. Blasphemy is, for example, a capital crime in these countries.

Ideologically based violence, when the state apparatus applies it, is political violence with practically no chance of being moderated. In fact, moderates are often among the first victims of violence. Such violence has frequently worked against the very interests of the regime producing it. During World War II, the German government was intent on exterminating all the Jews it could get its hands on. So much materiel and personnel were diverted to catching, transporting, and murdering Jews that the German war effort was seriously impaired.

Another genocidal example is the Pol Pot regime in Cambodia (1975–1979) which caused the deaths of nearly two million people of a population of seven million by executing them or by enforcing government-sanctioned and coordinated starvation. The goal of this madness was to create a new agriculturally based society by cleansing the old society of useless people such as physicians, teachers, engineers, and intellectuals—in short, anyone who couldn't easily become a farmer. Before it was overturned, Pol Pot's government had concluded it might be worth killing nearly everyone over the age of eighteen to achieve an agricultural commonwealth free of anyone who might retain memories of the previous "corrupt" society. (How the executioners over the age of eighteen were going to be persuaded to eventually kill themselves remains a mystery.)

These examples are far from atypical. When a regime that is strongly motivated by ideology comes to power, it is almost certain to be insecure because of its correct perception that large segments of the population may not endorse the ideology. Such a regime almost always comes to power through a revolution and is usually especially insecure in the immediate aftermath. Upon achieving power, such a revolutionary regime often engages in a "reign of terror" to eradicate all known opposition.[16]

The term **reign of terror** originated with the French Revolution (1789–1799); wholesale and state-sanctioned terror occurred from 1792 to 1794. Thousands of people, many of whom were apparently guilty of no crime and who had no interest in politics, were publicly executed. To the revolutionary regime, it didn't matter—the goal was to rid society of a social class, in this case the landed aristocracy, and anyone viewed as the aristocracy's retainers, sympathizers, or supporters. Similar phenomena occurred after the revolutions in Russia, China, Cuba, and numerous other countries that have come under the sway of self-righteous regimes.

---

[16] For a well written and readable analysis of what happens after a successful revolution, see the classic work by Crane Brinton, *The Anatomy of Revolution* (New York: Vintage Books, 1965).

Of course, the installation of a democratic political structure doesn't necessarily mean the end of a country's ideologically inspired violence. The newer democracies that appeared in the early 1990s in places as diverse as Russia and Nicaragua are instructive examples. Both countries have democratically elected executives and legislatures, yet plenty of nondemocratic residues remain in both countries.[17] Look at these countries closely and one can see plenty of ideologically minded individuals in the bureaucracy, police, and army who have not given up on restoring their preferred political system.[18] Moreover, both countries are continually faced with regional insurrections among people uninterested in accepting and deeply resentful of authority from the political center, regardless of whether the authority was earned through the democratic process.

Nor are countries that have developed a solid tradition of democratic processes immune from ideologically based violence. Many ethnic, religious, and linguistic minorities in India have violently expressed their desire for increased autonomy or outright independence frequently during the first half-century of the country's independence.[19] It is still possible that India could disintegrate into several smaller states.

A small country can disintegrate into fiefdoms controlled by warlords who vary between being politically violent themselves and exerting a force for stability. Since 1975, Lebanon's central government, for example, has had minimal or no control over much of the country. The neighboring powers Israel and Syria, whose agents control the southern half and northeastern parts of the country, respectively, have haphazardly replaced some of the authority of the Lebanese government. Much of the country, though, has been divided by local sectarian militias, each of which controls anywhere from a few square city blocks in Beirut, the capital city, to a few hundred square miles in the country's hinterland. Each militia subscribes to a radical ideology or belongs to a radical religious sect that does not tend to favor political compromise or the peaceful resolution of disputes.

THE VIRTUE OF MINIMAL POLITICAL VIOLENCE

A political regime that can govern with minimal or no violence is an effective one. It is either a regime that has so ruthlessly suppressed its opposition that it has little need to invoke violence or, and more preferably, a regime whose political institutions enjoy such widespread and voluntary support that violence becomes totally unnecessary. Neither extreme model exists in reality.

Political and social order is what nearly all regimes strive for and sincerely desire. But democratic and nondemocratic regimes go about achieving this goal in different ways. One scholar of the subject has suggested that order is

---

[17] Hendrick Hertzberg, "Nicaragua's Second Act," *The New Yorker*, September 23, 1996, pp. 7–8.

[18] Ibid.

[19] "The State We're In," *The Economist*, September 14, 1996, p. 40.

achieved either through a **coercion** or **consensus theory of order.**[20] In the coercion theory of order, might makes right, whereas in the consensus theory, widely accepted and institutionalized norms and values maintain order. Democracies such as the United States, according to consensus theory, have satisfactorily resolved the issues strong enough to threaten or destroy the national consensus that has taken generations to establish. Issues such as abortion may still detract from the overall consensus, but they aren't able to destroy the public's confidence in the generally accepted institutions available to deal with the issue.

Coercive theory often assumes that a large part of the country must be subdued to create order. The regime may enforce a value system, with violence if necessary, on an unwilling or resistant segment of the population, persecuting or forcibly converting religious, ethnic, economic, or sociocultural minorities to another value system or ideology. The regime might choose to leave them alone if they simply keep quiet and tacitly accept a less than equal place in the political system.

Order, however achieved, is not always the most desirable quality. In societies where slavery was a thriving institution, such as ancient Rome or the American south of the eighteenth and nineteenth centuries, there was usually order, but the order actually oppressed a large proportion of the population. More recently, millions of former Soviet citizens enjoyed reasonably comfortable, orderly lives even though they lived under a stagnant bureaucratic system that gave them little personal liberty. Some Russians actually miss the order that is now missing from their lives. The Chinese communist regime, in contrast, has provided enough economic excitement through its advocacy of the free market[21] to sustain its preferred form of totalitarian stability.

TERROR: THE FULLEST EXPRESSION OF POLITICAL VIOLENCE

In the last third of the twentieth century, political terrorism has become the most explicit form of political violence. It is a phenomenon that has existed for centuries, tracing back to Roman times.[22] Modern versions of terrorism are many times more horrific because of the availability of increasingly lethal weapon systems. No longer are terrorists simply political assassins or isolated bomb throwers. Nor are their targets individual if important officeholders. Terrorism terrifies because, in its modern version, anyone and everyone is a potential target.

---

[20] Sederberg, *Fires Within*, pp. 14–15.

[21] The Chinese leader, Deng Yao-ping (1904–1997) has stated that "it is glorious to get rich," a radical opinion for a communist, but an excellent one for a politician.

[22] David C. Rapoport, "Fear and Trembling: Terrorism in Three Religious Traditions," *The American Political Science Review*, vol. 78, no. 3 (September 1984), pp. 658–76.

Terrorism has many characteristics and forms. For the purposes of this chapter, we will introduce two of the most general expressions of terror: state and nonstate. While the two occasionally overlap, each has distinct features and activities. In this section, we will examine the basic essentials of each.

Nonstate Terrorism

Nonstate terrorists are usually individuals who have determined it is no longer worthwhile to try to accomplish political objectives within the law, a law which to them represents the power of an immoral and/or illegitimate regime. They are contemptuous of the society's political institutions and practices. While such characteristics could simply make someone politically apathetic or a disillusioned but harmless recluse, a minority of those who feel politically alienated also consider themselves at war with not only the prevailing power structure, but the structure of the entire society. Before someone becomes a terrorist, he or she must first believe that society is so corrupt it is irredeemable; it must instead be destroyed, root and branch. If this sounds harsh and unreasonable to most of us, it is because we prefer the society we live in, with its faults, to an unknown and perhaps worse environment.

Nineteenth-century terrorists confined themselves to shooting or bombing high-ranking government officials, including U.S. President William McKinley (1897–1901). The current age of political terrorism is generally considered to have begun in 1968 as airplane hijackings reached almost epidemic proportions. Remarkably few people were seriously injured or lost their lives in these hijackings, and as airport security improved (at least in most places), hijackings rapidly decreased in frequency.

Unfortunately, as terrorists become frustrated in one area, they tend to develop newer, progressively more lethal methods. They also learn from one another:

> *Analysis of terrorist incidents indicates that many groups consciously apply lessons learned from previous terrorist incidents. For example, terrorist tactics are changing constantly in response to changes and improvements in the ability of the authorities to manage particular types of terrorist incidents.*[23]

Pan Am flight 103's destruction in 1988, caused by a bomb placed in its cargo bin, is a frightening example of escalating terrorism. The bombing of a federal facility in Oklahoma City in 1995 is another. Moreover, a disconcerting number of religiously inspired terrorists, convinced they will immediately enter paradise upon physical **martyrdom,** are willingly dying for their causes. In Israel during the spring and summer months of 1996, Arab suicide bombers carrying explosives climbed aboard public buses, killing themselves and dozens of other people. After a lull, more suicide bombers appeared in 1997 blowing themselves up along with unsuspecting Israeli shoppers in crowded marketplaces.

---

[23] Grant Wardlaw, *Political Terrorism: Theory, Tactics, and Countermeasures,* 2d. ed. (Cambridge: Cambridge University Press, 1989), p. 172.

We can summarize several critical and somewhat interrelated differences between the older and newer forms of terrorism:

1. *Civilians are the target of choice.* Many terrorist organizations no longer consider civilians innocent bystanders. Instead, no one is innocent in a depraved society. If a terrorist views a society as corrupt or immoral, he or she is likely to view everyone in that society as a contributor to the corruption and immorality, or at least as a willing collaborator. Since individuals are as bad as the system, individuals should be destroyed along with it. Thus, civilian aircraft, department stores (a favorite target of the Irish Republican Army), or public buses (a target of the Hamas organization in Israel) have become legitimate targets. The only really innocent people are those self-righteously terrorizing the rest of the population. Murdering random civilians also has a practical aspect. In doing so, terrorists demonstrate that no one is safe and no government is capable of protecting its own citizenry from their violence.

2. *Terrorist organizations believe in and occasionally practice maximum lethality.* Because terrorists now go after civilian populations, it is inevitable (and, from the terrorist's standpoint, desirable) that people of all genders and ages will be killed or injured. The terrorist's objective is to insure that no one feels secure going to work, going shopping, or attending school, since there are no safe places. Making people afraid to venture from their homes and even making them feel insecure inside their homes is the ultimate goal.

Most successful terrorist organizations tend to enjoy at least a degree of state sponsorship. Iran, North Korea, Libya, and Syria are countries that have often been linked to terrorist organizations. State sponsors are often much like the terrorists themselves: self-righteous in the face of the international community's condemnation. Some organizations have actually enlisted several states as sponsors. Why do some governments employ known terrorists? Several reasons apply:

1. *State sponsorship is cheap.* A government can provide a terrorist organization with relatively low-cost assistance by supporting training camps and providing safe houses and financing. Moreover, a government can withdraw its support at any time. It need not provide explanations. Once a government decides continuing support is no longer in its best interests, it can cut the organization.

2. *State sponsorship often serves a government's foreign policy objectives.* The Iranian government, for example, has provided support to organizations such as Hizbollah in Lebanon as part of its quest to extend both Iranian influence and the Shiite Muslim faith. Syria for decades has sponsored terrorist groups that attack Israeli civilian targets. It has also used terrorism to pressure Israel to comply with the Syrian government's foreign policy goals, including the removal of the Israeli presence in the Golan Heights, located on the Syrian-Israeli frontier.

3. *State sponsorship can be denied or withdrawn.* It is difficult to demonstrate links between a government and the terrorist organizations it sponsors, and no government prefers to make its support of terrorism public. A few governments may actually acknowledge a link, but they deny that they are sponsoring terrorism, arguing that they are supporting "freedom fighters" in their just struggle against a powerful enemy.

With the passage of time, most terrorist organizations have come and gone. It is difficult to be sure at any given time how many terrorist organizations exist or how threatening they are to the governments and societies they have targeted. To confuse the authorities, some organizations commit an outrage and then simply reassemble under a new name. Some have been known to claim credit for the acts of others.

During the 1960s and 1970s, the most public terrorist organizations were motivated by secular ideologies on the extreme left and, to a somewhat lesser extent, on the extreme right. The Baader-Meinhoff gang in Germany, for example, targeted members of both the business and political establishments, arguing their leaders were conspiring to exploit and abuse the masses of working people under their control. The Red Brigades in Italy took a similar approach, singling the same kinds of people out for kidnapping and extortion and shooting public figures in the kneecaps and groin. (A former Italian prime minister, Aldo Mori, was kidnapped and eventually murdered in the most famous case of Italian terrorism.) Most of these groups have either faded from the scene or have seen their members apprehended and imprisoned.

The winding down of the Cold War helped curtail the activities of many of the ideologically driven groups. Moreover, the arrival of radical religious regimes, first in Iran in 1979 and several years later in Sudan and Afghanistan, to an appreciable extent shifted the focus of terrorism. Most if not all major religions have extremist movements: Shiite Muslims in Iran, Hindu nationalists in India, Jewish settlers in the West Bank, and a few Christian sects in North America have inspired some terrorist activities.

These movements often target democratic societies they view as corrupt and decadent. The cleric regime in Iran, for example, constantly refers to the United States as the "great Satan" (Israel is the "little Satan"). Religiously inspired terrorists are, it seems, even less likely to object to dying than their secular cohorts. A devout Muslim, for example, who perishes while attacking an enemy of Islam believes he or she goes immediately to paradise. Martyrdom is encouraged in this life and rewarded in the next.

State Terrorism

A government may have some very practical reasons for imposing a violent regime on its citizenry. The more brutal and sustained features of state terrorism are areas of concern that represent an underdeveloped area of research,[24]

---

[24] See John F. McCamant, "Governance Without Blood: Social Science's Antiseptic View of Rule; or, The Neglect of Political Repression," in Michael Stohl and George A. Lopez, eds., *The State as Terrorist: The Dynamics of Government and Repression* (Westport, Connecticut: Greenwood Press, 1984).

although there is a growing awareness that a government that commands a bureaucracy, secret police, and armed forces is capable of committing all sorts of crimes, often with impunity.

Terrorism was practically institutionalized under the Nazi regime in Germany and the Stalinist regime in the Soviet Union. Both succeeded in ridding themselves of anyone suspected of less than loyal support and even encouraged children to inform on their parents if they displayed any lack of enthusiasm for the regime. Terror in a totalitarian regime is a politically useful tool to maintain the regime's power.

The state as terrorist is neither a new concept or a new phenomenon. The state is obviously capable of doing substantial harm for long periods of time. This certainly gives the state a great advantage over nonstate terrorists, who have to keep shooting people and blowing up buildings to insure they have the attention of the public and the authorities. The state, in contrast, is a permanent fixture whose agencies are constantly in the public eye.

A government that perpetuates a policy of political violence by imprisoning or executing people for their political opinions and/or religious and racial backgrounds can get away with it for a long time and can commit more violence than any other social agent. After all, a government typically commands and often monopolizes the resources required for perpetuating violence. Moreover, some governments that have an active policy of terror count on a degree of popular support or at least neutral acquiescence, as both the Nazis and communists did.

State terror can assume different versions and intensities. We can identify at least three general gradations of terror:

1.   *Intimidation:* This usually occurs through the state's control of the electronic and print media and security forces. The media provide instructions for proper political behavior and ruthlessly discourage dissent. They also make the penalties for misbehavior clear. In China, for example, those who protest loudly against government policies may well be shipped off for a three-year visit to a labor camp. If a labor camp inmate can be "reeducated," that person may return to society.

2.   *Coerced conversion:* A revolutionary organization such as the Bolsheviks in Russia or communists in China may take power and call for a complete overhaul of the national economic and social life-style. Those who don't or won't fit in are frequently sent to "reeducation camps." They often don't return. Iran provides another recent example of coerced conversion. The regime of clerics since 1979 has instituted dress codes for all females. It has also invoked criminal penalties on the entire population for immoral behavior as defined by the Koran: for example, those guilty of adultery or blasphemy are stoned.

3.   *Selective genocide or autogenocide:* The most serious and frightening policy of state terrorism is the elimination of entire communities within a national population. The genocidal activities the Nazi regime undertook against the Jewish population of Europe (1939–1945) and the Stalinist purge of the peasant class of kulaks in Ukraine (during most of the 1930s) caused the deaths

of millions of civilians. Autogenocide—extermination of one's own people—occurred during the Pol Pot regime in Cambodia from 1975 to 1979, as indicated previously.

These three categories often overlap. Intimidation can eventually lead to genocide. Before the Nazis decided to physically destroy Jews, they first barred them from professions such as law, medicine, and teaching. Eventually, German Jews were forbidden to purchase milk, own pets, or cultivate private vegetable gardens. Finally, they were forbidden to live. Misery and humiliation preceded and prepared them for extermination.

State terrorism challenges the Western political and philosophical traditions of humanitarianism, toleration, and protection of individual and natural rights. The terrorist state may simply be a new formulation of the old conflict between despotism and democracy; between the point of view that the state precedes and is superior to the individual, and the classical concept of individual sovereignty.

SUMMARY

1. Important differences separate criminal and political violence. Political violence is minimized in the western or western-style democracies, while criminal behavior is often minimized in systems whose governments are capable of the worst forms of violence for any infraction of the law.

2. Democracies tend to have governments that subject themselves to the laws they have legislated. Nondemocratic governments tend to enforce the law fairly and consistently except when it comes to political crimes—opposition, dissent, or belonging to a distrusted minority community.

3. State-sponsored violence exists in a number of countries. Yet, as in China during the Great Cultural Revolution, even a totalitarian government can lose control of its own systematic violence once it develops an overly enthusiastic following.

4. State authorities may ignore or even sanction gender violence, and even the institution of slavery is alive and well in several countries. In such instances, the state, even if it wishes to end a horrific practice, may be reluctant to

pursue the matter because it doesn't want to confront time-honored and entrenched traditions.

5. Ideologically driven violence is perhaps the most lethal when perpetuated by a political regime. Even citizens willing to completely subscribe to the government's policies may not be allowed to do so if they belong to a racial, religious, or social grouping the government wants to eliminate.

6. Nonstate political terrorism in its most contemporary apparition assumes that no one in a "corrupt" society has a right to claim innocence. Therefore, anyone is liable to become a terrorist target.

7. Nonstate terrorists often have substantial longevity and lethal capabilities because they enjoy state sponsorship. If adopted by a state, terrorists can forcefully and indirectly express the state's foreign policy agenda.

8. State terrorism can produce incredible misery for a population. It can manifest itself in several ways, ranging from intimidation of selected minorities or entire populations to their physical extermination.

GLOSSARY

coercion theory of order   A theory stating that a political regime can maintain order by forcing its values on a resistant or unwilling population that is unlikely to voluntarily accept them.

consensus theory of order   A theory stating that a political society can maintain order with minimal or nonexistent political violence when it has established a widespread acceptance of political values and norms.

death squads   Murderous gangs that exterminate a regime's political opponents, even though the death squad is not an official agent of the state.

enforcement violence   The ability of a political regime to sustain itself by applying force whenever necessary to both maintain its existence and secure social order.

martyrdom   The willing death of an individual in order to further a radical ideological or theological message.

illegal violence   Violence that violates the law and that is exercised by unlawful and unconstitutional agents. Sometimes illegal violence causes the deterioration of a political regime. At other times, it surfaces after the breakdown of the regime.

legal violence   Violence the state commits in keeping with the law. The state sometimes has the responsibility to apply violence to maintain order in the society, to protect its citizens, or to remove from society those who have injured others.

reign of terror   Arbitrary violence institutionalized by a newly installed revolutionary regime that is both insecure and ideologically driven.

The International Situation at Century's End

••

*T*hese two chapters review the current status of international politics as well as what immediately preceded it (Chapter 12) and pinpoints ethnicity and ethnic conflict (Chapter 13) as a feature that seems destined to characterized international relations well into the twenty-first century. Both chapters examine the aftermath and residues of the Cold War. They are exploratory in that students of international relations are attempting to learn what comes after the Cold War. A new paradigm is being developed that questions old assumptions about the nation-state system and may devise new definitions of what really constitutes sovereignty.

• • •

• • •

The International Constellation

Even before World War II ended in 1945, the main features of the postwar international system were becoming very clear. Major European powers such as Britain, France, Germany, and to a somewhat lesser extent, Italy, along with Japan, had dominated international politics for about a century. But they had so exhausted themselves in the conflict that their entire economies had been devastated and their populations decimated. Of the major participants in the war, only the United States had escaped becoming a battleground and emerged with its economy intact.

Britain had not endured a German occupation but was exhausted nonetheless. Within two years, Britain would ask the United States to accept traditional British responsibilities to protect the Middle East and southeastern Europe. This request soon led to the **Truman Doctrine,** a strategy for containing Soviet expansion. France had experienced a four year German occupation (1940–1944); no sooner had it begun its recovery than its colonial empire in southeast Asia and north Africa began to unravel. Not until 1958, with the advent of the Fifth Republic, would the French again achieve political stability. Germany was completely wrecked. The Nazi regime's excesses had alienated most of the European peoples. The Germans faced the future as a country divided into East and West, despised and distrusted by millions of their neighbors, and with the daunting task of becoming a sovereign state again. Japan, like Germany, was in shambles. Although Japan had never before lost a war, it was now militarily occupied and had become the only country in history to experience nuclear warfare.

The collapse of so many great powers in such a short period of time marked the end of an age. Two superpowers, the Soviet Union and the United States, emerged as the only countries able to exert power on a global scale. For most of the next half-century, international politics would be characterized by superpower rivalry. Then, rather suddenly and almost quietly, one of the superpowers disintegrated.

In this chapter, we will explore the immediate and potential consequences of yet another unprecedented situation: the United States as the sole superpower without serious rivals, but not without problems and challenges. We will try to identify some of these challenges as well as explore their possible consequences and outcomes. The international constellation of the first few decades of the twenty-first century will look very different from its counterpart in the last decades of the twentieth, but will still grow out of the dominant features that characterize the global picture of today.

THE INTERNATIONAL ARENA

About three and a half centuries ago, the Treaty of Westphalia (1648) ended the Thirty Years War in Europe. It was in Europe that the modern state system first took form. The rough outlines of the system developed during and immediately after this period. Of course, Europe in 1648 looked quite different from the Europe of 1945; even the Europe of 1995 barely resembles the Europe of 1945. Many current states did not exist 350 years ago or even a century ago. Some that did exist no longer do. Moreover, the rest of the world almost exploded with new countries in the post World War II period, particularly in Africa (see figure 12.1).

Very few countries that existed in 1914 when World War I began had the same national boundaries at the end of the twentieth century. Losing or winning a major conflict can cause noticeable changes in a country's borders—in fact, the change can be so severe that the country is literally wiped off the map. Poland, for example, disappeared at the end of eighteenth century after its predatory neighbors, Austria, Prussia, and Russia, partitioned it, only to reappear at the beginning of the twentieth century.

We live in a world with nations that are or were "stateless," as well as with nations that live within a state and are often in conflict with it. Kurds and Palestinians in the Middle East and the Karen people in Myanmar (Burma) are excellent examples. The Kurds are actually in conflict with at least three states—Iraq, Iran, and Turkey—since their nation spills over several borders. Still, the world today lives in what passes for a **nation-state system** because there is no part of the globe that some sovereign state hasn't claimed jurisdiction over. In other words, there is no reprieve or escape from a state's presence no matter where one goes. A nation-state

> . . . *may decree that a person dies; with no less effort, it may offer the protection that enables a person to live. . . . Whether it be to be born, to live, or to die, no one can do so without official recognition—the recognition of the nation-state.*[1]

Notice that in all of these life events, the *state* is the final arbiter. There simply is no higher secular authority. States create and enforce laws and mete out punishments for misconduct. But what governs the relationships *between* sovereign states?

---

[1] John D. Stoessinger, *The Might of Nations: World Politics in Our Time*, 10th ed. (New York: McGraw-Hill, 1993), p. 6.

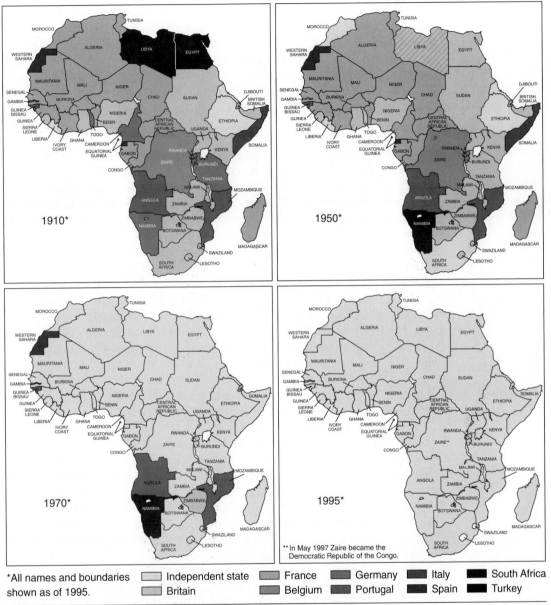

Source: John L. Allen, Student Atlas of World Politics, 2d. ed. (Madison, Wisconsin: Brown & Benchmark, 1996), p. 25.

Figure 12.1

Africa: Colonialism to Independence, 1910–1995

A body of international regulations and laws suggest how governments ought to behave toward one another. Interestingly, most countries regularly and voluntarily adhere to these standards. For example, health regulations offered by the World Health Organization (WHO) and aircraft security, landing, and take-off facilities coordinated by the International Air Transport Association (IATA) are nearly universally accepted. Many of these governing and regulating organizations are under the auspices of the United Nations. Others, including environmental organizations, are independent, but they often publish widely agreed upon regulations.

With rare exception, the world's nearly two hundred countries work within international guidelines because it makes sense for them to do so. International understandings facilitate trade and commerce, encourage multilateral cooperation, and generally make life easier for untold millions of people in numerous countries. This is not to say we are seeing the beginning of the end of the sovereign state. In fact, we could argue that international cooperation actually helps to sustain sovereignty, since cooperation must serve the national interest of the cooperating state or it wouldn't be involved.

Cooperative measures work only as long as participants see advantages. Volunteerism goes a long way, but once it stops, what happens? No sovereign authority is available to enforce compliance with an international law or practice. The International Court of Justice, for example, can hand down a judicial decision against a particular country, but the country, especially if it is a strong one, can completely and safely ignore the decision.

The United Nations General Assembly can also pass resolutions against a particular regime, but these resolutions achieve little practical effect. The UN can even expel a member, but, short of taking collective military action against a renegade regime—an infrequent event—the UN cannot do much to change the behavior of any government. In 1950, the United Nations authorized a multinational military force (under American leadership) to resist North Korea's invasion of South Korea by undertaking a "police action." Such decisions usually have restrained goals; in Korea, the UN settled for the North's expulsion from the South rather than an occupation of the North. Similarly, in 1990 and 1991, a twenty-eight-member coalition (again under American leadership) aligned to remove the Iraqis from Kuwait, but the coalition did not attempt to get rid of Saddam Hussein altogether.

The revolution in communications technology has critically influenced the international arena and the foreign policy expressions of individual states. The United States during the Vietnam conflict provided the first nationally televised war in history. Watching the news during the dinner hour became for millions of American families the decisive factor in determining whether they supported their country's presence in Vietnam. Increasingly, in great part because of television, Americans found themselves questioning what the United States was doing in Vietnam and why it was necessary to send young soldiers to endanger themselves there.

Image matters in international politics, as do perception and misperception. World War I cost perhaps 25 million lives and unfurled as governments developed different perceptions about their neighbors. The war began with the assassination of the designated successor to the emperorship of Austria-Hungary; this caused the Austrian armed forces to mobilize against Serbia, Austria's age-old enemy, whom the Austrians suspected of complicity in the assassination. Germany felt honor-bound to mobilize on behalf of its ally, Austria. Likewise, Russia felt morally obligated to come to the aid of a fellow Slavic country, Serbia. Then France and Britain decided to mobilize because Germany was threatening the neutrality of Belgium. Some of this may sound disconcertingly familiar. In the 1990s, Russia was still supportive of Serbia, while Germany supported Croatia, both regions of the former Yugoslavia long at odds with one another.

No government that ordered military mobilization in the late summer of 1914 anticipated the horrific casualties that followed over the next four-and-a-half years. In the end, no one was sure why the war happened at all.[2] The most murderous century in history was well underway.

To avoid a repetition of 1914, the western democracies attempted to placate Germany as it undertook a military and economic revival during the 1930s by feeding Czechoslovakia to it. This policy of **appeasement** didn't work, and Europe fell headlong into another war. The bad memories of appeasement endured well into the 1960s as those who were young soldiers during World War II came to power in the United States and Western Europe. American foreign policy makers in the 1960s accordingly decried concessions to communism in southeast Asia. The result was Vietnam and the divisions within American society over whether the war was necessary. The "Vietnam syndrome" was still around a generation later. President Bush in 1990 and 1991 went out of his way to assure the American people that the U.S. involvement in the Persian Gulf conflict would not result in "another Vietnam."

Foreign policy formulation is guided, then, by past failures and successes. The problem is that international politics, like so much else in life, is constantly changing. If contesting powers possess nuclear weapons, it is important to prevent an international crisis from flaring to the point that no one feels able to back down (in other words, to avoid a possible replay of 1914). Simply put, any prevailing country must give an opponent a face-saving device to avoid conflict. President John Kennedy (1961–1963) did this in 1962 when he allowed Soviet leader Nikita Khrushchev to gracefully retreat from a decision to ship Soviet missiles to Cuba to aim at the United States. This moment was as close as the two superpowers actually came to nuclear war.

PREREQUISITES OF STATE POWER

Becoming a superpower is a rare occurrence. Because it was one of the few countries in the world that possessed nearly everything required to be a superpower, the United States achieved the status in relatively short order and

---

[2] For an excellent treatment of this subject, see Barbara Tuchman, *The Guns of August* (New York: MacMillan, 1962).

without the terrible sacrifices required of the Soviet population. Most countries with ambitions to become a "great power" need what one would expect: a fairly large and skilled population, a goodly amount of natural resources, including those resources required for a substantial industrial infrastructure, and able political leadership. A certain amount of good luck doesn't hurt, either. Being left alone to exploit and develop natural resources during the first century of its existence certainly helped the United States become a global power. The geographical location of the United States guaranteed its insulation from foreign attack until well into the twentieth century and probably until the nuclear age.

Suppose, though, that a country lacks many of these advantages and still wants to be a power, at least in its own region, or is convinced it must become a power to guarantee its own survival—what can it do? Consider two impressive if sometimes controversial examples:

1. *Israel:* By nearly all accounts, Israel is a country with a serious shortage of natural resources (Israel has lots of sand, beaches, and religious shrines—hardly the hallmarks of power). During most of its first half century of political independence, Israel was surrounded and vastly outnumbered by countries sworn to its destruction. Forced by circumstances to rely primarily on itself for survival, Israel developed the strongest and most efficient armed forces in the Middle East and positioned itself as a center of agricultural and technological innovation. Israel also acquired the ability to deliver at least a hundred nuclear missiles to their targets. (The Israelis consistently deny this last point, but military experts believe they have this capability.)

2. *Japan:* Defeated in World War II and deprived of the East Asian empire that provided it with vital resources, including oil and rubber, Japan from the 1940s on was reduced to its home islands. Japan has always been incapable of feeding itself—it is a country the size of California with four times the population. Land is in such short supply that rice is grown on mountainsides and in-ground burials are not permitted. And Japan is completely dependent on overseas sources to supply 95 percent of its energy needs. The Japanese understood that to recover from a disastrous war and retrieve their status as a regional power, the country would have to excel in trade and the efficient manufacture of affordable, good-quality products. Even without its own supply of raw materials for its growing industries, Japan still achieved a rapid economic resurgence. It now has the largest skilled labor force of any democracy outside the United States.

MULTIPOLARITY, BIPOLARITY, AND UNIPOLARITY

Since we are seen to be, for better or worse, a part of the nation-state system, it seems natural to want to understand how the system works. Over the last several decades, the world has become increasingly complicated. In 1945, just over 2 billion people lived in fewer than sixty countries and several extensive colonial empires. Half a century later, the colonial empires were gone, replaced by more than another hundred sovereign countries, and the global population had

The Congress of Vienna 1814 where European leaders constructed a political power lasting a century.

exploded to nearly 6 billion people. With the significant exception of the Soviet Union, the major participants in World War II had more than recovered and were again among the economic and political leaders of the world. Japan and Germany reconstituted themselves as democracies and developed the world's second and third largest economies, respectively, while the Soviet Union stagnated economically and politically before its final collapse as a hopelessly incompetent and corrupt system in 1991.

The current international system is a product of processes that trace back perhaps as far as the Congress of Vienna (1814–1815), when the political foundations of modern Europe began to appear and Britain became the world's wealthiest power. Possessing the world's largest navy, economy, and colonial empire, the British also kept the international system in balance, assuring that no continental power could achieve overwheming hegemony in Europe. Britain allied itself with Russia to defeat the French during the Napoleonic wars (1799–1814), joined the French to defeat Russia in the Crimean War (1853–1856) and united with both the French and the Russians to defeat Germany in World Wars I and II (1914–1918 and 1939–1945). Britain was thus widely viewed as the balance in a situation characterized by **multipolarity,** or competition between several nations for regional supremacy. The major European countries, however, took increasing notice of rising powers such as Japan and the United States which, by the beginning of the twentieth century, had acquired significant global status. As World War II ended, it was clear that only the United States and the Soviet Union could project national power on a global scale. The international system had transformed into a situation characterized by **bipolarity,** or competition between two superpowers for global supremacy.

With the dissolution of the Soviet Union, it is tempting to conclude that during the early 1990s we entered an era of **unipolarity,** with an unchallengeable United States taking the role of sole superpower. In one sense, of course, this has happened. The United States is the world's premier military power, its largest economic power, and monitors numerous countries to ensure that international predators (such as Iraq, North Korea, and Serbia) don't aggress against their neighbors.

At the same time, we seem to be returning to multipolar situation. The United States faces no plausible military challengers, but Japan and Western Europe pose impressive long-term economic competition. On the horizon, China, and to a lesser extent, India, are rapidly modernizing their economies. It is hard to predict the international constellation of the future.

One of the most serious problems facing the United States—one that promises to have significant staying power well into the next century—is nearly the opposite of the challenge to American foreign policy during the Cold War. Instead of confronting monolithic communism, the United States now faces the political disintegration of a number of supposedly sovereign states. This deterioration has especially affected Eastern Europe and the former Soviet republics (FSRs), as well as Third World regions in which conflicting ethnic groups commit violence against one another. This much more complex and unpredictable picture may present more problems for the United States than communism did.

Even the First World has difficulties with disintegration. The two countries bordering the United States are contending with separatist movements. A majority of French-speaking Quebecois may secede from the Canadian federation. In Mexico, a rebellion that began in 1995 among indigenous peoples in the southern part of the country provided a wake-up call that signaled Mexico's incomplete national unity.

Of course, if Quebec leaves Canada, it will do so in a peaceful secession (many English-speaking as well as French-speaking Canadians favor Quebec's secession). The breakup of Czechoslovakia into the Czech Republic and Slovakia in 1993 was a quiet "velvet divorce." Yet most of the three dozen or so wars going on at any given time are within rather than between countries. Iraq in the Middle East, Sudan in Africa, and Sri Lanka in South Asia are all examples of countries in which ethnic and religious feuding has partitioned states, possibly on a permanent basis.

COLLECTIVE SECURITY

In the end, there is good reason to conclude that no one country, regardless of how strong or how committed to using its power in the global arena, can control world events. When the United States decided to dislodge Iraq's occupation of Kuwait, it did so in concert with a coalition of twenty-eight countries, including most Arab states. While a superpower may find it natural and may be expected to lead, it cannot lead alone.

The Zapatista Liberation Army stand guard in southern Mexico—rebelling against the central government in Mexico.

The notion of **collective security** has existed for a long time. The idea is simply this: a number of countries interested in preserving the international status quo combine efforts to stop the one or two countries interested in challenging it. Most of Europe joined forces against France from 1799 to 1814 to achieve collective security, and the same sort of phenomenon occurred in World War II. The suggestion that a regime such as Nazi Germany would dominate the continent was unacceptable to other European states. While the Nazis represented an especially odious regime, even a Germany less ideologically disagreeable but eager to annex or occupy countries on its border would have found itself facing an array of forces.

Iraq supplies a more recent example. Saddam Hussein's regime in 1990 threatened the existence of several countries in the Persian Gulf region, none of whom were capable of repelling an Iraqi invasion (Saddam's army had more soldiers than the entire population of Kuwait). The industrialized democracies dependent upon the flow of oil and natural gas from the Gulf could not abide Iraqi dominance of a huge proportion of these valuable natural resources.

The objectives in actions taken to achieve collective security can differ. Nazi Germany was so thoroughly evil, it was persuasively argued, that it had to be destroyed and its leadership permanently removed from power. In Iraq's case, the Saddam Hussein regime was also considered evil, but the coalition that fought it did not consider it as menacing an evil as the Nazis. Thus, while it was necessary to evict Saddam from Kuwait, it was unnecessary to oust him from power, however desirable the international community (and probably most Iraqis) might find the prospect.

The notion of "safety in numbers" can apply to international relations. A dominant regional or global power does not take kindly to challengers. Neither do lesser powers that have carved a comfortable and respectable niche for themselves in the international arena and that have a cordial relationship with the one or two major powers around. Let's review some telling examples of each of these situations:

1.   *France (1789–1815):* The 1789 French Revolution shook every throne in Europe. The execution of the royal family, the declaration of radical revolutionary themes such as liberty and equality, and the rise of Napoleon united most of Europe against France. The coalition was so strong that in the end it defeated Napoleon, a leader widely regarded even by his enemies as a military genius. France at one point was fighting against the combined forces of Austria, Britain (the unofficially acknowledged leader of the coalition), Prussia, Russia, Spain, and Sweden. None of these countries was prepared to tolerate the domination of much of the continent by a single power, but none alone could have defeated France.

2.   *Germany (1914–1918 and 1939–1945):* Germany made two attempts to dominate Europe during the first half of the twentieth century. In both cases, the United States had to assume the leadership of the coalition that prevented German supremacy in Europe, especially during the second conflict when the German army occupied most of the continent. In effect, the United States replaced Britain as the power most capable of coordinating collective security arrangements and leading a coalition against any country attempting to upset the balance of power.

3.   *Soviet Union (1945–1990):* Germany lost its bid for continental hegemony but upset the balance of power anyway. During the Cold War, the intention was not to defeat the Soviet Union in a military conflict—an insane notion in the nuclear age. Instead, the United States and its allies strove to contain Soviet expansion in the hope (not unrealistic, as it turned out) that the communist state would mellow or eventually collapse under its own self-defeating ideology. During the Cold War, the United States became the "leader of the Free World" and busied itself with building containment coalitions such as **NATO,** or the North Atlantic Treaty Organization.

Following the end of the Napoleonic wars in 1815, Britain emerged as what passed in those days for a superpower. No other country could compete at that moment in history with British military and economic strength. The century that followed, from 1815 to 1914, was known as the *Pax Britannica,* or British peace. Remarkably few wars broke out during this period. Of course, old habits are hard to break, and European countries fought one another occasionally, but these conflicts did not threaten to destroy Europe's overall balance of power. Most of the time, the larger countries were involved in building colonial empires and violently eliminating opposition to their authority in their colonies. From 1914 through 1945, though, tensions produced two world wars, followed by a haphazard and incomplete *Pax Americana.*

Long before the Cold War ended, the world realized that collective security would have to be modified. During its last years, the Soviet Union had too many problems to threaten other countries. In all likelihood, it no longer had any desire to do so. Collective security now focused on local or regional threats to the status quo, as in the Persian Gulf conflict.

THE NEW WORLD ORDER

Think for a moment about how the Cold War simplified international relations. The United States had a menacing enemy available at all times that it could blame for problems in the world or even at home. In many ways, the Soviet Union was a perfect focus for American foreign policy:

1. It was a totalitarian system equipped with an ideology that predicted and actively worked towards the doom of the capitalist economy most of us enjoy.

2. The Soviet system was nondemocratic and therefore the opposite of the type of system our political culture admires.

3. The Soviet Union was a nuclear power that posed the first mortal challenge to the United States in its history.

4. The Soviets were devoted to challenging and damaging American interests on a global scale.

When the Soviet Union dissolved, Americans no longer had an adversary to loathe and fear. For decades, the Soviet Union had provided us with simplicity and certainty; everyone knew that the Soviet Union was a competitor and a threat. We also enjoyed a confidence that the Soviet system was evil and ours was good and right. In other words, it was reassuring for both sides in the Cold War to have a worldview that divided people and cultures into irredeemably good and bad sides: each side saw itself as pure and noble and the other as corrupt and antagonistic to the best interests of the human race. Such a dichotomy is difficult to replace.

The challenge facing the United States was how to respond to a world without challenges, or at least none that were life-threatening. In retrospect, this had been the situation almost all along. The Soviet Union had always been an "incomplete superpower."[3] Currently, and for the foreseeable future, the United States is "in a class of its own economically and perhaps militarily."[4]

---

[3] David Reynolds, "Beyond Bipolarity in Space and Time, " in Michael J. Hogan, ed., *The End of the Cold War: Its Meaning and Implications* (Cambridge: Cambridge University Press), p. 248.

[4] Paul Kennedy, *The Rise and Fall of the Great Powers* (New Haven: Yale University Press, 1982), p. 514.

Even if it stays there, a fast-changing world will continue to provide unanticipated problems.

What may evolve during the next few decades is an America as a sole superpower with serious competitors. Regional power blocs have already appeared, disappeared, and may reappear (figures 12.2 and 12.3). A sizable power bloc could compete with the United States.

Since the Soviet demise in 1991, the assurances the Cold War provided have been absent. Does the United States now have an enduring enemy to focus on? Clearly, the answer is no. Of course, Fidel Castro, the septugenarian Cuban dictator, and Saddam Hussein, the unstable Iraqi dictator, still remain in power. Such names, though, fail to strike fear in the world community because the countries they control are small, poor, and without allies or powerful sponsors.

The United States and the international system have entered a new and different era. While no monolithic superpower challenges and competes with the United States, current and potential movements can easily guarantee sleepless nights for policymakers. Even before the Soviet collapse, both superpowers had begun to appreciate the limits of their substantial power. The United States from 1965 to 1975 experienced tremendous frustration in the Vietnam War as the determination and ruthlessness of a Third World military force induced an American withdrawal. The Soviets a decade later withdrew from a similarly disastrous conflict in Afghanistan, another Third World country. The invasion had relentlessly drained military personnel and resources. Neither the United States nor the Soviet Union risked the full level of military commitment each possessed, probably for lack of popular support at home and because each country had no clear objectives for fighting the war in the first place.

The international system that seemed to solidify in the early 1800s began to show signs of wear by the time the twentieth century dawned. We may still be within the unraveling process. For at least a century, European powers had energetically planted their flags across the globe. While most of the British, Spanish, and Portuguese empires in the western hemisphere secured their political independence from Europe during the late eighteenth and early nineteenth centuries, they were not yet in a position to compete with their former colonial masters, who still dominated the eastern hemisphere.

However, some interesting signs of change cropped up. The United States and Japan were definitely rising powers by 1900, and Europe itself was still precariously divided into rival blocs that seemed to be daily coming closer to an armed continental conflict. The two world wars finished Europe as the most important and powerful political force in the world, but only temporarily. Combined, the countries of Western Europe have as large a population and skilled labor force as the United States and Japan together. Moreover, Europe may be through fighting wars, except for occasional but contained conflicts such as the one in Bosnia. The European Union is anticipated to eventually include most if not all the countries of Eastern Europe. Germany, France, Italy, and Britain represent the third-, fourth-, fifth-, and sixth-largest national economies in the world. With the threat of Soviet communism gone, Europe

ARCTIC OCEAN

Reykjavik • ICELAND

ATLANTIC
OCEAN

SWEDEN

NORWAY

FINLAND

Helsinki •

Leningrad •

Oslo •

Stockholm •

BALTIC
SEA

Tallinn • ESTONIA

LATVIAN SSR
Riga •

Kaliningrad

LITHUANIAN SSR
Vilnius •

USSR

Northern
Ireland

NORTH
SEA

DENMARK

Copenhagen •

IRELAND

Dublin •

UNITED
KINGDOM

London •

NETHERLANDS

Amsterdam •

Brussels •
BELGIUM

Bonn •

GERMAN
Berlin •
DEMOCRATIC
REPUBLIC

Warsaw •

POLAND

LUXEMBOURG

Paris •

FEDERAL
REPUBLIC
OF
GERMANY

Prague •
CZECHOSLOVAKIA

Bay of Biscay

FRANCE

Bern •
SWITZ.
LIECHTENSTEIN

Vienna •
AUSTRIA

Budapest •

HUNGARY

ROMANIA

Bucharest •

BLACK
SEA

ITALY

Belgrade •

YUGOSLAVIA

BULGARIA
Sofia •

MONOCO

ANDORRA

Corsica

VATICAN
CITY
Rome •

Tirane •
ALBANIA

GREECE

TURKEY

PORTUGAL

Madrid •

SPAIN

Lisbon •

Balearic
Islands

Sardinia

MEDITERRANEAN SEA

Sicily

Athens •

Crete

AFRICA

| 0 | | 250 | | 500 Miles |
| 0 | 350 | | 700 Kilometers | |

Source: John L. Allen, *Student Atlas of World Politics,* 2d. ed. (Madison, Wisconsin: Brown & Benchmark, 1996), p. 21.

The Cold War Alliances, 1955	**Post–World War II Polish Territorial Annexations**	**Post–World War II Soviet Territorial Annexations**
NATO members	From Germany	From Czechoslovakia
Warsaw Pact members		From Finland
Non-alliance countries		From Germany
- - - - 1939 boundaries		From Poland
——— 1955 boundaries		From Romania
		From Estonia, Latvia, and Lithuania

Figure 12.2
Post-World War II Europe

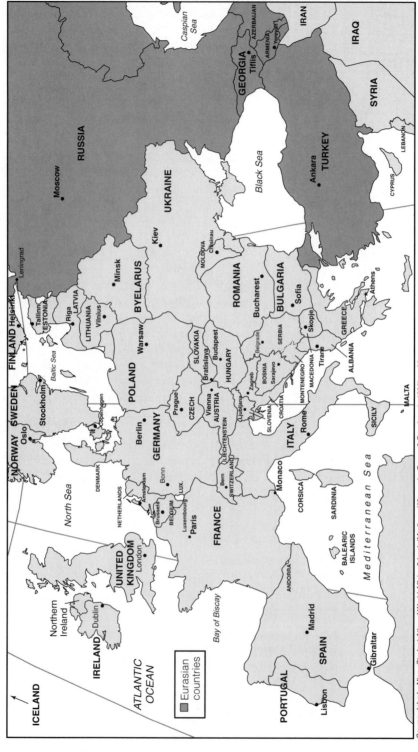

Figure 12.3
Post-Cold War Europe

Source: John L. Allen, *Student Atlas of World Affairs*, 2d. ed. (Madison, Wisconsin: Brown & Benchmark, 1996), p. 22.

may once again come into its own, especially if it can maintain the peace and achieve the political unity many Europeans desire.

INTERNATIONAL POLITICS IN THE TWENTY-FIRST CENTURY

No one in her or his right mind confidently predicts the future. By the same token, no wise person ignores the lessons of the past. The history of international politics can be viewed as a long story of great economic and military powers that rise and fall.

Paul Kennedy's thesis in *The Rise and Fall of the Great Powers* is that "imperial overstretch" ruined the chances of great powers to remain great. A global presence through colonial empire (as Britain did) or through unprecedented military expenditures (as the United States did) can simply be too costly for any country to sustain. The cost for the Soviet Union, which may have devoted as much as 50 percent of its economy to military preparedness, became overwheming after several decades for an economy that was already in serious decline.

Potential powers always loom on the horizon. Large countries with substantial resources, such as China, Brazil, Indonesia, and Nigeria, could become dominant regional powers. However, able political leadership, usually in short supply even in the most powerful countries, may not be available when needed. China's political elite is known to be seriously split over future political and economic directions. Brazil has a history of sliding away from its focus on development. Indonesia has been governed for a third of a century by one family, guaranteeing a lack of solid political institutions. And Nigeria remains deeply divided along ethnic and tribal lines unlikely to evaporate very soon.

While it can be treacherous to make predictions, it is not unreasonable to assume that in the next century governments will still compete with one another on regional and global scales for the resources necessary to improve the material welfare of their citizenries. Governments seem almost programmed to compete against one another for the necessities they are obligated to provide for their citizenries. Both governments and their capabilities as well as the resources themselves may change over time. In the Middle Ages, wars were fought in the Near East over religion. This century has witnessed much competition and not a few wars over oil. During the next century, it is hardly rash to assume that Near Eastern countries with exploding populations and ambitious plans for economic development could violently compete for the resource of water, an even more precious commodity than oil. Clearly, there is a lot to think about.

A NOTE ON THE NUCLEAR NIGHTMARE

The end of the Cold War was not the end of international dilemmas and dangers. In the following chapter, we will briefly explore the renewal of ethnic and religious conflict and the problems these conflicts pose for world peace and

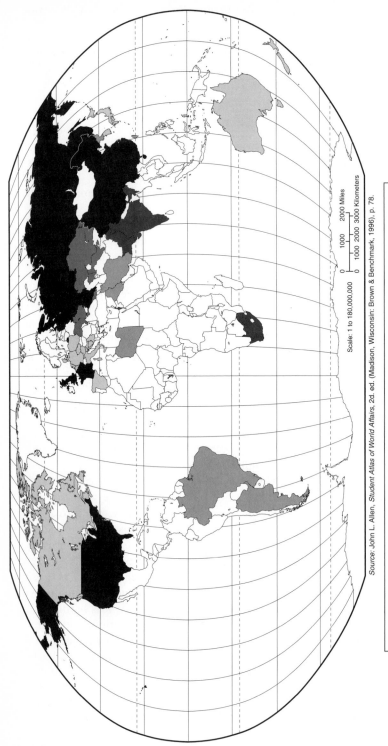

Source: John L. Allen, *Student Atlas of World Affairs*, 2d. ed. (Madison, Wisconsin: Brown & Benchmark, 1996), p. 78.

The Nuclear and Near-Nuclear Nations

Major nuclear powers: medium to large stocks of nuclear weapons and effective delivery systems (planes and missiles).

Countries that possess nuclear weapons manufacturing and delivery capacity: small stocks of weapons.

Countries probably possessing some remaining nuclear stocks after the breakup of the Soviet Union.

Countries with stated intent to develop nuclear weapons and a high probability of nuclear weapons manufacturing and delivery capacity in the near future.

Countries with the technological capacity to manufacture and deliver weapons but without nuclear weapons programs.

Scale: 1 to 180,000,000

0   1000   2000 Miles

0 1000 2000 3000 Kilometers

Figure 12.4
Nations with Nuclear Weapons

stability. The collapse of communism was a dream come true for most advocates of democracy. Yet, as we know, the resolution of one problem inevitably produces others. Several international difficulties resulted from the Cold War's demise.

Rather suddenly, "loose nukes" arrived on the scene. Instead of two presumably responsible superpowers who supposedly knew better than to go to war and controlling the world's nuclear arsenal, nuclear weaponry was dispersed into the hands of several governments. After the Soviet collapse, four former Soviet republics—Russia, Ukraine, Kazakhstan, and Belarus—inherited nuclear installations. Most weapons were transferred to Russian control. Occasional lapses in security, though, could cause one to conjure up images of terrorists stealing (or even buying from an impoverished Russian government) nuclear devices. This scenario is, of course, unlikely to materialize, but as one bumper sticker has suggested, "One nuclear explosion can ruin your whole day." One imaginative smuggler was able to hide a substantial amount of uranium in his underwear, taking it from Moscow all the way to Prague before he was discovered and detained.[5]

A second and more realistic danger concerns governments who develop their own nuclear technology. As figure 12.4 suggests, nuclear technology is already widely available. It is probably futile to hope that earth will one day be completely rid of nuclear weapons and the potential for self-destruction. We cannot ensure that democracy and prosperity will be the wave of the future unless we have some assurance that our survival as a species is also part of the wave.

SUMMARY

1. The international constellation is in a constant state of flux as major national powers rise and fall. The current situation is no exception; a seemingly permanent post-World War II confrontation ended peacefully when one of two superpowers disappeared from the scene.

2. The nation-state system is alive and well. More sovereign entities exist than ever before.

3. Though countries still jealously guard their sovereign status, the overwhelming majority actively participate in international bodies, including the United Nations, that are crucial in regulating increasing numbers of global areas of commerce and technology.

4. At any given moment, international politics is the result of historical events—some planned, some unintended—that leave important and memorable residues that affect the outlook of entire countries.

5. Most countries are not as fortunate as the United States and lack a number of qualities that can make them great powers. Many accept their roles as second-tier countries, while others feel compelled to make the most efficient use of the resources they do possess to insure national survival.

---

[5] Walter Goodman, "Worrying About Russia's Uranium," *The New York Times*, November 19, 1996, p. B3.

6. Through the twentieth century, international politics has been characterized by multipolar, bipolar, and perhaps unipolar situations. It is unclear whether we are now in a unipolar climate or are reverting to multipolarity.

7. Collective security is an important and defining feature of international stability. When it is working well, collective security helps to guarantee that no country or group of countries emerge that are menacing to peace or threatening to the balance of power.

8. The immediate future of international politics is fraught with uncertainty now that the Cold War has ended. New powers are almost sure to emerge at some point, as they always have in the past. Even new democracies may pose challenges to the United States.

9. The demise of the Cold War did not mean the end of the nuclear threat to civilization. The threat may have even increased because of the real possibility that more governments will acquire nuclear technology, along with the ability to deliver nuclear weapons to designated targets and perhaps to terrorist organizations.

GLOSSARY

appeasement   The idea that a hostile nation can be persuaded to maintain peaceful relations if other countries give in to some of its demands. The British and French governments' attempt to placate German territorial ambitions enjoyed substantial popular support in the late 1930s. The guiding notion was that it was only fair to meet at least some German demands since Germany had been so harshly treated by the Versailles Treaty at the end of World War I.

bipolarity   An international situation in which two superpowers challenge each other for global supremacy. Usually, each is too strong for one to eliminate the other or to be challenged by any other power.

collective security   The idea that countries interested in preserving the status quo can ally to defeat a country trying to challenge it.

multipolarity   An international situation in which several powers compete against one another for regional supremacy. Multipolarity may divide countries into various contending coalitions.

nation-state system   While many nations do not have their own states and many states are composed of numerous nations, some type of sovereign jurisdiction has extended to the entire earth's surface, creating a network of nation-states.

NATO   The North Atlantic Treaty Organization was created in 1949 to thwart any Soviet designs on Western Europe. NATO was part of the containment strategy formulated in the Truman Doctrine.

Truman Doctrine   Promulgated in 1947, this plan provided a strategy for containing Soviet communist expansion in southeastern Europe and the Near East. Later it was extended to western Europe through NATO.

unipolarity   An international situation in which a single superpower has unchallenged global supremacy, commanding a disproportionate share of military force and economic dominance.

Ethnic Conflict and the International Constellation

··

As we have discussed previously, the collapse of Soviet and East European communism brought new problems and challenges to the international scene. It seemed like an opportune time for democracy to spread across the globe without interference. Simultaneously, a clamor arose among ethnic and subnational communities for political autonomy. This clamor grew more strident than it had been at any previous time in history.

This chapter seeks to analyze how these two processes affect one another. The various ethnic conflicts flaring up across the globe are defining the character and some of the ingredients of future international politics. As we examine these events, we will review the effects of nationalism, subnationalism, and ethnicity on the political process, and we will discuss the difficulties so commonly found *between* nation and state.

THE NEW WORLD ORDER REVISITED

In the post-Cold War era, revised definitions of what constitutes a state and sovereignty may be in the offing. Consider the following actual or potential challenges to international stability:

1. Between 1800 and 1945, the number of sovereign states in the international community increased from about 25 to 60. Between 1945 and 1995, the number tripled to more than 180, and the end of this expansion is not yet in sight. More and more new states are territorially and demographically small, and many, perhaps most, are less than economically viable. Some lack established or permanent political institutions. A few states exist in name only, completely lacking any effective political institutions. This raises the question to what degree they may contribute to or detract from overall instability in their respective regions.

2. The multiplication of sovereign states takes into account only a tiny fraction of the hundreds of ethnic communities that are either clamoring for a stronger degree of political independence or at least a greater degree of autonomy, both cultural and political. These communities generally desire more separation from a political center they feel is controlled by a rival or ineffective ethnic community.

3. Ethnic minorities may no longer regard as legitimate national boundaries the international community has long assumed are fixed in concrete. These ethnic minorities often consider the central government's presence invasive, uninvited, and alien.

4. The Soviet empire's collapse has produced a largely unexpected impact: an unsettling of the state system as ethnic minorities assert or reassert their desire to control their own political destinies. Simultaneously, a lack of global leadership has developed; other countries are either unable to fill this role, or, like the United States, are reluctant to accept it.

5. The territorial state is itself a questionable entity. It is misleading to look at a multicolored map of the world and assume that the boundary lines always imply central government control. A government, by virtue of its military and the support of its population, may indeed control all the territory its borders outline. But that isn't the entire story. As one scholar has pointed out: "The distinction between *power over people* and *power over territory* is a useful one to make, for it singles out two aspects of sovereignty that are best addressed separately: disputes involving the right of peoples to self-determination and territorial disputes among them."[1]

Put another way, political situations are not always what they seem. In earlier chapters, we stressed the point that there are important differences between terms such as *nation* and *state*. This chapter highlights the idea that these differences can be so substantial that conflicts occur as often between nations *within* states as they do between different sovereign states.

COMPETING NATIONALISMS

The disagreeable truth of ethnic conflict is that **ethnies,** or ethnic communities, often conflict because two or more of them turn up at about the same time on the same land and then argue about who really owns the territory. This tendency has been in ample evidence for centuries. When Europeans "discovered" America five centuries ago, they also discovered long-settled inhabitants.

The Amerindians were the indigenous peoples of the Americas. They numbered in the neighborhood of 75 million, considerably more than Europe's total population at the time. These were the descendants of the original inhabi-

---

[1] Gidon Gottlieb, *Nation Against State: A New Approach to Ethnic Conflicts and the Decline of Sovereignty* (New York: Council on Foreign Relations Press, 1993), p. 15.

tants of the western hemisphere who had first crossed over from Asia 15,000 to 20,000 years ago. The Amerindians were quickly decimated, mostly by diseases such as smallpox, that the European settlers brought with them. Not until the last decades of the twentieth century did these indigenous peoples begin to make a demographic comeback.

When two cultures collide, one inevitably and arrogantly thinks of itself as superior; sometimes, they both do. Technologically speaking, one culture usually is superior. As a rule, Europe was able to subdue a good part of the world for several centuries because of its technological advancement in military weaponry. European hegemony ended as modernization and nationalist aspirations progressed in the developing world.

Ethnic conflict was not simply a case of white European Christians versus everyone else, even during Europe's dominant period. Ethnic conflict has often prevailed within Europe itself. (World War II could be considered a huge ethnic conflict and certainly provided an example of "ethnic cleansing.") As the Soviet Union dissolved, long-subdued mutual loathing between various ethnic communities came quickly to the surface. As a seasoned observer of Soviet and Russian affairs put it:

> *In Tallin, I heard Estonians describe Russians as cretins and brutes, and Russians describe Estonians as Nazi collaborators. In Yerevan, Armenians were sure that Azerbaijanis had deliberately "set off" the earthquake that killed at least 25,000 people with an underground nuclear test and were about to carry out an Islamic crusade against them more bloody than the Turkish massacre of Armenians in 1915. In Baku, Azerbaijanis knew with absolute certainty that the Yerevan government was preparing to grab all its territory and assert an Armenian kingdom with the help of emigre millionaires in Los Angeles.*[2]

Even the territorial integrity of the Russian Federated Republic, which contains about half the population and two-thirds of the territory of the old Soviet Union, is constantly beset by non-Russian ethnic minorities in various regions of the country. During the mid-1990s, Chechnya had a strong separatist movement even though Russia physically surrounds Chechnya on three sides. Nor is Chechnya alone. As the map in figure 13.1 suggests, the Russian Federated Republic contains numerous non-Russian communities.

Even the more than 1 million Chechens are divided: the separatist movement enjoyed popular support only in the southern third of the country. Russia's presence was actually welcomed in the northern third, while the middle third of the country was a mixed bag. Though a small country, Chechnya is divided into regions under one hundred *teips*, or clan leaders, who fight for control of four hundred villages.[3] The Russian government must contend with an

---

[2] David Remnick, *Lenin's Tomb: The Last Days of the Soviet Empire* (New York: Random House, 1993), p. 89.

[3] "Chechnya, No Man's Land," *The Economist*, October 7, 1995, p. 56.

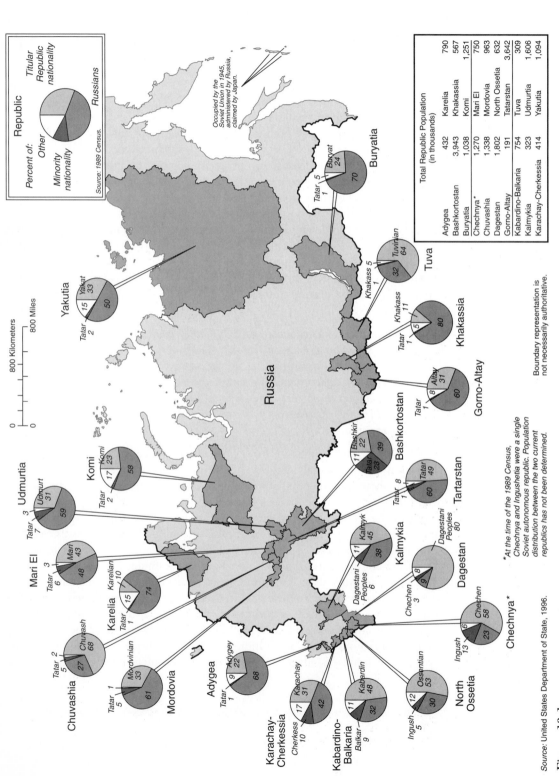

Figure 13.1
Russia's Ethnic Republics

Republic

Percent of:
- Titular Republic nationality
- Russians
- Other
- Minority nationality

Source: 1989 Census.

Occupied by the Soviet Union in 1945, administered by Russia, claimed by Japan.

Russia

Total Republic Population (in thousands)			
Adygea	432	Karelia	790
Bashkortostan	3,943	Khakassia	567
Buryatia	1,038	Komi	1,251
Chechnya*		Mari El	750
Chuvashia	1,338	Mordovia	963
Dagestan	1,802	North Ossetia	632
Gorno-Altay	191	Tatarstan	3,642
Kabardino-Balkaria	754	Tuva	309
Kalmykia	323	Udmurtia	1,606
Karachay-Cherkessia	414	Yakutia	1,094

Boundary representation is not necessarily authoritative.

*At the time of the 1989 Census, Chechnya and Ingushetia were a single Soviet autonomous republic. Population distribution between the two current republics has not been determined.

Source: United States Department of State, 1996.

Buryatia
Buryat 24
Tatar 5
70
1

Tuva
Tuvinian 64
Khakass 5
32
1

Khakassia
Khakass 11
Tatar 1
80
5

Gorno-Altay
Altay 31
Tatar 1
60
8

Yakutia
Yakut 33
Tatar 2
50
15

Komi
Komi 23
Tatar 2
58
17

Udmurtia
Udmurt 31
Tatar 7
59
3

Mari El
Mari 43
Tatar 6
48
3

Karelia
Karelian 10
Tatar 1
74
15

Chuvashia
Chuvash 68
Tatar 5
27
2

Mordovia
Mordvinian 33
Tatar 5
61
1

Adygea
Adygey 22
Tatar 1
68
9

Bashkortostan
Bashkir 22
Tatar 28
39
11

Tatarstan
Tatar 49
60
8
1

Kalmykia
Kalmyk 45
11
38

Dagestan
Dagestani Peoples 80
Dagestani Peoples 6
9
8
3

Chechnya*
Chechen 58
Chechen 9
23
6

Karachay-Cherkessia
Karachay 31
Cherkess 10
42
17

Kabardino-Balkaria
Kabardin 48
Balkar 9
32
11

North Ossetia
Ossetian 53
Ingush 5
30
12

Ingush 13

800 Kilometers
800 Miles
0

Chechnya: In modern warfare civilians in any ethnic community are easy targets.

unruly province, while the Chechen government has little control over a good part of what is supposed to happen to its legal jurisdiction.[4]

Few countries are completely immune from at least occasional ethnic tensions. Frequently considered the most successful story of ethnic integration, the United States, reveals signs of being something less than a melting pot. As noted American historian Arthur M. Schlesinger, Jr., has incisively written,

> *The cult of ethnicity has reversed the movement of American history, producing a nation of minorities—or at least of minority spokesmen—less interested in joining with the majority in common endeavor than in declaring their alienation from an oppressive, white, patriarchal, racist, sexist, classist society. The ethnic ideology inculcates the illusion that membership in one or another ethnic group is the basic American experience.[5]*

Ethnicity is an undeniable and critically important feature of the modern state system. It may even prove to be the instrument of the system's future

---

[4] Russians and Chechen nationalists may hate each other, but both have to contend with the "English myth" that has been transmitted between generations since sometime in the eighteenth century. Somehow, a number of Chechens are convinced that sooner or later they are destined to come under the jurisdiction of the British crown. Thus far, no one in the British government has suggested that the country is ready to annex Chechnya. "Weekend Edition," National Public Radio, December 8, 1996.

[5] Arthur M. Schlesinger, Jr., *The Disuniting of America* (New York and London: W. W. Norton, 1992), p. 112.

alteration into more and smaller states in which political stability and consensual regimes may be rarities.

NATIONALISM AND ETHNICITY

Nationalism—one's identification with a politically or culturally distinct group of people—has for generations been a crucial determinant of international politics as well as a defining feature of who and what we are. Even if we do not individually think of ourselves as Americans, for example, many non-Americans regard us as such. It's not unreasonable: if we speak a particular language, live in a particular geographical area, and belong to a particular political economy, we are most likely to affiliate with other people who share the same traits. Even more importantly,

> *nations exist much more in time than in space. The history of common triumphs and suffering evokes powerful bonds of solidarity for nations large and small. Common suffering seems to be more important in this respect than are victories. The Civil War was probably the most tragic experience of the American nation. Yet both North and South have come to regard this grim American tragedy as a period of glory.*[6]

It is possible that the United States would be a less unified country had the Civil War never occurred. The war's unforeseen length and wholesale devastation gave both sides a common if horrific reference point for national coherence. The viability of nationalism apparently depends a great deal on widespread, shared suffering.

National coherence is frequently based on a country's "finest hour," to use Winston Churchill's famous phrase. Russia still memorializes its defeat of Nazi Germany at the cost of at least 20 million Russian lives; Israel maintains the memory of 6 million Holocaust victims; and China continues to officially honor the surviving veterans of the Long March during the 1930s, which cost hundreds of thousands of lives but saved the communist cause. It may be trite, but it is still accurate to conclude that a people who endure great privation together tend to stay together. There is nothing like a mortal danger to a country (or the lingering memory of one) to keep a people unified.

Nationalism frequently invokes a "heroic age" that comes close to deifying a country's founders. In a dictatorship, deification is actually insisted upon—huge statues and banners as big as city blocks display images of the country's current or past leaders. Democracies are hardly immune from this practice, though it is usually both more dignified and more modest. The United States, for example, inculcates respect for its founders, the wise assemblage of persons who created the country's successful political and legal institutions. Other

---

[6] John G. Stoessinger, *The Might of Nations: World Politics in Our Time*, 10th ed. (New York: McGraw-Hill, 1995), p. 8.

countries may have a problem in this regard: the Russian tsarist regime that ended in 1917, for example, was characterized by a royal family uninterested in and totally out of touch with the people and thus is not a period Russians would regard nostalgically; nor did the early communist leaders such as Lenin provide enduring idols.

Nationalism has great staying power. Both communists and democrats have been monumentally wrong about nationalism, for similar reasons. Each assumed that nationalistic fervor would gradually and quietly dissipate as economic prosperity increased and was more equitably distributed. Once widespread prosperity was achieved, the thinking went, loyalties to one's ethnic community would be reduced to insignificant and peaceful levels. Leaders expected that parochial boundaries based on ethnicity or religion would gradually dissolve as economic and technological improvements became available to more and more people.

To some extent and in several places, this phenomenon did occur. Many individuals have become more concerned with their stock portfolios than with the skin pigmentation, accents, or religious beliefs of their neighbors. The difficulty, of course, is that economic progress is not a given. Once an economic downturn occurs, as it did in several western European countries during the 1990s when unemployment accelerated to 10 or 12 percent, there is rarely a shortage of political opportunists to blame the economic problems on any newly arrived immigrants, especially those of a different color or religion.

The idea that people who achieve material prosperity tend to forget their nationalist attachments can be pervasive, but it is also wrong.[7] Part of the delay in fully integrating the member states of the European Union is the reluctance of several countries to accept what they view as infringements on their national sovereignty. One of the most divisive issues in the 1997 British general elections, for example, questioned whether Britain's submission to a single European currency would detract from or endanger its national sovereignty.

Ethnicity's Revenge

In coming years, the 1990s may be recalled as a decade when nationalism intensely asserted itself as soon as it had the chance. Hundreds of ethnic groups, seemingly dormant for long periods of time, are loudly insisting that their entire communities accord them ultimate loyalty. It's all rather ironic: the global economy is relentlessly expanding, and countries are becoming increasingly interdependent through commerce and trade; yet the countries and the ethnic communities within them work all the harder to emphasize their distinctiveness, protect their special traditions, and separate themselves from what they regard as unwarranted interference.

---

[7] For a superb explanation of how wrong, see Isaiah Berlin, "The Bent Twig: A Note on Nationalism," *Foreign Affairs,* vol. 51 (October 1972).

A global society has both advantages and disadvantages. However, some ethnic communities interpret the advantages and disadvantages differently. For example, some communities might regard integrated and interrelated communities and global development in technology as benefits; others view them as encroachments and sources of instability. Instead of breaking down ethnic cultures, modernization is in a curious way reinforcing them. Millions of people throughout the world, most noticeably in the developing countries, are unnerved by the sudden technological penetrations into their lives. Their reaction is personal and visceral: they cling steadfastly to the core of their community's defining features. The ties to community become the ultimate loyalty, while the outside world is viewed with hostility and suspicion.

An ethnic group's desire for recognition and autonomy is both natural and understandable. Unfortunately, it is also provocative and unnerving to a national government fearful of dismemberment. Even worse, ethnic aspirations may destroy international stability and raise some disturbing questions. How many sovereign entities can the international system comfortably or reasonably support? How far can the widespread desire for sovereignty be taken? How big should an ethnic community be to possess a territorial state? One scholar suggests that

> *The emergence of states like Slovakia, the collapse of other states, like Somalia, and the continued existence of insignificant ministates confirm that statehood is no longer a "big deal."* [8]

At the same time, it is clearly impractical for thousands of identifiable ethnies to establish their own territorial states. There is some doubt that all or even most of them really want one. Many do because they feel uncomfortable in their current political situation. Iraq, Canada, and Sri Lanka, for example, all have ethnic minorities distinct from the majorities in terms of language, religion, and overall culture. In all these places, an ethnic or religious minority is struggling to preserve its identity.

These are only three of perhaps dozens of states that face or have already endured partition. We examined the problems associated with partition in a previous chapter. What alternatives to partition exist?

1.   *State collapse:* Somalia in eastern Africa unraveled in the early 1990s as clannish loyalties, always stronger than state loyalties in Somalia, became undisputed first attachments. A state collapses when a central authority no longer exists, or does not receive much attention or respect if it does exist.

2.   *Regional secession:* The breakup of Czechoslovakia in 1993 into the Czech Republic and Slovakia was a peaceful process; Quebec's possible departure from Canada may become another one. These are exceptions, though; most secessions involve a prolonged conflict. The secession of Bangladesh from Pakistan in 1971 was successful but not without a war. A regional secession oc-

---

[8] Gidon Gottlieb, *Nation Against State*, p. 19.

Figure 13.2
A Proposed Division of Italy

curs most often because the region's ethnic community is distinct from the rest of the country in culture, religion, language, history, and possibly all of these. Even long-standing and relatively stable democracies such as Italy's have strong separatist movements. In Italy's case, the Lombard League is determined to peacefully separate the northern and most prosperous third of the country from the rest (figure 13.2).

Cyprus represents another possibility. Turkey occupied the northern third of the country in 1974 to protect the Islamic Turkish minority living there from what they perceived as the political and economic domination of the Christian Greek majority. Cyprus has been a divided country ever since and shows no likelihood of reuniting (figure 13.3).

3. *State dissolution and "refederation":* It is possible that a state's disintegration makes good sense over the long term. Nothing engraved in concrete says that any state must have a single center of political authority. Local jurisdictions often manage their affairs well, and arbitrarily drawn frontiers—say, those in Africa that Europeans designed—aren't always considerate of tribal or regional divisions.

A recent case in point is the Democratic Republic of Congo, formerly Zaire. By the end of 1996, the country was disintegrating into its various regional parts, such as East Kasai and Shaba. Local leaders controlled the regions

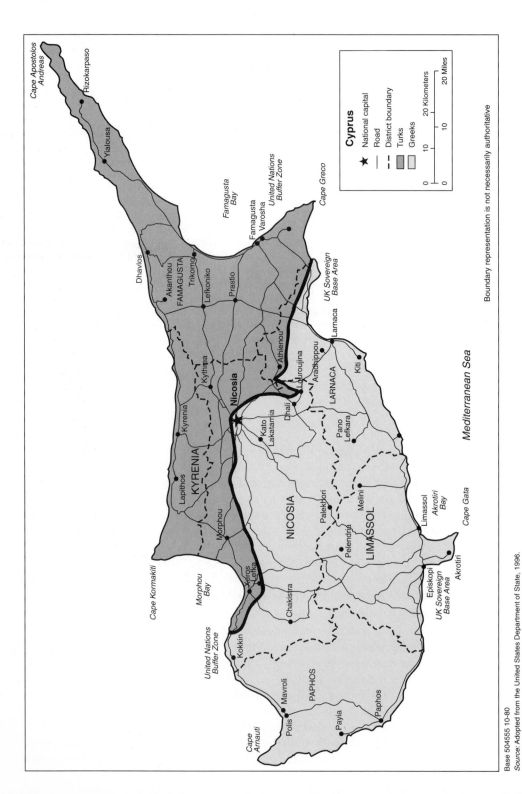

Base 504555 10-80

Source: Adopted from the United States Department of State, 1996.

Figure 13.3
The De Facto Partition of Cyprus

and didn't bother with a formal secession from the central power.[9] Eventually, in 1997, the Congo central government fell and was replaced by a new regime led by Laurent Kabila. (One of Kabila's first problems was how to deal with charges that his regime allowed or condoned a massacre of Rwandan Hitu refugees.)

Local leadership is not a perfect situation. In the best scenario, local leaders are indigenous to the areas they control with paramilitary personnel (whose loyalty is usually to these particular leaders rather than to an overall political regime or set of institutions). This is not exactly the sort of environment conducive to political democracy, but the local chieftains do tend to provide the people with helpful things, such as public schools and medical services, that the central government itself, not usually a beacon of democracy, will not or cannot provide. Considering that there must be stability before democracy has a chance, this may not be an especially bad compromise.

Ethnicity and Religion

Most ethnic communities are characterized by a particular religious doctrine. However, one must be careful not to get carried away with what can be a stereotype. Plenty of Israelis aren't Jewish, many Irish aren't Catholic, and lots of Egyptians aren't Islamic. While westerners usually assume that Indians are Hindu, India is also the second largest Muslim country in the world.

Stereotypes can sometimes persist no matter what the reality. Ethnies who belong to a religion that the state finds disagreeable can face severe discrimination or worse. In fact, religious differences are capable not only of producing ethnic conflict, but even of spawning ethnic communities themselves. Consider the dreadfully familiar example of Bosnia: powerful religious differences have created ethnic divisions. The reason Bosnian Croats, Muslims, and Serbs tend to be physically indistinguishable from one another is because they aren't very racially or historically different. All three "speak the same language and share the same land and much of the same history."[10] Given the right set of circumstances, usually engineered by unscrupulous, ruthless, and manipulative political leaders, religion can furnish a sort of artificial but pervasive ethnicity that can be every bit as competitive and violent as the real thing.

Ethnic communities, even in pluralist societies such as the United States, tend to be closely associated with a dominant religious faith. A combination of religion and ethnicity is not in itself necessarily or inevitably violent. The religious factor though, has the potential to aggravate perceived or real differences between ethnic groups. Fear of "the other"[11] intensifies when the other's

---

[9] "Polls to Nowhere," *The Economist*, November 23, 1996, pp. 20–21.

[10] William Finnegan, "Salt City," *The New Yorker*, February 12, 1996, p. 48.

[11] "The Pope Speaks at U.N.: Human Rights and the 'Risk of Freedom,'" *The New York Times*, October 6, 1995, p. A16.

religious practices *and* ethnic background differ from those of the prevailing majority.

It is far from a coincidence that ethnic conflicts usually have a religious dimension. Israeli Jews versus Palestinian Muslims and Christians, and Bosnian Muslims versus Serb Orthodox and Croatian Catholics, are only two of many prominent examples. The Egyptian Coptic Christian community, increasingly under attack from radical Muslims, considers itself ethnically as well as religiously separate from the country's Islamic majority. Many Copts believe themselves the only authentic Egyptians, take pride in the fact that Egypt was the first country to convert to Christianity, and consider themselves the direct descendants of the country's ancient inhabitants. They regard Muslims as invading Arabs and latecomers, unwelcome and uninvited arrivals.

From all of this, we can draw some tentative conclusions about the links between religion and ethnic revivalism:

1.   In the overwhelming majority of cases, religion reinforces and, on occasion, even predominates ethnic perspectives on the world. India may be the largest and most important example of this phenomenon. India and Hinduism preceded Christianity by at least fifteen hundred years and Islam by two thousand. India's cultural and, later, its national character developed in tandem with the ethical and social features of Hinduism. Indian nationalism is inseparable from Hinduism, as far as India's more conservative Hindu elements are concerned.

2.   Religion and ethnicity reinforce one another both culturally and politically. If one is attacked, the other is, too. European Christians crusading against Arab Muslims certainly demonstrated this phenomenon. At the same time that European Christians were attacking Arab Muslims, Turkish Muslims were attacking Indian Hindus. In each case, the objective was nothing less than the destruction of a faith and culture.

3.   Whenever one religion is fighting to expand, another feels it is under negative and perhaps violent attack. Indian Hindus justifiably felt persecuted by Muslims in much the same way Arab Muslims believed European Christians were terribly aggressive during the Crusades. Entire civilizations consider themselves in a fight for their very survival.

4.   Religion combined with ethnicity can become a catalyst for civil war if a minority feels it is put upon or abused by a country's political center. A minority may not be a minority in certain sections of the country. In some Indian states, for instance, Muslims are a numerical majority; in the western Chinese province of Xingxiang, Turkish Muslims are a numerical majority. The Indian and Chinese governments worry with reason that these communities may attempt to secede, a prospect that often receives encouragement from kindred peoples on the other side of the border.

Of course, different religions that feel beleaguered can find it convenient to support a common cause. In the southernmost region of Lebanon, which is simultaneously Israel's "security zone," Lebanese Christians have joined with the Israeli Defense Forces to fight Shia Muslims.[12] Even aside from this conflict, Lebanon is a country divided and subdivided into sectarian communities, as we discussed in a previous chapter. Lebanese Christians and Israelis alike are convinced that the military expression of the radical Shiites, the Hizbullah, is a mortal threat. Lebanon is a country politically defined by its religious divisions (figure 13.4). The southern Lebanese conflict indicates how durable religious conflicts can be: this particular war has been going on and off since the middle 1970s, and no end is in sight after a quarter-century of fighting. The roots of the conflict, of course, go even further back, perhaps to the Middle Ages.

Ethnic Conflict and Migrations

National borders are more porous than they have been in much of modern history. Citizens of the fifteen European Union member states are moving with greater ease across borders than ever before. Hundreds of thousands of Americans and Canadians cross their three-thousand-mile frontier daily. Yet these examples pertain to western countries, many of which have taken strong measures to seal these same frontiers against anyone they don't want to let in. At the same time, the numbers of people who desire to emigrate (or whose governments have "encouraged" them to leave) have exploded, along with their levels of desperation.

During the eighteenth century, British courts exiled criminals and prostitutes to sparsely inhabited and economically backward places such as Australia and parts of America both to get rid of them and to help settle vast stretches of territory. While this model has little to do with ethnicity, other governments have applied it in a selective and often vindictive fashion; during the summer of 1980, the Cuban government sent hundreds of its most violent criminals to a place the Castro regime felt richly deserved them—the United States. Similarly, shortly before World War II, the Nazis, who were experts at ethnic cleansing, sought to remove Jews from Germany. They placed nearly a thousand on a "ship of the damned" that no country allowed to dock.

Whether they are thrown out of or sincerely desire to leave a country, immigrants have sometimes become a remarkable asset to a country and have sometimes presented a serious social and economic problem. The movement of so many people exposes reluctant or hostile governments unprepared to receive them. Extensive migration in the closing years of the twentieth century influences both the domestic and foreign policies of numerous governments.

What is causing the movement of so many people—perhaps as many as 17 million in the mid-1990s—across borders around the globe? The numbers are perhaps unprecedented since the fall of the Roman Empire fifteen hundred years ago. The complete answer would probably take several additional chapters. Be of good cheer, though; we only have the space to provide a cursory analysis.

---

12 "Israel's Forgotten War in South Lebanon," *The Economist*, July 15, 1995, p. 27.

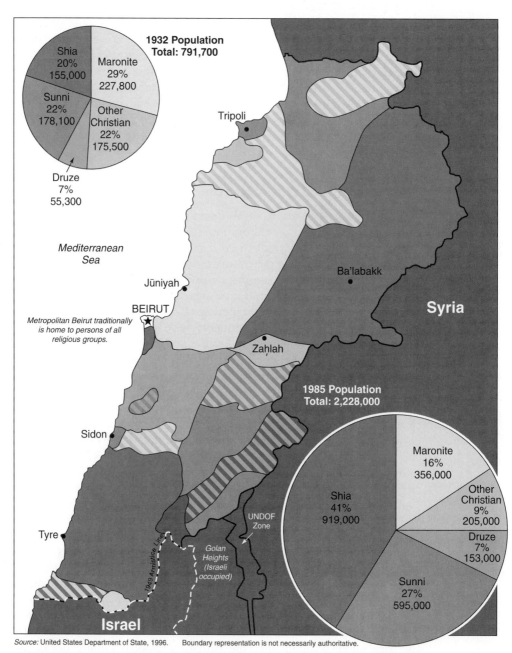

1932 Population
Total: 791,700

Shia
20%
155,000

Maronite
29%
227,800

Sunni
22%
178,100

Other
Christian
22%
175,500

Druze
7%
55,300

*Mediterranean
Sea*

Tripoli

Jūniyah

BEIRUT

*Metropolitan Beirut traditionally
is home to persons of all
religious groups.*

Ba'labakk

Syria

Zaḥlah

1985 Population
Total: 2,228,000

Sidon

Maronite
16%
356,000

Other
Christian
9%
205,000

Shia
41%
919,000

Druze
7%
153,000

Sunni
27%
595,000

Tyre

1949 Armistice Line

UNDOF
Zone

*Golan
Heights
(Israeli
occupied)*

Israel

Source: United States Department of State, 1996.   Boundary representation is not necessarily authoritative.

Figure 13.4
Contemporary Distribution of Lebanon's Main Religious Groups

The most persuasive response is that the international state system is and always has been incomplete. There are probably hundreds of ethnic communities of substantial size that are unhappy with, feel trapped by, and are violently opposed to national boundary lines that the global community officially recognizes. The farther one is removed from the more familiar and oldest part of this system (Europe, North America, and a few other areas), the less certain the state system becomes. Take Central Asia, composed of countries most Americans are unfamiliar with and, unless they hurry, may not get a chance to know. As one observer has pointed out:

> *Central Asia looks more like a medieval map, in which geography and ethnicity—defined by highly ambiguous and ever-shifting centers of power—will matter increasingly more and fixed borders will matter less.*[13]

Central Asia contains the six former Soviet republics that are predominantly Muslim. Our ignorance of the region is even more astounding considering the amount of natural wealth it possesses. These republics are experiencing turmoil based on ethnicity, which seems to override religious affiliation; conflict is also arising over tribal attachments, which seem to override ethnic loyalty.

The resultant civil wars have created a form of forced migration as large numbers of refugees flee from warring sides and the usually simultaneous collapse of the central government. Numerous states from Turkey to India are in peril.[14] Some are experiencing a decline in stability as central governments lose control of large stretches of territory and population.

Trouble is brewing even in supposedly stable countries. In previous discussions, we have mentioned the separatist tendencies in safely democratic countries such as Germany, Canada, and Italy. The situation in Germany is especially volatile. East and West Germany were separated for about forty-five years along ideological and political lines. West Germany grew to become the third biggest economy in the world, while East Germany languished as a communist society. When the two parts united in 1990, West Germany undertook to rebuild the eastern economy. East Germans have resented what they see as condescension on the part of West Germans. West Germans have resented the resentment of the *Ossis*, as the East Germans are called.

It seems safe to say that after a period of adjustment, Germany will eventually become a thoroughly united country. But the Germans demonstrate that even very similar cultures can, over a period of time, become very distinct communities. When the Berlin Wall was standing (from 1961 to 1989), Ossis used to risk their lives to escape to the West. Since the Wall came down, Ossis have grown apprehensive about the West's rampant materialism and accelerated pace of life. Unity quite understandably ended migration but, unpredictably, created other difficulties.

---

[13] Robert Kaplan, "Countries Without Borders," *The New York Times*, October 16, 1996.
[14] Ibid.

Berliners sing and dance on top of the Berlin Wall to celebrate the opening of East-West German borders on November 10, 1989.

What conclusions can we draw about ethnicity and migration? Several come to mind:

1. Migratory patterns since the 1970s have acquired an increasingly ethnic character. Millions of North Africans have moved to France and Italy, West Indians and South Asians have moved to the United Kingdom, Turks and other Middle Easterners have gone to Germany, and Latin Americans have migrated to the United States, often because they were officially or unofficially encouraged to do so. Menial jobs were available in the new homeland, and within a generation or two, the children and grandchildren of these immigrants rose in economic and social status to white-collar professions.

2. By the mid-1990s, a sort of reverse immigration began. This one was again ethnic in nature, but the pattern was to move *away from* western countries, an idea nearly unheard of a generation earlier. Well-educated individuals from Europe and North America who possessed "transferable skills"—usually computer and financial expertise—were on the move to East Asian and other rising economic and technological powers. A wave of blue-collar migration also began around this time, British skilled and semiskilled workers, for example, began moving to places such as Hong Kong to accept relatively good-paying jobs that the indigenous Chinese labor force didn't want.[15] The immigration of

---

[15] "Marketplace," National Public Radio, October 14, 1996.

skilled people in substantial numbers is probably a healthy sign for the global economy. Unfortunately, these are the exceptions rather than the rule of migration—at least, so far.

No matter which migration patterns prevail, hospitable welcomes can become scarce, especially in times of economic hardship. In the United States, California has opted to deny even legal immigrants some social services. The long-held notion that we would always welcome immigrants in the United States—where we are all the descendants of immigrants, where immigrants have historically strengthened and vitalized the economy, and where newcomers have made useful social contributions—was in serious jeopardy by the 1990s. Many people began concluding that the United States had received all the immigrants it could handle and that their presence was straining public services. This idea gained momentum during the 1990s, especially in states, like California, that had accomodated a large proportion of the new residents.

During the last months of 1996, the 104th United States Congress passed several pieces of legislation that restricted or abolished the social and educational services legal immigrants could receive. New York City, with nearly half a million legal immigrants (about 5 percent of the city's total population) and an unknown number of illegal ones, felt particularly singled out. Legal immigrants have by most accounts continuously revitalized New York. Its mayor, Rudolph Giuliani, instructed city attorneys to file suit in federal court on the basis that the congressional legislation was unconstitutional.[16]

In sum, ethnicity definitely plays an important role in a substantial and growing anti-immigrant bias. By 1996, Germany had about 7 million foreign residents within its borders, about 60 percent more than a decade earlier.[17] The proportion of foreigners had been fairly level in the decade prior to 1985. The explosion of the immigrant community coincided with a period of rising unemployment. This combination predictably increased expressions of intolerance toward foreigners. Some of these expressions became violent and seemed disconcerting reminders of Germany's Nazi era.[18]

Compared to France and Germany, which have seen anti-immigrant biases erupt into violence, the United States suffers a mild case of anti-immigrant feelings. French and German youths, mostly unemployed (and perhaps unemployable because they lack skills and education) and often inspired by racist ideology, have occasionally resorted to beating up foreign workers from North Africa and the Middle East. These outbursts are probably at least partially traceable to economic conditions. During the mid-1990s, France and Germany

---

[16] The suit is based on the Fourth Amendment of the United States Constitution, which states that "The right of the people to be secure in their persons, houses, papers, and effects, against unreasonable searches and seizures, shall not be violated . . ." Ultimately, the courts may base their decision on how the term *people* is legally defined.

[17] "Welcome and Stay Out," *The Economist*, May 14, 1996, p. 55.

[18] Ibid.

experienced double-digit unemployment rates, while the United States maintained a rate of only 5 percent.

Some ethnic communities are integrated into a society's political economy more easily than others. In countries such as Canada and the United States, integration occurred with a minimum of acrimony. In places such as Japan or Iceland, integration doesn't occur at all because foreigners either are unwelcome (Japan) or because few people want to immigrate (Iceland). The political impact immigrants make can be severe and enduring. Authoritarian regimes are often unhesitatingly brutal in throwing out or even committing genocidal acts against unwanted ethnic and religious communities.

Finally, immigration in the closing years of the twentieth century, and most likely in the early years of the twenty-first, will certainly be a permanent component in considerations of ethnicity. With millions of people on the move either as legal immigrants or as refugees fleeing war zones, economic impoverishment, or natural catastrophes, it is inevitable that the most developed parts of the world will have to deal with the impact. National debates on immigration will increasingly take on an ethnic flavor as large groups of people from Third World and destabilized countries attempt to improve or save their lives.

SUMMARY

1. The international state system has expanded rapidly since 1945, multiplying the number of states in the world. Some countries have arisen without establishing reliable political institutions.

2. Mutual fear and loathing between different ethnic groups surfaced dramatically as the Soviet Union collapsed. Many of these feelings are based on myth but have long ancestries.

3. A nation often is unified by a people's history of common suffering. Once nationalism is firmly established, it tends to override a society's other considerations, including economic self-interest.

4. In the post-Cold War era, a state's collapse is no longer unusual. Countries with no viable government, such as Somalia, are countries in name only. Other countries with competing ethnic communities may survive in partitioned or fragmented form.

5. Religion plays a significant role in the division of people into groups. Many of these groups perceive themselves and others as different

ethnic groups, even though physically and historically the groups belong to the same ethnic background.

6. Ethnic conflicts have caused increasing numbers of people to migrate. Millions of people are on the move across the planet.

7. In modern times (since about 1500), migratory patterns have chiefly emphasized the movement of Europeans to the Americas. Current migratory patterns emphasize the movement of migrants from developing nations to both Western Europe and North America.

8. The influx of large numbers of nonwhite and non-Christian immigrants is significantly changing the demographics of several western countries. Extremist and nationalist political elements resent this development and are quick to take political advantage of an unfavorable economic environment, blaming economic woes on immigrants.

9. The immigration patterns of the 1990s will likely continue well into the twenty-first century.

GLOSSARY

ethnies   A term of abbreviation applied to ethnic communities. An ethnie is simply an ethnic group distinguished and united by its religion, culture, language, or common history of suffering.

nationalism   A people's psychological bonding with symbols of a common ancestry or of other identifiable links with one another, usually accompanied by a widespread pride in a nation's accomplishments.

Summary and Conclusions

Although this is the long-awaited (and perhaps long-hoped-for) last chapter, the issues raised in this text are likely to be with us for a long time. The United States and much of the rest of the world are constantly reinventing themselves. A similar phenomenon occurred in the late 1940s, when the Cold War began, and is occurring again in the aftermath of the Cold War.

Politics is itself a manifestation of reinvention; it has to be because of the nature of humankind. Just over half a century ago, Americans regarded Germans and Japanese as monsters and murdering psychopaths. Today, these two nations have stable democracies and have become military and political allies of the United States, as well as our economic partners and competitors. Similarly, two generations of Americans viewed Russians as menacing and malevolent adversaries. Now we generally see them as people in need of encouragement to democratize their political system and modernize and privatize their economy. This list of contrasts could easily go on.

This chapter offers some concluding remarks and observations about the overall themes of this text—democratization, ethnic conflict, authoritarian and democratic political institutions, political ideology, and the American role in the global political economy. The chapter also tries to make some projections. Given the less-than-predictable nature of human endeavors, making projections may be risky. But one thing we can say with certainty: the pace of political change is increasing on a global scale, and interesting and unprecedented times are undoubtedly ahead of us.

THE AMERICAN DEMOCRACY
IN A NONDEMOCRATIC WORLD

During the half-century between 1939, when World War II began, and 1989, when the Berlin Wall came down, signaling the end of the Cold War and the collapse of European communism, the world changed in drastic ways. A hundred or more new states appeared during these five decades. Several others—East Germany, the Soviet Union, Yugoslavia—dissolved. The decade that followed the end of the Cold War has been a period of transition that poses both challenges and opportunities for democracy.

We have seen that once democratic institutions and processes are solidly in place, they tend to stay that way. We spent several chapters, for example, reviewing how executive, legislative, and judicial structures can work to enhance democracy once their integrity is established. Yet it is also apparent that even political leaders who sincerely desire to institutionalize democracy can put off doing so if they are unsure whether either they or their country will be around in a few years. For all of that, though, democracy—or at least varying forms of democratization—has made noticeable progress over the last decade and more (figure 14.1).

We have also observed how the political and overall culture play an important role in firmly establishing and sustaining democratic institutions and processes. At times, these processes can all go terribly wrong. In 1848, a strong reformist movement in much of Europe led to democratization in several Western European countries. In the German states, however, many reformers were driven underground or emigrated to America, where they were quickly integrated. Some political historians view this dismissal of political reformers in Germany as an important factor in the absence of strong democratic traditions, the Nazi experience, and, in Eastern Germany, nearly half a century of communism.

We have learned, sometimes the hard way, that individuals affect the world

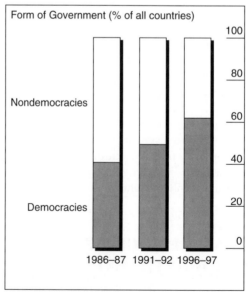

Source: "Human Rights and Diplomacy: The Bloodhounds of History," *The Economist*, April 12, 1997, p. 20.

Figure 14.1

Government by the People: the Increase in Democracies

Soviet leader Mikhail Gorbachev, right, and American President Ronald Reagan say farewell in Reykjavik, Iceland, October, 1986, after four sessions of talks effectively signaled the end of the Cold War.

whether they live in democratic or nondemocratic countries. British Prime Minister Winston Churchill (1874–1965), for example, was struck by a taxi cab in December 1936 while crossing a street in New York—a challenging activity then as now, but made even riskier by Churchill's habit of jaywalking. The cab was going only 35 mph; Churchill might well have been killed had the cab been zooming along at 45 or 50 mph. Who, then, would have led Britain through its darkest days in World War II? And what if Churchill's great enemy, Adolf Hitler, had died in 1938, before launching World War II? Would he be remembered as a leader who restored the German economy and national morale, even if in a brutal fashion, rather than as a mass murderer and sociopath who ended up blowing his brains out in a Berlin bunker?

Former Egyptian President Anwar Sadat's trip to Jerusalem in 1977 ended thirty years of hostility between Egypt and Israel. Richard Nixon's visit to China in 1972 helped begin the improvement and normalization of relations between that country and the United States. The fact that the last leader of the Soviet Union, Mikhail Gorbachev, and President Ronald Reagan personally liked each other helped trust grow in the relationship between the two nuclear superpowers. The friendship overcame Reagan's view of the Soviet Union as the "evil empire"; Reagan discovered that Gorbachev was not himself particularly evil. Together, they helped end the Cold War and consequently helped produce a somewhat safer world.

A personalized style of diplomacy doesn't always work, but that doesn't mean that two sides can't reach some agreement. National leaders may thoroughly detest each other—Hafez al-Asad of Syria and Saddam Hussein of Iraq are a good example—but still work out mutually satisfactory arrangements. The trick is to exercise **pragmatism**—experimenting with solutions that benefit both sides—rather than try to fulfill an ideological mission. Personalities matter: while Gorbachev was neither an ideological fanatic nor a paranoid, one of his predecessors, Joseph Stalin, was both—and each left an indelible mark on his country's history.

Political democratization remains an incomplete and far from global process. In fact, there is not even universal agreement that democracy, especially the western variety, is always a good thing. In December 1996, Chinese government officials escorted a group of American journalists on a visit to a newly built dam the Chinese were particularly proud of. The Chinese wanted to brag about the benefits the dam would bring, such as less seasonal flooding and better irrigated agricultural systems. The American journalists were more interested in asking questions about the amount of environmental damage ecologists said the dam was causing as well as about the more than 1 million people who were given no choice but to leave their homes to make way for the dam's construction. The Chinese authorities had not considered or taken an interest in these issues, and they certainly didn't want to respond to questions about them. One official abruptly ended the discussion by suggesting to the journalists that "you Americans have too much freedom."[1]

The discussion is instructive—it reveals the great disparity between two very distinct political cultures. The Americans were shocked because no governmental agency in the United States would have had the authority, let alone the nerve, to move large numbers of people without their consent. The Chinese were chagrined that outsiders were questioning their effort to modernize on moral or legal grounds. The remark that Americans have too much freedom was not simply a casual or isolated observation. Clearly, the Chinese believed the American journalists had a lot of gall to make judgments about their actions, and the journalists were incredulous that the Chinese would pursue modernization at the cost of the environment and their own people.

China has the biggest population in the world and one of the fastest growing economies. Over the last decade or so, it has become an increasingly substantial American trading partner. But it also has shown no discernible interest in any political reform that would lead to democratization and its inevitable result—the denouement of communist party control (and the power and privileges such control provides) in China. These factors pose a dilemma for an American democracy whose consumers are eager to purchase Chinese products, but who also object to the slave labor system used to produce those goods.

The United States, as the world's military superpower and still the largest economic power, will continue to have to make some morally difficult choices: is it more important to have an economically healthy relationship with China or to use economic incentives to wean the Chinese government from its less-

---

[1] "Weekend Edition," National Public Radio, December 14, 1996.

than-humane policies regarding economic development? Both positions tug at the formulation of American foreign and economic policy and at the essence of America's political culture.

ON THE HORIZON

The end of superpower rivalry does not mean the beginning of boredom in international politics. We have already reviewed the challenges that such critical and widespread phenomena as ethnic conflict and the rise of religious radicalism pose to stability. These phenomena are not usually conducive to either democratization or to economic development. In some cases, though, neither of these processes is a priority to movements and governments who desire ethnic cleansing, the installation of a religiously orthodox regime, or both.

Very little is static in international relations. The Cold War's termination is not the end of history, but simply the start of a new and quite different epoch. To begin with, some disconcerting and rather durable aftereffects have trailed the Cold War:

1. The menace of nuclear war has been considerably reduced but is far from eliminated. The United States and Russia, for example, had each reduced its nuclear weapons inventory from 27,000 in 1990 to 15,000 in 1996, but this was still more than enough to destroy the world several times over. Both were scheduled to reduce this total to about 12,000 by the beginning of the twenty-first century.[2] While neither country wants a nuclear confrontation with each other or anyone else, both still have an abundance of weaponry.

2. Unpredictable groups or governments have the potential to acquire nuclear weapons, perhaps from a cash-strapped Russia known to lack top-of-the-line security at its nuclear installations. Moreover, a disconcerting number of countries are already on the **nuclear threshold,** or on the verge of acquiring nuclear weapons or the ability to build them. Some of these countries—Iraq, Iran, Libya, and North Korea, for example, are governed by regimes with long and demonstrative records of irrational and aggressive behavior in the international arena. Some also support political terrorists who would be keenly interested in acquiring a nuclear option.

3. While the larger democracies, known as the G7,[3] currently dominate the global economy and possess unquestionable military and technological superiority over any combination of adversaries, they are far from unanimous in their concerns and objectives. For example, France and the United States are often at odds in their foreign policy expressions. In 1996, each tried to block

---

[2] Edward L. Rowny, "A New START with Russia," *The Wall Street Journal*, December 11, 1996, p. A22.

[3] As indicated in the chapter on the political economy, the G7 includes the United States, Japan, Germany, France, the United Kingdom, Italy, and Canada.

the other's preference for the United Nations Secretary-General. Even more seriously, the two governments argue over the post-Soviet role NATO will play. The French want NATO to focus more on the Mediterranean theater because of their understandable concern with the political instability and economic difficulties of North African countries. France and other NATO members such as Italy fear that a large influx of illegal immigrants will precipitate economic dislocations and increase political terrorism.[4] The United States, in contrast, focuses more on the possibility of political instability in Eastern Europe and the former Soviet republics and the resultant opportunities for communists or extreme nationalists to come to power. Former communist states such as Bulgaria are strong candidates for **political implosion,** or complete governmental collapse, as the economy continually deteriorates and democracy has not gained enough of a foothold to offer alternatives.[5]

   4.   Political fragmentation as the result of ethnic and/or religious divisions will continue to require American attention and, on some occasions, American intervention. Consider the example of Bosnia. Only a few hundred miles away from a mostly stable, democratic, and prosperous Western Europe, Bosnia is a place where violence lurks everywhere. A NATO official on duty in Bosnia once observed, "If you need combat soldiers to escort you to your residence, it's not the kind of place where you're really going to feel at home."[6]

   This list is far from all-inclusive. It does suggest, though, at least some of the difficulties that will confront and challenge the United States as it formulates and implements foreign policy in the near future.

PERCEPTION VERSUS REALITY

The perceptions one group of people have of other groups make history and drive both national and international politics. Germans between 1933 and 1945 tortured and murdered millions of Jews, even to the detriment of Germany's national interest, because they were convinced that Jews were an evil scourge.[7] The conviction was a complete fantasy, but it was also one that had a history stretching back to the Middle Ages. Unless we perceive reality with some sense of rationality, individuals as well as entire nations can become victims of dangerous misconceptions.

   Millions of Americans during the early decades of the Cold War assumed

---

[4] Gail Russell Chaddock, "Paris Tries to Direct NATO's Club Med," *The Christian Science Monitor,* December 9, 1996, p. 6.

[5] Robert D. Kaplan, "Limited Options in Serbia," *The New York Times,* January 14, 1997, p. A15.

[6] Colin Woodward, "Bosnia's Uneasy Peace: One Year Report Card Shows Gains, Failures," *The Christian Science Monitor,* December 4, 1996, p. 7.

[7] To read more on this example of self-destructive national hatred, see the controversial study by Daniel Jonah Goldhagen, *Hitler's Willing Executioners: Ordinary Germans and the Holocaust* (New York: Alfred A. Knopf, 1996).

that Soviet communism was a pervasive threat to their way of life. In this case, a Soviet challenge to American military power actually did exist (although there was never a viable threat that the Soviet economic system would catch up to the American standard of living). This was, as we saw earlier, a containable challenge, yet the perception that communists were somehow able to subvert and destroy American society persisted for decades. Paranoia overcame common sense for a time as not a few Americans stocked canned goods in fallout shelters in case of communist attack. Some even convinced themselves that the fluoridation of water was a communist attempt to weaken the physiology of American citizens.

There are often significant divides between perception and reality. One expert considers the division a serious component in the conduct of international politics. He defines this component as

> . . . *a vital dimension of international relations: the frequent and highly significant differences between the way nations perceive one another and the way they really are. For the titanic struggles among the nations of our time are not only waged on the basis of objective realities. They are also fought out in the realm of imagery and imagination.*[8]

Images matter, and they can linger for a long time. When NATO was created in 1949, its purpose, as its first Secretary General explained, was "to keep the Russians out, the Americans in, and the Germans down."[9] Half a century later, the concerns are much the same but less intense. Western Europeans still occasionally worry that an economically desperate Russia might strike out, that the Americans will recover their isolationist perspective and remove their military units from Europe, and that the Germans, with the region's largest economy, will again become predominant and militaristic.

Certainly, real differences existed between the United States and the Soviet Union during the Cold War. These differences reflected a division in ideology, military and political rivalry, and national interest—all objective and understandable realities. But many perceptions magnified and distorted these realities. Soviet dictator Joseph Stalin (1923–1953) was a paranoid and sociopath who assumed that the United States was striving to destroy him. For their part, Americans during the 1950s needed to become better educated about the goals and history of the Soviet Union to more accurately evaluate the Soviet challenge, rather than spend their time searching for communist infiltrators in American industries.

Stereotypes can influence people and nations and can even gradually be transformed into reality. The Arab-Israeli conflict is an excellent case study. For

---

[8] John G. Stoessinger, *The Might of Nations: World Politics in Our Time*, 10th ed. (New York: McGraw-Hill, 1996), p. 402.

[9] Quoted in A. Hyde-Price, "Future Security Systems for Europe," in C. McInnes, ed., *Strategy and Security in the New Europe* (London: Routledge, 1992), p. 42.

many years after Israel's establishment in 1948, Arab governments accused Israel of conspiring to seize Arab territory and threatened to "drive the Israelis into the sea" before this could happen. The Israelis, unreceptive to the idea of being destroyed, launched successful preemptive wars in 1956 and 1967 to forestall an Arab attack. The result was that Israel did come to occupy more Arab territory—exactly what the Arabs feared and what, ironically, might not have happened had the Arabs not threatened Israel. Several decades later, Israel is still in the process of gradually returning Arab lands. This is a perfect if rather depressing case of a self-fulfilling prophecy.

INTEGRATION AND FRAGMENTATION

It is safe to assume that the international situation will continue to change, substantially and rapidly, in the early years of the twenty-first century. The impact of such change will strongly influence the process of American politics. As the one remaining superpower, the United States will be expected to fully participate in the global economy, the continuing and expanding technological revolution, and democratization. Problems that are difficult to resolve and in fact may not be completely or permanently resolvable will continue to challenge the United States, including ethnic conflict, religious nationalism, and the rise of innovative forms of political sovereignty. We may be in the midst of a lengthy era of collapsing empires that began a century ago—the latest being the Soviet empire—and we may continue to watch as new (or renewed) states come into being.

The United States and much of the rest of the world may find themselves in a situation characterized by a dynamic contradiction. On the one hand, a strong **supranationalism** appears to be rising, in which countries voluntarily compromise national sovereignty for the mutual benefits of pooling their economic and political resources. The European Union is thus far the most successful example of this process, but it is confined to Western European politics. In some of these countries, such as Denmark and the United Kingdom, large segments of the population are hesitant about full involvement in a movement that may diminish national sovereignty. Others, such as the Czech Republic and Slovenia, are enthusiastically applying to be admitted to what they regard as an exclusive and prosperous club.

Countering supranationalism are the fragmentation and disintegration occurring elsewhere. Instead of becoming more unified, some countries, as we have seen, are falling apart. Instead of becoming more integrated into an economic or political region, some countries strongly guard their peculiar forms of ethnocentrism and isolationism. North Korea's regime, for example, prefers to remain removed from the mainstream of the global economy rather than open the country up to economic and political changes that would undermine the government's control.

During the 1990s, it became apparent that these two opposite political phenomena were occurring across much of the world. Organizations such as the North American Free Trade Association (NAFTA) and the European Union (EU) were enabling countries to affordably trade with one another to mutual advantage as tariff barriers were eliminated. The EU, as we saw in an earlier chapter, is working toward political as well as economic integration, highlighted by a functioning though limited European Parliament that since the 1980s has gradually acquired more and more authority.[10] Both NAFTA and the EU seem poised to expand as more countries qualify economically and politically (that is, possess workable democratic processes) apply for membership. This kind of integration has enabled economies to grow and technologies to expand for mutual benefit.

At the same time, fragmentation is increasingly commonplace. Some countries are either dissolving into smaller sovereign units or are trying to avoid dissolution by granting more autonomy to various regions. India, for example, divided its ethnically troubled northeastern state of Assam into five separate states. The division ultimately satisfied no one, and elements of the largest ethnic group in Assam (there is no majority) want to secede from India altogether.[11] India is only one of several sizable and diverse countries that may experience partial or total disintegration in the future.

Neither process, integration or fragmentation, has any end in sight. Each is destined to be a strong dimension of international politics in the early decades of the twenty-first century. Both phenomena will impact and be influenced by the United States. As the first (and so far the only) **universal nation,** with peoples from all over the globe integrated into society, Americans will continue to be viewed by both admirers and adversaries as the cornerstone of political change.

When it comes to integration and fragmentation, the American experience remains instructive and perhaps even prophetic. During most of the last half of the twentieth century, the United States was caught up in a sometimes painful effort to achieve racial integration and harmony. Technically, virtually no remaining legal barriers to integration exist. Yet, disconcerting signs indicate that the "disuniting of America"[12] may actually be occurring and that some ethnic communities in the United States may welcome it.[13]

The American purpose is not always received with great enthusiasm outside of the country, either. The United States often and sometimes blatantly views itself as a moral nation. This view grew out of a philosophy Americans adopted at the beginning of the country's history that the United States was the "New Jerusalem" where the corrupt and autocratic habits of the old countries would never take root. Instead, America was a special place. In the colonial period,

---

[10] "Looking for Legitimacy," *The Economist,* January 11, 1997, pp. 49–50.

[11] "Beyond the Brahmaputra," *The Economist,* January 4, 1997, p. 38.

[12] Arthur M. Schlesinger, Jr., *The Disuniting of America* (New York and London: W. W. Norton, 1992).

[13] "The Ebonics Virus," *The Economist,* January 4, 1997, pp. 26–27.

Common expressions such as "New-English Jerusalem," "American Jerusalem," "God's American Israel," "American Canaan" connoted from the superior virtue of the people of the colonies and their superior well-being, a sure sign of their election.[14]

Many Americans also don't understand why any country is reluctant to be like America if it has the opportunity to do so:

While few countries would take issue with the tenets of democracy, many have balked at U.S. insistence that their systems should resemble American-style democracy in order to be legitimate. U.S. emphasis on multiparty elections, a pristine human-rights record, and a free-market economy becomes a point of resentment, if not contention.[15]

Still, the United States remains the most critical player in international politics. As Secretary of State Madeline Albright once observed, the United States is the "indispensable nation," whose role in international politics must be "between disengagement, which is not possible, and overextension, which is not sustainable."[16]

The United States is also the most successful democratic experiment in history. It will almost certainly be called upon to support democratic movements wherever they occur. American support may be what makes the difference between stability and implosion for some fledgling democracies. We have ended this text with a brief emphasis on the American role because its prevailing presence in world affairs will likely continue, and because democracy, for all the perils that lie ahead of it, is moving forward. Today's college students may be the generation that sees the firm establishment of democracy across the globe.

GLOSSARY

nuclear threshold   On the verge of acquiring nuclear weapons or the technical ability to build them.

political implosion   The complete collapse of a political system as the governed lose respect and support for the institutions and personnel of government.

pragmatism   A practical approach to politics and diplomacy as opposed to an ideological style. Pragmatists often experiment to see what works and what doesn't.

supranationalism   A phenomenon in which several countries in a region pool their resources and agree to be monitored by the same institutions. Some believe supranationalism will succeed nationalism in global politics.

universal nation   A collection of diverse peoples from throughout the world who have migrated to one country and made a place for themselves and their descendants. The United States is the first (and at present, only) universal nation.

---

[14] Liah Greenfield, *Nationalism: Five Roads to Modernity* (Cambridge, Massachusetts: Harvard University Press, 1992), p. 407.

[15] Adonis Hoffman, "Increasingly, U.S. Finds Itself Whistling Alone," *The Christian Science Monitor*, December 13, 1996, p. 18.

[16] "Albright's Perch," *The Economist*, January 11, 1997, p. 30.

Credits

Chapter 1
TA 1.1, p. 4: © AP/Wide World Photos; TA 1.2, p. 5: © Superstock; TA 1.3, p. 16: © AP/Wide World Photos.

Chapter 2
TA 2.1, p. 37: © Culver Pictures, Inc.; TA 2.2, p. 43: © AP/Wide World Photos; TA 2.3, p. 47: © Culver Pictures, Inc.

Chapter 3
TA 3.1, p. 61: © McGraw-Hill Higher Education/Photo by James L. Shaffer; TA 3.2, p. 63; TA 3.3, p. 68: © AP/Wide World Photos.

Chapter 4
TA 4.1, p. 75: © Reuters/Corbis-Bettmann Archives; TA 4.2, p. 76: © Nick Cornish/Globe Pictures; TA 4.3, p. 91: © Culver Pictures, Inc.

Chapter 5
TA 5.1, p. 103: © Everett Collection; TA 5.2, p. 105: © UPI/Corbis-Bettmann Archives.

Chapter 6
TA 6.1, p. 124; 6.2, p. 129; 6.3, p. 138: © AP/Wide World Photos.

Chapter 7
TA 7.1, p. 146: © AP/Wide World Photos; TA 7.2, p. 151: © Reuters/Corbis-Bettmann Archives.

Chapter 8
TA 8.1, p. 166; 8.2, p. 176: © AP/Wide World Photos.

Chapter 9
TA 9.1, p. 195: © AP/Wide World Photos; TA 9.2, p. 206: © Robert E. Murowchick/Photo Researchers, Inc.; TA 9.3, p. 209: © Visual Departures, LTD./Photo Researchers, Inc.

Chapter 10
TA 10.1, p. 213: © Superstock, Inc.; TA 10.2, p. 217: © UPI/Corbis-Bettmann Archives.

Chapter 11
TA 11.1, p. 230: © AP/Wide World Photos; TA 11.2, p. 234: National Archives (11-SC-203583), Courtesy of USHMM Photo Archives. Courtesy U.S. Holocaust Memorial Museum.

Chapter 12
TA 12.1, p. 251: © Ewing Galloway, NY; TA 12.2, p. 253: © AP/Wide World Photos.

Chapter 13
TA 13.1, p. 267; 13.2, p. 278: © AP/Wide World Photos.

Chapter 14
TA 14.1, p. 285: © AP/Wide World Photos.

Index

C
.....

European Union (EU)
  governments in members of, 173
  migration within, 279
  nationalist attachments and, 273
  purpose of, 294, 295
  representation within, 260, 263
Executive selection
  in France, 127–130
  by legislature, 110–112
  methods for, 127
  in United Kingdom, 132–134
  in United States, 130–132
Executives. *See also* President, U.S.;
  Presidents; Prime minister, U.K.
  bureaucracy and, 139–142
  constitutional restraints on,
    137–138
  overview of, 119
  in parliamentary system, 106
  powers of, 136, 137–138
  recruitment of, 112–113
  self-selected, 134–136. *See also*
    Dictatorships
Expansionist policies
  due to threats to sovereignty, 220,
    222
  justifications for, 222–223
  reasons for, 218–220
Extremist political parties
  coalition governments and, 174
  explanation of, 172, 187

F

Fascism, 47–48
Federal courts, 158, 159
Federalist Paper 51 (Hamilton), 3
Female infanticide, 14, 15
Fillmore, Millard, 132
Finland, 226
Firearms, 59
First Amendment, U.S. Constitution,
  168
First World countries, 193, 207
Forbes, Steve, 123, 131
Ford, Gerald, 110, 115
Former Soviet republics (FSRs). *See
  also specific countries*
  economic development in, 193,
    195
  establishment of, 223
  ethnic turmoil in, 281, 292

political disintegration of, 256
Russians living in, 224
France
  expansionist policy of, 221
  following World War II, 249
  foreign policy of, 291–292
  foreign residents in, 18, 154,
    283
  judicial system in, 158–159, 160
  legal system in, 152
  legislature in, 101, 102
  monarchy in, 126
  Muslims in, 154
  nuclear testing by, 130
  political culture in, 51, 68
  population of, 207
  power of president in, 137
  referendum in, 99, 186
  selection of president in, 127–130
Franco, Francisco, 47
Free Democratic party (Germany),
  170, 175
Free markets
  democratic process and, 77, 78
  explanation of, 93
  in nonwestern regions, 197
French Revolution of 1789
  forces allied against, 258
  political terms originating from,
    33
  reign of terror during, 237, 245
Fukuyama, Francis, 73
Fundamentalism. *See* Religious
  fundamentalism

G

G7. *See also specific countries*
  economic development and,
    197
  explanation of, 212
  objectives of, 291–292
Gaza Strip, 23, 218
Genocide
  central government's commitment
    to, 6
  explanation of, 24
  selective, 243–244
German Civil Code, 152
Germany. *See also* East Germany;
  Nazi Germany; West Germany
  bureaucracy in, 141

democracy in, 89
economic miracle in, 84
electoral system in, 183–185
expansionist policy of, 219–220,
  223
fear of Czechoslovakia by, 220
forces allied against, 258
foreign residents in, 18, 55,
  283
interest groups and, 168
Jews in, 16, 156, 236, 243, 244,
  279, 292. *See also* Nazi Germany
judicial system in, 159, 160–161
legislature in, 102–103
Nazism in, 47–48, 61, 78, 155. *See
  also* Nazi Germany
partitioning of, 225
political culture in, 55
political parties in, 168, 170,
  173–175, 178
reunification of, 174, 225, 281
selection of executive in, 110
terrorist organizations in, 242
World War I and, 253
Giscard d'Estaing, Valery, 139
Giuliani, Rudolph, 283
Golan Heights, 241
Goldwater, Barry, 121, 177
Gorbachev, Mikhail, 6, 8, 289, 290
Gottleib, Gidon, 19
Government
  in ancient Greece, 28–33
  explanation of, 2–3
  nature of, 5–6
  overview of, 1
  politics vs., 2
  in post Cold War Era, 2–12. *See
    also* Cold War
Grant, Ulysses S., 123, 131
Great Britain. *See also* United
  Kingdom
  European Union and, 273
  expansionist policy of, 221
  following World War II, 249
  immigrants in, 55
  origins of democracy in, 83–84
  Palestine and, 225
  as world power, 255, 258
Great Depression, 62, 121
Greece. *See* Ancient Greece
Green party (Germany), 173
Greenfield, Liah, 296
Grenada invasion, 122
Grotius, Hugo, 153
Gush Emunim (Israel), 66

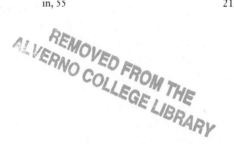